BOUDICA

Vanessa Collingridge

EBURY
PRESS

First published in Great Britain 2005

1 3 5 7 9 10 8 6 4 2

Ebury Press, an imprint of Ebury Publishing.
Random House, 20 Vauxhall Bridge Road, London SW1V 2SA

Random House Australia (Pty) Limited
20 Alfred Street, Milsons Point, Sydney, New South Wales 2061, Australia

Random House New Zealand Limited
18 Poland Road, Glenfield, Auckland 10, New Zealand

Random House South Africa (Pty) Limited
Endulini, 5A Jubilee Road, Parktown 2193, South Africa

The Random House Group Limited Reg. No. 954009

www.randomhouse.co.uk

A CIP catalogue record for this book is available from the British Library.

Cover design by Two Associates
Typeset by seagulls

Every effort has been made to trace and contact the copyright holders of photographs featured in
the book. If notified, the publisher will rectify any errors or omissions in subsequent editions.

ISBN 0 091 89819 6

Papers used by Ebury Press are natural, recyclable products made from wood grown in sustainable forests.

Printed and bound in Great Britain by Clays of St Ives PLC

BBC Panorama interview with Diana, Princess of Wales: text reproduced
with kind permission, © BBC Panorama, 1995

Extract from Winston Churchill's *The History of the English-Speaking Peoples*,
Cassell 1956, reproduced with kind permission of Curtis Brown Ltd, London on behalf of
The Estate of Sir Winston Churchill © Winston S Churchill, 1956

Extract used with permission from Arthur Grimble, 1922, *Women as Empire Builders*,
United Empire XIII

Extract from Richard Hingley & Christina Unwin's *Boudica – Iron Age Warrior Queen*,
Hambledon and London Ltd, 2004, reproduced with permission

Grateful acknowledgment is made to the following for permission to reprint
the excerpt from *Women of the Celts*, by Jean Markale, tr. A. Mygind, C. Hauch, and P. Henry
(Rochester, Vt.: Inner Traditions, 1986), translation © 1975 by A. Mygind, C. Hauch, and P. Henry

Extract used with permission from Elizabeth Newbery's
Lookout Guide to the Quarrelling Celts. Jarrold Publishers, Andover

Extract from Lewis Spence's *Boadicea – Warrior Queen of the Britons*,
Robert Hale Limited (1937), used with permission

"Whoever were the first inhabitants of Britain, whether natives or immigrants, has never been answered: don't forget we are dealing with barbarians"

Tacitus, *Agricola*, xi.

For my parents, Gordon and Irene,
and their redheaded tribe of Collingridges.

CONTENTS

TRIBAL
BOUNDARIES OF
EARLY ROMAN
BRITAIN

CALEDONIA

BRIGANTES

Eboracum
(York)   PARISI

Lindum (Lincoln)
CORITANI

DECEANGLI
CORNOVII   Venta (Caistor)
ORDOVICES   Viroconium   Ratae (Leicester)
             (Wroxter)   ICENI

                    DOBUNNI   CATUVELLAUNI   TRINOVANTES
DEMETAE   Verulamium
             SILURES   (St Albans)   Camulodunum
                                             (Colchester)
                         Calleva
                       (Silchester)
              ATREBATES   Londinium
                   BELGAE   (London)   CANTIACI
                                  REGNENSES
       Isca (Exeter)
              DUROTRIGES
    DUMNONII

© V. COLLINGRIDGE

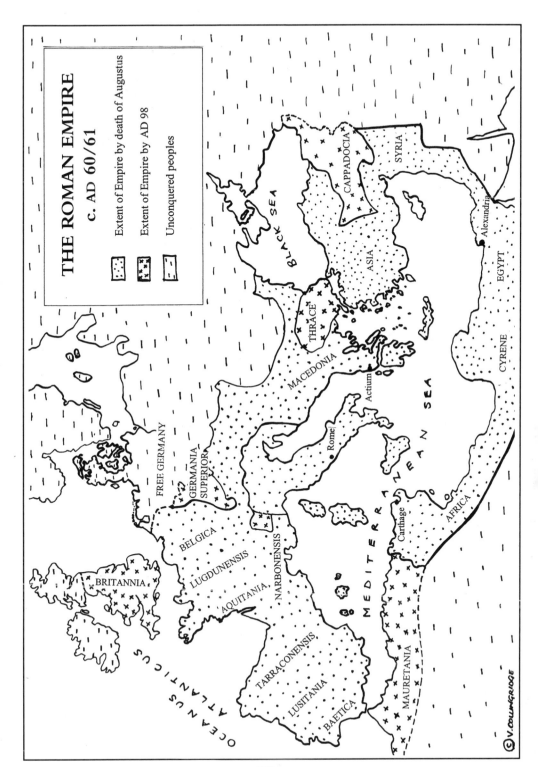

THE ROMAN EMPIRE
c. AD 60/61

Extent of Empire by death of Augustus

Extent of Empire by AD 98

Unconquered peoples

BLACK SEA

CAPPADOCIA

SYRIA

ASIA

THRACE

MACEDONIA

Alexandria

EGYPT

CYRENE

Actium

Rome

FREE GERMANY

GERMANIA SUPERIOR

MEDITERRANEAN SEA

BELGICA

LUGDUNENSIS

NARBONENSIS

Carthage

AFRICA

AQUITANIA

BRITANNIA

TARRACONENSIS

LUSITANIA

BAETICA

MAURETANIA

OCEANUS ATLANTICUS

© V.COLLINGRIDGE

LIST OF ILLUSTRATIONS

TIMELINE

BC

1000	Bronze Age Urnfield culture exists throughout Europe
800	Iron Age Celtic Hallstatt culture appears in Europe and expands
600	The *Massiliote Periplus* is written in the Greek port of Massilia (Marseilles), describing two distant islands of Ierne (Ireland) and Albion (Britain)
550	Hillforts built across southern Britain, including Danebury Ring, Hampshire
500	Greek writer Hecateus describes the Keltoi
	La Tène culture evolves and starts to spread through Europe
c 400	Celtic tribes "The Gauls" invade northern Italy
c 390	The Gauls sack Rome
c 325–320	The voyage of Pytheas, who describes Britain and Ireland as the Pretannic Islands
218	Celts ally with Carthage in Second Punic War
c 200–100	Development of large fortified settlements called *oppida* in Europe
	First Belgic migrations from the Continent to Britain
	Romans fight and finally defeat the Cimbri and Teutones
	Danebury hillfort is abandoned for unknown reasons
60	First triumvirate: Pompey, Crassus and Julius Caesar
58	Julius Caesar campaigns in Gaul
55	Julius Caesar's first invasion of Britain
54	Julius Caesar's second invasion of Britain
52	Gaulish rebellion led by Vercingetorix; defeated at Alesia
	Commius flees to Britain
49	Caesar crosses the Rubicon
46	Vercingetorix is paraded through Rome and then executed
44	Julius Caesar murdered by fellow Romans; end of Roman civil war
43	Second triumvirate: Marc Antony, Lepidus and Octavian
31	Battle of Actium: Antony and Cleopatra defeated by Octavian
27	Octavian becomes first Roman emperor, Augustus

AD

9	15,000 Roman soldiers wiped out by native Germans in Teutoberg Forest, ending Roman expansion in region
14	Augustus dies; Tiberius becomes emperor
37	Tiberius dies; Caligula (Gaius Caesar) becomes emperor
40	Emperor Caligula abandons invasion of Britain at French coast
41	Emperor Caligula murdered; Claudius takes imperial throne
43	Emperor Claudius invades Britain; Caratacus leads resistance
47	First revolt by the Iceni tribe, soon quashed by Romans
	Publius Ostorius Scapula leads military action against tribes of Britons
48	Romans help Cartimandua retain power as Brigantian Queen
c50	London established as Roman trading port
51	Caratacus finally defeated in battle, handed to Romans by Queen Cartimandua of the Brigantes
54	Emperor Claudius dies, probably poisoned; Nero becomes emperor
52–58	Conquest of Wales continued under Aulus Didius Gallus, then Quintus Veranius
57	Cartimandua's husband, Venutius, rebels against her
59	Emperor Nero has his mother, Agrippina, murdered
58–61	Gaius Suetonius Paulinus becomes governor of Britain
60	Client King Prasutagus of the Iceni dies, leaving his lands jointly to Nero and his two daughters. His Queen, Boudica, attempts rule in his place
	Suetonius invades Anglesey to extinguish Druid resistance
	Boudica rises up in revolt against the Romans, sacking Colchester, London then St Albans before being defeated and dying
	Widespread retribution against the rebellious tribes of Britons
68	Nero commits suicide
68–69	"Year of the four emperors"; finally, Vespasian becomes emperor
69	Venutius splits from Cartimandua who takes Vellocatus as her new consort; Venutius leads army against her; she is rescued by Romans but disappears from history
71	Romans defeat Brigantes under Venutius and annexe territory
79	Mount Vesuvius erupts; Vespasian dies; Titus becomes Emperor
81	Titus dies; his brother Domitian becomes Emperor
84	Tacitus claims that Agricola, provincial governor of Britannia, defeats Calgacus's army of 30,000 Caledonian warriors at Mons Graupius
122–30	Hadrian's Wall built
410	Roman Britain ends

INTRODUCTION

The red layer was the colour of African earth. Flecked with shards of blackened pottery and charcoal, it could have been the debris of any human settlement anywhere on the continent. But this was not in Africa, or the blood-red clays of India, or the deserts of South America: this was in Britain and deep underground in the basement of a hotel in Colchester. The last sun that this soil had seen was a faint disc of light through a choking blanket of smoke. Two millennia ago, fire had wrapped up the town's population and all their belongings in a thousand degrees of burning – a temperature so unimaginably hot that it could melt glass back into a liquid and cook the clay of the buildings into the rock-hard ceramic bones of death. This was the mark of an Iron Age Zoro; this was the destruction layer of Boudica.

Boudica – the Iron Age queen of the Iceni tribe – left her indelible signature on the landscape of Britain in the form of a layer of charred, red earth in Roman Britain's largest three settlements, which she burned to the ground. But much more than that, she has also branded her legacy into the British psyche to the extent that almost two thousand years on, we are using her name as a byword for strong women leaders, fictional characters – even as the epitome of the nationalist or Celtic patriot. Dramatically, she is cast as another Braveheart, rolled back in time and space to the lands of East Anglia and the time of the Roman conquests; in reality, Boudica was a collaborator turned rebel and then infamous warrior queen.

But until recently, for someone with such a tight grip on the British imagination, we've known very little about the real woman from antiquity; in fact, we still don't even know her real name. We grew up calling her "Boadicea" which turns out to have been an early gaffe after a scribe mistook her name in

Latin and transposed two vital letters; however, it sounded right so it stuck for centuries until we realised the mistake. Over the past few years, she's been correctly renamed "Boudica" from the Celtic word "bouda" or "victory"; it's a chorus that was allegedly chanted again and again before warriors went into battle – but we still cannot even say for sure whether this was her real name or just a title.

Boadicea, Bonduca, Boudicca or Boudica, she's a figure who has not only been cherished from our past but one who has been continually reinvented to serve as a "woman of our age". Such is her draw that whenever there has been a strong or high-profile woman in power (whether politically, economically, or in any other field), Boudica has been the reference point or role model in both words and pictures. Boudica may mean different things to different people but her brand image is so great that she is instantly recognisable across the generations and throughout much of the western world and the Commonwealth.

The trouble is, when we blow the dust off our schoolbook knowledge, it quickly becomes apparent that we know only the headlines about Britain's most famous warrior queen: here was a Briton who fought the Romans, had some big battles – and then died. The few scant details of her story can be made to fit the relevance of almost any latter-day political scenario of queens, empires or fights against oppression – yet the more we pick our way through myth, folklore and other people's histories to get to the real story of Boudica, the more we realise that the pared-down truth behind the stories has a power and resonance that surpasses even legend.

Archaeological discoveries of the twentieth century have added much intriguing flesh to the bare bones of her story – but as our knowledge of the "real" Boudica builds and grows, what has emerged are the parallel but entirely *distinct* lives of a real historical woman versus the fictional characters we have created in her name for the last two thousand years. Until the last few decades, Iron Age Britain was thought to be the almost passive recipient of waves of immigrants from a more developed mainland Europe who introduced a new, more sophisticated culture and ideas. However, as the scientific rigour of archaeology has improved, the reality in the ground tells an altogether different story: an Iron Age Britain rich in regional diversity and complexity, with social, economic and military links that extended for thousands of miles into Europe and the Mediterranean and for a privileged part of the population at least, a geographical mobility that would be impressive today. Whatever the Romans chose to believe, these people were certainly not "barbarians" in any modern sense of the word. Suddenly, the world of the late Iron Age and early Roman period becomes a deeply textured, fascinating blend of influences and ideas: the Boudica of antiquity emerges as the product of her time, her contacts and her noble class – most likely a wine-drinking, fashion-conscious, bi-lingual Roman citizen with a sophisticated palate and relatively cosmopolitan tastes – far removed from the raw stereotype we were taught about in school, and all the richer for that. But in whittling down the legend to find the real Boudica the debris should not be discarded: just like tea leaves in the bottom of a cup, what is left behind can have an intrinsic value of its own. The cultural and political accretions that have been forced on her story over two millennia tell their own story of the hopes, dreams and prejudices of the chroniclers throughout the ages who built Boudica into the icon she still is today.

Instead of a single biography of Boudica, this book explores the search for the *biographies* of Boudica – who created them, and why. And the story that emerges is much more than a tale of a woman who led her people against a foreign army: it's about our culture and ourselves, and how we shape our heroes to serve specific purposes, regardless of whether or not othe facts actually fit the story at all. The story of Boudica is therefore both the exemplar and the allegory for how we make our histories.

The legend of Boudica's revolt against the Romans ticks all the boxes of a modern epic: with its sex and violence, agony and ecstasy, glory and honour – and the tension of certain doom, it's a swashbuckling, heart-rending *morality* tale of two radically different worlds colliding. The lead character is a true freedom-fighter in the mould of Scotland's William Wallace, struggling to protect a cherished way of life and waging some valiant battles against a seemingly invulnerable enemy right down to the same tragi-heroic ending. But what has made this story endure for almost two thousand years are the twists that still entrance us today, for not only does the hero ultimately lose – the defeated fighter was a woman.

This point might seem obvious but it is critical to the understanding of Boudica's place in the history books. Jenny Hall, Roman curator at the Museum of London, agrees: "The Roman army was heavily defeated by Boudica's army; now that was bad enough, but to be heavily defeated *by a woman* was extremely embarrassing. So, to alleviate some of that embarrassment they had to build up her story even further, making her out to be absolutely terrifying. That's not to take away from her achievements, though – she really did cause them serious problems, almost wiping out a whole legion and destroying their three most important towns."

While the Iceni queen was ruling over her people in what is now East Anglia, further west another Briton was raising an army against the Romans. Caratacus was a mighty warrior who led a remarkable war of resistance against the foreign invaders for almost a decade. In many ways, he outshone Boudica completely: he managed to unite disparate tribes into an effective force of freedom-fighters and then lead a successful guerrilla campaign against the Romans which diverted their attentions from empire-building to mere survival. It took one of the best armies in the world eight long years to defeat this legendary fighter and by the time of his eventual capture, he was revered throughout Rome and her provinces as a great soldier and leader of men. Yet two thousand years on, his name is little more than a wisp of memory in the wake of the warrior queen because he was just another male insurgent. His lesson – never to take on the Romans in a pitched battle – was ignored by Boudica to her cost but while she failed to benefit from his tactical skills, she did benefit from the mystique that built up around him. To Rome, Caratacus was a product of the dark and dangerous island of Britannia where wild, hostile landscapes were teeming with savage, painted and fearless fighters. So while his harrying attacks may have made him famous for a few years, his real legacy was in shoring up the myth of a barbarous Britain: this set the scene for something even more alien and threatening to the patriarchal Roman mindset – a *woman* who dared to step outside the "normal" role of wife and mother, and to take up arms against Rome. For not only the Romans, but also the Anglo-

Saxons, the Elizabethans and today's Britons, her sex is not just a point of curiosity, it is fundamental to understanding her longevity and why she has endured the snakes-and-ladders of fame and infamy over the last two thousand years.

The key to understanding her tumultuous journey through history lies not in Boudica's story but the broader context of Roman culture. As sure as David beat Goliath, in great world myths and legends the underdog is meant to win; such are the ways in which heroes are made. And according to this formula, Boudica should have earned her place in history by beating the Romans in that last, fateful battle and sending them scurrying back to Rome. But that is to read the history books from a British point of view; to the Romans who were writing the first accounts of the warrior queen, *they* were the underdogs, grossly outnumbered and facing a ferocious and barbaric enemy. They needed to win to preserve their honour as the occupying force, but more importantly, they needed to beat Boudica precisely because she was a woman: a further defeat would be the ultimate ignominy. Had she beaten them, she *could* have been the most powerful woman in the western world; instead, she became one of the most infamous.

It was this infamy that brought me to her story over twenty years ago when we learned of her at school. Growing up in the Seventies and Eighties, there was inevitably an undercurrent of discussion about the role of women in society throughout my childhood which I absorbed like a sponge, unwittingly at first but then as a more deliberate act of enquiry. From the feminist movement to the Indian bandit queen Phoolan Devi and the British Prime Minister, Margaret Thatcher, the whole spectrum of what women could achieve in life was now being questioned. And along with that questioning came my search for new and "edgier" role models who challenged the traditional gender stereotypes that straddled the boundaries between the sexually "incontinent" vamp and the housewife indoors.

Ironically, my growing passion for what was then endearingly called "women's issues" came from my father, who was as far from the liberal fringe as it was possible to get. Our family was large and rumbustious and between us we held pretty much every shade of political persuasion which made for years of very noisy dinner-table discussion. As the youngest and arguably the most extrovert of the children, I didn't see why any avenue should be barred to me, not least on account of my sex – and what started as a strong-willed desire for independence became a fully-fledged, bra-burning (if only I had been old enough to wear one) mentality.

Certainly, I cannot remember a time when I wasn't acutely aware of the inherently political nature of women's position in society and – much to my father's disgust and my now extreme embarrassment – by the grand old age of twelve, I would proudly read *Cosmopolitan* magazine and call myself a feminist!

Against this backdrop, it's hardly surprising that learning about a warrior queen called Boadicea had a particular resonance with a young, impressionable child on the look-out for strong and feisty mentors. To me, she represented so much more than just a rebel leader: she embedded herself in my world view and sharpened my antennae for women who dared to challenge the status quo. It was a high-falutin basis on which to start my lifelong interest in Boudica but there was something a little more down to earth that made me pin my colours firmly to her mast.

There are not many female heroes in our history books and even fewer were known for having the same untamed thatch of red hair that cursed my childhood. I was too much of a tomboy to be drawn to stories of damsels in distress or cloistered princesses yet here was a queen who fought for her people on muddy and bloody battlefields; a perfect role-model for an ungainly ginger child. Boudica – or Boadicea as she was to us then – became my personal mascot, someone who I could look up to with a quiet sense of communion. The girls could have their blonde-haired Barbies; I would have my kick-ass carrot-top Queen.

It might at first seem a trivial point but Boudica's red hair is as much a part of the whole Boudica legend as her other symbols – the scythe-wheeled chariot (a nineteenth-century invention) and the spear; and, whether it was true or not, the mere fact that she was *said* to have red hair is highly significant as it marks her apart from the Roman "norm".

Although two classical commentators recount Boudica's story, we only know of the trademark red hair by the writings of one of them: the Greek historian, Cassius Dio, who died around AD 235 – one hundred and seventy-five years after

6

Boudica's final battle. He gives us our only physical description of the woman who almost drove the Romans out of Britain:

> "In build she was very tall, in her demeanour most terrifying, in the glint of her eye most fierce, and her voice was harsh; a great mound of the tawniest hair fell to her hips; around her neck was a large golden torc; and she wore a tunic of many colours upon which a thick cloak was fastened with a brooch. This was her general attire."
>
> CASSIUS DIO BK 62: 2

The scene is awe-inspiring – a powerful piece of imagery that has shaped our views of Boudica for almost two millennia: here is the classic picture of the warrior queen. But while it makes great drama, it is almost *too much* of a classical portrait, built on the widely held stereotypes and myths that abounded in the writings of the day about the "barbarians" that lived in the lands of Gaul and Britannia. Again, what seems unique by itself is in context just more Roman propaganda. How much of Cassius Dio's description was a genuine account and how much a romantic embroidering of the facts will never fully be known but some "facts" do ring true. The "large golden torc" is credible enough, as precious torcs dating back to the late Iron Age and early Roman period have been

"Stroppy Cow. Just because we pronounce her name wrong."

found in buried hoards, presumably because their owners wanted to keep them safe in times of trouble (the fact that they were never reclaimed suggesting that their owners' grim judgement of the situation had been correct). As for the tunic, we know from archaeological evidence that the ancient Britons were show-offs and did indeed favour brooches, the more richly decorated the better; and they used to weave a kind of plaid or tartan, the best of which would certainly be of "many colours" to show off the design.

However, rather than painting an impressive picture, everything in Cassius Dio's description seems designed to instil the reader with an awe that is also tainted with disgust: like the Amazons to the Greeks, everything about the other culture was upside-down and just plain *wrong*. To a Roman audience, a woman ruler was a vile oxymoron as only men were fit to govern: queens, with their deadly blend of sex and power, represented a perversion of the natural order. The mere fact that the Britons had monarchs was a sign that they were culturally backward: according to the Roman version of history, Rome had got rid of its monarchy more than five hundred years earlier, when it found the system was inherently corrupt. They had then progressed from the high ideals of the Republic to the magnificence of the Roman Empire, both of which had the moderating influence of the Senate to provide the necessary checks and balances on the supreme power of its leaders. As the most powerful nation on earth (so they thought), their system of governance was clearly superior.

What's more, no Roman (and for that read "civilised") woman would have spoken with a "harsh" voice or allowed her hair to go untamed; and what Roman female, let alone a queen, would have been flattered by being referred to not as "stately" or "powerful" but as "fierce"? The underlying suggestion of barbarism is never far below the surface in the classical texts about Boudica in an attempt to underline the fact that she's from a less cultured, less developed and less worthy race than the Romans. Everything about her signals her "otherness". Even the reference to her "tawny" hair – interpreted through the ages as meaning "red" – sets her apart from the more "normal" darker Latin hues.

The exotic savagery of the redhead is underlined in a popular story about the Emperor Caligula who so embarrassed by the small number of prisoners he had to display at his victory parade that he collected together the tallest of his

Gaulish prisoners and made them firstly grow their hair then dye it red, so the Roman crowds would know that he had conquered the mighty barbarians. Here, red hair was the ultimate symbol of an inferior race, and one that contrasted with the obvious glory of Rome.

But it wasn't just uncivilised people who sported red hair, though it was likely to be symbolic of a flaw in their morality. There is a popular belief that one of the most infamous queens of all time, Cleopatra, may also have been ginger as a result of her Macedonian ancestry stretching back to the famous fellow redhead, Alexander the Great. Although there is only a slim chance that this was true, any red hair she sported would have been most likely dyed with henna in the custom of the day. According to the Greek historian and biographer, Plutarch (AD 46-126), Cleopatra dressed herself and liked to be *addressed* as the "new Isis" after the most powerful of all the Egyptian deities. This idea is supported by the discovery of a figurine of the goddess with gilded hair and heavy, red-coloured eyebrows which was excavated from Pompeii. We know that Cleopatra took great pride in her appearance and, as the last in a line of Greek rulers in Egypt – and with at least two high-profile Roman lovers and her own Macedonian ancestry, she certainly had a number of "looks" to draw upon for inspiration; she may well have chosen to dye her hair red. This seemingly unconnected fact takes on a more ominous tone when put in the context of the events of AD 60. Cleopatra died in 30 BC so the twenty-one years of her rule that gave Rome so much cause for concern were still very much within political and folk memory by the time of Boudica's revolt. Queens *per se* were problematic to Rome – but red-headed queens? They would have been condemned by their very existence.

It wasn't just Romans who were chary of those who looked different, though their legacy may have compounded the prejudice. All over Europe throughout the next two thousand years redheaded people were somehow perceived as dangerous. At best they were "abnormal"; at worst, a manifestation of evil. The trend towards demonising those with red hair was accelerated by the spread of Christianity throughout the Old World: Judas was said to have been a redhead and he went on to betray Jesus Christ, an act which was enough to condemn an entire genotype.

By the Middle Ages, the negative associations between hair colour, Jews and the Devil are well-recorded: despite their prevalence in northern Europe, there are numerous historical examples of redheads being witches, redheads being unclean and something best avoided and also redheaded women bringing bad luck to sailors and fishermen. Even today, the currency of the colour holds true throughout the western world: red signifies danger and devilment. It's a shorthand sign of warning that would not have been wasted on readers throughout history, and certainly not on readers of Cassius Dio's description of Boudica: here was a woman who stood in stark contrast to the Roman ideal. The truth is that Boudica may not have had red hair at all; but just saying that she did was another warning that marked her out as strange, foreign and dangerous.

Of course, the history of Boudica that has come down to us today was originally written by those who defeated her and they selected their facts for more reasons than mere reportage. "Tawny" hair is merely one example; embedded within the lines of Tacitus and Cassius Dio are all the prejudices, coded beliefs and covert politicking that you would expect from the editor of a modern tabloid newspaper. Classical texts were written to make the writer and patron look as good as possible; they were constructed as entertainment, as likely to be read out to an audience as quietly to oneself and were therefore full of drama, rhetoric and moralising. They are certainly *not* a statement of the truth, however hard their tags of "annals" or "histories" may try to convince.

Unlike the Romans who prided themselves on their literary culture, the Britons and, indeed, their Celtic-speaking neighbours in mainland Europe had no strong tradition of writing things down: knowledge was largely the preserve of the elite band of Druids who were their political and spiritual leaders. This means that while we have the two main Roman documentary sources of Tacitus and Cassius Dio, in terms of written evidence from a *British* point of view (and even the term British, we will see, is problematic), there is precious little from the period leading up to – and immediately after – the Boudican revolt. What scant writing survives comes not from books at all but from inscriptions on coins and memorial stones and while these might provide important information in terms of dates, dynasties and cultural influences, they are severely limited in what they can add to the narrative of Boudica's life.

However, a string of exciting discoveries has meant that we are now far from reliant upon solely the two early historians' version of the story. Balancing the classical writings of the day, other forms of "evidence" we have for Boudica and the revolt of AD 60/61 are the material remains from the early Roman era in Britain, some from archaeology and more recently, from metal detectorists. It is these *material* finds that provide us with a more genuine insight into the lives of the ancient Britons and offer a window into a world that is breathtaking in its juxtaposition of material simplicity and cultural complexity. Over the last eighty years, since Sir Mortimer Wheeler championed the modern, systematic dig, archaeology has been transformed from the former gentleman's pursuit of antiquarianism into a science – and transformed along with it has been our understanding of the Iron Age and the impact of the Roman conquests on the population of Britain. The legacy of this change in revealing the true story of the past cannot be overstated: archaeology has made history sharpen up its act.

In turn, archaeology has been challenged by another mode of study. Until the last two decades or so, metal detectorists were the pariah of the archaeological world; archaeologists claimed they were ruthless profiteers who blundered and plundered their way through the British landscape with careless regard for the context of their finds and in so doing destroyed potentially important information from the sites where their "treasure" had been found. These accusations were on top of the more basic charges of often not keeping good records of the find's location so it was lost again to history – or simply hunting treasure for money rather than pleasure or understanding. Archaeologists wouldn't talk to the detectorists – and the detectorists wouldn't talk to the archaeologists. This stand-off did no one any good and undoubtedly encouraged some detectorists to indeed bypass the academics when they made an interesting find. However, it could not be denied that the technology itself was useful in turning up metal finds buried perhaps for centuries or even millennia in the ground – and it was doing this with relentless success.

Thankfully for both sides, a sea change which had begun in the early 1970s now began to gain momentum – and it centred largely on the very region of the country that was once Boudica's homeland. Realising that both sides were losing out in the archaeological stand-off, the Norfolk Museums Service began to forge closer relationships between the amateurs and the professionals, with museum staff sharing their knowledge in exchange for detectorists showing their discoveries. Within months, the scheme was paying dividends with all manner of amateur finds – from coins and brooches to pieces of horse gear – being brought to the attention of curators. As well as adding to the general basket of knowledge about Norfolk through the ages, the significance of this move was that for the first time in thousands of years, the rank and file of Iron Age Britain were given the chance to have their own voices heard, through the material remains of their daily lives. Until this point, the history of Iron Age and early Roman Britain was known largely through the classical texts and archaeological discoveries such as stone buildings and rich funerary sites, which inevitably focus on the stories of the wealthy and those of high status. Now, through schemes like the Norfolk one, which was expanded to a national network of so-called Finds Liaison Officers under the Government's Portable Antiquities Scheme, ordinary British people are going out and (on the whole) responsibly digging up the stories of ordinary people's lives – and then working with the museum service to put that knowledge into the public domain.

This democratic making of history through finds of everyday lost items and deliberately buried hoards has hugely advanced our understanding of the time when Boudica rose up, gathered her vast army of warriors, farmers, smithies, labourers – and other women – and turned on the foreign invaders. By sharing that knowledge, the amateurs have forged a connection with professionals who can then synthesise and collate all of the pieces of information to help recreate the jigsaw of knowledge about everyday life around the time of the Roman invasions. Just as importantly, however, this new relationship has also built up a strong connection between local people and their local history, giving people a real sense of ownership over the past that, in turn, fosters a desire to learn even more. Suddenly, history has become deeply personal – and the irony is that by making it personal and focussing on real, ordinary people, it's sometimes easier to see the bigger picture of what was happening two thousand years ago.

When it comes to the story of Boudica, that bigger picture is an intricate tapestry of imperial designs, firstly by the Roman Empire and then by the British.

INTRODUCTION

These are explored in the first few chapters of this book. It took little more than a century for the people in what would become Rome to move from living in small wattle and daub huts to living in proto-urban settlements with streets flanked by brick and stone houses. This rapid transformation would continue apace: just over four centuries later, Rome was perhaps the most lavish city on earth with an empire that was without rival across the western world. This immense achievement was not down to luck but good resources, confidence and design. From their earliest days, Romans tended to be cosmopolitan and outward-looking, always hungry for the best of whatever was on offer elsewhere. For ambitious politicians in need of military success, geographical barriers were merely barriers in the mind, to be overcome in the relentless pursuit of glory, wealth and the slaves that were needed to keep the empire functioning. The limits of Romanisation would be rolled forever outwards until the power at the centre began to fail and the whole system became too unwieldy. But until that time, Rome needed ever-more lands to plunder in the same way a growing foetus will continue to feed from its mother even when she is starving.

Caesar's conquest of Gaul laid the basis for his raids on Britain, and these were followed almost a hundred years later by the invasion of the Emperor Claudius in AD 43 that led, in turn, to the Romanisation of almost the entire country. And what couldn't be achieved militarily was achieved by economic, political and cultural contacts, and by the sheer weight of time. But this rolling-out of Empire wasn't achieved in a monochrome, even fashion: progress was patchy with some serious clashes in style, but it is precisely when there is a check to the grand design that it becomes most interesting to pause and take a closer look: these are the moments when there is most to learn about both sides, when strengths and weaknesses are forced into the limelight. These are the moments when the entire pattern of history can change.

It is into this context of two cultures clashing that the long, colourful threads of Boudica and her fight against the Romans are carefully woven. But before we can understand the importance of this British tribal queen in her own lifetime and beyond, we need to follow the threads of her story back to the very origins of Rome as a city – and as an idea – for it is only by understanding the Roman mind that the story of Boudica makes real and meaningful sense. These threads stretch back to over a thousand years before Boudica was even born. The stories of how Rome came to be are known as "foundation myths" and it is these that encapsulate the dreams, aspirations and prejudices of a people trying to make sense of who they are and how they got there. What *actually* happened between 1000 and start of the Roman Republic in 509 BC is almost less important than what was *said* to have happened: in the myths lie all the clues we need to understand not only how, but *why*, the story of the Iron Age queen became so much a part of the fabric of Roman Britain – and then Britain to the modern day.

This book aims to unravel both those stories and their contexts: it's an exploration of how – and why – we make the histories we do; but more than that, it is also testament to the belief that ancient history can be just as surprising today as it was two thousand years ago when the story of a woman's desire for justice for her daughters, herself and her people captured the imagination of one of the greatest empires on earth.

My own search for the real Boudica has taken me from Britain to Rome, from libraries, museums and archives to muddy fields, ancient ruins and spectacular earthworks. I've toured the ivory towers of academia and the homes of metal detectorists in a effort to present the full-bodied history of an Iron Age queen. My aim was to distil the essence of Boudica – to be able to look through her to the landscapes, peoples and times in which she was living. But the more I searched for clarity, the more I realised how much of the story is based on ignorance and unquestioned tales. The few books that recounted her story seemed merely to repeat the age-old mythologies and cultural stereotypes rather than present any fresh insight or hard, rigorous evidence – and I knew I would have to start my research from first principles. Then, as I was being driven demented by the kaleidoscope of storylines refracting off one another, I spoke with the Iron Age coin expert, Dr Philip de Jersey.

Philip and I were at university together in the Eighties so it was easy to be frank and explain my frustrations, but his reaction took me by surprise: he laughed, saying that, yes, the Iron Age could be a complete nightmare even for the experts. "It was so much easier in the past when we just had forty or so coins to work with," he said. "That way we could base our theories on a nice, neat

The alleged 'Boudica' coin, complete with moustache

set of data but it's always a lot more fluid in reality than people think – in fact, it can sometimes feel like the more we find out, the less we know."

He went on to describe a case in point: in the late 1980s, there was a flurry of excitement when a coin from Boudica's Iceni tribe was ascribed to the warrior queen and classified as "the coinage of Boudica". It appeared to be the right date and bore the trademark Iceni horse on one side and a face on the other. So was this the real, tangible proof of the queen that experts had long been searching for? Alas, no. Sadly, it was more of a case of wishful thinking: on closer inspection the "female" face clearly sported a moustache. However, it's a salutary lesson in being willing to accept a convenient truth over a complex reality.

This book is the product of that desire for a deeper and ultimately more honest and rewarding search. At times it might seem as though I've taken a detour but it's always for a reason: sometimes it's only by taking the "scenic route" that we can get the fresh insight and gather a new understanding that brings history alive. At times, too, we simply do not know what really happened to the characters as the facts were never recorded, or have been lost. All we can do then is suggest the most likely motivation or course of events, based on the best available evidence. My hope is that by taking in the wide panorama, I've captured more of the feel of the landscape.

My journey to discover the truth behind the many legends of Boudica spans two cultures, two continents and more than two millennia. It's the story of two worlds colliding and what is left when the white energy of violent fusion finally starts to fade. Separating these two worlds – the safe and civilised, and the unknown and unimaginable – is a stretch of water which we call the North Atlantic but the Romans called *Oceanus*, or "the Ocean". And lurking in the waters that so terrified them lay the dark and mysterious island of Britannia – a land of mythical creatures and potential riches. But to the Romans, Britannia was much more than this: just as Rome was an idea as well as a physical place, so was Britannia. And while crossing *Ocean* to get there required an almost heroic leap of faith, a successful conquest was like conquering the Gods themselves.

The story of the conquest of Britannia is therefore the essential prologue to the story of Boudica. And while the main action may have been played out in the green, marshy lands of Britain, its origins – and the reasons for the great imperial love affair with Britain – are thousands of miles away, in the dusty hills that would one day become the great nerve-centre of Rome.

CHAPTER 1
OCEAN

"But the most famous example of his courage was his expedition to Britain, for he was the first man to bring a navy into the western ocean, the first to sail into the Atlantic to wage war with his army, and then by invading a mysterious island which historians doubted even existed other than in name and fable, he coud be said to have pushed the Roman Empire beyond the limits of the known world."

PLUTARCH WRITING ON CAESAR IN "LIVES"

In the beginning, there was *Ocean* – the father of all waters and the mighty river-god that encircled the flat earth. Within the firm reach of his arms lay the glorious Roman Empire, the one true civilisation divided into its rightful order of rulers, citizens, freemen and slaves. Also encircled within the great limbs of *Ocean* were the lands of the barbarians – strange, primitive peoples lacking in both culture and vision who must one day fall to their superior Roman neighbours until the mighty Empire pushed against *Ocean*'s shores from north to south and east to west. These shores of Europe, Asia and Africa marked the edge of the world; beyond lay the unknown, a void in knowledge filled by fear and mystery, the entrance to the darkness of the other world.

The origins of *Ocean* and its fundamental role in the beliefs of the classical world dated back at least to the earliest Greek geographies and mythologies and go a long way to explaining the dramatic hold that the Atlantic and especially Britain had in the ancient mindset. To their way of thinking, the Mediterranean Sea was the crucible of all the "civilisation" that bubbled out on to the surrounding coastal lands. For millennia, sea journeys would be made along these coastal fringes for trade and exploration, but in their small boats in

Reconstruction of Marcus Vipsanius Agrippa's Roman map of the world from AD *20, commissioned by the Emperor Augustus*

the era before maps or charts, sailors would hug the land searching for the well-known reference points of headlands, bays and rivers. But the limits of this safe, civilised world ended at the Pillars of Hercules: these marked a physical and emotional gateway, beyond which lay what the fifth-century BC Greek poet, Pindar, called the "dark west", a limitless stretch of dangerous water punctuated by petrifying Gorgons and sea monsters and legendary islands of dead heroes. Although *Ocean* encompassed the world, the so-called *Atlantic* or western section of the great water was named for Atlas who stood "at the limits of the earth", holding the broad heavens above his head. And sailors knew enough about those waters to know that they were best avoided…

But for centuries, if not millennia, what lay beyond the Mediterranean lands was merely of interest to philosophers. Intellectuals and poets could spend their time pondering on *Ocean* with all its strange creatures and islands but for most of the classical world, *within* the Pillars of Hercules there were lands and riches aplenty. Inside this world were great cities and civilisations that surely could not be surpassed. If you wanted unimaginable wealth, you merely had to conquer one of your neighbours – and then use its treasures to feed an ever-hungry city that was growing fat on power.

And to the Romans of what is now western Italy, the world was centred upon and radiated out from Rome. But Rome was much more than a city – it was concept, an ideal, a whole way of life. Of course, Roman civilisation was not the first major culture to try to dominate the Old World, though it was arguably the most successful. The Greeks, Egyptians, Etruscans and the Babylonians had all spawned major civilisations which had risen then fallen, giving way to internal stresses and external forces. The Romans had taken what they admired from earlier cultures and made it their own, dismissing the rest as "foreign" and therefore inferior. From the Etruscans they drew their religion, the trademark purple togas of high office and the infamous gladiatorial games; from the Greeks, the Romans took much of their arts and sciences – and even the foundation myth for Rome itself.

Straddled between the thin dorsal fin of the Appenine mountain range and the warm waters of the young Tyrrhenian Sea lies the dry and rocky landscape that once formed the cradle of the Roman world. Humans have lived here for two hundred thousand years, though continuous habitation was interrupted by the last Ice Age. When this ended some ten thousand years ago, early humans flowed back into the lowlands and plains of the region. At first the population was sparse and patchy until the arrival of more settled Neolithic farmers around 5000 BC and the much later phase of population growth during the Iron Age.

From prehistoric times, however, people have made their homes in the shadow of the highest peaks of the Appenines – the snow-covered Gran Sasso d'Italia; rising to almost three thousand metres, this "Great Rock" dominates the region. Early Neolithic hunters could roam the marshy river valleys or hunt the bears and wild boar that can sometimes still be found in the dense beech, oak and pine woods that flank the mountain slopes.

By the Bronze Age, partially settled farmers worked the fertile soils that lie along the wide valley of the River Tiber and grazed their animals in the green valleys before moving up to higher pastures for the dry summer months. The climate for those early settlers was essentially the same as it is today: in summer, the flatter lands of the coast would bake in temperatures that can reach thirty-five degrees celsius while the hot, dry winds desiccated the earth until it turned to dust; spring and autumn are still the rainy seasons while the winter brings the stormy tramontana winds, often accompanied by flurries of snow.

By the dawn of the Iron Age in around 800 BC, the local population had grown both in numbers and in wealth through trade and agriculture – and this spawned more changes: people started to live in small, clustered settlements on the higher, more easily defended hills. These were not primitive people: they drained the marshes and developed political hierarchies, probably based around the *paterfamilias* or oldest male; they also developed religious cult-associations or federations, focusing on deities such as Diana, Jupiter and Venus. Evidence of their rectangular, wattle-and-daub huts containing hearths and charred cooking utensils have been found throughout the region; three such huts have even been uncovered on the Palatine Hill itself from where Rome would soon rise up as both a city and an idea.

By around 650 BC, with the coming of the Etruscans from the north (and with Greek influences permeating up from the south), the region began to adopt some of the cultural and political structures which would become embedded in Roman culture for the next thousand years: aristocracies, ruling magistracies and a Senate, or Council of Elders. On the domestic level, the *paterfamilias* ruled with complete omnipotence: he was within his legal rights to put his wife to death or sell his children into slavery. However, the evolution of the region's society was not restricted to these "developments" – and the pace of the change is almost beyond belief: within just a hundred years, the settlements were transformed from clusters of traditional huts to whole urban townscapes, with planned streets of brick houses with more lavish homes for the wealthy. Grand public buildings and religious temples began to rise up, made of vast blocks of skilfully carved stone, sometimes decorated with coloured terracotta. It was also around this time that the higher-status inhabitants began to use the alphabet to write things down – and the lingua franca used was not Etruscan at all, but Latin. Though it may have faced periods of foreign domination, this was a confident society: it took what was useful, and discarded the rest.

This was also a land that was rich in resources, both cultural and material: there were plentiful stocks of fish and easy transport in both the river and the sea, the brown alluvial soils supported abundant agriculture, while from the long mountain reaches came all the raw materials for building the great cities of the future: water, limestone, wood – and the famous Italian marbles. By 500 BC, the fifty or so communities in the region had been distilled into around a dozen powerful settlements which dominated the surrounding lands of the region – and the most powerful of all was Rome.

There were many legends about the actual foundation of Rome; the most popular myth blended stories both from Rome and Greece, and ran as follows: around 1184 BC, Troy was destroyed by the Greeks after a ten-year siege that ended in the famous episode of the wooden horse; however, the Trojan hero Aeneas managed to escape the slaughter along with a band of men. While searching for a new home, a vivid dream instructed him to head west in search of a new land where the River Tiber flowed and after years of wandering around the Mediterranean, the group finally arrived at the Tiber where they were warmly received. The king of the region was a man called Latinus; he was impressed by the young man and soon offered Aeneas his daughter's hand in marriage. Despite some initial opposition from the locals who were less sure about the new arrivals, the Trojans settled, intermarried with the native women and then became the "Latins". Aeneas founded the city of Lavinium, named after his new wife, and located nineteen miles south of modern-day Rome.

This foundation myth gained popularity during the years of the Republic from around the fifth century BC as it well suited the purposes of the budding civic leaders. Not only did it give the Romans an impressive classical pedigree; the Trojan angle fitted nicely with their desire to be seen as distinct from the Greeks. But the myth caused a problem for this new version of official "history": the dates simply didn't add up. The start-date for the Roman Republic relied upon records of its annual list of magistrates; from this, the republic appears to have originated around 509 BC; before that the Romans believed that the area was ruled by a series of seven kings, leading back to the creation of the actual city of Rome by Romulus in 753. That date was arrived upon by using Greek methods of genealogical reckoning: mathematicians worked out that the period of time taken for seven kings to rule would be somewhere in the region of two hundred and fifty years, meaning that the first of the seven kings – Romulus – must have ruled from the middle of the eighth century BC. The year of 753 was eventually agreed upon as the official start-date of the so-called "Regal Period". However, that meant some creative historiography was needed to breach the four hundred year gap from the fall of Troy in 1184 BC to the "official" foundation of Rome in 753 BC – and to make the "facts" fit the official version of history.

The answer was to devise a series of twelve fictitious kings who ruled over the general area, all of whom descended from a royal line starting with Aeneas and ending with the arrival of the twin brothers, Romulus and Remus, who founded the actual city of Rome itself. Once again, the engineered solution fitted the bill both numerically and also in terms of a classical pedigree: Rome had grown up from a land of heroes who had fought bravely to overcome tyranny; who could ask for a more fitting, more auspicious start in life for the ancient world's most famous city?

The legend ran as follows: good King Nutimor was the twelfth king after Aeneas and ruler of the area which would one day be called Rome. However, he was deposed by his wicked and megalomaniacal brother, Amulius. In a vain attempt to hold on to his ill-gotten power, Amulius then forced the former King's daughter, Rhea, to become a Vestal Virgin; in that way she had to remain celibate and so there would be no possibility of her continuing Numitor's royal line and threatening his brother's position. However, she became pregnant by the god Mars and gave birth to the twins, Romulus and Remus. When he heard about the existence of the boys, a furious Amulius gave orders for the babies to be drowned in the River Tiber but the basket in which they were placed floated off downstream instead of sinking and the boys' river journey ended at what was to become the future site of the city of Rome. There, on the banks of the Tiber, the twins were suckled and fed by a she-wolf and a woodpecker until a local herdsman tending his sheep chanced upon them and took them home where his wife reared the boys as her own.

As they grew up, Romulus and Remus played with the children of the area and soon became the leaders of an adventurous band of young men. Romulus was fearless and warlike, and eventually he and his brother managed to kill Amulius and restore their grandfather to the throne. To honour their victory and to mark the site where they had been saved as babies, they founded a new city on the Palatine Hill, bounded by a large stone wall. However, this wall was to be Remus's undoing: during the building of the city, the brothers quarrelled and when Remus jumped over the city wall, his brother killed him. Romulus was now free to build and populate the city as he deemed fit and he quickly consolidated his power, becoming Rome's first King in a line of seven that became known as the "Regal Period".

Seven kings; seven hills. The so-called regal period of Rome all made perfect sense to those writing it down in later years, from its official start date in 753 BC to its conclusion in 509 BC when the last royal ruler – the vile and tyrannical king Tarquinius Superbus – was overthrown. Once more, the popular story of the end of the Regal Period fitted nicely with the need for a sea change in Roman government: Tarquinius Superbus was an evil despot who ruled Rome through fear. When his son raped the beautiful Lucretia, a much-respected noblewoman, it was one outrage too many for the population to bear. A group of senators led a revolt to overthrow the king, and he and his family were finally expelled from the city. In reality, the end of the hated Etruscan monarchy did not mean the immediate cessation of Etruscan influence: the city still expressed itself in Etruscan styles of art for at least another fifty years while the wealthy continued to demand Greek pottery and ceramics; fine temples were still being built and some of the elected officials sported Etruscan names. However, all across the region, ruling monarchies were dissolving into oligarchy, with the noble families vying for political power. This was now a society where wealth and power were inextricably linked – and the gap between the haves and have-nots was growing ever wider. The irony is that while the years of monarchy which had become so corrupting were now over for good, the same elite band of families was rocking the city's administrative cradle; inside, swaddled in their noble raiments, lay the hungry infant that would grow up to dominate the Ancient World. Freed of the sins of its forefathers, Rome was now entering the next phase of its moral evolution: the republic.

If you were lucky in the early republic, you would be the one in ten who was born into privilege. Archaeological evidence shows that you would live in a fine house, supported by serfs and slaves, you would look out on to swathes of your family's land and you would know that beyond your destiny in public office, you would never, ever have to work. Life would be a genteel shaping through tuition, conversation and observation until you were fully moulded into a Roman patrician. Of course, if you were born a woman, your destiny would be to marry well, keep a good home, discreetly support your husband in his political duties and raise the next generation of civic leaders and their wives. The theory did not always work out; a number of famines reduced even the aristocracy to dire financial straits. However, for the bulk of the population who scraped by in the peasant economy, such crises literally could be fatal. In some cases, if you failed to repay a loan, your lender could have you executed; your lands would be repossessed and your dependents left homeless and sold into slavery "across the Tiber". The republic may have been a moral ideal but its version of morality was far removed from ours today.

Hard facts and written records are few and far between for the period of the early republic; much of the history as we now know it is the result of what archaeologists call "the spade", augmented by scraps of surviving administrative documents of varying degrees of reliability. From around the end of the third century BC, formal "histories" began to emerge from writers like Fabius Pictor and Cincius Alimentus, and the poets Ennius and Naevius. These were all written in Greek – largely because there was no great literary tradition in Latin but also because their purpose was as much to educate the Greeks about Rome as their own countrymen about their origins.

However, all that was transformed by the reactionary statesman and orator, Cato the Elder (234-149 BC): he was both vehemently anti-Greek and fiercely proud of the old Roman traditions – factors which go a long way to explaining why his version of Roman history was the first ever to be written in Latin. Although only portions of his major work, *Origines*, survive today, his writings formed the basis of research for subsequent annalists. They reconstructed much fuller histories using personal elaboration and pure invention, often as flattery to their patrons' families who were aggrandised along with the list of Rome's successes.

For these historians – and countless others throughout time – personal allegiances and the events of the day coloured the way that the city's "history" was laid down. Factual information was fleshed out with folklore, plumped up with politics and re-versioned to suit the desires and need of the contemporary audience. In some cases, it appears that whole swathes of fact might have been edited out of history altogether in order to save embarrassment and tell a more pleasing story: theorists are now suggesting that the ending of the Roman monarchy didn't come from a popular uprising against the king at all but as a result of an invasion by a neighbouring Etruscan king, Lars Porsena of Clusium. According to this somewhat less glamorous version of events, Porsena defeated the Romans and captured the city but before he could establish himself as the new king, Porsena was forced to leave the city. However, rather than ask Tarquinius to return from exile, the Romans chose to do away with the monarchy altogether – thereby establishing the Roman Republic. Clearly, this telling of history would have been less flattering to Rome than the version they later adopted as "fact" – and it's no surprise that, if true, it was dropped in favour of a more illustrious legend.

By the latter half of the first century BC, Rome had found a new stability that enabled learned scholars to work there in relative peace. The great historian Livy (59 BC – AD 17) and his Greek contemporary Dionysius of Halicarnassus were the first writers to attempt to strip away the embellishments in order to create a more factual history of Rome – and while their success at this may have been limited, their work has been a major influence on Roman knowledge and understanding for the last two thousand years. Another essential source of reference about Rome's ancient past is the Greek historian Diodorus Siculus who also flourished in the first century BC. His three volumes of detailed Roman history up to the time of Julius Caesar are not only valuable in their own right, they are even more important as they draw upon the works of others which have since been lost. Together, these three writers form a keystone of modern knowledge about Roman history to the end of the republic and they would have been required reading for anyone who presumed to call themselves "educated" right up until the eighteenth century. Today, those histories are augmented by archaeological discoveries which have helped to transform our understanding of life in early Rome.

The Rome of the republic may have lost its kings but it retained many of its traditional features of politics and administration. No longer under the absolute control of a monarch, it was now governed by a system of two consuls, or senior magistrates, who held power for one year only, and who were advised by a senate of, at times, three hundred men who were the heads of influential local families. In reality, though, it was the senate itself that was the cauldron of all power and prestige, and the senate that gave Rome its unique modus operandi.

As a city, Rome was confident and aggressive in both its own defence and its attacks on its neighbours. It prided itself on only fighting "just" wars, that is, wars where it was forced to defend itself; but with honour and glory being so intimately tied up with military success, it was often hard for politicians and generals to resist stirring up, or even manipulating, its neighbours and rivals into a course of action that would "justify" direct military action. While it might have been a worthy ideal, this moral framework was incompatible with what was basically an expansionist state.

Bellicosity was in the blood – or at least built in to the Roman system of beliefs. With no royal line, one's status had to be at least partly earned – and with military success came personal power and all the trappings of wealth an aspiring Roman could desire.

As for women, they were firmly excluded from the military and political spheres and therefore from much of civic life. In general, Roman women had fewer freedoms than their Etruscan predecessors, whatever their social status. Childhood would end abruptly between the ages of fifteen to eighteen when a girl would be married off – some ten or more years before their brothers married; by the menopause (around fifty years old) they were classed as having entered old age and tended to be depicted in art as the stereotypical hag or grotesque prostitute. But in many ways all that was immaterial: with average life expectancy around twenty-five to thirty years, and high rates of maternal mortality, few women would have to worry about growing old at all – and once past the age of fifty, at least they were no longer legally required to re-marry if their first husband died. The liberating factor was money – and not caring what others thought; however, while she was dependent on her husband or *paterfamilias*, a woman was subject to his legal control and restricted to the domestic or religious domain.

Women were looked down upon in both literature and society; even the word was used as a term of abuse. The satirist, Juvenal, who flourished in the early years of the Roman Empire mocked a friend for getting married and subjecting himself to a woman's "bitch tyranny" while more than a century beforehand, following his time as consul, the staunch moralist and conservative, Cato the Elder, supported a law called the *lex Voconia* of 161 BC which put a check on women's financial freedoms. This was no aberrant misogyny: in his classic treatise *On Agriculture* written around 160 BC, he laid out his strong views on wifely duties that would have struck a chord with the majority of men in the Roman Republic and beyond:

> *"Make her be in awe of you. Stop her from being extravagant. She must visit the neighbouring and other women very rarely, and not have them either in the house or in her part of it. She must not go out for meals or be a socialite … she must be neat herself and keep the farm clean and tidy. She must sweep and arrange the hearth every night before she goes to bed … "*
>
> CATO THE ELDER: *ON AGRICULTURE*, C. 160 BC

However, with Rome's fervent militarism, the reality for many soldiers' wives was frequently living alone, often for years at a time, waiting for their husband's return and meantime running farms, businesses and households as ably as any man. Women like these helped keep Rome fed and clothed but there were few ancient historians who would celebrate their achievements; instead, the stories of these *de facto* female heads of households have been cast aside and left to blow away like dried-out seed pods.

But not all of Roman life was about exclusion: despite being bounded by the usual city walls, Rome had always been uncommonly outward-looking to other peoples and places. Although Latin was the dominant language of the region, a whole range of different languages, dialects and accents would have been heard in its bustling streets as a result of strong trade links and military activity, its location at the meeting point of three major population groups (the Latins, the Etruscans and the Sabines) and also at a stategically important crossing point of the River Tiber on the land route from the Appenines to the sea. Furthermore the Greeks had established colonial towns and cities across the south of Italy, adding to the constant interplay of trade, ideas and military skirmishes. The ancient world was certainly not a place of tranquillity.

Of all the ancient cultures, Rome was possibly the most cosmopolitan and inclusive – as long as you had the right credentials, contacts or value to the state, you could be welcomed as a Roman citizen, regardless of where you were born. Perhaps because of the broad mix of population it encompassed as a result, it also had a more expanded world view than many of its political rivals – a world view that would one day have Rome at the beating heart of a mighty empire.

Over the five hundred years before the fall of the republic and the rise of the Roman Empire in 27 BC, this self-confident city would grow to be a world superpower, changing the social and political landscape of the Mediterranean and even further afield almost beyond belief. From its starting point as a patchwork of small, jostling states with tribal and strategic alliances, it was transformed by the Romans' growing thirst for land, wealth and power into a vast administrative empire with a tight control over financial, political and military security.

There were, however, what even the most bullish Roman would have to admit to as being "setbacks" – and one of these in particular had a profound and lasting effect on the Roman psyche and the political geography of Europe.

For the first hundred or so years after the formation of the republic, things had been going pretty well for the Romans: with their victory over the neighbouring city of Fidenae (437–426 BC) they won their first major war against an established and organised state which brought one of their main neighbours under their control along with a large slab of land; next was Veii, a large Etruscan town nearby which fell to Rome after an alleged ten-year war (406-396 BC). Possession of Veii almost doubled the amount of land now under Roman control and strategically it also opened what are now Tuscany and Umbria to further Roman influence.

But before the Romans could capitalise on their hard-won gains, disaster struck. While Rome was busy dominating its near neighbours, trouble was brewing to the north where a marauding army of Gauls was sweeping down through the Po Valley. Gauls were a different breed of enemy from the normal Etruscans or Greeks. Whereas the latter were similarly urbane and cultured, the Gauls were largely rural people with little in the way of stone-built towns. But what they lacked in material refinement, they made up for in bravery: they were both famed and feared for their impressive warrior culture which had already dominated most of Europe down to the north of Italy and would occasionally be felt as far south as Sicily.

By around 390 BC and under the strong command of their leader, Brennus, the Gallic army had successfully reached what is now west central Italy and surrounded the town of Clusium – the former home of the Etruscan king, Lars Porsena. Clusium was now effectively in the stranglehold of a Gallic siege.

As news of the siege of Clusium spread westwards to Rome, a by-now very nervous republic sent the high-born politician and commander, Quintus Fabius Ambustus, along with two of his kinsmen from the influential Roman Fabii family to meet with the Gauls. The diplomatic efforts did not quite work out as the Romans had intended: Quintus Fabius became embroiled in a skirmish with the Gauls who demanded that Rome should hand over the guilty parties. Instead of punishing the culprits – and in a complete rebuff of the Gaulish request – Rome instead elected all three men tribunes. Outraged by this flagrant insult, the Gauls then set their sights on Rome itself, giving the Romans a drubbing at the battle of the Allia River about 12 miles from Rome before marching on to capture the city.

Crucially, however, Brennus's campaign lost momentum: the Gallic commander appears to have waited for a few days after the victory at the Allia River before making the final assault on Rome – thereby giving the Romans the chance to fortify the Capitoline, one of the city's famous hills. While the city below was well and truly sacked, it took a further seven months for the Capitoline siege to be resolved. At last, Rome wearily accepted the Gauls' demands for ransom in gold and Brennus was able to leave with his honour and fortune intact. For the Romans, it was a disastrous blow to both their city and their treasury but the most damage was done to the Roman sense of pride. Until now, they had thought themselves almost invincible; from this point on, the Gauls would be one enemy that would stick in the Roman craw.

Meantime, the Romans set about rebuilding the city, redoubling their efforts to gain control of the region's land and wealth – and rewriting their history books, claiming that the soldier, statesman and hero, Marcus Furius Camillus, had actually defeated the Gaulish invaders.

With each passing century, Rome rolled it borders further and further out from its base in today's Italy. It took around forty years of hard fighting for Rome to recover the power lost during the Gaulish defeats, and then the three major Punic Wars between Rome and the Phoenicians of Carthage before the republic was the unquestioned ruler of Italy and master of the Mediterranean. By then, the Gauls had once again been a thorn in the Roman side, assisting Hannibal in his devastating victories against the Romans during the Second Punic War of 218-201 BC.

Hannibal was the son of a great Carthaginian commander, born in what is now a suburb of Tunis, today's capital of Tunisia. According to the Greek historian, Polybius, and his Roman counterpart, Livy – the two main sources of information about his life – when Hannibal was still a child, his father made him swear eternal enmity towards Rome and he had spent his early years doing everything in his power to upset the growing Roman control over the Mediterranean in favour of the Phoenicians. Carthage was a serious rival to Rome's power and imperial ambitions: both states desperately wanted control over the entire Mediterranean basin and lands – and along with these, the rich trade that flowed through there.

Hannibal's big chance to score a victory over Rome came during his efforts to win the Iberian peninsula for Carthage: Rome took exception to his siege of the Iberian city of Saguntum which they considered to be one of their allies.

Although Hannibal was defeated and severely wounded in the battle that followed, he managed to escape. The Romans were furious at this double insult to their hegemony, insisting that Hannibal be handed over to them immediately – and when this did not happen, they declared war on Carthage.

The response by Hannibal is one of the greatest military feats of the ancient world. Almost single-handedly, he took control of his great army of men and led the assault against the Romans throughout mainland Europe, making the vast crossing from the Pyrenees in Spain, then across the Alps of France and Italy, then down into the Po delta and the Italian peninsula itself. In what can only be described as a storybook expedition through the mountains and rivers of this treacherous landscape, he had to cope with guerrilla tactics from warring Gallic tribes, precipitous mountain passes, rockfalls and landslides, let alone the snow and ice that made his multi-cultural and multi-lingual army feel very far from home. In a major feat of military command, Hannibal somehow managed not only to successfully navigate the five-month journey intact – including floating his warring elephants downstream on earth-covered rafts – but to encourage the Gaulish tribes of Insubres and the Boii of northern Italy to join forces with him against the Romans. Even so, the original (alleged) ninety thousand infantry and twelve thousand cavalry – and infamous thirty-eight elephants – that had left Spain some five months before were now reduced to just twenty thousand infantry, twelve thousand cavalry and a handful of elephants. But what he lacked in sheer force, he made up for in guile: a series of impeccable military decisions and dramatic victories by Hannibal devastated a Roman army of up to perhaps eighty-five thousand men until – by the winter of 216–215 BC – his army had reached as far south as Capua on Italy's western coast.

Capua was the second greatest town in Italy, located sixteen miles north of modern Naples, and it had been under Roman control for over a hundred years; however, its population had a long tradition of opposition to its official rulers and when Hannibal reached the town, its people joined with him against the Romans. His army now contained Phoenicians, Iberians, Gauls and Capuans: to the enemy, it must have appeared that all the world was uniting against them.

Rome was almost paralysed with shock: from being one of the most successful states in the Mediterranean, it had suffered the biggest losses in the history of the republic; but it had also now learned its lesson. Rather than trying to engage Hannibal's seemingly invincible army in a series of decisive battles, it moved to a policy of slowly trying to recover what it had lost. The defeats thus far were blamed on the wrath of the gods at Roman irreverence, to be propitiated by the sacrifice of a Gallic and Greek man and woman and the burial alive of two Vestal Virgins; the senate must now be steadfast, the army resolute.

Already Hannibal's army and supplies were nearing exhaustion; his men were now forced to spread themselves even more thinly in order to defend what they had won while, in contrast, the superior numbers of Roman soldiers quietly held both their nerve and their ground. Even with the help of Celtic tribes from the north, the next few years of hard graft reaped Hannibal little in the way of victories and soon his losses began to outweigh his gains. In 211 BC, Hannibal was forced to march to relieve a Roman siege of Capua – but despite his efforts, in a defining moment for his whole campaign, the city fell to Rome along with Syracuse in Sicily and Tarentum in southern Italy.

Realising that he had now lost the initiative but desperate to fight on, Hannibal withdrew from central Italy to Bruttium in the South where he held out until 203 when he finally left Italy for North Africa. From there and locations around the southern and eastern Mediterranean, he continued to rout the Roman army until his eventual defeat and death by poison around 183 BC – around the same time that the northern lands of the Celtic Boii and Insubres were finally colonised by their victorious southern enemy.

Following the demise of Hannibal, there was one last effort by the Carthaginians to stop Roman dominance across the Mediterranean in the third and final Punic War of 149-146 BC. Almost inevitably, this war was short and decisive: in just three years, Rome finally burned the ancient city of Carthage to the ground, enslaved what remained of its population and ritually scattered salt over the entire area to prevent anything growing there again. A great city – and a great era in the history of civilisation – was now in ashes beneath the hungry fire of Romanisation. Roman influence now extended from the Balkans to North Africa, through a series of colonies, treaties and bilateral alliances; she had proven not only her military might but her commercial stranglehold over the whole Mediterranean basin.

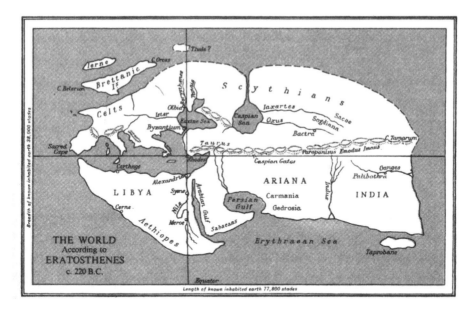

Eratosthenes World Map c. 220 BC (reconstruction)
The known world of the Ancient Greeks and Romans stretched from Ireland
(Ierne) down to Sri Lanka (Taprobane). Though little of it was under direct
Mediterranean control, Roman traders and envoys had made contact
with vast swathes of this supposed super-continent

The landscape of the ancient world was now far removed from that of 509 BC when the Roman republic first came into being. What was then a patchwork of largely agricultural tribes, small villages and trading routes was now a vast network of Roman civil and military power – and a well-oiled machine for both labour and wealth extraction from the periphery to the core.

As for the institution of the Republic itself, as it stretched its boundaries further and further afield, cracks started to appear in its very heart: the city of Rome. The gravest concerns were over issues like the supply of manpower for the military and for the production of food for the townspeople. As the army drained increasing numbers of men from the land and those who were left were attracted to a job that paid hard cash rather than subsistence, the region was heading towards a crisis. The slump in agricultural production left Rome dependent upon grain from Sicily and Africa – and its price yo-yoed according to supply. The days of eating cereal porridge were fading into history: now the population wanted bread as their staple, with olive oil, greens and meat if they could afford it. However, while the countryside was left depopulated and unproductive, restless peasants crowded streets of the capital. Here, they crammed themselves into the jerry-built wooden shacks hastily put up by entrepreneurs with an eye for the desperate buyer. Fire was a constant hazard, sweeping mercilessly through row upon row of homes and workshops, increasing the misery of the immigrant communities. Unless you were fortunate enough to be wealthy, life in the city was harsh, unpredictable and dangerous.

An unemployed, hungry population is a threat to domestic security – or at least the security of the status quo. As the privileged in Roman society grew fat on the riches of their military or political winnings, the poor became unhappy and increasingly frustrated. With no ready employment and having given up the self-sufficiency of peasantry, there was no way out for the landless proletariat. For the rich and powerful, the seemingly endless supply of foreign slaves solved the immediate problem of a pliant workforce and insulated them against any personal distress. As for their roles as civic leaders, they merely tried to placate the common folk by providing what the satirical Roman poet, Juvenal, called "bread and circuses", that is, free bread and public entertainment to keep the mind occupied and the stomach at least partly full.

The result was inevitable: internal strife and a series of civil wars ensued and in the political manoeuvrings that followed, the seeds were sown for the destruction of the republic. With its eyes firmly fixed at the edges of its influence, Rome had failed to notice that its heartbeat was growing fainter and more erratic: the republic was now the sick man of the old world.

Meanwhile, in the uneasy political atmosphere of Rome, a rising star was winning the attention of both the military and the ruling classes. In around 100 BC, on the thirteenth day of the month of Quinctilis – a month that would later be renamed July in his honour, Gaius Julius Caesar was born. Unlike others of his class, his home was not a vast country estate on the Palatine but an *insula* or apartment house in one of the poorest, most overcrowded and multicultural districts in Rome. The busy, jostling townscape of his childhood offered little in the way of prestige but it did provide him with an ability to mix easily with people of all classes and nationalities – skills that would serve him well for manoeuvring through both politics and the military.

However, despite his seemingly humble origins, his was an old patrician family, one of Rome's original aristocracies whose name they claimed could be traced back via an ancient clan line to Aeneas and then to his mother, the goddess Venus herself. Around the fourth century BC, the family had merged with the so-called *plebeians* – or commoners – of Rome and had risen through the ranks to become part of the city's ruling noble classes. But by all accounts, although they were privileged, by the time of Caesar's birth the family was neither hugely wealthy nor particularly influential. In a society where connections were everything, there was yet another fly in the ointment for this ambitious young man: critically, his family refused to align itself with the nobility that by now ruled not only Rome but its vast hinterlands with an audacious level of arrogance and corruption. Bereft of this social advantage, the young Julius Caesar knew he would have to earn his own status, and the only way to do that was through politics, the military or preferably both. Luckily he was well armed for the job with a sharp intellect and a skill for manoeuvring through the murky waters of power play that bordered on genius.

Julius Caesar was not a man who accepted the hand life dealt him. In his mind, boundaries were as much mental shackles as physical restraints – and he was not a man to be hemmed in by tradition, especially when a few audacious risks here and there could be balanced against huge personal and political gain. As someone who was starting out with more ambition than real influence, he needed to work his way up the hard way – by earning vast sums of money to fund his political goals. For that he needed a success on the scale of Alexander the Great, an achievement that would ensure his name echoed around the senate in tones of hushed reverence, something that would quell the doubters and win him the position he felt he deserved: public office to create a new kind of Rome – a Rome that would be restored to all its former moral glory.

In 84 BC, the tall, slim young Caesar pinned his political colours squarely to the mast with his marriage to Cornelia, the daughter of a radical, revolutionary nobleman who had dared to oppose the much-feared Lucius

Cornelius Sulla. Although Caesar seems to have genuinely loved Cornelia, it would prove a dangerous match: Sulla was one of the most important (and, many would argue, despised) men in the republic, who would go on to become Rome's first dictator to rule without the imposition of a time-limit. What is more, he was a man who did not take kindly to being publicly challenged by a novice politician without a pedigree. He now demanded that Caesar divorce his new wife; Caesar refused but equally knew he had made a powerful enemy. The only solution was to leave Rome and do military service in Asia, then in Anatolia, until Sulla's death in 78 BC.

His return to Rome was marked by his growing notoriety as a legal advocate, prosecuting some extremely powerful but corrupt officials, including one ex-consul, while earning the respect and gratitude of the general public. Still only in his twenties, he pursued his conventional politicking – carefully choosing his allegiances, steadily working his way up through public office and paying the necessary "expenses" to keep his supporters and patrons on-side. It was also rumoured that he gave generous "presents" to a whole raft of mistresses.

Following the death of his wife, he married Pompeia, a distant relative of Gnaeus Pompeius (Pompey) with whom he had now allied himself. Pompey was one of the most powerful and successful commanders in Rome and a rising political figure who had begun his career fighting for Sulla and had now, in a spectacular *volte face*, changed sides. An able politician, Pompey was a key figure in Caesar's own bid for success.

By 62 BC, Caesar's plans were working well: he had been elected praetor, one of the key judicial positions in the government of Rome which now meant the coveted top job of consul was in sight. Every year, two consuls, or magistrates, would be elected to rule Rome and the position was a passport to the highest stratum in society as well as more lucrative and prestigious assignments in the provinces. But then, in December of that year, disaster struck. According to the Greek historian, Plutarch, at a women-only party hosted by Pompeia to celebrate the goddess of fruitfulness, a troublesome politician named Clodius allegedly entered Caesar's house, disguised as a female harpist. The deception was quickly noticed and news of the intruder, when it broke, caused a major scandal which echoed around the streets of Rome by morning. Caesar immediately divorced his wife but his enemies rejoiced: here was a public embarrassment and religious infringement that would surely cut him down to size. Clodius was hauled in front of the senate but although he was acquitted, Caesar was resolute: he could not afford to have a wife who was not "above suspicion" (he's said to have coined the phrase) at a time when public image was everything for an aspiring politician.

By 61-60 BC, with his reputation shaken but intact, Caesar had landed the plum job of the governorship of Far Spain (modern Andalusia and Portugal) which not only brought him huge power but enormous wealth – enough to give bonuses to his soldiers, pay off all his debts, give money back to the treasury and, most importantly, enough money to stand for the consulship the following year. This position gave him huge political clout and prestige, and it almost guaranteed his name would go forward to be a provincial governor once his term in office had ended – and with *that* position lay the massive wealth that in turn could lead to unrivalled power.

It was as if the gods that his wife had so offended were now smiling on Caesar: he was duly elected consul, negotiated a secret pact with Pompey and crowned it with the master-stroke of uniting Pompey with his hugely influential arch-enemy, Crassus. But he did far more than just excel in a game of political chess; with a genuine belief in greater fairness for the common man, he forced through new laws on land distribution and, much to his enemies' annoyance, a curb on the abuses of the nobility.

And then finally came the reward he was looking for – governorship of Illyricum (in modern Albania, Croatia and Slovenia), Cisalpine Gaul (the land between the Appenines and the Alps) and then Transalpine Gaul (all of modern France and Belgium, along with parts of Switzerland, Germany and the Netherlands) as well. This was a vast swathe of land stretching from the Mediterranean to the Atlantic and the Pyrenees to the Rhine, challenging in its terrain, terrifying in its inhabitants but teeming with resources and potential plunder. Not only that, it was also near enough to the seat of power in Rome to keep a close eye on his political rivals. Caesar knew he had been handed the perfect opportunity to push back the boundaries of Roman power and earn the plaudits of the senate, for this wasn't just land: this was a grudge-match.

Ever since the sack of Rome in 390 BC, the Romans had both feared and hated the Gaulish people of Europe, and this was only compounded by their role under Hannibal in the Second Punic War. As an enemy they were brave, unpredictable and terrifying but they had one major strength that was also their major weakness: it was widely reported that Gallic tribes could never stop fighting, whether against the Romans or more likely, against each other. This was their Achilles' heel and Caesar was about to exploit it to the full.

At first, it seemed that the odds of subjugating the Gauls were not stacked in Caesar's favour: at forty-one years old, he was well past the age at which most men made their military reputations and he had never actually fought a pitched battle; moreover, his army was smaller, less equipped and arguably less skilled but what he lacked in military might, he made up for in strategy. Roman discipline was the envy of armies across the ancient world and Caesar was a born commander who knew how to fight a chaotic enemy and get the best out of his men.

His plan was to make his reputation by picking off the Gauls tribe by tribe, either through fighting, fear or alliances until he had conquered whole swathes of territory, along with its wealth and its manpower. But even Caesar could not have known the full extent of the action he was about to take. In a move that would subjugate the peoples of Europe for the next five hundred years, he was about to launch what history and he himself would come to call "The Gallic War".

His first chosen victims were the Helvetii of Switzerland who were planning a mass migration almost due west across the mountains and major river valleys into western Gaul to escape the marauding Germanic tribes. Together with some neighbouring bands of Celts, around three hundred and sixty thousand men, women and children had massed on the banks of the Rhône with all their possessions and animals, ready to cross the water to their new lives. But this crossing into a Roman province gave Caesar all the justification he needed to wage a war in "self-defence" even though the Helvetii had yet to encroach upon Roman soil. After a forced march through the night with his troops to reach the water's edge, he launched a dawn attack that slaughtered a quarter of the Gaulish migrants and left the remainder scattered in the neighbouring woods in such a state of profound shock that even those bellicose people tried to sue for peace.

Caesar was happy to halt the fighting, at least temporarily: he knew he had won the initiative and it suited his plans to wait until his new legions were positioned in a much stronger location before the real battle commenced. In the meantime, his army dogged the tail of the long line of migrants as they wove their way northwards around the mountains to the flatter region of their promised land, but all the while he was growing shorter and shorter of food. Caesar now knew he had to change his plans: he was left with no option but to divert his troops to the Gaulish stronghold at Bibracte. These were the lands of the friendly Aedui tribe in modern Burgundy – somewhere he knew he could find supplies for both his men and his animals. However, the diversion was a feat in itself.

This is a highland region, part of the Massif Central that stretches its thick arms toward the Paris basin. The mountains might have been rounded by time but they are unforgiving, rising up to nearly a thousand metres and frosted with thin, rocky soils. In Caesar's day, the lower slopes were thickly wooded and crossing the region was made more difficult still by the long deep valleys which bisect the Massif as well as treacherous swamps which have since been drained. The Romans not only had to contend with the area's harsh geography, they had to do so while carrying up to thirty kilos/sixty pounds of equipment, including their weapons, spare clothing, food rations, their camp and cooking gear, some rope, a shovel and a wicker basket for carrying earth. This would have made their passage cumbersome and laborious – but what happened next was, according to Caesar, either due to the Helvetii believing the Romans were weakened or because the Helvetii themselves overestimated their strength.

Along with their allies, the Boii and the Tulingi, the Helvetii suddenly did an about-turn and attacked the Roman troops; Caesar quickly sent his cavalry to hold them in check while he organised the remainder of his force for what was about to become the first pitched battle in his career. He knew that he had to maintain a calm discipline amongst his men – many of whom were new and inexperienced – and his ability to keep his head at a point of crisis would be a talent that marked him out as one of the greatest commanders of all time. He positioned his men up a slope in three lines, eight men deep, with the most experienced soldiers at the front; the least experienced – located at the back of the lines at the top of a hill – were ordered to dig a protective trench around the mounds of supplies and personal effects, and stoically waited for orders.

Caesar now showed he was no ordinary leader: whereas the usual protocol was to address one's troops, inspiring them to bravery and instilling in them the fear of dishonour should they display anything other than extreme courage, Caesar proved beyond all doubt that he was indeed a "soldier's soldier". To a stunned silence in his ranks, he dismounted and ordered all his officers to follow his lead, thus proving by their own actions "that the dangers would be the same for everyone". With that, they faced the enemy.

The charge, when it came, was fierce and terrifying: a phalanx of Helvetii roared up the slope towards the Romans, their shields tightly held together to present a solid defence while they readied themselves for their attack with their swords or spears. It must have been a terrifying sight even for the experienced legionnaires who made up the front rows of the Roman ranks, but they knew what they had to do: when the Helvetii reached a line around thirty metres away, the Romans unleashed a deluge of javelins, specially designed with spearheads of soft iron so that when they punctured a shield they crumpled and wedged themselves in so firmly that they couldn't be easily removed. The Gauls were left with no option but to throw down their shields and submit themselves to unprotected combat and thereby sealed their fate.

For Caesar, this was a perfect battle, the savage outcome slowly unfurling itself on the plains of that spring day in Burgundy – just as it would a century later against a valiant but doomed army of Britons led by a redheaded warrior queen. Now, the phalanx of the Helvetii began to break down as the Roman forces set to work. As soon as one line of legionnaires tired, the next would move forward in its place, stabbing and slaying the enemy with ruthless efficiency.

The Helvetii knew they were defeated; those who could fled the field up a narrow valley to a nearby hill where they could regroup and buy some time – but all the while they were pursued by the relentless Romans. Meantime, it was the turn of their allies, the Boii and the Tulingi, to come on to the battlefield but their hopes that they would do any better were brutally extinguished: the rear third of the Roman forces now raced down the slope and dispatched them with their swords and a similar lack of mercy. As the afternoon turned into evening and the landscape became drenched with blood, the ringing of metal and screams of the Gauls crescendoed into a feverish cacophony of desperation. In a last bid to defend themselves, the Gauls barricaded themselves behind their carts and wagons but even this was futile. The roaring finale, when it came, signalled their total defeat and as the soldiers broke through the cordon, they slaughtered anyone who couldn't escape.

The Romans now had fire in their veins, hunting down and dispatching the Gauls in a monotony of killing that continued well into the night. At last, the oppressive hush of death muffled first the cries and then the final breaths of the wounded. And then it was over: three-quarters of the Helvetii had been butchered – and Caesar had won his first major victory that would earn him the plaudits of Rome. Or at least, this is the way that Caesar's version of history tells it. There are no other documents which lay out in such detail the events of 58 BC; all we have to rely on today is the first book of Caesar's *Gallic War* which he wrote up that winter when the weather made fighting almost impossible and he at last had time to draw breath. And of course, what Caesar wrote was designed to show him in as good a light as possible. As one commentator puts it, he was setting himself up as not only a commander of an army, but his own war correspondent, editor and publisher as well. The way that the *Gallic War* is written cleverly gives the impression of it being historical fact and not autobiography; the style is factual, the writing plain and Caesar writes in the third person so the reader can quickly forget that he was the actual author at all. As reportage, it is convincing; as a work of self-publicity, it is inspired.

However, almost inevitably the reality fails to live up to his claims. For example, by extrapolating the population densities of the local tribes at the time, Caesar's details about the numbers of migrating Helvetii now appear to be wildly exaggerated. While he claims there were around three hundred and sixty thousand tribespeople, even the most generous figures that historians can come up with today suggest the real number would have been closer to around two hundred and fifty thousand. Given that around half of those would have been women and not all of the men would have been of an age and condition to fight, the Helvetii army would almost certainly have numbered much less than a hundred thousand men, with more realistic estimates at around forty thousand.

In other words, the Celtic and Roman armies would have been roughly the same size: less dramatic but much more credible a scenario.

Whatever the truth of the situation, the impact of Caesar's victories over the Gauls in 58 BC raised eyebrows in the Senate: he was now a man to be watched – both by his supporters and his enemies.

The Roman army was arguably the greatest invention of the ancient world. Professional, proud and disciplined, it was a prime reason why Rome was the dominant force across the whole of the Mediterranean and now increasingly across northern Europe. Originally, in the time of the kings, the army was mustered from the ancient clans of Rome. Three tribes each provided a thousand men for infantry which were further subdivided into *centuries* of around a hundred men, together with three smaller and less-important squadrons of mounted soldiers (the Romans were never known for their cavalry). In the early days, fighting was haphazard and "heroic" based around a throwing spear and probably a long shield; however, during the sixth century both the structure and equipment of the army were completely reformed, largely under the sixth of the seven kings, Servius Tullius (578-534 BC). He reportedly doubled the number of soldiers, increased the cavalry and levied them (*legio* is from the word for "levy") according to tribal wealth rather than family group. It was also around this time that the infantry became more heavily armed like their Greek counterparts, sporting swords and a round shield, clipped to the forearm which in turn encouraged new styles of fighting.

Servius was wise enough to see that one of his biggest problems was recruitment, and here he faced an anachronism: although Rome's population was increasing sharply, this was largely due to immigration. However, the army could only recruit from the old local clans and given Rome's military ambitions, they simply could not keep pace with demand. The solution was to reorganise the three clans into a new group of twenty clans, many of which were based not only on family lines but on where you lived. This meant that new, untapped sources of manpower could be exploited by the military – and the new recruits would gain access to social and political mobility. Throughout the republic, the army grew in skill and strength becoming, like Rome itself, a force to be feared.

Service in the military evolved from being the realm of the "privileged" to being a career in itself – and this, in turn, conferred improved stability and loyalty on the army. By the time of Caesar, legions were as much loyal to their commanders as to the state; they were, in effect, private professional armies where the men would gamble on surviving the twenty-five years of service to receive their ample pensions along with Roman citizenship (for those who didn't already have it) and frequently a tranche of land as well. In addition, if your commander was successful in his military service there was also the chance of receiving significant *donativa*, or bounty, which helped to guarantee further loyalty along the way.

Though the potential rewards were good, life on the ground was harsh: the average soldier's pay was roughly that of a labourer – but from this was deducted the cost of his food and equipment. Groups of eight men would form a soldier's *contubernia*: throughout the campaigning season, they would march together, eat together and sleep together in a small leather tent which became wetter and colder the further north they pushed. Together with their heavy leather jerkins and woollen tunics, thick leather sandals and shin guards, they must have grown weary of the constant feel of the damp against their skin.

Given the conditions under which the soldiers were expected to live and work, discipline had to be tight – and it is no surprise that the best army in the world was also the best organised. The structure was hierarchical, just as it is for most armies today, with smaller, manoeuvrable building-blocks combining tier by tier to form a legion. At the bottom of the pyramid were the *contubernia* or tent-parties; these formed *centuriae* or "hundreds" (which were actually groups comprising around eighty men though this number could change from thirty to over two hundred). Two of these "hundreds" formed a *manipula* – literally translating as a "handful" – and three *manipuli* comprised a "cohort" of generally some five or six hundred men. To make a full legion required ten such cohorts amounting to around six thousand men, with cohort number one considered the elite band of fighters.

With his legions relaxing in the relative comfort of their winter quarters, Julius Caesar at last had the opportunity to ponder on what he had achieved: he had won some good battles and proved himself as a commander against Rome's old enemy of the Gauls; what's more, he knew the best was yet to come. The coming season would see him push even further into the Celtic lands, further than any other Roman commander had ever been.

If the success of his first year's campaigning had got him noticed, the mettle of his second year in Gaul would establish his reputation as a great tactician and commander of men. From his base in northern Italy, he now ordered his newly expanded army (from six legions to eight) who had overwintered in Vesontio – modern Besançon, on the Doubs River of eastern France – to prepare themselves again for the coming season. For their part, the Gauls sensed what was coming; why else would the Romans base themselves so blatantly on the Gaulish side of the border? Joining them in early summer, Caesar and his vast army of eight legions pushed north through modern Burgundy to the river Marne to execute some of the finest military action in the course of the Gallic War. This time, the pretext for war was even flimsier: in his own words, "frequent rumours" that a large coalition of Belgic tribes was conspiring against Rome.

The Belgae, whose name comes from the Celtic for "proud", occupied the area north of the Marne and Seine rivers, with some groups spreading across the Channel into Britain. Typically, however, not all the Belgic peoples were happy to unite against a common enemy: the Remi tribe from the area around modern-day Rheims caught up with Caesar as he marched through their lands and pleaded for his protection, alleging that a force of three hundred thousand men had been raised by the remaining Belgic tribes in an attempt to drive his legions out of Gaul once and for all.

The Remi might have been wise to seek protection but in doing so, they guaranteed the wrath of their compatriots who attacked and besieged one of their neighbouring towns. Caesar immediately called some of his men to its defence – and the Belgae responded by turning their fury against the Romans. The battles which followed were the Gallic War in microcosm: fierce but shambolic fighting from the Gauls and tight, precision warfare by Rome that devastated an entire people, and left them in no doubt that the era of Celtic supremacy had passed.

The key to Caesar's military strategy was his inspired use of the very best in Roman warring technology: siege towers on wheels, bridges, defensive trenches and giant catapults, the likes of which had never been seen by the enemy, and all designed by his chief engineers whose creations left the Gauls so completely outclassed that they knew they were beaten. Man to man, they had a chance against the Romans; man to machine, they were at Rome's mercy. As word of each defeat quickly spread throughout the region, and stories were told about the giant, iconic structures, Gallic resistance began to crumble. Tribes throughout the north of Gaul submitted to the Romans, falling one after the other like a giant house of cards until Caesar was the undoubted master of the entire region, from the Alps to the Channel. Yet at no point in Caesar's commentaries does he mention the engineering brilliance of Mamurra of Formiae or Cornelius Balbo or the large part they played in bringing Gaul to its knees. The two men and their role in winning the Gallic War were edited out of history – and the glory went to its author, Gaius Julius Caesar.

Yet another glory that would soon be attributed to Caesar was the first major crossing of *Ocean* to the shores of the land the Romans called "Britannia". His "invasions" of 55 and 54 BC would be trumpeted throughout Rome and the provinces as the first real conquering of *Ocean* and the first Roman incursion on to British soil; strange, then, to learn from the great geographer Strabo and historian Diodorus Siculus that during the winter of 57-56 BC it appears that the brilliant Publius Crassus, son of Caesar's triumvirate partner and leader of his Seventh Legion in Gaul, undertook an exploratory expedition to Britain in search of the famous tin mines. Crassus the first Roman in Britain? That wouldn't fit with Caesar's plans at all, not when so much was to be gained by being renowned as the man who held both *Ocean* and the far-flung Britons in his sway. So the voyage of Publius Crassus gains no mention in Caesar's *Gallic War* and his name slips quietly into oblivion.

CHAPTER 2

THE MIGHTY COLOSSUS

"Why, man, he doth bestride the narrow world like a Colossus; and we petty men walk under his huge legs, and peep about to find ourselves dishonourable graves."

CASSIUS ON CAESAR IN SHAKESPEARE'S *JULIUS CAESAR*, ACT 1 SCENE II

The slave-dealers sniffing behind Caesar's entourage like dogs on a scent now slavered with delight: with so many Gaulish tribes vanquished, they fell on the broken tribespeople in a frenzy of consumption – men, women, even young children – snapping them into the long iron neck-chains and shipping them back to the flesh markets of Rome. Slowly and systematically, Gaul was being drained of its lifeblood to feed the hunger of the Roman world and prepare the ground for the next stage in its expansion.

Caesar was now the unquestioned (and enormously wealthy) hero of the day. Not only had he essentially brought the whole of Gaul under the control of Rome, the vast caravans of slaves and rich booty parading home through the streets of the capital meant that no one could be in any doubt about the magnitude of his achievements. He was undoubtedly "Conqueror of Gaul" – and in thanks to the bountiful gods the Senate decreed a ream of sacrifices, festivals and a fifteen-day public holiday – the greatest accolade a Roman general had ever received.

His enemies were less pleased with Caesar's successes in Gaul and his growing reputation as one of the Republic's greatest leaders. Behind the scenes of jubilation over the winter and spring of 56, Caesar was engaged in a deadly power struggle to confirm Pompey and Crassus's positions as consuls for the following year and his own position as governor of Gaul for another five years which would bring with it vast wealth and his own personal army, as well as protecting him from any threat of malicious prosecution from his adversaries. Once again, none of the dramas being played out in sotto voce made it into the limelight of *The Gallic War*.

Political machinations in Rome were matched by those among the supposedly conquered lands of Gaul. The campaign season of 56 BC was largely taken up with revolts by the Celtic tribes who were far from happy with their new overlords and the grip the Romans now had over them. Most agitated were the Armoricans – the collective name for the northern Gauls of modern Brittany and Normandy that translates from the Celtic as the "people beside the sea". Until their defeat by the Romans, they controlled the lucrative coastal trading routes along the Atlantic seaboard plying European wine, amber, pottery, glassware and other luxury goods in exchange for British tin, cattle, hides and hunting dogs.

The Armoricans are a people who fascinate Celtic coin expert, Dr Philip de Jersey: "One of the most interesting things about the Armoricans is that all the tribes used a bizarre human-headed horse on their coins. This pattern really was very specific to Armorica – you just don't see it anywhere else, and each tribe had their own variation of the basic shared symbol. Unfortunately, of course, we can't say what its meaning was but it all adds to the mystery of these

Armorican human-headed horse – a silver stater of the Aulerci Diablintes

people who were clearly expressing some kind of huge cultural symbolism. And other than their coins, which would have been crucial to them as traders, we really don't know a great deal about them beyond what Caesar reported – but he seems to have been pretty accurate in the way he described them. They *were* good sailors, in fact very skilled seafarers, and using a kind of flat-bottomed boat they were pretty much able to dominate the coastal trade around the north Breton coast, though doubtless there were still spats with rival tribes trying to muscle in on the act. Nothing would have been very cut and dried among the tribes when it came to dividing up trade."

Although Britain may have been a land of myths and legends for the Romans, among the Celts there had been a long tradition of trade between Britain and continental Europe. This trade was both buoyant and valuable with all the seafaring tribes keen to have their slice of the action. "This must have made it quite piratical at times," says archaeologist Philip de Jersey. "I imagine that some tribes were desperate to capture as much of the trade for themselves as they could – a bit like the nautical equivalent of cattle-raiders." It's not hard to imagine how they felt about the Romans muscling in on their patch.

The leading tribe in the region – and the tribe that would lead the revolt against the Romans – was the Veneti, according to Caesar, the undisputed masters of the seas. With their vast fleet of sailing ships, they had grown rich on the proceeds of that trade and now felt under threat for both their lands and their livelihood. But those ships gave Caesar a problem: Rome had never fought a battle in the Atlantic and Caesar had neither the ships nor the experience to fight one. However, if he wanted to achieve the next step in his great plan for himself and the republic, he needed to dominate not only the lands of Gaul but the seas and their bounty as well – and that meant creating a navy from scratch. But the rewards were well worth the trouble: in his sights was not just the wealth that geographers had talked of in the lands beyond *Ocean*, the really glittering prize across the water was the domination of Britain itself.

There was nothing that Rome liked better than the expansion of its empire, and Caesar knew that the Senate would shower triumphs on the man who could deliver this. His own future was therefore bound to that of Rome which badly needed the manpower and wealth of the new lands to support the hungry structures of its modus operandi. The core could not function without the slaves, trade-routes and wealth. But subjugation had to be total: any tribe who stood in the way of the state's imperial ambitions had to be cut down – not just because they dared to oppose Roman might but also because in the relentless march to keep expanding its borders outwards, the army could not be diverted to keeping peace back in the provinces. And that meant Gaul had to be enslaved by whatever force or brutality was required, as an end in itself and as a stepping stone ever-northwards to Britain.

The spring of 56 buzzed with industry as Caesar set in motion his ambitious plans against the Armoricans. Before he could even think of building a navy fleet – something he would have to pay for largely by himself – he first needed somewhere to build it, so thousands of legionaries and Gaulish slaves were put to work constructing a gigantic shipyard and then an entire naval fleet on the banks of the Loire river in what is now north-west France. Unlike the Celtic ships which were solely powered by sail, Caesar ordered his men to build triremes – large wooden ships almost architectural in beauty, with three banks of oars below deck and two giant square-rigged sails above.

Triremes had a long tradition in the Mediterranean: they were used to deadly effect during the Phoenician and Greek wars of the fifth century BC, their lightweight construction affording both speed and manoeuvrability of the bronze-clad ram at the bow that would pierce an enemy's hull like a pin through a balloon. With speeds of up to seven knots or more, they could chase and harry an enemy for miles while the power of the oars meant freedom from the tyranny of the wind. The classic trireme reached its height with the ships of the Athenians: just over thirty metres/one hundred feet long and around six metres/eighteen feet wide, these were propelled by one hundred and seventy oarsmen (freemen, not slaves) divided into the classic three levels: sixty-two rowers called *thranites* formed the top tier of the ship, then there were fifty-four *zygians* in the middle and a further fifty-four *thalamians* at the bottom, each rowing to the rhythm of a drum or a flute. Alongside the musicians on deck would be a complement of soldiers carrying spears and bows, ready to attack the enemy and if they drew close enough, board their vessel for hand-to-hand combat. Gradually, the armed deck soldiers had become so important that all the rowers were placed below decks, making the ships much heavier and less manoeuvrable but giving more space above for the naval army.

The ships themselves were one of the great classical conundrums. No wrecks of a trireme have ever been found and no naval plans survived from antiquity. Many archaeologists refused to accept that a ship could organise a hundred and seventy oars in three tiers and still be able to function, so after years of intense debate, a British charity called the Trireme Trust – in conjunction with the Greek Navy – reconstructed what has been called a "floating hypothesis": a full-scale three-tiered trireme based on pictures from fragments of pottery found on the floor of the Aegean Sea, the famous Lenormant relief from the Acropolis and references from classical literature, with the remains of ancient construction sheds which gave the overall proportions of the ships. The magnificent craft, *Olympias*, was launched in 1987 and received its first major sea trials at the Greek naval base at Poros in the baking hot summer of that year with a crew of young oarsmen and women from rowing clubs all over Britain.

I was one of those rowers lucky enough to be involved. For weeks, we took her out twice a day, dragging ourselves from our bunks at the naval barracks as dawn was breaking in order to get our work done before the sun grew too hot and then repeating the trials in the fading light of the late afternoon. The trireme looked incongruous against the modern grey ships of the Greek Navy. She hugged the dock, honey-coloured and majestic, with her sculpted lines etched out against the bluest of sky and sea. We would line up on the dock in strict order, file on board and then clamber down to our seats which were allocated according to height and ability. Being at the shorter end of the scale, I was down in the bowels of the ship as a *thalamian*, rowing for hours in what seemed like a dark and humid wooden cage with the raw sap dripping from the beams and covering our bodies with its sticky residue. But once we hit our rhythm, none of that mattered: from the glimpses of blue I could see through my port-hole as the oar connected with the water, I knew we were cutting through the Aegean like an unstoppable force, one hundred and seventy oars, working their way through the water in perfect synchronicity. This vessel, based on a two thousand year old design, was now the youngest ship in the Greek Navy, but she proved herself in both manoeuvrability and with speeds of up to seven knots from our scratch crew. To us, she was impressive; to an enemy, she would have been terrifying.

Such were the ships now under construction by Caesar's men and slaves but even that vast workforce could not supply him with all the vessels he wanted. Despite working flat out all spring, at least a hundred merchant ships also had to be requisitioned from the subjugated Gaulish tribes, along with the sailors and pilots to crew them in these unfamiliar waters.

Officially, the reason for building the giant fleet was to suppress the revolt by the Armoricans who were unhappy at the threat to their virtual monopoly over the region's coastal trade; unofficially, it is most likely that Caesar had already decided to invade Britain and the Gallic revolt was just an excuse. Moreover, historians have recently suggested that he may have deliberately switched the order of events to give the impression that he was responding to a threat (and thereby justified in his future actions) rather than precipitating the revolt himself

The reconstructed Greek Trireme awaiting her crew
(including the author) at Poros Naval Base, Greece, 1987

by building a fleet that would destroy the powerbase and trade routes of the Atlantic Celts. Again, a skilled politician like Caesar would know that how you present the "facts" in the official version of events can be as important as the "facts" themselves, and if a little creativity can help you win more votes in the senate – and hence more power – then so be it.

Whatever the true order of events, the effect was the same: by the time Caesar joined the fleet in May of 56, the Gauls were preparing for war. He quickly sent troops to quell the revolt in Normandy, dispatched a cavalry north-east to prevent the Belgae from joining their Armorican compatriots and then sent further troops to the regions of Aquitania and the Garonne River in south-west France. As for who would lead his new fleet, that honour befell a young man who had captured Caesar's attention: a certain Decimus Junius Brutus Albinus, who twelve years on would become infamous for his part in Caesar's assassination, and some fifteen hundred years later would be immortalised by William Shakespeare as the man whose treachery broke Caesar's heart, evoking the words "Et tu, Brute? Then fall, Caesar".

Meanwhile, Caesar set his sights on the Veneti and took his remaining legions towards their lands in modern-day Brittany. Once again, his battle plan was reliant on the skill and creativity of his structural engineers as the Veneti had retreated to their cliff castles along the coast. Fortified settlements, or *oppida*, were used throughout the Celtic world, offering their people's lands, farms and homesteads protection with a series of dykes and ramparts which made a useful barrier against warring chariots and horses. But the cliff castles of the Veneti had an added surprise to keep their inhabitants safe: for much of the day, they were completely surrounded by water, with only a causeway for access at low tide. But a man like Caesar wasn't about to let the sea get the better of him: in a game of technological cat and mouse, he ordered his men to build siege works and huge dams "as tall as the walls of their *oppida*". However, when it looked as though the Romans were about to get the upper hand, the Veneti would retaliate by sending in ships to evacuate all their valuables and inhabitants, relocating to yet another cliff castle so that the Romans would have to start their siege all over again.

Philip de Jersey takes issue with Caesar's version of his war against this tribe from Brittany's southern coast. "Undoubtedly the Veneti were good seafarers and didn't want to let go of their control of that part of the coast, but in terms of the archaeological record, here Caesar's account just doesn't stack up. There is actually very little in the way of material evidence for these people, so I'm suspicious that they were really as dominant in the region as Caesar suggests. The bulk of the trade to Britain was via Brittany's north coast, not their southern one, and there's also the fact that there is precious little left behind by the Veneti. Surely, if they were as important as Caesar claims, then we would be finding more in the way of coins and other artefacts today. They did exist and they were controlling this section of the coast but I'm afraid it looks like Caesar's been over-hyping them to make his victory over them seem more critical than it really was."

All summer this attack by land and the counter-attack by sea continued with the Romans soon losing any ground they had won. But like the mouse being tossed about by a cat, the Veneti knew Caesar was not merely toying: whatever the personal misery for the tribe with all their children and elderly, possessions and animals, they had to keep moving. They knew they were now battling for survival – and to begin with, it looked like they were winning. This was a situation Caesar had not anticipated and in terms of time could not afford to happen if he wanted to secure the Channel for the bigger goal of the invasion of Britain that season. Growing tired of the stalemate, he resigned himself to the fact that the only way to make any headway would be to play by the Veneti's rules and attack them at sea. Trouble was, this was much more than the crossing of *Ocean* to Britain: this was a naval battle in a foreign sea on the enemy's terms – three things that put the Romans at a serious disadvantage. While their army was feared throughout North Africa right up to northern Gaul, the Roman navy was relatively weak and inexperienced; what is more, it had never had to cope with the ebb and flow of the tides, let alone the capricious weather along the coasts of northern Europe. As for Caesar, he had never even dipped a toe – let alone sail – in the waters of the Atlantic but if he wanted to crush the Veneti, he had no choice but to beat them at their own game. And what he lacked in experience, he would have to make up for in imagination and tactics.

The strength of the Veneti was in their vast fleet of ships but to Caesar, this was also their Achilles' heel. Unlike the fast and manoeuvrable triremes that were waiting in the shipyards of the Loire, the heavily built Gaulish fleet was reliant on windpower only. To beat them, Caesar would have to have both skill and luck on his side – and on this occasion, both his tactics and the weather came up trumps. From his base on the heights above Quiberon Bay in the Bay of Biscay, he and his men watched Brutus sail out of the Loire and along the coast of Northern Gaul to meet the Veneti fleet face to face. Brutus had ordered the Roman armourers to prepare their men with long poles leading to a sharp-pointed hook like a scythe. In their light and speedy triremes, the Romans were able to get alongside the enemy, hurl missiles on deck and then use the hooks to grab on to the lines securing the Veneti's yardarms to their masts; once secured, the triremes would row quickly away from the ship with a burst of power so huge that the ropes would stretch and then snap like elastic bands, rendering the sails of the Veneti useless. As if the harrying alone was not enough, the wind that had been strong all day suddenly died away, catching the Veneti unawares and leaving them utterly helpless.

Unable now to sail away to safety, the Gaulish fleet was picked off one by one by the Roman navy until their crews had been slaughtered and their ships set on fire. According to Caesar, two hundred and twenty enemy ships were totally devastated; only a handful had managed to escape. The only answer for the rest of the tribe was surrender, with the leaders put to death and people sold into slavery. Caesar had won himself and the Romans their first ever battle in the Atlantic – and it seemed he was now invincible.

As word of his victory was passed back to Rome, in the opposite direction came the welcome news that his armies had managed to put down the rebellions in Normandy and the south. Piece by piece, the final components of his plan were falling into place: Caesar now had control of almost every tribe in Gaul – and most importantly – of the coastal waters leading across *Ocean* to the holy grail of his campaign: the conquest of Britain.

The end of the campaigning season of 56 BC was spent in pursuit of the last two Gaulish tribes to remain undefeated. The Morini and the Menapii occupied the coastal lands leading to the Rhine – and Caesar had them firmly in his sights. However, this time luck was against him: as the weather closed in and Northern

Gaul became a mudbath, even this tireless commander realised it was time for his legions to head back to their winter base camp in the more central and much drier Seine; meanwhile, he changed his attention from military to political warfare to secure the consulship of 55 BC for Pompey and Crassus, and another five years for himself as Governor of Gaul. Caesar now had what he wanted: his so-called "triumvirate" or gang of three controlled not only the richest provinces Rome had to offer, but the supreme power of all of its twenty legions as well.

Just in case he was beginning to think himself charmed, his celebrations were interrupted by news of migrating tribes of Germans who had crossed the Rhine into not only the lands of the Gauls but the very lands from which he had hoped to launch his invasion of Britain in the coming campaign season. Rumour had it that not only were they settling in these new lands, they were supplying arms and manpower to the Gaulish resistance. He immediately headed north to counter the threat and clear the way for his greater ambition.

Caesar was under no illusions that he was unanimously popular in Rome; he knew his enemies were just waiting for a mistake or sign of failure to use as his gibbet. Now he risked losing the Atlantic seaboard which he had worked all year to secure – and with that, risked queering the pitch for his invasion of Britain. Caesar raced to meet the Germans and held initial talks with their leaders in a bid to resolve the dispute peacefully; in reality, peace was far from his mind. In retaliation for an assault on some of his men, Caesar ordered what would become one of the biggest slaughters in his career. An alleged four hundred and thirty thousand migrating Germans, including women and children, were cut down in an attack of such severity it shocked Rome to the core. As details emerged that every last woman and child was being hunted down and killed in a move that could hardly be called "justifiable", a stunned senate cancelled all the proposed victory celebrations leaving Caesar in no doubt that he was on the verge of ruining the reputation he had worked so hard to create. To repair the damage, he needed a masterstroke – and that came in two shapes: another piece of technological wizardry – the bridge over the Rhine, and one further invasion.

At four hundred and fifty metres/five hundred yards long and twelve metres/forty feet wide, the bridge his men built over the Rhine was a major feat of engineering but just as important as this piece of Roman iconography was the fact that it allowed Caesar to become the first Roman general to cross what until then had been a river boundary into the lands of the Germans. Iconography and prestige: these were the only trophies to come out of Caesar's excursions into Germany, but they were enough. After a mere eighteen days of rampaging through German farms, fields and villages, his troops crossed back over the bridge they had built, and then destroyed it. A point had been made and Germany had served its purpose. It was time to move on.

On the coast of what is now the area between Boulogne and Dieppe in northern France, the year-old Roman naval fleet was waiting for its commander. On his journey from the Rhine to the sea, Caesar was met and accompanied by one Gaulish leader whom he had come to respect, trust – and use. Commius was a member of the tribe of Gauls known as the Atrebates and, as such, had much in common with the tribes of southern Britain including the same language and many cultural traditions. To Caesar, he would be the perfect person to soften up the British as part of an advance party and tell them all about the benefits of Roman suzerainty, for Caesar was about to take one of the biggest risks of his career: the conquering of *Ocean* and the invasion of Britain.

As the summer 55 BC began to wane, a few miles to the south of what is now Calais, Caesar massed his naval fleet and made his final preparations for a journey that would leave Rome wide-eyed in amazement. His actions may have seemed rash to those around him; when it came to strategy, Caesar was not in the habit of consulting others and tended to keep his plans to himself. While it may have shaken his officers, the idea of invading Britain had probably been formulating in his mind for the last few years and was most likely the real reason behind the creation of his navy the previous year. By now, he had conquered Gaul and crossed the Rhine – crossing *Ocean* and conquering Britain would give him the final jewel in his crown.

However, even Caesar would have to admit that he knew very little about the large island that lay to the north. In desperate need of good intelligence, he summoned the local Gaulish traders to his quarters and quizzed them about the waters, coastline and peoples of the strange land across the sea. Where were the good harbours? Were they big enough for his fleet? What hazards should he expect to encounter from the strange people and even stranger tides? The traders either didn't know or refused to share their information with their brash new Roman overlord.

Caesar had no choice but to send one of his own trusted men, Gaius Volusenus, ahead to scout for a suitable route and landing spot for the Roman troops. Volusenus spent just short of a week in the Channel and along the exposed, sweeping coastline of Kent, searching for the best harbour for the invasion but according to Caesar, he did not land: as before, the honour of being the first Roman on British soil had been strictly reserved for one man only.

By now the invasion was an open secret. Over the next few days, envoys arrived at Caesar's camp from Britain with offers of hostages and submission to Rome; in exchange, they received "fulsome promises" and valuable hostages including the Atrebates aristocrat, Commius. His job was simple: aided by thirty cavalry troops, he was to "visit as many tribes as possible, to encourage them to seek Rome's protection, and to tell them that Caesar would soon be arriving in Britain".

The steely resolve was no doubt as much for his own benefit as for Commius and the Britons. Caesar was about to launch out on a mission that could jeopardise everything he had fought for. The campaign season was ending, the weather was against him and he still had not managed to extinguish the last seeds of rebellion in northern Gaul which left him horribly exposed. And yet, *Ocean* and Britain called out to him like the Sirens.

Around midnight, on the August 25 or 26, 55 BC, the Roman fleet caught the ebb tide from the harbour and set sail. On board the eighty transport ships and dozen or so warships were the Seventh and Tenth Legions, along with around two thousand well-armed auxiliaries. The weather was calm, the waters still and an almost full moon lit the way ahead with its silvery trail.

Even Caesar had to be impressed with the giant cliffs that snubbed their flat white noses at his arrival into Kentish waters of modern-day Dover. Fringing their tops were rows of angry Britons and he quickly realised that this was no welcome party; rather than sail into a hostile harbour, he ordered his Gaulish pilots to sail on and find a suitable beach to launch a full-scale military invasion before meeting up with his ambassador, Commius. But unbeknown to him, Commius had met an equally hostile reaction from the native Britons who had taken him and his Roman cavalry hostage. There was no brokered peace, only fear, hatred and a readiness for war.

There is much speculation about the precise site of the landing – and the bloody fight between Britons and Romans that followed immediately on its heels. The strongest contender is the long, shingle beach near Deal which lies about ten miles north along the coast from Dover. "There's pretty much a consensus that Caesar made his landing somewhere around here," explains Dr de Jersey. "However, there's a frustrating lack of evidence as to any exact spot. We do get occasional finds of Roman republican coins which could have come from the first or second invasion, but then again, they *could* be much later deposits. What we'd really like, to prove where and when the landings took place, would be something like a marching camp – but there's nothing at all like that so we're left with good old guesswork based on Caesar's writings. Without those, though, there'd be precious little evidence of the landings at all."

Here the fleet would have arrived in the afternoon as the sun was beginning to dip towards the horizon. It's hard to imagine the feelings of those onboard: his troops were already unnerved by their first crossing of *Ocean*; now they had to face the prospect of landing in this dangerous, mythical and legendary country. Even Caesar reports how, for the Romans, the thought of a landing neck-deep in water, weighed down by weapons and armour, unable to get a secure footing on the large pebbles and facing merciless attack from hosts of blue-painted Britons was absolutely terrifying – and for a while after he gave the order to jump down from the boats, his men stood rigid, frozen with fear. And it is easy to see why: on the beach in front of them were near-naked, screaming foot-soldiers hurling their spears and brandishing swords; not only that, many of Caesar's men would be seeing for the first time the Britons' lightweight chariots swooping down from behind to deliver their warriors before retreating at lightning speed to re-arm. Caesar now needed to draw on every resource he had – from the archers, slings and catapults on his warships, to the patriotic bravery of his Tenth Legion's standard bearer who made a brief prayer to the gods and then jumped overboard and led his men down into the foaming water. The first ever battle for "Britain" had begun.

Hours of savage fighting ensued – and in a rabble of hand-to-hand combat with swords, daggers, spears and stones, even Caesar had to admit that the execution of his strategy was far from his usual cold, clear discipline. Abandoning his original battle-plan, he now sent in flotillas of troop-filled support-boats wherever they were needed and gradually this talent for quick and flexible thinking edged his men ahead. After a night of sailing the Channel, a day skirting the coast and the last hours of sunlight fighting against all odds, the Roman army at last pushed the Britons off the beach and back inland. The first battle was over – Rome had successfully invaded Britannia, if only by just a few hundred metres. And there they spent their first night on British soil, exhausted, wet-through and unsure of all their futures. To the Romans, fresh from the glory of their victories in Gaul, the people of this savage land were even stranger than the stories that abounded of this cold, dangerous place that lay beyond the edge of the known world. To the Britons lurking in the darkness of the shadows, this was *their* world – and they didn't want to share.

CHAPTER 3

THE LAST OF
THE FREE

"We, the remotest people on earth, the last of the free, have been proteccted by our distance and obscurity until this day. Now, even the furthest reaches of our island are exposed to our enemies ... Thieves of the world, not content with emptying the land with their cupidity [the Romans] now plunder the sea ... Robbing, butchering and looting they falsely name government; they make a desolation and call it peace."

TACITUS'S VERSION OF A SPEECH BY CALGACUS, LEADER OF THE PICTS
IN THE BATTLE OF MONS GRAUPIUS, AD 84. TACITUS, *AGRICOLA*, 30

For the Britons licking their wounds after the first battle of Britain, this was what they had both feared and expected. This was a known enemy: many of their warriors had fought with the Veneti and other Gaulish tribes as mercenaries so were only too aware of the threat presented by the enemy force now resting in their camp below. They knew they should have taken them, pushed them back into the foaming surf, driving them back on to the ships that brought defeat and death to their comrades across the water. Was it now their turn to be butchered? The clamour of the fighting still rang in their ears but the Britons needed to clear their minds, to think of a strategy – one that would succeed where their allies had failed. They were proud fighters, boastful of their bravery, steeped in traditions of war and a cosmology where there was little fear of death. Even so, that first night sharing their soil with the enemy must have proved a long one.

Although Britain was isolated from continental Europe by its geography, it had long been part of what can be *loosely* termed the "Celtic tradition" of the Continent, influenced by the language and culture that had dominated Gaul for the five or so centuries prior to Caesar's invasion. Rome may have portrayed the Iron Age Celts as savage, uncivilised barbarians but the reality was far more sophisticated. This Celtic culture was not uniform and homogenous – there were marked differences even between neighbouring peoples, but the term is a generality that had been applied to the inhabitants of the larger part of Europe since the earliest writings of the classical world and then again in the modern era as a descriptive term for those ancient peoples who shared a common Celtic root to their language.

This so-called Celtic culture had been developing and dispersing from the heartland of what is now Italy, Switzerland and Austria to the farthest fringes of Europe, sometimes by means of the migration of the people themselves but even more significantly, when it came to reaching Britain, by contact with their commodities and ideas. However, this was no smooth, continuous wave of influence: while some aspects of Celtic values, practices and products were picked up by other traditions, these were often incorporated into pre-existing cultures to create a deeply textured pattern of regional variation from the Alps to the outermost reaches of Britain.

While ancient history talks of a "Celtic" Britain, no classical writer ever described the ancient Britons as being "Celts" like their Continental neighbours – and certainly the ancient Britons themselves never used this term to define their own identity. In fact, this label only developed in Britain from the eighteenth century onwards and it glosses over the reality of archaeological discoveries. The evidence on the ground suggests that at the time of Caesar's invasion, not only did the population speak different "Celtic" languages, but Britain was composed of a number of distinct communities with differing cultural practices, often markedly different from those of the Continental Celts but sometimes sharing their themes or individual fashions.

One clear example of this regional diversity is the discovery of grain pits and also wheel-thrown pottery in the tribal lands of the south and east of Britain, which seem to be proof of a productive agricultural economy; yet further north, in the vast region of the Brigantes tribe which dominated the land astride the Pennines, the economy seems to have been based less on crops and more on animal husbandry, with no substantial evidence of growing and storing grain. Here, the livestock was farmed using a system of nomadism or transhumance – moving between (lowland) winter bases and (upland) summer pasturelands in an annual cycle. Today, high on the Yorkshire moors, it's still possible to see the caves that provided shelter to these wandering farming communities. Meanwhile, the native pottery that has come to light seems to be coarser and hand- rather than wheel-made. However, Barry Cunliffe, Professor of European Archaeology at Oxford University, argues that these differences don't reflect a more simplistic culture: "No doubt most of the containers were made of wood basketry and leather – materials more appropriate to the pressures of pastoral mobility." When the Brigantes wanted fine pottery, they simply imported it instead.

The first major work from someone with direct experience of the peoples of the British Isles comes from Julius Caesar, who discusses the similarities between Britain and the coastal lands of the Gauls, and how there had been some recent Gaulish settlers who had migrated over the Channel. However, he also comments how the Britons further inland regarded themselves as indigenous, that is, not migrating Celts at all. As for the Romans, they certainly regarded the Britons as a collection of different peoples, with *Brittones* in the north and *Britanni* in the south.

However, there was one connecting factor between the British and European Iron Age communities that cannot be disputed: the exchange of products through trade and gift-giving. Though most of the Celts relied predominantly on agriculture for their day-to-day survival, the diversity of landscapes and natural resources throughout Europe meant that tribal groups began to specialise in their production. From that specialisation came reciprocal exchange, barter and fully-fledged trading routes stretching the full length and breadth of the continent and beyond, from the Baltic as far as India and China.

It was these trading routes that provided much of the information about other peoples and other lands; and it was also trading routes that Caesar was hoping to control when he conquered the Armorican regions along the coast of northern Gaul. The strange island that lay within the embrace of *Ocean* at the end of the trade-line was well-known for its mythology, but within that mythology was an enticing array of resources: the exquisite pearls, the hunting dogs, the nuggets of precious tin which were mixed with copper to make bronze and – for the Romans in particular – the vast, untapped supply of slaves.

It is estimated that as much as forty per cent of the population of Rome was made up of slaves. In fact, the social structure and the whole economy of the republic were completely dependent on this 'free' source of labour. The formula was simple – as more and more men were drained from the land to serve in the ever-expanding army, which in turn was needed to conquer and then defend increasing amounts of new land, an equivalent number of slaves had to be harvested from the new provinces and sent back to feed the labour market. Without slaves, and without the riches that were plundered from the newly conquered provinces, the whole system of the republic would come crashing down.

By the time of Caesar, the "equitable" ideals of the republic had degenerated to such an extent that the powerful politicians, provincial governors and commanders of the legions could manipulate the system to generate vast wealth and private armies for themselves. And while the key to power was wealth, the key to that wealth rested on slavery.

The trade in human beings was not, however, solely a Roman tradition. The Celtic peoples throughout Europe also had their slaves who were similarly the vanquished tribes of this warrior culture. But unlike Roman society where you were either a slave or "freeman", there was little meaning to the word "free" amongst Celtic populations, even for tribal leaders. Instead, you were born and bound into that society in a complex and hierarchical network of obligations that linked families, tribes and whole regions in a three-dimensional game of chess, played out by the fortunes of warrior "champions" both within and between each community. The fate of you, your family, your tribe and its lands could thus rest on the fate of just one chosen man.

It is often said that devastation of the Celts was due to the fact that they would just as soon fight each other as unite as one people and fight the Romans. While true at some level, it ignores one underpinning theme in the Celtic world: there was no such thing as a Celtic society. Instead, there were Veneti and Helvetii and Atrebates and Belgae and any number of other tribal groups who may have shared a core language and a common history and even a common culture but there was no widespread sense of having a shared identity as a Celt. From about the sixth century BC, the Greeks had written of their Alpine neighbours, the *Keltoi,* which is the first time the word comes to our attention, but there is scant evidence of its general usage among the so-called Celts themselves and even its modern use as a handy moniker for classifying the general ethnic group has been severely criticised as imposing a modern-day construction on to pre-historic peoples.

In terms of their response to the Roman threat, the fluid movements of Celts around the time of Caesar's invasion that resulted in Britons fighting in Gaul and Gauls trading and settling in Britain were more likely the result of temporary allegiances or concerns over trade and jobs as mercenary soldiers rather than any sense of being one people under "foreign" attack. Clearly, some of the migrating Gauls who came to Britain around this time were displaced people seeking a new place to live, but these incomers were often far from welcome to the existing population and were perceived to be as much of a threat as any Roman.

The Celtic world was thus a continuum (albeit a lumpy one), from the most Romanised lands closest to Italy to the more "traditional" Celtic lands at the fringes of Europe. And with Britain being not only at the edge of the known world, but to many Roman minds in the seas *beyond* it, it was hardly surprising that it was viewed as being among the most "foreign", savage and barbarous lands on earth.

What we do know from the archaeological record – for example, artefacts, earthworks and often relic patterns of settlement agriculture in the landscape – is this: from the late Bronze Age (around 1200-800 BC), the peoples of Britain were becoming increasingly sedentary and growing in number from the days of their former hunter/fisher transient lifestyles. Like their Continental partners, they were largely farmers tending herds and growing crops in relatively small fields but instead of the rectangular houses that were common in central Europe, Britons tended to live in round or oval homesteads – eminently more streamlined for the windier, wetter climate. As the centuries rolled on, some areas developed defensive hillforts with a whole range of functions – like the spectacular Maiden Castle in Dorset, where the key tribal players could live or retreat in relative safety or corral their livestock – and here there is some evidence of more complex social organisation required not only for their initial construction but also to maintain the community of up to two hundred families who lived at times inside them. Other communities marked out their lands or retreated behind series of fortified dykes, designed to slow the warrior and confound their chariots, but in general, there was little in terms of politics, religion or economy to tie the disparate homesteads together as one people. By the early Iron Age, even the sacred, ceremonial sites that had once created some bonds for their ancestors – sites like the Neolithic monuments of Stonehenge and Avebury – had been abandoned, their purpose and meaning lost in the gentle erosion of three thousand years.

With the passing centuries, the trend towards sedentary lifestyles under a ruling warrior elite was becoming an established fact of life. By the seventh century BC, it seems that as an ancient Briton you would live and work with your family or clan group for all your short life, defending yourselves when necessary from any warring bands or neighbours and being almost wholly self-sufficient. Typically, your world view existed as far as the edge of your clan's land; beyond that lay the unknown. There was little in the way of established centres of regional power and communications were relatively constrained. However, social and political organisation through *local* tribal hierarchies certainly existed, and evidence for this is to be found in the sheer complexity of earthworks and field systems which would have required co-operation on a large scale just to build the giant structures that sprawled across parts of Britain at this time.

There was also a long tradition of trade (or more correctly, gift-giving and exchange) for the rare commodities that couldn't be made or found locally. The trade routes themselves were well-established, focusing particularly along the coastal fringes of Britain and inland along waterways which provided an easier mode of transport. Precious objects such as jewellery and the long, slashing bronze swords from this early "Hallstatt" Iron Age period (thus called from the site in Austria where a rich collection of late Bronze Age/early Iron Age artefacts were discovered) found their way across the Channel. For most of the rural population where life was a daily monotony of tending the animals, working the land and caring for family members, the arrival of traders would have been an occasion in itself; these growing points of contacts with the outside world were not only important for the exchange of goods, they were also critical for transferring ideas from other peoples and places in a network that could reach for thousands of miles across seas, mountains and plains.

From around the fifth century BC, the manufacture, trade and use of iron increased and spread across the whole of the ancient world, including Britain. It was also around this period – a generally accepted date is around 500 BC – that people in the so-called Celtic world started adding designs to their possessions that demonstrated the now-iconic swirling or curvilinear designs labelled La Tène style. This is what many people think of as classic Celtic artform: organically shaped animals, mystical beasts – and a feeling that you could trace your finger along the lines and never come to a stop. Vestiges of this rich and expressive artform persisted in Ireland until the ninth century AD and can still be appreciated today in the remarkable Book of Kells. It was also adopted by craftspeople in Britain who became widely regarded as masters of the art. In England – for example at Desborough in the Midlands and Holcombe in the

The Birdlip Mirror was buried with its aristocratic female owner around AD 50 in Gloucestershire. Exquisitely fashioned from highly decorated bronze, its a masterpiece of native British craftsmanship

south-west – exquisitely decorated bronze mirrors in La Tène style have been discovered which have one side, where the metal has been polished to make it reflective while the other side explodes with a profusion of glorious organic detail. Clearly, precious objects like these are not the artefacts of a backward society, however primitive those societies may appear to be; although rare, when they *are* found such items are frequently in the graves of women, with many experts positing a spiritual or shamanistic function as well as being used to see oneself. But while the full extent of their use and meaning remains unknown, their quality of craftsmanship and symbolic importance denote a degree of cultural sophistication that confounds the derogatory attitudes of many of the classical writers from the Roman and Greek worlds.

However, in the pick-and-mix of ideas from the Continent, not everything "foreign" was perceived as an improvement and the Britons often held on to their strong local idiosyncrasies in terms of how they lived their day-to-day lives and how they buried their dead, leaving behind them a rich, if sometimes frustratingly diverse, archaeological record.

This case was argued strongly by J D Hill, Iron Age expert at the British Museum as we walked together through its galleries. His unconventional journey to the discipline – including his years spent working with children on schools' archaeology projects – has resulted in an almost raffish delight in challenging unquestioned lines of thinking about the period, and he pounced on evidence in the displays to prove his point. We were discussing the increasing trend for "kings" in Britain around the time of the Emperor Augustus – a trend that Hill believes could well have "opened up spaces for women like Boudica and Cartimandua" because it relied on passing the crown down to one's successors, some of whom were naturally going to be female. "Take these coins: we're seeing a time when the coin record is obsessed with claiming a kin relationship: they say 'son of' this king and 'son of' that king, so there was clearly a really strong desire to keep power in the family," he said. "But while the *idea* of kingship might have come from the political structures of Rome – which were becoming more focused around individuals as the Republic was breaking up – the Britons chose to emulate the new kind of Roman leaders in a very *British* way. It may have been based on a Roman model, but what resulted was *uniquely* British. And it could be argued that Cartimandua was just more politically sophisticated than Boudica in working the new system and holding on to her power." Though Boudica has since become more famous, it was hard to disagree.

From about the third century BC, the speed of change had begun to increase and the traditional lifestyles of the ancient peoples of Britain took on new dimensions that have left more of an imprint in the modern landscape. An increase in the number of settlements went hand-in-hand with a rise in agricultural activity; new areas were cleared and colonised and more drove routes appeared, connecting settlements in a network that can only imply more surplus and economic exchange. But rather than creating a monolithic culture across the whole island, these changes seem to have gone along with an *increase* in local and regional diversity. While the south and parts of south-eastern Britain often adopted and adapted ideas from the Gauls, the north and west tended to retain their own distinct styles of living, some of which were maintained right through to Roman occupation.

With the increase in wealth – at least for some members of the groups – came power, and the umbrella in this potent cocktail was a huge rise in the use of adornment and the symbols of status. It seems that the ancient Britons of this time had a love of display equivalent to any 'wide boy' entrepreneur today, matching bravado with conspicuous decoration.

Classical commentators talk of giant golden torcs, drunken feasting and ornate, boastful charioteers, the material evidence for which has since been thrown up in the archaeological record. This is where the concept of the warrior culture – found in a range of societies from the Samurai of Japan to the Middle East – has its clearest expression: a time when subsistence had been transformed by surplus (at least for a minority) and people were thus freed from the production of food to take on specialist roles within their communities, be that warrior, seer or craftsman.

Conspicuous consumption, an obsession with celebrity and living for the moment: perhaps we are not so very far away from Iron Age aspirations today. But paradoxically, the display culture in Britain was not materialistic in the way we think of it now – a difference demonstrated by the other marked change of this period: the development of an Iron Age version of our throwaway society. Although we dispose of vast quantities of possessions every day, the key distinction is that while we throw away what we no longer value, our ancestors threw away the things they held most dear.

During the Iron Age, precious metal objects were increasingly deposited as votive offerings to the gods, in streams, rivers and bogs. The spiritual world seems to have become suddenly more important, though whether that is just because this was the first time that people really had non-perishable votive goods to deposit (and for us to find two thousand years later) is hard to gauge. What's more, the changes weren't just reserved for the living: funerary rites which had tended to involve cremation or laying the dead out in the open were also shifting to burials in individual graves, sometimes accompanied by rich collections of personal artefacts to assist them in the afterlife. The argument has raged in academic circles whether these changes were the result of waves of migrations of Celts coming to Britain from Europe with their new ideas about warrior societies and hierarchies – or whether these foreign influences were actually just *ideas* that were imported and included into the indigenous cultures, rather than foreign peoples physically migrating here themselves. However, in the last few decades the lack of direct evidence for waves of invading Celts, combined with the often piecemeal way the new ideas were incorporated into the existing local culture, has tended to suggest that our long-held view of the population of Britain being refreshed by immigrants is overdue for renewal.

However, archaeologist Richard Hingley urges caution. "In the last thirty years or so, the invasion hypothesis has become really unpopular but I think perhaps now the reaction has gone too far the other way. We know for a fact that people in Rome were often *really* mobile, that governors would travel thousands of miles to a province just for a year or so, so why not people in Gaul and Britain? In the late Iron Age there's a lot more going on than we've given them credit for and we're now just starting to realise that. Still – that's what's so great about archaeology: it never stays still."

Votive offerings, grave goods, conspicuous consumption: this is the Iron Age legacy which is now helping to unlock the past. As I travelled around the country and talked to professional and amateur archaeologists, it soon became clear that discovering a coin, a piece of pottery, let alone something more substantial like a house or farmstead, was a special kind of experience – one whose memory still evoked a twinkle in the eye on the telling, even years after the event. John and Pat Wells are typical of the sparky, enthusiastic characters I met. Living close to King's Lynn in the Norfolk countryside, they have an intimate connection with the land of Boudica's Iceni tribe and a remarkable knowledge of the material record from around her time. The couple have been on archaeological digs together for more than forty years – and for the last eleven years, John has also been an active metal- detectorist, finding six previously unknown archaeological sites. He's built up an impressive collection of coins and around twenty brooches, some of which are extremely rare.

"It's not the monetary value of the finds," he explained to me while laying out his collection across his sitting room furniture and carpet, "it's the fact that I'm the first person to see them in perhaps two thousand years. Your mind starts to spin: who dropped this, what were they doing, what kind of life were they leading at the time. With some of the sites I've found, there have been so many objects that you start to think, 'This place must have been *really* heavily populated', and wondering what it was like. It opens up a whole new world – but it's a world that *you* are now connected with because you're the one who has just uncovered their personal possession."

He showed me his favourite discovery – an unusual three-legged mount probably once forming part of a belt. It was shaped like the modern symbol for the Isle of Man but found in a piece of ground close to his home. "You get such a strong feeling for metal-detecting that you can almost sense where the good sites are going to be. It's a very personal kind of link with the past that actually has nothing to do with what an object's worth – though of course, it would be nice to find that hoard of buried gold!" As John later showed me his metal detector in action, it was obvious as he swung the device low to the ground evoking a series of electronic beeps, that he was looking at the surrounding Norfolk countryside like a seer would look into tea leaves. But he wasn't reading the future: his eyes were looking into the ancient past of Boudica and her tribespeople, reading the landscape as though it was a letter from a long-lost friend. "I'm convinced that she's buried here, you know, even though they would have had to have done it in secret. And one day we will find her. This area's too holy – there are too many temples and too many finds for this not to be a special place. Where better to bury your queen than her homeland?"

We might not know the precise mechanism for change during the Iron Age, but the end result was a significant increase in population numbers and also in social complexity. Particularly in the south and east of Britain, La Tène style and culture was being picked up, adapted and integrated into not only the impressive artwork of the ancient British peoples but also in terms of the way people were organising themselves and living their daily lives. Here, and apparently for the first time, there was a growing stratification of their societies. Where once were dense clusters of homesteads where everyone would tend to collaborate, communities were now becoming more specialised and often developing new tiers or strata *within* themselves. Status became more of an issue, and this social difference was expressed through material goods and cultural practices. From farmers to craftspeople to members of the nobility, you sported all the fine accoutrements and imported products that befitted your place in society.

There also appears to have been a more physical change in the geographies of the later Iron Age Britons, again especially in the south and south-east. New centres of population were becoming established in previously unpopulated areas such as southern Suffolk down to Essex and much of Kent and across to Buckinghamshire – but these changes were not simply a matter of expansion: unlike the older settlements that surrounded them, these new settlements seem to have been fundamentally different, reflecting the new cultural developments in Iron Age Britain. The landscape frequently began to *look* different, too: where once was open farmland, the terrain became compartmentalised into smaller fields and paddocks. Along with the changes in field systems came a trend in some areas towards more individual rather than expanded farmsteads – a pattern also reflected inside the home which now began to show more individual patterns of eating using separate and specialised utensils and portioned meals which replaced the communal bowl of stew or porridge. As Iron Age expert J D Hill is keen to make clear, this change was not imposed by any wave of migrating overlords, nor were the Britons passive recipients of a dominant foreign culture: the changes might have come from outside but the demand for them most certainly came from within those societies in ancient Britain. In the lead up to Roman invasions, therefore, the landscape and its people were dynamic *and* evolving.

As old relationships between groups of people – and between people and the land – was being redefined, communal forms of living began to give way to more individual lifestyles which have left their mark in the archaeological record of the period. More individual plates, cups and other cooking and dining wares show that not only was the use of space within the home being transformed, but it also meant that the roles of women (as the primary domestic carers) were changing in order to spend more time at the hearth and less time taking part in communal work in the fields and farmsteads.

Over-arching these social changes were ones involving political reorganisation: often developing in a fluid pattern though certainly more visible by the time of Caesar's invasions in 55 and 54 BC, there appear to be distinct *tribal* identities linked to a specific "people" or territory, such as the Trinovantes of modern Essex, rather than the family groupings that seem to have previously characterised the Iron Age way of life. These labels may not have meant much to the average man or woman as you only need a name for your tribe if you encounter other peoples and what is more, they seem to fluctuate with the changing relationships of power between the tribes but one thing is certainly true: these political structures with leaders ruling over tribes of vassals made it much easier for the Romans to enact their plans for the political domination of Britain. Pick off the ruler … and the people, the lands and the wealth came too.

However, our knowledge of the politics of the Iron Age is being challenged by a surprising source. Businessman John Talbot is a prime example of how an amateur can revolutionise the accepted wisdom about a particular period in pre-history. Now an authority on pre-Roman coinage, he started collecting about eight years ago. "I got into it totally by chance – I met someone selling coins and couldn't believe that you could buy Iceni coinage so cheaply. I then got to know Philip de Jersey in Oxford and recorded the coins that I had bought on the Celtic

Coin Index. I was surprised just how big the gaps in knowledge were – so I started researching just one small group of Iceni coins and ended up looking at the whole series!" Credited by professional archaeologists with doing some leading-edge research, John is now publishing papers in academic journals. "What really interests me is trying to link coinage to political relationships – there appear to be linkages between certain Iceni coin issues and those of tribes to the north and south of their territory. I have been carrying out a systematic die study of the iceni coins and have now completed something like seven thousand coins out of the seven and a half thousand in the coin index. It is clear that much of the symbolism on the coins is not accidental or random and that you can order the coinage using these symbols. Interestingly, they also reveal clear links between certain streams of Iceni coinage and that of the Trinovantes and the Catuvellauni; these and other aspects of the coinage strongly suggest a political relationship between these groups. The work is also revealing some fascinating details relevant to the Boudican period, suggesting that native coins were being used right up to the revolt. A further aspect of the work is showing that the coinage consisted of an ordered group of related denominations at most times while it was being produced. Now, this might not seem much at first, but it suggests that people in the late Iron Age may have been using money in a sophisticated way and not just as token gifts or a store of wealth." It is interesting that some of the buried coin hoards which in recent years a number of authorities have doubted come from the time of Boudica's uprising now look like they were – and that's surely an indication of the general and widespread feeling of unrest that Britons must have been feeling around that time. So much human information from something so metallic and tiny: small wonder, then, that coins can unlock the past.

So what would the Iron Age peoples of Britain have known of the strange men on the even stranger ships, now standing off the coast of Kent?

They knew that they were a ruthless, hungry people who had invaded and conquered the tribes across the water. They knew, too, that the army was different from anything they had fought against, with giant structures that could cross rivers and scale even the fortified heights of the tribal *oppida*. The Britons also knew that this army had not come here for peace, as it had driven many people across the water to seek sanctuary in their own tribal lands. Some of the warriors lining the clifftops that day might even have fought as mercenaries for the Celts in Gaul alongside tribes who were now vanquished and sold into slavery. Others might have heard the stories from Armorican traders about how the army came from the same part of the world, many months of travel away, that was the source of the large amphorae of wine that some of the higher-ranking nobles had taken to drinking instead of the traditional ale. But without doubt, while they may have been happy to have Roman exports, having the Roman army and their ships lined up less than a mile away was another matter altogether.

And what about Caesar's men, looking back on their momentous first day in Britannia? As they had craned their necks on deck to look at the massed warriors roaring at them from the Dover Cliffs and then as they had come in towards that shingle beach, what did they know about the fabled land and mythical people they were about to invade?

Mediterranean traders had visited Britain from at least as early as the fourth century BC, bringing back stories along with their goods. The history of contact might stretch back even further with an account by one explorer from the Greek port of Massilia (Marseilles) of the strange island called "Albion". Around 300 BC, the Greek geographer, Pytheas of Massilia, circumnavigated the island garnering some detailed information about the land and its inhabitants and he recorded its name as The Pretanic Isles after its people, the Pretani – possibly a Celtic word translating as "the people who paint themselves". This was later mis-spelled by Caesar and others as Britanni or Britannia. But other than Pytheas, few had penetrated much further inland than the coast – and what right-minded Roman would want to? Apparently, the people there were half-men, half-animal so no matter how crammed full the islands were with tin and hides and hunting-dogs, it was not the kind of place you'd *choose* to visit. Not that Caesar's men had any choice at all – their commander had cursed the Britons for aiding the Gauls in their fight against Rome and for offering sanctuary to those high-ranking warmongers he had driven off their lands after the Gaulish revolt two years earlier; now they had to come here to finish the job in the name of Caesar and in the name of Rome. However, there was also the softest whisper that he was really coming to lay his hands on the fabled pearls that grew here.

The rumours about what they would find when they managed to get inland still abounded on the eve of the invasion – and beyond, such was the power of these shadowy islands over the Roman imagination. Even half a century later, when the men of the much-loved general, Caesar Germanicus, were shipwrecked and washed up on the beaches of Britain,

"not a man returned from the distance without his tale of wonders – violent whirlwinds, mysterious birds, enigmatic shapes half man and half beast: things seen or things believed in a moment of terror."

TACITUS: *ANNALS 11.24*

The stories and beliefs about this land at the edge of the world would persist for the entire duration of the Roman Empire. Almost half a millennium after Julius Caesar, in AD 396, St Jerome described Britain in his letters as one of his four corners to mark the end of the world, along with India, the Atlantic and the "ice-bound north". However, for Caesar's men sailing across the Channel with an invasion fleet, many on deck still believed, along with many of their republican compatriots, in ideas that stemmed from the writings of Hesiod, one of the earliest Greek poets who flourished around 700 BC. He wrote of certain "islands of the blest" that lay in the far *Ocean* and to which "happy heroes" journeyed after death. It was not a great leap of imagination before those islands of the blessed became the islands of Britain and Ireland to which Caesar's men had set sail. Steeped in classical mythology even then, Britain stood for far more than just bad weather and painted warriors.

In the meantime, even the crossing of the mighty river-god *Ocean* was sacrilegious enough for the ordinary Roman soldier whose belief in the gods was profound and resonated throughout their every action. For them, there was no precedent; few would have known if any Roman before Caesar had ever sailed the waters before – and according to Caesar's version of events, no one really had (if you exclude the merchants like Pytheas, Publius Crassus's tin-hunting trip two winters previously and of course Gaius Volusenus who had just spent a week scouting the coast of Britain on the orders of his commander). Crossing *Ocean* was like challenging the gods themselves, and that's something no man would take on lightly, especially a military man who needed all the divine help he could get. The following year, in 54 BC, Cicero would receive a letter from his brother Quintus, then on campaign in Britain with Caesar. Even to a man of learning and experience like Cicero, the descriptions fuelled him with such awe and intrigue that he wrote back "the ocean terrified me, and I was petrified by the Coast of the island!"

As to what the gods of this strange land thought of their arrival, that too was an unknown. Roman soldiers, like all Romans away from home, were respectful towards the local deities, often adopting them as their own. But what kind of gods were watching – and how would they react to this incursion? The Romans had yet to find out who governed the hearts of the enemy though they knew their Druid priests from the conquered lands of Gaul. One thing was certain: they understood the warriors well enough to know that within their camps there would be a current frenzy of communing with the spirit-world to divine the will of their gods.

As the soldiers looked around them, wide-eyed with anxiety, they realised there were other points of correspondence between the place they had just left and where they were now: even in the half-light of the breaking dawn they could see that this very green island was like a more densely populated version of northern Gaul. The rolling hills and valleys were crammed full of impenetrable thickets, woods and giant forests of beech that spread for miles in every direction, punctuated with broad clearings where the fields were laid out like floorboards with yellowing rectangles of the stubble of the late crops of cereals. The mode of farming was also similar to that across the ocean – small fields surrounded by drainage ditches and hedges, animals grazing freely or yoked in pairs to a light plough. As to what lay further inland – they had no idea but, if the gods were pleased with them, it would not be long before they found out.

CHAPTER 4

BEYOND THE DEEP SEA

"[Caesar] gazed across at the island of Britain and enquired of those standing about him what land it was and what folk inhabited it. When he had been told the name of the kingdom and of its inhabitants, he went on gazing out to sea. "By Hercules," he exclaimed. "Those Britons come from the same race as we do... All the same, unless I am mistaken, they have become very degenerate when compared with us, and they know nothing at all of modern warfare, living as they do beyond the deep sea and quite cut off from the world."

GEOFFREY OF MONMOUTH, RECOUNTING THE MYTH THAT
BRITONS WERE A "LOST TRIBE", DESCENDING FROM AENEAS'S GRANDSON,
BRUTUS. TAKEN FROM *THE HISTORY OF THE KINGS OF BRITAIN, IV, 1*

On their first night on British soil, both in their tents or outside on watch, the Romans had their first opportunity to reflect on the magnitude of their achievement. Caesar had taken them across the infamous *Ocean* into what many believed was the end of the world, in many ways the ancient Britons had turned out to be just another set of people like the warring Celts of Gaul. Physically an impressive bunch: they seemed to be much taller than the Romans, often light-haired and long-headed with piercing blue eyes that set them immediately apart from their Mediterranean invaders. Their nobles seemed to take much pride in their appearance, shaving their faces clean but leaving a long, flowing moustache, while the warriors stiffened their hair with lime until it stood up from their heads in a terrifying manner. They also used the infamous war chariots that had often been talked about but never actually seen by Caesar and most of his men – and the sight was impressive in both its speed and skill, especially to Romans who were never at ease with fighting on horseback.

But over the next few days, the Roman soldiers began to see a more rounded picture of the local population as they feigned disinterest towards their invaders and went cautiously about their business as usual. Now the naked, blue-painted warriors faded into an unfurling domestic scene: men and women going about their work in the fields, dressed in coloured or plaid tunics and cloaks, fastened by a brooch and without any of the conspicuous finery sported by their superiors. But whether labourer or warrior, theirs was essentially an agricultural lifestyle – there were no obvious signs of towns like the Romans were used to and there was little of the opulence that would be visible in a city like Rome, though the warriors and overlords would try their best to give off a good show of power and might.

In the watchful peace that followed the two sides' first battle on the beach, no one could guess whether the truce would last, not least Caesar who as a standard precautionary measure had oriented his tent as usual to the east to take full advantage of the good omens that were meant to hail from that direction. In the meantime, the soldiers at least had the security of one hundred acres carved out for their heavily defended camp. Whatever threats and dangers lay beyond the ditches and palisades of its perimeter, inside this bubble of Roman civilisation, however artificial, every man knew his place and his job. Too much thinking wasn't going to achieve anything – and it certainly wasn't encouraged by their superiors.

As for Caesar, he knew only too well the enormity of what he had taken on. Militarily, he was nearing the end of the summer campaign season so he knew that he wasn't going to get far inland before the worsening weather drove him back. But this invasion was conducted as much for political as military ends and that was where the real bounty lay. While slaves, tin and other precious metals all helped to shore up his power, the iconography of "conquering" Britain was what had driven him here and it was the reaction back in Rome that would be the final arbiter on whether or not his campaigning had been a success. The PR exercise would come with his dispatches to Rome and his account of the Gallic War. After all, it was up to him to define what he had achieved, and as skilled a self-publicist as Caesar was not immune to a little surgery to make the account more pleasing to Roman eyes. The fact that he had left his invasion too late in the year and that Commius had failed to soften up the Britons, leaving his men facing a fierce battle before they had even reached dry land, was ... unfortunate. It was clear that the Britons would not willingly help them augment their scant food supplies and despite the silence that now descended outside, the hostility from the locals was palpable. Caesar knew without thinking that his plans were already hamstrung.

So how to spin? It seems the answer was: "effortlessly".

"The summer was almost over, and winter arrives early in these regions because the whole of this part of Gaul faces north. Nevertheless, Caesar went ahead with plans for an expedition to Britain because he knew that in almost all the campaigns in Gaul our enemies had received reinforcements from the Britons. Even if there would not be enough time for conducting a campaign that season, he thought it would be most useful to have visited the island, to have seen what sort of people lived there, and to gain some knowledge of the landscape and the harbours and landing places."

CAESAR: *GALLIC WAR, IV, 20*

Morning broke and with it came something genuinely positive in the shape of his captured ally, Commius, along with the thirty cavalry who had been taken hostage at the same time. For over a week they had been held in chains but now they provided the Britons with the perfect opportunity to make a formal peace with this massive foreign army, blaming the capture of Commius on the ignorance of the "common people". This supplication allowed Caesar to be magnanimous: he reproached them for "having started hostilities without provocation" but told them they were forgiven as long as they sent some hostages of their own as proof of their good word. Then, in a masterstroke of aggrandisement, he adds that

"chiefs began to arrive from all parts of the island to seek Caesar's protection for their tribes and themselves. With this, peace was established."

CAESAR: *GALLIC WAR, IV, 27*

79

Although he had effectively captured no more than a beach, to history – at least to the version of history that would enter Roman legend – Caesar had conquered the proud warrior tribes of Britain with his military strength and personal munificence.

Then, just when things seemed to be going his way, disaster struck: four days after the initial landing, a violent storm blew up during the highest tide of the month; the fatal combination of wind and tide all but destroyed his fleet that was languishing not far from the camp, either pulled up on the beach or moored a little out to sea; just as disastrously, it also drove back to Gaul the crucial eighteen cavalry transport ships that were due to follow Caesar to Britain to enable him to push further inland.

Already effectively besieged in their camp, the ferocious storm only compounded the Romans' worries. Now stranded with precious little in the way of supplies and with no hope of assistance from the follow-on fleet, Caesar was left with no choice: whether or not the Britons were going to attack them, he had to repair his fleet and prepare his escape. Assigning one legion to do this, the other he sent out into the alien wilderness in search of food, all the while knowing that time was running out and soon the Britons would realise just how vulnerable the invaders really were.

And the Britons weren't slow to catch on: the attack, when it came, was swift and angry. While the Roman soldiers were out collecting grain, they were surprised by hordes of enemy warriors and charioteers who had been lurking in the nearby woods. By the time the remaining forces came to their aid, the legionaries were completely surrounded and facing a deluge of spears and stones. However, the mere sight of some two thousand armed men marching towards them was enough to drive the Britons away and as soon as it had started, the crisis melted away.

Even though there was now the appearance of calm, violence was in the air. As the weather again turned bad, the wind and rain slapped the faces of Romans and Britons like an angry spirit, dampening the mood for any more pitched battles; but behind the curtain of rain, each side was making itself ready: the Romans for departure; the Britons for revenge. Warriors had been filtering down to the coast from the neighbouring areas waiting for the skies to clear and the sun to glint on their swords. To the eerie sound of the horn and drum, the warriors launched their attack on the Roman camp. It was a futile gesture. The great Romanophile Napoleon Bonaparte would write in his memoirs that during ten or twelve centuries of Roman history, there is not a single case when one of their camps was overrun. And so it was to prove now. Despite their greater numbers and some heroic fighting which employed the full armoury of British warring tactics, the Roman camp with its watertight defences and highly trained troops was completely impervious to the native assault. Chariots, spears and maniacal shouts came to nothing; then the Romans moved in, slaughtering anyone who could not flee and leaving a trail of fire and destruction in their wake.

As the sun set on the smoking devastation that was once the fields, farms and homesteads of the Britons, Caesar received an envoy from the enemy asking for peace, which he agreed to in exchange for yet more hostages. Then the victors struck camp, loaded the rescued ships with men and equipment, and sailed decisively back to Gaul, taking with them nothing but experience. The Roman biographer and essayist, Plutarch, would later write that the Britons were so "miserably poor" that there was nothing worth taking anyway. In less than three weeks, they had fought three battles, almost lost their entire fleet and faced starvation and ruin in a desolate land – and in all that time, with all that effort, they had never got further than the beach. While the Britons might have watched the departing ships thinking the enemy had been expelled, the Romans knew that even this botched landing was far from being the end of the story. As for Caesar, he had achieved the one thing that really mattered – the glory of being the first commander who dared to invade Britain. With his reputation riding high, and a firm hand on the factual account of the whole "expedition", the ground was now laid bare for another invasion the following year.

The reaction in Rome was unprecedented. News that Caesar had not only crossed *Ocean* but had invaded the fabled land of the Britons stunned the local population in what can only be equated to the moon-landing some two thousand years later. The senate voted a holiday of twenty days of thanksgiving to the gods – and along with an orgy of feasting, games and entertainment, the population voraciously consumed any details of this land beyond the edge of the world. For the time being at least, Britannia was reeling under Roman sway.

That winter, Caesar did not need to spend months in the capital; his stock was high enough to overwhelm even his enemies and anyway, he had a more illustrious goal in mind: he wanted to make best use of his time preparing for another assault on Britain as early as possible the following spring.

With six hundred transport ships and twenty-eight warships – ten times his fleet of the previous year – this time the Romans would be invincible. In addition to the military vessels, around two hundred private ships joined the fleet as "hangers-on", hoping to make their fortunes by supplying the army and collecting booty for a home market hungry for anything British.

It was already June by the time that Caesar arrived at Pas de Calais. En route, he had been forced to sort out a disturbance among the tribes in what is now modern Germany but finally he and his men were ready for war. With a military contingent estimated at around seventeen to almost thirty thousand soldiers and sailors, Caesar was on the verge of setting a record for taking troops across the Channel that would stand for nearly two thousand years until the troop movements of World War One.

However, as if fated by the gods, the weather once again was against him, forcing the fleet to wait three weeks for a suitable southerly wind. At last, the winds turned – but a last-minute escape by the Druid hostage, Dumnorix, further delayed his departure. The Druid was eventually recovered and summarily executed; Caesar had no more time to spare. On the last day of July, just as the sun was setting, the ebb tide from Gaul carried with it a vast Roman armada as eight hundred ships set sail once more for the shores of Britain. Such was the power of Caesar that it seems his force had no authority from the senate to carry out the planned invasion – but this did not matter to him: he had determined to be the conqueror of Britain and nothing would stand in his way; not Druids, not the weather, not even the most powerful body in the whole of Rome.

To the Britons shrouded in the undergrowth watching the flotilla approach the Kentish shoreline, it must have been an awesome scene. Like ants pouring from a disturbed anthill, the ships spewed out the five legions of men, along with thousands of horses, cattle – and perhaps even an elephant in a never-ending stream that spread up from the beaches and on to dry land. To modern eyes, it would be spectacle enough: to the ancient Britons, it would have sent the ice of pure fear through their veins. However, if their eyes had spotted the face of the young nobleman, Mandubracius, from the British tribe of Trinovantes located around modern-day Essex, their terror might have turned to anger. Mandubracius had come to the attention of Caesar when he sought refuge in Gaul. His father, a Trinovantes chieftain, had been killed in a battle with their Catuvellauni neighbours and now he was seeking revenge. Caesar knew the power of go-betweens when dealing with the complexities of foreign clans and although there is no written evidence to prove it, it seems likely that he had offered the young man "protection" – along with his tribe back in Britain. Mandubracius either didn't guess or didn't care about the consequences of inviting the fox into the chicken run.

Meanwhile, this time the progress of the Romans was unimpeded: a year on from that dreadful battle in the surf, the troops now had the luxury of the second landing being unopposed by native warriors although even the most confident legionary must have known that they were being watched. With safety in their huge numbers, they pushed up the beach and started to build their second camp on British soil possibly around the region of modern-day Worth, a few miles north along the Kentish coast from the camp of the previous year.

However, this was no holiday: a scouting party soon found a small band of locals who informed them that a much larger group of warriors was lurking nearby – probably those who had been watching the second landing – and realised there was no point in attacking such a large army. The tribesmen had based themselves about twelve miles inland at one of their existing strongholds on a wooded hill, almost certainly what is now the twenty-five acre plateau at Bigberry, near Canterbury, which still bears the fortifications and artefacts of its Iron Age past.

Leaving his fleet at anchor, Caesar headed directly to find the Britons who now retreated inside their stronghold assuming they were safe to launch an attack of spears and stones on to the Romans below. At first it seemed as though the warriors had the advantage but they were about to see at first hand the Roman tactics that had won them the whole of Gaul; the legionaries merely put their shields over their heads like a giant tortoise-shell to protect them from the raining missiles while others simply filled in the ditch with baskets of earth.

The Britons could do nothing: as they watched with mounting horror, the Romans built up a series of ramps until they were able to flood into the hillfort and slaughter any warrior who couldn't escape into the surrounding woods. It was a textbook piece of warfare and its success was unequivocal. When the fighting was over, the Romans did not even bother to go after the fleeing men; the weather was closing in and so first they needed to finish their camp – the enemy could wait until tomorrow.

Oxford professor Barry Cunliffe is a world authority on the Iron Age peoples of Britain and Gaul. "Caesar found that fighting such a foe was difficult. Even greater problems were posed by the natives' use of chariots, of which Cassivellaunus is said to have had four thousand under his control. Evidently, this kind of warfare was new to Caesar. He describes how the Britons drove about wildly to create a din and to inspire fear while throwing their javelins at the enemy. They would then drive out through their cavalry and jump down to engage the enemy on foot while the charioteers retired a short way, positioning themselves so as to be able to swoop in and rescue their masters if required."

The one thing that seems to have impressed Caesar the most was the agility of the highly skilled charioteers who could run out along the chariot pole, stand on the yoke and get back into the vehicle even when it was racing along at top speed. As well as a necessity, this kind of warfare was clearly a passion – part of their whole identity and being. "Like the Celtic personality, it was daring, fierce and brave but lacked staying power," Professor Cunliffe argues. "It was impetuous and instinctive rather than considered. When faced with the grinding solidarity of the Roman military machine, the British resistance melted into the forests to engage in guerrilla warfare." But as Caesar was beginning to find out, the gods seemed to be on the side of the British.

The next morning, as a party of men were getting ready to go in pursuit of the fleeing warriors, Caesar received urgent word that – just like the last time he was here – a storm in the Channel had devastated his fleet. While they had been sleeping, the winds had whipped the waters into such a frenzy that the eight hundred ships had smashed into one another, broken their anchor-chains and been hurled on to the beach. Caesar had no choice but to head back with his legions to view the carnage.

The sight was enough to sink his heart: forty ships had been totally destroyed and the remainder were nearly all in need of repair. Once again, they were stranded in this wild and tempestuous country. Sending word back to Gaul to build more ships as quickly as possible, he gave orders for every single man to set to work immediately, cannibalising wood from the ships that were beyond saving to mend those that could still be rescued. According to Caesar's account, they worked in shifts around the clock for ten days and nights, continuing by lantern-light when the sun had long since set — but the full repairs would take weeks to complete.

Caesar's plans were now scuppered. He had probably hoped to be able to sail around Kent and up the Thames estuary to the Trinovantes' lands to the north in today's Essex; however, with his fleet and his plans in tatters, he was left with no option but to make the long journey by foot — which would be both dangerous and time-consuming. With the delays in Gaul, the campaigning season was already nearing its end: the weather was worsening and the nights getting longer but now he was here, there was no way he could return to Rome without a significant military success to justify the second invasion. He had to take Britain — or lose his hard-earned reputation. Leaving one legion to continue working on the ships, he took the other four plus his cavalry and all their baggage and supplies and began the long march inland.

In all probability, it was the young Trinovantes prince, Mandubracius, who led the way through Kent, across the Thames and north-eastwards towards his homeland. Along the way, they faced a bombardment of guerrilla tactics by the Britons who appear to have been organised under the brilliant warrior-strategist, Cassivellaunus, who according to Caesar had his territory "about seventy-five miles from the sea … separated from the maritime tribes by a river called the Thames." The actual location where the Romans crossed the River Thames en route to the tribal lands of the Trinovantes is lost in history but suggestions have covered a wide range of options from upstream Weybridge to East Tilbury near its mouth; with water levels lower at the time by perhaps as much as fifteen feet, there would have been a range of possibilities, despite Caesar's protestations that he only had one difficult choice, made even harder by the sharpened underwater stakes the natives had driven into the riverbed. Archaeology has since thrown up numerous examples of this type of technology being used along the Thames though whether the stakes were defensive, or part of another structure like a bridge, dock or fish-trap remains uncertain. Meanwhile, some commentators have questioned that he ever crossed the Thames at all, alleging that he mistook the River Medway for this most famous of British waterways.

Having crossed the water, Caesar's men had to push their way through the dense forests of oak, thick with undergrowth and the ever-present danger of bands of spearmen and charioteers launching guerrilla attacks on the column of Roman troops. With the vast train of soldiers and hangers-on in a line probably stretching for several miles along the rough tracks and drove roads, there was no hope of going unnoticed but the cavalry did their best to protect their ranks from any surrounding threat. Meanwhile, Cassivellaunus's warriors diverted much of their efforts into driving their fellow Britons and their livestock out of the path of the Romans and into the forests to prevent their capture and use by the enemy.

As Caesar advanced towards the land of the Trinovantes with Mandubracius at his side, they were met by emissaries from the tribe with offers of surrender and supplies of grain; they also asked that Mandubracius be allowed to return as their ruler – all in all, a perfect result for Caesar who also demanded some hostages as the icing on the cake, just to make sure they kept to their word. As news of the treaty spread, five neighbouring tribes also turned up at the Roman camp, offering to submit to this almighty foreign force in exchange for their protection. But just as important as them yielding to Caesar was the information they provided – information about a fortified and well-stocked settlement belonging to Cassivellaunus, set amongst woods and swamps but within reasonable striking distance. With an opportunity like that, how could Caesar refuse? Now rested and restocked with food and water, the Roman army was once again ready to be on the move.

The *oppidum* of Cassivellaunus was an impressive sight: well-fortified and securely barricaded against attack; the only factor lacking was readiness but this one thing would cost them dear. With the elements of both sheer numbers and surprise on his side, Caesar's four legions together with his cavalry charged up the slope, smashed through the defences and rained down on the Britons like hellfire. Realising there was no hope of beating the invaders, those who could ran out the far side of the stronghold into the surrounding fields and woodlands, hotly pursued by some twenty thousand Romans who showed no mercy to any that were caught. It did not take long. Soon the land was covered in bodies, blooded and still, but the corpse of Cassivellaunus was not among them. Caesar knew that could mean only one thing: a revenge attack, but even he had not anticipated just where Cassivellaunus would strike next.

When he learned of the British plans, even this mercurially minded commander must have realised he'd been outwitted, for the Britons were regrouping to launch a surprise attack – not on his legions but on his precious naval fleet. With no way of spiriting over four legions of men back down to the Kentish coast, Caesar could do nothing but rely on the one legion he had left defending the camp. Fortunately, those men were not as impotent as their general and the tight military discipline quickly overcame the piecemeal native attacks. Meantime, a surviving exchange of letters between Caesar and his statesman and scholar-friend, Cicero, gives the lie to the coolly confident *official* account of what he portrayed as a mere inconvenience; from a discrepancy in the dates which proves Caesar arrived in Kent much earlier than expected and without his full army, it seems he had in fact raced to the coast with a troupe of horsemen to see for himself the threat his naval camp faced. However, to admit to panic would only give ammunition to Caesar's enemies back home so, once again, this detail was edited out of his "history" and no doubt his formal dispatches back to the senate as well; when it came to defending his reputation back in Rome, the pen was indeed mightier than the sword.

Meanwhile, Caesar had survived a potentially lethal threat both in Britain and by implication in Rome. On hearing of the failed attack at the base-camp, Cassivellaunus realised that there was no longer anything to be gained by fighting against the invading army who were not only larger and better equipped than the tribal warriors, but whose discipline seemed to make them impervious to attack. With the trickle of defecting tribes turning into more of a torrent, he realised the game was up. With the pro-Roman Commius as an intermediary, he sent envoys to Caesar to sue for peace.

The news of Cassivellaunus's submission doubtless brought a sigh of relief even for someone as super-coolly confident as Caesar. Meanwhile, the campaigning season was almost over, over-wintering in Britain was not a viable option and with the collapse of the native defence, he could at last withdraw with honour. His invasion of Britain was hardly the success he had wanted but he could accurately report that he had brought another region under Roman control, with hostages and annual tributes to be sent back to Rome.

Striking camp, he knew he could not rely on the integrity of the Britons but it would be foolish to leave any troops in this cold, hostile and stormy land. On September 25, 54 BC, Caesar wrote to Cicero that "Britain is finished off". He would never see it again, nor one suspects, would he have wanted to. Leading his men to the coast, they boarded the ships – now fully repaired – and, after a delay caused by yet more storms, they sailed as quickly as they could back to Gaul. In total, they had been in Britain for less than two months.

For almost a century after the first two Roman invasions, things settled back into the familiar patterns of old: lots of feasting, some fighting with your neighbours – but mainly just farming. There were changes, such as a growing use of coins in payments for goods and services and as a store of wealth, and more Roman products such as drinking vessels and wine which had been imported from Italy and were popular among the tribal elite. However, these changes tended to be most felt in the upper echelons of society; for the average peasant working the land, the days and years were mapped out just like their forefathers' had been. What's more, the Romanisation of Britain would have happened to some degree even if the legions had never dared to cross *Ocean*, just as it had happened in Gaul. The military invasion was far less important than the cultural invasion that was already long underway from the Continent.

Likewise, and to Caesar's frustration, his invasion of Britain had little real impact on his own standing or that of Rome. After the triumphs of the previous year, news of Caesar's conquests in 54 BC met with little enthusiasm back home: they had found nothing that would set the traders' hearts racing, nothing that would encourage citizens to leave for Britain in search of a better life and nothing that would add to the glory of the republic. In all, the whole last year of campaigning had been a bit of a damp squib.

But Caesar's bad fortune was not to end there. On his arrival back in Gaul he learned of more insurrection from the supposedly conquered Gauls which would need urgent attention; and on a personal level, he also learned that his beloved daughter, Julia, had died in childbirth, with her baby son dying shortly afterwards. His grief was compounded as her death removed the important family link with his triumvirate partner, Pompey, who now owed Caesar no loyalty whatsoever.

Over the next year, while Caesar was away campaigning in northern Gaul, political strife in Rome led to calls for Pompey to be named chief magistrate or emergency "dictator". As if this was not destabilising enough, over in what is now Turkey, the third man in the triumvirate, Marcus Crassus, was killed by the Parthians in the worst defeat the Roman army had suffered since the days of Hannibal.

The tripartite power structure engineered by Caesar was now gone for good. After much pressure from a city descending into chaos, the senate had abandoned elections and appointed Pompey as sole consul. The republic – with its high ideals and inherent checks and balances to prevent the abuse of power – was crumbling into ashes, and all the while Caesar was stuck in Gaul trying to quell a growing rebellion. He might have been leading the greatest fighting force in the history of Rome but he was only too aware that the real war that would decide his fate was being played out a thousand miles away in Rome where the battlefields were corridors and the weapons mere whispers.

For the whole of 52 BC, Caesar was battling against the growing strength of the young Gaulish rebel leader, Vercingetorix, who had managed to unite the disparate peoples of Gaul into a proud and giant army. Unlike in times past when one tribe would fight against another, this time the rebellion gathered momentum and size like a snowball hurtling down a mountain. In a rare example of military indiscipline at Gergovia in what is now south-central France, Caesar suffered the first outright defeat of his whole Gaulish career, as well as taking heavy losses amongst his men. The Romans were seriously outnumbered but they had one weapon which proved the key to turning the tide of fortune: tried and tested siege tactics. Vercingetorix now made his fatal error and withdrew to a mountain stronghold to the north-east at Alesia, in the modern-day *départment* of Côte-d'Or. From here he sent word to all the Gaulish tribes to provide men in support, gambling on defeating the Romans by sheer might, trapping them in a vice by attacking from the surrounding plains while his own men swept down from the mountain.

And to begin with, it looked like his gamble was going to prove successful. Even Commius, that leader of the Atrebates and one-time friend of Caesar, answered the call – part of a consignment of an alleged forty-three tribes or quarter of a million men. But after three failed attempts to rout the Romans, Vercingetorix realised he was now trapped in the *oppidum*. Food was running out, along with their options. As the besieged Gauls fell prey to starvation, Vercingetorix knew the only way out was surrender or death. Dressed in his finery, on a perfectly groomed horse, he rode up to Caesar and sat motionless in supplication at his feet. The Gauls had been utterly defeated in a year that marked the beginning of the end for the Celts of mainland Europe.

The Romans were never again in serious danger of losing control of Gaul. Scuffles continued but no leader rose up to take the place of the youthful but brilliant Vercingetorix. He was paraded in chains through the streets of Rome as part of Caesar's *triumph* of 52 BC and then finally strangled six years later when even his iconography of total Gaulish defeat was not enough to save him; at execution, he was probably aged just twenty-six.

The following years in Rome were plagued by civil war between Caesar and Pompey as the city broke up into political factions and bitter internecine conflict. However, on Pompey's defeat and later death, Caesar finally achieved what he had always wanted: to be elected supreme ruler of all Roman lands. His political success had been matched with conquests in his private life: while pursuing Pompey in Egypt, he had started an affair with Cleopatra, the infamous Egyptian queen whom he now set up in a villa across the Tiber and later flattered with a golden statue in his ancestral temple in Rome. Having headed to Spain to stamp out the last of the Pompeian opposition, he returned triumphantly to Rome where the senate declared a fifty-day holiday in celebration and changed his birthday month of *Quintilis* to *Julius* (our July) in his honour.

But under the veneer of jubilation was an undercurrent of mounting resentment. Caesar was portraying himself as a king and consorting with not only a queen but a *foreign* queen at that. The aristocracy now seethed in scornful anger and fermenting jealousy: more power for Caesar meant less power among their own ranks. Some harked back to the halcyon days of the republic; others thought they could lead Rome to a better future. Meanwhile, the conspicuous displays of wealth and privilege along with Caesar's growing irascibility stuck in their craw and brought them to choking point: something had to be done, and soon. In February 44 BC, the situation reached breaking point when Caesar was given the title of *dictator perpetuo*; he was now effectively Rome's ruler until the end of his natural life – but that life was about to be cut short. On March 15, 44 BC, as Caesar was seated on his golden throne in the Senate House a group of conspirators lurched forward and stabbed him in a deluge of knives. As his body was ripped open by the blades, the real and final pain was in seeing that among the conspirators was Decimus Brutus – his former friend and trusted colleague. A broken-hearted Gaius Julius Caesar died from his wounds, and Rome had lost its most famous statesman and military commander.

If the conspirators had expected that his death would herald a new dawn of peace and prosperity, then they were badly mistaken: thirteen years of civil war followed his murder and the power vacuum sapped both strength and wealth from the city. And while Caesar's legacy to Rome marked the effective end of the republic, his remarkable career had also ended native rule in the vast swathes of land that were once Celtic Europe. His defeat of Vercingetorix had not only won the battle, it had broken the spirit of the Gauls. Without a new leader rising up from the ranks, resistance was futile and the region submitted to the yoke of their foreign overlords. In fact, it would be another hundred years before Rome's hegemony in the provinces was seriously challenged – and that challenge would come not from Gaul but from Britain, and not from a warrior king like Vercingetorix but from Boudica of the Iceni – history's most enduring warrior queen.

CHAPTER 5

ONE HUNDRED YEARS OF SOLITUDE

Britain 54 BC to AD 43

"Cassivellaunus, the King of the Britons, sends his greetings to Gaius Julius Caesar. The cupidity of the Roman People, my dear Caesar, is really quite beyond belief. They have an insatiable thirst for anything that is made of gold or silver, to the point that they cannot leave us alone, although we live over the edge of the world and far beyond the perilous seas... We have become so accustomed to the concept of liberty that we are completely ignorant of what is meant by submitting to slavery... If you start attacking the island of Britain, as you have threatened, you must clearly understand, Caesar, that we shall fight for our liberty and for our kingdom."

GEOFFREY OF MONMOUTH (D.1155), *THE HISTORY OF THE KINGS OF BRITAIN*, IV, I – A CURIOUS MIXTURE OF LOOSE FACT AND MUCH FICTION, BASED ON A "MYSTERY" DOCUMENT HE WAS GIVEN

During a particularly wet week in February 1982, David Bunting was digging for gravel to fill some potholes in the road. He farmed the land near the modern-day village of Kelvedon in Essex, which lies fifteen kilometres to the south-east of Colchester, and the field in which he was working stretched up a hill with commanding views of the surrounding countryside. However, today the view was the last thing on his mind: it was cold, the ground was sodden and his major concern was just getting the job done. But as he cut down through the waterlogged earth, he made contact with something hard and metallic that was solid enough to stop him in his tracks: scraping away the dirt, he found what looked like a sword.

Jim Bennet was a retired policeman from the area who was well known for his keen interest in archaeology. Suspecting that he might have uncovered an ancient relic, David invited him to come and have a look at the find, and Jim immediately started excavating the site. Even as an amateur, Jim knew that the farmer had made a significant discovery – but he had no idea just how unique the discovery was: for this was the grave of an Iron Age warrior – substantial at two metres square and complete with magnificent sword, spear and shield, and a fine bronze bowl.

Warrior graves are few and far between, but what made this one truly special were the stories behind the weapons that had been buried with their owner whose body had long since been eaten away by the acid soil. The story has been pieced together carefully by Dr Paul Sealey, Boudica expert and archaeologist at Colchester Museum, who was almost jumping with excitement when I met him on a similarly cold, wet winter's day.

"This really is an incredible set of finds: here is a man who was clearly revered as some kind of great warrior or chief, who died and was buried in a lavish grave to mark his status in the community. Now, that would have been interesting in itself but when we got the results of the weapons, I could hardly believe my eyes." Paul searched on his desk for a moment and then drew out a line-drawing of the grave goods. "Look at this – the iron sword had a bronze scabbard which sported a strip of tin that had been fused right the way down its length – now that's something I've never seen or even heard of before. It's an amazing piece of craftsmanship: it must have looked spectacular in its day with silvery tin set against the golden-yellow of the bronze. But what really stunned me was where all this weaponry came from. Here is a guy who clearly had his finger on the pulse of the latest European fashions: he had a shield boss and spear that were *Gaulish* – but the sword had been wrapped up in linen which is something we've only ever seen in two sites in *Guernsey*. The scabbard was made in *Britain*, or at least in the British style – and then there was an imported *Roman* bronze bowl in the grave to boot."

It all seemed a confusing mêlée of cultural influences – so who *was* the Kelvedon warrior? Paul sat back in his chair and smiled. "That is the question. We know from the style of the goods that the grave dates to the mid-first century BC – so what we're talking about here is a couple of generations before Boudica was born. Was he therefore some kind of wealthy refugee fleeing from Caesar's Gallic Wars? Or was he a British mercenary who had fought on the Continent and had now returned home? He really is a complete amalgam of European styles but if we like to follow fashion today then why shouldn't men in the Iron Age, too? What he does do is give us some pretty clear evidence that for the elite, at least, there was incredible mobility and a far-flung social network. It may sound fanciful, but it's nice to think that after his time spent fighting overseas, his Trinovantian tribesmen buried him up here in a magnificent funeral so that this great warrior could overlook their village, and perhaps keep them safe even long after his death."

Little by little, the picture of Iron Age Britain – and the years leading up to Boudica – were taking a more human shape; and with the story of the Kelvedon warrior, my search to understand the nature of the queen and her people had just moved a step closer to the truth.

It would only have taken a couple of months for news of Caesar's demise to have reached the shores of Britain and the ears of Cassivellaunus – and it is hard to imagine that he shed any tears over the death of his Roman adversary. There is no evidence that he had ever sent the taxes to Rome decreed by Caesar as part of their settlement for peace – and even Caesar himself reported in his *Gallic War* that only two tribes ever sent the hostages they owed. But from Rome's point of view, there was nothing to be gained by going back to retrieve forcibly any missing dues. In fact, the Greek geographer and historian Strabo went as far as suggesting that there was really no point in going back to Britain at all as the cost of establishing it as a genuine province, with all the military and administrative layers that it would require, was simply throwing good money after bad.

So Britain languished behind the scenes as a mere footnote in the classical histories and geographies of a Roman world that was struggling to put its own house in order. But while the bureaucrats may not have been interested in keeping a close account of "Nearer Britain", the landscape itself was bursting with dynamic activity. The regular traders kept up their journeys to and from the islands, chieftains came and went, then evolved into kings, and the coalition of Cassivellaunus broke down into tribes that went back to war against themselves. For almost a century, the general population went about its daily life against a context of possibilities for radical change, especially for those higher up the social strata. Some communities chose to maintain their ancient traditions, others seized on the new cultural trends that had already started before Caesar made his symbolic crossing of *Ocean*. It didn't matter that the Romans had left before the shock of invasion could permeate the depths of the distinctive tribal cultures: Iron Age Britain was not standing still.

Out of sight and for the most part out of mind of the Romans, Britain also became a useful place for the Druids of Celtic Europe to come in search of sanctuary. Druids had formed one of the few international structures in Europe, holding a yearly court at Chârtres where they would gather to discuss Druidic business and settle simmering disputes. But with Roman domination, their institutions were being broken up and they themselves were being squeezed out of Gaul. Britain provided a refuge both for Druid practitioners and their ideas. They built up a powerful stronghold on the sacred Isle of Anglesey where as well as teaching their dark arts of divination, they festered with hatred against the godless Romans who were trying to extinguish their whole mode of life and who had forced them from their native lands.

Despite the lack of a written Celtic language it is possible to piece together a mosaic of information to give a picture of what went on in Britain after the curtain of Roman history had been re-drawn. While snippets from the classical authors tell fragmentary stories from a Roman point of view, the landscape of Britain throws up its own evidence in terms of coins, archaeology and relic patterns on the ground – and these can tell us so much about the hidden history of late Iron Age Britain.

Even without the direct presence of the Romans themselves, the people of Britain were changing in response to a range of influences, including Romanisation, and particularly affected were some communities in the south-east. The size of farms was tending to increase (though the fields themselves were often increasingly subdivided) while the crops that were grown were shifting from the ancient wheat of einkorn, to spelt and also emmer – a staple part of the diet of the Roman army, which used it to make bread. Far from being nutritionally substandard, these grains had a protein value double that of modern wheat and were ground using a heavy stone quern with its two stones grinding the cereals down into a versatile and fibre-rich flour. Experiments at Butser Iron Age farm in Hampshire has shown how these "primitive" wheats can actually give fantastic yields of over sixteen hundred pounds per acre – which is two thousand pounds more than was being achieved by British farming in the period leading up to the Second World War, before the introduction of mechanisation and artificial fertilisers.

Meanwhile, if the politics of Rome was growing more complicated, they were more than matched by the political machinations in the land that Caesar had so willingly left behind. In the last few decades BC, parts of Britain were experiencing what appears to be a new phenomenon in their cultures: the rise of kings and monarchical dynasties. Instead of becoming chief of a tribe by warring prowess or merit, the top layer of the political hierarchy was able to hand down its power to their offspring in a fundamental reorganisation of the structuring of those societies. And for the people living under the new kings' sway, tied in to the monarch's inherited power came inherited loyalties and servitudes that forged complex new identities.

The personal story of Commius, the leader of the Atrebates tribe from what is now Belgium, is a prime example of the changing geopolitics of the late Iron Age. Assuming the Commius on record is that same person throughout, his catalogue of shifting affiliations demonstrates just how fluid the politics of the Celtic-speaking peoples was in the period from the first Roman invasion under Caesar to the second invasion under the Emperor Claudius. It also underlines how mercurial the Ancient Britons could be in keeping to their strategic alliances – something the Romans would learn to their cost all too soon with their "friendly" pro-Roman queen, Boudica.

Having sided with the Romans and won the respect and trust of Caesar during his Gallic War, Commius failed in his attempt to mollify the Britons in advance of Caesar's first expedition to the coast of Kent; far from being welcomed with his Celtic connections as "one of them", he had been seized by the British, held in chains and only handed back to Caesar once they realised they had been defeated. But rather than bear a life-long enmity towards his British captors or swear undying fealty to Caesar, Commius then swapped sides to support the Celtic rebel leader, Vercingetorix in his Gaulish uprising against the Romans in 52 BC. As if his life wasn't already complicated enough, this Teflon-coated aristocrat then survived two attempts on his life by the furious Romans, sought refuge from the Germans with whom he joined forces, then surrendered to the Romans, and eventually fled back to Britain around 51 BC where despite having come as the Romans' emissary a few years before, he managed to win enough support to establish his own kingdom amongst the Atrebates. There is a popular belief that this was centred on Calleva Attrebatum near modern Silchester in Hampshire, although this is not supported by any direct archaeological evidence. Recent excavations suggest that it developed from scratch in around 25 BC, which makes it hard to tie him in with its foundation but the settlement was soon growing in size and sophistication: over the years between 25 BC and the turn of the new millennium, a whole network of streets grew up, along with further signs of Mediterranean-style urbanisation that continued apace during the rule of his son and successor, Tincomarus. However, Commius left something other than his flesh and blood, a Roman-style settlement and a list of exploits like a Celtic superhero: he also became notable to archaeologists for probably being the first leader in Britain to mint coins bearing his own name.

After a remarkable life, Commius's legacy was a personal dynasty that went on to rule the area through his son, Tincomarus, who was king from around 25 BC to AD 5 or 6 from his own base near Chichester. In an astonishing volte-face, *he* now managed to switch his allegiance once again and reunite firmly with the Romans, albeit this time under the power of the Emperor Augustus. In an extraordinary half century, this quisling family had come full-circle: Tincomarus had now become so Romanised he was importing a steady stream of Roman products and minting his own coins that depicted his portrait in typical Roman fashion. But the story of the family was not to end there.

Although the chronology and facts now become incredibly unclear, one version of events suggests that Tincomarus fought with his so-called brother, Epillus, who

Gold Stater of Commius, leader of the Atrebates
and both friend and foe to the Romans

ruled from a base at Silchester and seemingly had control over the whole of Kent, too. Who won is hard to gauge – but Epillus started minting coins bearing his own portrait instead of his brother's. However, despite the fact that Tincomarus raced to Rome to complain to Augustus of his brother's behaviour, Epillus seems to have somehow managed to curry favour with the Romans – or at least to ape them – and he was soon using the Latin title *Rex* on his coins. But even this currency was not current for long – Epillus was then expelled in turn by Verica – according to his coins yet another alleged son of Commius (though probably really the son of Tincomarus). Verica once more managed to win the approval of the Romans and to hold firmly on to his rule until AD 43; however, the dynasty was finally driven out of their lands by the Catuvellauni, once ruled by the great British king, Cunobelin, who was Verica's rival on the north side of the Thames.

The convoluted political shenanigans are enough to make even the Iron Age coin expert, Philip de Jersey, laugh at their complexity. As we pored meticulously through all the evidence and the dates, he was almost apologetic to reveal that it's now thought that it was actually Cunobelin's brother, Epaticcus, who drive the Atrebates from their lands "But maybe that's one king too many," he added, mischievously.

In the final twist to this extremely exhausting family tale, it is also claimed that Verica fled to Rome which was by now under the control of the Emperor

Claudius, thereby giving this most unmilitary Roman leader an excuse to mount the second major invasion of Britain.

While the experience of Commius's dynastic troubles might have been extreme, it seems that the Atrebates of modern Hampshire were not the only tribe to flee to Rome begging for help. As more and more archaeological evidence comes to light from this period, academics are having to re-think the relationships between Britain and Rome in the period between the invasions of Caesar (55 and 54 BC) and Claudius (AD 43). While it seems clear that what is now Scotland, Wales and the north of England maintained strong independent tribal control – either directly or through confederacies of local tribes, there is a growing feeling that many of the ascendant nobility in the south and east of England would have had close connections with Rome, both diplomatic and even educational, sending their sons there in an Iron Age equivalent of the finishing schools of the modern era. Here they would have joined the ranks of the wealthiest Roman families, educating their sons in Roman law and customs, mathematics, Latin, Greek (which they had to learn by rote) – and for the richest and most able students – rhetoric and public speaking. Ironically, the sons of British nobles might also have received

Gold Stater of the Romanised King, Tincomarus (top)
Silver unit of Epillus REX (bottom)

physical instruction to prepare them for war – their masters little knowing that the boys' skills might one day be turned against Rome.

It is not known how seriously the Britons took their pledge of taxes to Caesar but it's likely that throughout this time there were some reciprocal ties in terms of money and 'gifts' between the ruling classes of two cultures to maintain at least friendly bonds. And, as had been the case so often in Gaul, the British tribes would rather increase their power by making social and military pacts with the foreign power of Rome than unite with their own neighbours; the Britons either failed to see or refused to see that across the Channel this had resulted in the eventual annihilation of not only those individual tribes but of independent Celtic rule throughout the whole of continental Europe.

North of the River Thames in what is now Hertfordshire lies some of the most dramatic Iron Age scenery in Britain. But it's not a great building or a town that stuns onlookers into silence; instead it's a series of breathtaking earthworks that dominate the landscape like giant cavernous tunnels. The largest of them all has a mouth that gapes so deep and wide it easily swallows the vast, thick-waisted beech trees that now litter its flanks. The Devil's Dyke, as it has become known, is a super-sized ditch like an inverted cathedral: up to forty metres wide at the top, it runs for over four hundred and fifty metres through the woodlands and fields of Wheathampstead – though in its day the network would doubtless have extended further. Two thousand years after its construction, it still has the power to shock both in terms of magnitude and symbolism: here is the work of a seriously powerful people, and unlike the inhabitants of Rome who showed their prestige in marble temples, this was a graphic statement expressed by the raw energy of the earth.

I was encouraged to visit the earthworks by Dr Rosalind Niblett, a small, smiling woman whose intellect and passion streams out from her piercing eyes. An early authority on the Trinovantes and now the unquestioned expert on the Catuvellauni tribe and archaeology of Verulamium (now St Albans) – the final town destroyed in the Boudican uprising – Dr Niblett talks of having the same "strong feel" for the ancient landscape lurking beneath the surface that is common to many professional and amateur archaeologists. Her enthusiasm for her subject also displays a pattern similar to many of her peers: excited by the excavations of the Temple of Mithras in London in the 1950s, she chanced upon an article in the newspaper about a schoolboy digging up a rare pot. The effect of the story is still apparent today. "My immediate reaction was, 'I can do that!' even though I was only ten or eleven at the time. I didn't realise, though, that I could ever really be a real archaeologist – that seemed far too intellectual but I suppose that sense of search and discovery appeals to the detective part of the brain."

Off her own bat, she joined the Watford Archaeological Society and then "got on a bike and cycled off over the golf course" looking for the dig at a Roman Villa by the Merchant Taylors' Boys' School. "I was very determined," she laughed, "but they let me join the dig and despite the fact that I was much younger than them, they were all very nice to me." From there, her interest flourished until she found herself on digs with the eminent archaeologists Sheppard Frere and Sir Mortimer Wheeler. Before long, she was leading digs at Colchester – Boudica's first target in the uprising – before moving to St Albans where she has spent the last thirty years transforming our understanding of Verulamium in the Iron Age and during the Roman conquest. Six books and monographs later, she seems to be able to picture every inch of the ancient landscape that surrounds her. "It's about knowing the lie of the land. I don't really drive so I end up walking or cycling everywhere and that gives you a *feeling* for the landscape, its soils and its shape. And an earthwork like the Devil's Dyke is a really powerful statement in terms of its sheer iconography: it's saying, 'Someone really impressive controls this land'."

Wheathampstead was the former base of another great British tribe, the Catuvellauni, who by the first decades of the new millennium ruled over the lands to the north of the River Thames including modern Hertfordshire, Buckinghamshire and East Oxfordshire. They were the very same tribe which had led the British resistance to Caesar's second assault on Britain under their inspirational leader, Cassivellaunus. Following the death of this man who had done so much to unite the British counter-attack – firstly on Caesar and then on his abandoned naval fleet – the tribe was ruled by his son, Addedomarus, from around 40 BC to 20 BC and then by his grandson – a warrior prince called Tasciovanus – from around 20 BC to 10 AD.

There is some speculation about where Tasciovanus made his capital as he seems to have been somewhat peripatetic but a leading suggestion is that he based himself at what would become the Romano–British town of Verulamium, the mark for which appears on his coins; there are also coins of his bearing the mark for Camulodunum, modern-day Colchester, which became important from around AD 5 and then infamous with the revolt of Boudica in AD 60/61. However, one interesting possibility is that Tasciovanus was the high-status person who resided at the Iron Age site that still can be seen today between Puckeridge and Braughing in modern Hertfordshire; here, all manner of exotic Roman imports have been found, including fine Italian glassware, oil and wine amphorae, a favourite fish sauce from Spain, and north Italian pottery cups – imports suitable for a prince or tribal leader. Also found there were Roman toilet instruments called *ligulae*, pens and even graffiti bearing the name Graecus. This astounding find suggests that not only was trade with the Continent buoyant but that there were Romanised and literate people living there as well – hardly the cultural backwater sometimes portrayed for the British Iron Age.

By this time, the Catuvellauni were growing in power, with lands to the north of London expanding up towards Northamptonshire and down perhaps as far as Kent. And hand in hand with land went wealth. Like the Atrebates, they too were importing Roman goods and minting their own money bearing the face of their leader in the style of Roman imperial coins – a sign of the

Silver unit of Tasciovanus, leader of the Catuvellauni tribe

growing Romanisation of this once fiercely anti-Roman tribe. Tasciovanus died some time around AD 5-10 and was succeeded by his son, Cunobelin, who was to rule for almost forty years – a remarkable achievement given the constant state of flux that seemed to be a feature of neighbouring tribes.

Around the time of his accession, it seems Cunobelin conquered the next-door land of the Trinovantes, in what is now Essex, and transferred the seat of power, along with his personal mint, from Verulamium to Camulodunum. Despite the increasing numbers of Roman imports such as wine and olive oil in the homes of the wealthy, Camulodunum was a staunchly Iron Age settlement with buildings of wood and wattle and daub, protected by the traditional system of defensive dykes – and for the vast majority of its inhabitants, life would have been basic with none of the luxuries of their nobles and kings. The disparity in wealth has been further underlined by the investigation in 1923 of the so-called Lexden Tumulus – a giant burial site in a suburb of Colchester containing some of the richest burials in the area. Inside the tomb was a finely decorated funerary litter containing an iron-bound chest, chain mail, an artefact woven in golden wire, around a dozen amphorae for wine and some ornate metalwork. The *pièce de résistance* was a medallion which imitated a silver coin of the Roman emperor Augustus, minted around 17 BC – but to whom this finery belonged is a mystery.

Much more is known about Cunobelin than most of the previous tribal rulers. He was one of the great success stories of ancient British kings, with his influence and power so great that he was regarded by the Roman biographer, Suetonius, as *Britannorum rex* or king of Britain, from sometime around AD 7 to AD 40. Certainly his range seems to have been far with his coins found all over Essex and Hertfordshire, as far south as north-west Kent and as far west as Oxfordshire. Verulamium also grew and developed massively during this period. However, it seems that his power was not always used for the benefit of his fellow tribesmen. Three years before driving Verica and his Atrebatic dynasty out of their lands, Cunobelin (or his successor) had expelled his son, the young Adminius, from his kingdom. Stung with outrage, Adminius had then fled overseas to seek help from the infamous despot, the Emperor Caligula, who seriously considered using Cunobelin and his son as the pretext for another invasion of Britain.

However, it seems Adminius was alone in being so pro-Rome. Following

Silver unit of Cunobelin, a great leader of the Catuvellauni tribe

the death of his father around AD 41 or 42, his brothers Caratacus and Togodumnus both took a firm anti-Rome stance, with Caratacus becoming one of the great heroes of the British resistance after the second major Roman invasion under the emperor Claudius in AD 43.

The flat plains of what is now East Anglia contain some of the richest agricultural land in whole of Britain. Here, the fertile soils left by the glaciers and rivers of the last ten thousand years are warmed by the dry climate to almost optimum conditions for farming. By the Iron Age, humans had cleared much of the good farmland of its covering of trees, creating mosaics of open fields for crops and animals, divided and drained by a system of ditches and dykes. The wealth generated by the rich lands spawned distinct centres of populations – albeit often much smaller than their southern counterparts but displaying many of the same features of tribal dynasties, rich burials and complex social organisation. Although the low-lying landscape is still notoriously marshy, the region's coast and waterways provided a useful network for trade and communication, not just within the area and to much of Britain but eastwards, to Europe.

The lack of hills meant that the hill forts of southern England and the western fringe were not an option here; instead, settlements were sometimes protected by long earthworks which helped to mark them out in terms of powerful symbolism and to defend them from raids by rival warriors and

ONE HUNDRED YEARS OF SOLITUDE

chariots. And there was much here to covet: not only were the soils rich for agriculture, this was the land of wild horses that roamed the plains too wet for farming. If any creature came to symbolise the people who lived here, it was the horse – not the elegant, long-legged and streamlined beasts we think of today, but their small and stocky ancestors who still inhabit the desolate plateaus of Dartmoor and who could endure the boggy conditions and rough vegetation that typified the eastern marshes.

Within this landscape was a British tribe that would become famous – or rather, infamous – throughout two thousand years of history: the Iceni of modern-day Norfolk, north Suffolk and the north-eastern Cambridgeshire Fens. The Iceni don't appear to have been a particularly bellicose tribe, though it does seem that they were made up of several factions. Their land is unusual in that it has very little evidence of fortified settlements – leading to the conclusion that the politics of the tribe and their neighbours were relatively settled, at least for the time being.

However, all that was set to change. The Iceni receive their first explicit mention in the classical texts following a rebellion against the Romans in AD 47 though there is good reason to believe that they were the same people who were recorded by Caesar as being the Cenimagni, or Greater Iceni. They were one of the five tribes who submitted to the Romans after the Trinovantes had begged for Caesar's protection; a century later, they were the tribe that spawned King Prasutagus and his Queen, Boudica – after which time the tribe would never again be associated with peace.

CHAPTER 6

CLAUDIUS'S CONQUEST OF BRITAIN, AD 43

[Claudius] ordered the Britons,
Beyond the limits of the known sea,
And the Brigantes, blue with their shields,
To surrender their necks to Roman chains
And Ocean himself to tremble at
The new Laws of the Roman axe.

SENECA: APOCOLOCYNTOSIS 12.13-18

With Caesar murdered and the republic in tatters, it would be easy to think that there was a new political landscape in Rome. But that would be to underestimate the influence of Julius Caesar, whose legacy, relationships and "sons" would affect the course of the next stage in Roman evolution: the successor to the triumvirate of Caesar, Crassus and Pompey – the so-called *second triumvirate*. This ruling band of three comprised Caesar's trusted friend and first lieutenant, Mark Antony, his own adopted son, Octavian (brother of Mark Antony's wife, Octavia), and the seasoned pro-Caesar politician, Marcus Lepidus. Caesar may have been dead, but his thirst for power lived on.

This was a nervous period in Rome's history, where love and power would prove as lethally intoxicating as each other and where a whisper in the corridors of power could make or break your career, and even end your life. For the general public, going about their daily lives as normally as possible in the busy markets and streets of the city, this was a time where all the pride and the certainties of being at the centre of a megastate were suddenly stripped bare. It must have seemed as though the whole capital was at the mercy of political brinkmanship; meanwhile, all the ordinary people could do was keep their heads down and hope that the glory – and the economy – of Rome would be quickly restored.

Unlike Caesar's uneasy "marriage of convenience" first time around, the second triumvirate had official standing within Rome and gave the three men absolute authority and dictatorial powers. At first, the system appeared to function well but as each of the men vied for more power it inevitably grew unbalanced; eventually it slowly and painfully began to tear itself to pieces, just as it had done in Caesar's day. Marcus Lepidus was sidelined and effectively ruled out of the game, while Mark Anthony – in a move that had more to do with love than strategy – famously joined with the Egyptian queen Cleopatra in what Plutarch would later describe as a "dreadful calamity". Together this partnership of equals who minted their coins with one head on each side, united against the young Octavian. To the watching public in Rome, the new alliance showed just how dangerous and corrupting powerful women could be: love was not a respected affliction – it served only to enslave and emasculate powerful men. All unions should be made with rational heads on the basis of what could be gained by the match. Viewed in this light, Cleopatra offered little but trouble: the sexually voracious foreign queen had now ensnared two of the most important men in recent history – and her influence could only end in disaster.

And so it was to prove: this exotic, fiercely intelligent and beguiling woman was not only in command of a fabulously wealthy country and a strong military; now religious propaganda declared that she was the New Isis, the most powerful of all the Egyptian goddesses and one that was associated with the Greeks' Aphrodite and the Romans' Venus. The deification may have increased her awe and her links to the origins of Rome (as mother of Aeneas, the mythical founder of the city) but it also aligned her with Aphrodite's other traditions of sexual love, warfare and the sea. These were a dangerous cocktail that would combine to cause Cleopatra's ultimate undoing.

Although Mark Antony was forbidden by Roman law from marrying her, there is little doubt he was genuinely in love with Cleopatra, and his devotion was passionate *and* political: he needed her land and wealth to defeat Octavian, just like she needed his help to regain control over the old Ptolemaic kingdom. But many in the capital viewed Cleopatra as more of a threat than an advantage: when his dutiful real wife, Octavia, delivered both troops and money from her brother to help Mark Antony's military campaigns in North Africa, he refused to see her, and then divorced her. This move effectively severed his links with her brother, Octavian, and set the two men at loggerheads with one another. As a further sign of Mark Antony's growing distance from Rome, a lavish ceremony known as the Alexandrian Donations proclaimed Cleopatra as Queen of Kings, and her son Caesarian by Julius Caesar, King of Kings. This was more than just theatre: it was interpreted by their enemies as ceding control of Roman lands to a foreign, dynastic power. Octavian now retaliated with a masterstroke, producing Mark Antony's will which purported to show him favouring the children of Cleopatra over those of his own Roman wife, and citing that he should be buried in Alexandria. It may have been spurious but it besmirched Antony's reputation, branding him as "soft and effeminate" to have fallen under a woman's spell. With Mark Antony now publicly weakened, Octavian could take up the mantle of the virile and masculine soldier, and as the battle of words continued it polarised the already divided Roman political opinion and cleared the way for war.

With Octavian based in Italy and Mark Antony's men along the coast of Greece, any battle would have to be fought in the Mediterranean which left Mark Antony at a severe disadvantage: though he had strong support within the senate, his navy was less experienced than Octavian's and his troops were unhappy about the constant presence of his Egyptian queen. The result was inevitable: with every victory won by Octavian, Mark Antony's troops' spirit ebbed away. The final assault came at the Battle of Actium in 31 BC, where the lovers lined up their army and their fleet against Octavian's warships but the battle was lost before it was even started. With the outcome inevitable, Cleopatra ordered her ships to break for freedom and, joined by her lover, fled to Egypt.

For Octavian, the Battle of Actium delivered personal vindication and the basis for political supremacy; but he knew this was not enough. It took almost a year for him to track the lovers down in Egypt – and when he did, his forces finally won their revenge. Knowing he had no chance of victory and hearing rumours of his beloved queen's death, Mark Antony committed suicide. In a breathtaking piece of political desperation, Cleopatra then tried to win over Octavian with her sexual charms – but Octavian was not about to become her third Roman scalp. Knowing she had lost every power she ever had, on August 30, 30 BC, she took her own life.

Of the original gang of three, Octavian was now the sole surviving dictator and the most powerful man in the Mediterranean world but unlike his adoptive father, he did not let the power of ruling all Rome go to his head. In a canny PR exercise, he renamed himself *princeps* or "first citizen" to give at least the impression that he was a man of the people, and he set about restoring the stability of a land that had spent too many years at war against both enemies and, more recently, against itself. At last, under Octavian's steady hand, peace returned both to Rome and to its people.

In 27 BC, having won himself the plaudit of restoring the institutions of the republic (he had actually done nothing of the kind), he changed his name to Caesar Augustus in homage to his great uncle and adoptive father, Julius Caesar. He then went on to emulate his forebear not only in name but also in his expansionist policies in northern and central Europe until he was beaten back by the war with the Pannonians around Hungary in AD 6; another set-back came with the annihilation of three Roman legions by the Germans in the Teutoburg Forest in AD 9 which drove the Romans back to the west of the Rhine.

Around the time he became Caesar Augustus, he was flirting with the idea of an invasion of Britain – a fitting memorial to his honoured namesake and one that would soon turn the tide of British history forever. References by the poet Horace suggest that he had already started tugging at the diplomatic drawstrings that stretched between the two countries, drawing on the relationships that tribes like the Atrebates, Trinovantes and Catuvellauni had established with Rome. According to Strabo, some key British rulers had even set up offerings in the Capitol (perhaps via the presence of their sons), something that generally went hand-in-hand with ratifying treaties. Although the dating of this makes the accuracy of the statement uncertain, it does underline that some form of *entente cordiale* was building, with Rome as the superior power.

The best opportunity for making these relationships permanent and unequivocal came when Augustus was in Gaul. Here, he had not only the desire but the forces and proximity to make an invasion a serious consideration; however, he was instead diverted by trouble brewing in Spain and the moment was lost. Compared with Britain, Spain was much wealthier and more important, generating as it did much of the trade in gold and silver. At least for the moment, the cold, wet island in the waters of *Ocean* would have to be left uncrossed by his forces; his only invasion would be carried across the waves by the relationships he was building with its tribal leaders and, rather than sending soldiers, he would send Roman goods and ideas instead.

In AD 14, at the old age of seventy-seven, this first Emperor of Rome died and was added to the pantheon of gods, having transformed and modernised the administration of the state and its empire, and consolidated many of its provinces. Although not meant to be inherited, this most powerful of titles passed to his adopted son, Tiberius. Already fifty-six years old, he had lived a full life of public and military successes and personal disasters. Tiberius had lost his beloved brother, Drusus, who fell off his horse while campaigning in Germany. Though Tiberius raced four hundred miles to be at his side, he arrived just in time to watch his brother die. He then lost the other person most precious to him: his first marriage to Vipsania Agrippina stood out in Roman society as being a match made by love, not politics. She was the daughter of Augustus's son-in-law, Marcus Agrippa, and Tiberius's passion for her was fully reciprocated. But while they might have planned to spend the rest of their lives together, Augustus had other ideas in mind: when his much-spoiled daughter, Julia, was widowed, he forced Tiberius to divorce his wife and marry Julia instead. The union was not a happy one: his new wife had a reputation for adultery and quickly tired of her sober husband. Tiberius was caught in a delicate position – he could not divorce the emperor's daughter, nor be responsible for circulating rumours about her behaviour. Having lost the two people he loved most in the world, his only option was to ask for postings overseas to keep as far away as possible from his troublesome wife and the dangerous sexual politics she represented.

However, he never recovered from his broken heart and from that point on, his personality became increasingly cold and sullen. His reign was marked at first by prudent control of the military, the state and the treasury; in fact, by the time he died, he reportedly left twenty times the wealth that he had inherited as emperor. He had also inherited from Augustus the idea that it was more important to maintain the status quo than to pursue an expansionist policy and so no major efforts were made to push beyond the shores of Gaul once more into Britain. There was certainly still contact between the two countries during this time, with traders, diplomatic emissaries and doubtless more sons of tribal leaders visiting the capital, so it seems his policy was prudent: rather than go to the trouble of invading Britain, Tiberius had got the British aristocracy to come to Rome instead.

One contact that supports the idea of a growing connection between the two lands was that during the Rhine campaigns of the Roman commander, Germanicus, in AD 16: the typically stormy winds blew some of his troop ships across the North Sea to Britain where they were wrecked in the south coast. Rather than be attacked as foreign troops might have expected, they were treated with kindness and returned home, bringing with them the most incredible stories from that fabled land that only added to its mystique back home. As to the name of the tribe which treated their guests with a hospitality that was enshrined under Celtic traditions, there is no record – though the evidence from coins of the period suggests that the gesture might have been made by Commius's pro-Roman successor, Verica.

Whatever the links across the Channel, the news of contact by Germanicus's fleet didn't arouse any interest from the emperor to formalise the chance landing with a planned invasion of Britain. With advancing age and a dreadful skin condition that emitted pustulous boils and evil smells, he withdrew to the island of Capri where by all accounts he indulged in a reign of terror, delighting in vile and obscene executions and torture.

But even Tiberius's absolute power couldn't cheat time. Realising he was getting close to death, he starting looking for a suitable successor and decided that the best of a bad bunch lay in Gaius Caesar, a great-grandson of Augustus known as Caligula or Little Boot from his days as an army camp mascot. In a prescient dedication, he admitted: "I am nursing a viper in the bosom of Rome" – and so it was to prove. In the spring of AD 37, Tiberius injured himself in a ceremonial javelin game and fell into a coma. When doctors finally were allowed to examine him for the first time in half a century, they found him emaciated and close to death.

Immediately, Caligula was sent for and news of his succession was proclaimed. Trouble was, Tiberius then rallied, sat up and asked for something to eat – at which point the commander of the Praetorian guard finished the job properly by smothering him to death with the blankets on his bed. It was the end of a life of public success and personal failure; however, he left behind a Rome that was once again strong and ready to continue its march towards global domination.

The reign of Caligula, from AD 37 to 41, has gone down in history as that of a despotic, cruel and mad tyrant. He was rumoured to have made his horse consul which – although untrue – made a compelling story that fitted perfectly with the excesses of his bizarre but thankfully short time as emperor. In just four years he managed to squander all the funds in Tiberius's treasury and once they were gone he resorted to bribery and extortion to fund his chaotic lifestyle and even crazier schemes. One of these followed his exploits in Gaul where he had marched in AD 40 in order to plunder the wealth from its inhabitants. He planned to use the coast of Gaul as a base from which to launch his invasion of Britain. However, once they got to the beaches overlooking the Channel, he merely ordered his men to take off their helmets and scoop up seashells as the spoils of *Ocean* – and with that, they returned to Rome.

What his men made of the strange experience is hard to fathom; it is even harder to imagine what the ancient Britons made of the move: with their strong links to the Continent they would almost certainly have been well-aware of the massing army; what they thought of the threat of invasion and its subsequent whimsical end, is anyone's guess. They may even have been pre-warned of the emperor's madness – Cunobelin's son, Adminius, had fled across the Channel with a band of supporters around AD 39 after being exiled following a family bust-up. Cunobelin was well-known to the Romans who regarded him as "King of the Britons" – and presumably his son was considered quite a catch. Caligula was away campaigning (unsuccessfully) at the time but receiving this king's son enabled him to boast back to the capital that he had received the total surrender of the whole of the British Isles. Whatever plaudits it earned Caligula, it doesn't seem to have done Adminius much good: he effectively disappears from the limelight, though some commentators suggest that he returned to Britain shortly before the invasion in AD 43 where he may have been installed as a nominal governor of Cantium (Kent) and could even have lived in the lavish villa found at Eccles near the River Medway.

Meanwhile, with his strange and cruel behaviour, Caligula certainly wasn't making friends and in January AD 41, he was murdered by his own Praetorian guard (the personal army of the emperors) while watching the Palatine games. Few would mourn his passing.

The first few roller-coaster years of the Roman empire had demonstrated just how dangerous supreme control by one man could be. Impoverished and unconfident, Rome needed someone to lead it back into the success and prosperity that had marked the heyday of the Republic; what it got was Caligula's uncle – Tiberius Claudius Caesar Augustus Germanicus – otherwise known as its fourth Emperor, Claudius. It was not a promising start: growing up, he was ugly, clumsy and continually ill – in all, something of an embarrassment to those around him but this did have the advantage that he was allowed to drop out of the limelight and out of the pressures of being a pawn in the savage politics of Rome. Instead, in around AD 8 when he was about eighteen years old, Claudius was encouraged to study under the great historian, Livy, who had won the imperial attention of the then emperor, Augustus.

Under Livy's steady tutelage, the youthful Claudius developed into an accomplished historian, concentrating his time writing chronicles of Rome, the Etruscans and also some biographies until old enough and experienced enough to take a more active role in public life. Although he was made consul in AD 37, under his nephew and now emperor Caligula, the two were never close – something that probably played in his favour for on becoming emperor himself in AD 41 he had the full support of the army and also the public.

It is worth noting that one man who was not convinced by Claudius was the historian, Cassius Dio. His version of the way Claudius acceded to the imperial throne is so sneering that it borders on the humorous, describing his moment of glory with a pathos that totally erodes the new emperor's credibility:

"Meanwhile some soldiers who had come into the palace intent on looting found Claudius tucked away in a dark corner. He had been with Gaius [Caligula]

when he had left the theatre, and now, fearing the uproar, was hunkered down
in hiding. To begin with the soldiers thought he was someone else or had
something worth stealing, and hauled him out – but when they recognised him,
they hailed him as emperor and led him to the camp. Afterward with all their
comrades they handed him supreme power, inasmuch as he was from the
emperor's family and was considered suitable."

CASSIUS DIO: ROMAN HISTORY, BOOK LX

However, Dio's mocking humour about the way he came to power soon turns
to venom when describing the actual reign of Claudius. Having listed his
physical weaknesses which included shaking, sickliness, his faltering voice and
an inability to stand for any period of time, Dio goes on to add that:

"It wasn't the disabilities of Claudius that caused his deterioration so much
as the company he kept with freedmen and women, for more than any of his
peers, he was clearly ruled by slaves and women."

DIO CASSIUS: ROMAN HISTORY, BOOK LX

Though Dio is writing around a hundred and fifty years after the death of the
emperor, Claudius would have been aware that his credentials for ruling Rome
and its empire were less than impressive, and the poison so neatly articulated by
Cassius Dio would have been fermenting in the corridors of power even at the
start of his reign. Already unconventional in his background and appearance,
the accusation of being "ruled by slaves and women" would have been deadly
to his credibility. It may not seem much to a modern audience but to a citizen
of ancient Rome, this would have been a heinous charge. Roman society was
founded upon the unpaid labour of slaves and the firm rule of the *paterfamilias*
over his wife, daughters and his entire household: to encourage any inversion of
this hierarchy risked undermining the whole structure of Roman civilisation.

Claudius was only too aware of such views and of his own vulnerable
position. What he needed was to expand the empire to bring him the military
glory he was lacking from his largely academic lifestyle to date; such a feat would
also guarantee the support of both the army and the public, and might win

him more recognition from a sceptical and sometimes hostile senate. He was looking for a campaign that would achieve all this – but one that would also have the benefit of dampening the influence of the Druidic class of barbarian priests that Claudius believed was stirring up anti-Roman feeling throughout Gaul and the Celtic fringes of Europe.

Another factor that made Britain desirable for a renewed invasion was the rich trade that Rome was currently enjoying with the island, especially in products like Roman wine and pottery in exchange for British tin, lead, iron and other metals. They could certainly use a new source of silver, as their Spanish mines were being exhausted. However, without the lands being thoroughly explored, who knew what else lay waiting to be exploited by the Romans? To Claudius, the threat of crossing the dangerous waters of *Ocean* was more than compensated by the potential rewards of a spectacular political, economic and personal success.

In the end, he was given the perfect excuse for an invasion of Britain by the arrival at his court of Verica, the likely grandson of King Commius of the Atrebates. Verica had been expelled from Britain over a leadership challenge and had come to Rome seeking refuge and probably also revenge. He pleaded for help from the emperor who realised the excuse for an invasion had been handed to him on a plate: he could now be seen to show magnanimity towards the Briton – and prove to his detractors exactly what he was made of.

The army of around fifty thousand men massed nervously on the beaches of Gesoriacum in what is now Boulogne-sur-Mer. This well-established harbour now supplied much of the cross-Channel trade with Britain, via the Roman merchants who had dominated the routes since Caesar's annihilation of the Armoricans. Now, almost a century on, the fort on the built-up northern shore of the Liane River buzzed with activity as if the Roman harbour had always been there. It had witnessed the same scene just a few years before when Caligula had planned his own invasion of Britain before the bizarre volte-face that earned him the derision of his legions; this time, however, there would be no turning back. Like D-Day in reverse, the phalanxes of troops stood in uneasy silence, waiting for their turn to pile on board the naval ships built but never used by Caligula which were now loaded with supplies and ready to sail.

Leading the men was not the emperor himself but his respected commander, Aulus Plautius, who had all the necessary experience to launch what would be an audacious attack on the people of Britain. But while Plautius may have been confident about the forthcoming assault, his four legions plus auxiliaries of cavalry and infantry from the provinces were increasingly agitated: despite the two "successful" invasions by Julius Caesar, Britain and *Ocean* still played a powerful role in the Roman imagination. This was one journey they would rather not be making.

Also agitated would have been any Britons who happened to be on the wrong side of the Channel. In particular, the sight of the boarding troops would have hardened the hearts of the dominant Catuvellauni and Atrebates tribes of southern England: by now, they had carved out nice little "empires" of their own among their defeated British neighbours, growing wealthy on the trade opportunities offered by their Mediterranean friends. To all intents and purposes, they were already Romanised – and the prospect of a mass arrival of the Roman army was far less welcomed than their luxury food, wine and trinkets.

For their part, on board a fleet that would soon be known as the *classis Britannica*, the approaching forces of Aulus Plautius were not brimming with optimism either. Though sure of their military might, Britain was still the land of legends, separated from the civilised world of the established Empire by the unpredictable waters of *Ocean* with its strange tides so alien to the Mediterranean peoples, and the notoriously violent storms that almost left both previous invasions stranded and vulnerable to the barbarian Britons. While the glory of invasion propelled them forwards, the risks once they got there would be as high as the rewards.

The only sketchy account we have of the invasion of AD 43 comes from Cassius Dio's *Roman History*. While purporting to be a straight account from the founding days of Aeneas, the work is riven with personal feelings that are so bold they can at times come across as both shocking and humorous. It is clear that Cassius Dio was still no fan of Claudius, considering him to be cowardly and under the influence of his wives. However, even he could not deprive Claudius of the glory of successfully invading Britain, a feat that struck fear into the hearts of some of the bravest, most disciplined soldiers in the world to such an extent that they are reported to have almost refused to board their ships.

The difficulties in getting the legions to go to "outside the limits of the known world" delayed the invasion until late in the campaigning season. It was only the intercession of Claudius's freedman, Narcissus, that eventually drove the soldiers into action – not from any inspirational bravado but allegedly because they took extreme offence at being lectured by a freedman. But their troubles did not end once they had made the commitment to board the ships: having launched the first of their three fleets, they were soon blown off course by the treacherous winds in the Channel. Just like with Caesar's forces a century before, it must have seemed as though all the gods were against them. According to Cassius Dio, after all the fears and problems with getting underway, there was finally some good news on the horizon: a much-welcomed omen in the form of a comet which raced across the night sky from the east and auspiciously to the west – the direction where they were now headed.

It seems strange that the Romans were so nervous about crossing *Ocean* to Britain. As more and more graves of British Iron Age nobles are being dug up and examined, there is now a significant body of evidence that the tribal elites of ancient Britain were perhaps frequently making the journey in reverse – across the Channel to mainland Europe and Rome, for education and sometimes even as soldiers in the Roman army. Rosalind Niblett's work on the archaeological site at Folly Lane in St Albans shows the king or chief who was buried there had been such a soldier or auxiliary in the Roman Army, and he'd brought back home with him a love of the Roman way of life. This Romanisation of communities was a tried and tested method of increasing Roman control over foreign lands, and it seems likely that it was happening around this Iron Age settlement in modern Hertfordshire. There is even a suggestion that the Folly Lane king might have been a client ruler for the Romans – a fact that would link him to East Anglia and the future client kingdom of Boudica's Iceni tribe. So have we underestimated the extent of Roman influence in Britain before Claudius reached these shores? Rosalind Niblett is pragmatic: "Whether he was a client king or a *princeps civium* (chief citizen) is impossible to say, but we can safely assume that he was a man who had displayed sufficient pro-Roman sympathies at the time of the conquest to allow him to retain his wealth and position for over a decade after the conquest." And so it was to prove over in the Iceni lands of the east until Queen Boudica rose up with her people – and turned against the foreigners and the descendants of the soldier-king at the romanised town of St Albans.

The invading army of AD 43 arrived in the safe harbour of Richborough – the beachhead defences of which survive to this day – and from there, they quickly made their way inland – most likely along the ancient pre-historic track through the North Downs, now known as the Pilgrims' Way. They were largely unopposed by the British warriors other than the odd skirmish in eastern Kent when the Romans were left vulnerable in the swamps and forests. Just as in the days of Julius Caesar, the guerrilla tactics of the natives were the most effective way to try to combat the enemy. But on this occasion, the boggy landscape offered less impediment to the Roman forces; among the troops were soldiers from Germany who were well accustomed to wading through streams and even fast-flowing rivers.

Early into the march inland came the heartening news that the Dobunni tribe to the west were ready to submit – but just as the mood was becoming more optimistic, the troops arrived at the Kentish River Medway. While they waited for orders as to what to do next, they could see the enemy massed around five hundred metres away on the opposite side of the river, reportedly "bivouacked in a somewhat careless fashion". Just as they had done a century before under Cassivellaunus, disparate tribes of British warriors had united to form a vast army, this time under the leadership of two powerful Catuvellaunian "kings" who between themselves controlled much of southeast England – Caratacus and Togodumnus, the sons of the late king, Cunobelin. They had chosen this site believing it would offer them a strategic advantage – they knew where the shallows were while the Romans would not be able to cross without a bridge. But they had not reckoned on two things: the brilliant and crafty battle tactics of Aulus Plautius and the Batavian cohorts in the Roman army whose troops were able to swim, fully clothed in armour and carrying all their weapons, across the water.

While some of the Roman troops made the appearance of lining up to cross the river for battle, Plautius ordered the Batavians to head along the banks until they were out of sight of the Britons, and then swim across to hit the enemy at their rear. The plan worked perfectly: to the amazement and then terror of the British who realised they had been caught napping, the Batavians reached the far bank with enough strength to race out of the water and hit the warriors where it hurt the most – the ranks of chariots and horses that were positioned behind the enemy front line. As the Romans hurried to cripple the horses by slashing the tendons in their legs, the Britons were left without their most devastating weapon – their chariots. Prevented from making a full attack, they couldn't even make a rapid escape. Thoroughly trapped, large numbers of warring Britons were now cut down by the remaining Roman soldiers who had begun crossing the river under the leadership of the future emperor, Vespasian, and his brother, Sabinus.

The fighting continued throughout the day and late into the night when the Britons eventually dispersed and the Romans organised themselves in their new camp on the north bank of the river. But if the Romans thought that what would become known as the Battle of the Medway was over, then they were wrong. The very next day, the routed British returned with yet more warriors and fell on the Romans in another round of fighting that this time seemed to have neither a victor nor an end. Just as the Britons were getting the upper hand, the fortunes were reversed: the Romans managed to encircle the Britons, capturing them in a classic pincer movement, and finally took the day. During the fierce fighting that by now had now lasted two long days, Togodumnus was mortally wounded while the defeated warriors under Caratacus fled back towards the Thames where they melted away into the scrubland and marshes.

As much of a threat as the enemy themselves was the hostile landscape of Britain, with its dense woods and forests, swamps and rivers that put the advancing Romans in persistent danger of drowning or attack. While the Britons had the home advantage of knowing safe routes through the dangerous lands, the Romans, weighed down with armour and supplies, were less manoeuvrable. However, the Roman troops pushed on until they reached the Thames – but to the undoubted surprise of the Britons, here they stopped, set up camp and then sent word back to Claudius that he should make haste to Britain. And then they waited, in full knowledge that the delay in pushing north would merely serve to give the Britons time to organise themselves for the battles that would inevitably lie ahead.

Despite having effectively won control over much of southeast England, Aulus Plautius was now even more vulnerable – not only by the threat from Caratacus, enraged at this invasion and the slaughter of his brother and people, but also from being seen to deprive his emperor of the glory of successfully "taking" Britain. The official line runs that he became afraid and called for Claudius; more likely, this was a prearranged moment to enable Claudius to come in and scoop up the honours.

It took six long weeks for Claudius to make his way north through Gaul, across *Ocean* to Britain. Waiting in their anxious camp on the banks of the Thames, the sight of the emperor arriving with all his regalia – including a troupe of elephants – must have impressed even Plautius. The enlarged Roman army now headed north towards the major stronghold of Camulodunum, now Colchester in modern Essex. They stormed easily the prestigious British settlement and made it their capital – for this time, the Romans were not planning on leaving. Caesar may have become legendary for his invasion of Britain but Claudius had now achieved what Caesar never did: he really had "taken" the new province of Britannia – and almost four hundred years of Roman occupation was about to begin.

Like a house of cards, one British tribe after another now fell to Rome, either by force or by surrender. Amongst the tribes that were now pledging themselves to Rome were the Iceni – probably under King Antedios, and King Cogidubnus of the Regni and Atrabates, who had taken over the kingdom from Verica. No one knows if Verica survived long enough to be restored to his former lands but his successor, Cogidubnus, not only enlarged his kingdom but also received Roman citizenship, along with the appellations "Tiberius Claudius Cogidubnus" and *rex et legatus Augusti* as official recognition as the emperor's deputy in the new province. Also among the submitting Britons from around this time was a British queen, Cartimandua of the Brigantes, whose vast territories from the Midlands up to the north of England gave the Romans a valuable buffer zone between the pliant or conquered tribes of England and the warring tribes to the north and west. However, this relationship was to cost the Romans dearly and give the moralising chroniclers plenty of ammunition about warrior queens in general, and British ones in particular.

With safety if not completely guaranteed then at least established for the time being, Claudius returned to Rome leaving Plautius in charge as Britain's first Roman governor. As for the emperor, he had stayed in Britain for a mere sixteen days. However, none of that mattered back in the street of the capital where he was hailed as "Britannicus" and granted a triumph, with celebrations all over the city including athletic games, bear-baiting, horse racing and stage shows. Adding Britannia to the Roman empire was a huge cause for celebration – so big, in fact, that it was decided that one festival was not enough and they should henceforth be held annually to mark the occasion. And, just in case anyone had missed this great feat, two triumphal arches were built – one in Rome and one in Gaul from where the invasion was mounted – which bore witness to the eleven British tribes that had submitted and celebrated the crossing of *Ocean* and the paltry loss of troops. Even Claudius's son was proudly renamed "Britannicus" in honour of his father's achievements – a name which stuck until the day he died.

Meanwhile, *Britannia* was a meaningless term to the natives of Britain. They defined themselves not by the Roman name for the great island in which they lived but by their local tribes and affiliations, many of which had been in a state of flux during the last one hundred years since contact by Caesar. Since the previous invasions they had been left to fight out a tribal hierarchy between themselves, but this time even those who had accepted Roman suzerainty were under the fetters both of their own local king or queen who ruled on behalf of the Romans, and the Romans themselves under the guise of the provincial governor, Plautius, his tax-collecting administrators and his army. The double whammy was therefore both military and financial rule by Rome, and there was nothing the average Iron Age Briton could do about it. To be fair, the reality was that very few people in the tribal societies around the time of the Claudian conquest had any real concept of individual freedom, so they may well have hardly noticed that yet another level of serfdom had been imposed upon them. However, they would have noticed the new rules restricting their possession of weapons and the additional taxes extracted from them by the Roman procurator to pay for the military presence; and they would certainly have noticed the benefits of association heading directly to their tribal leaders in terms of exquisite goods, loans and wine by the amphora.

As I travelled around the country in search of Boudica and her story, it was becoming increasingly obvious that the myth of the Iceni queen fighting as "one of the people" was growing less and less convincing. All the pieces of the jigsaw from fieldwork, interviews and archives were building a picture that stood in stark and uncomfortable contrast to the clean-cut image of Boudica as a "Braveheart in a bra". If our queen had been on the side of the Romans during the Claudian invasion, she must have benefited in a similar way to the other client rulers who all sported fine imported luxury goods as a conspicuous display of their loyalties and often new-found wealth. This version of her story is far less glorious than the simplistic tale of a wronged queen who casts off her crown to turn freedom-fighter. Our cosy notions of Britain versus Rome, "them against us", of defending our nation and our independence – all these were beginning to wear thin under the friction of a mounting body of evidence of a patchwork of competing tribes and shifting loyalties that were a feature of her day. And as much as it revealed more of the *truth* about Boudica, it began to chisel away at the façade of nationalistic and peculiarly *British* pride that the warrior queen has been intimately linked with for the last five hundred years. Every step, every discovery that took me closer to the past took me further away from the very essence of the notion of "Britishness" that we use to define ourselves and our identity. It was not only Boudica who was being challenged – it was our fundamental myths of origin.

Britain was now developing as a two-tier society – those who were with the Romans and the rebels who were not. If your tribe supported Rome you could live peaceably enough (as long as you paid your taxes) under your usual tribal leader; if you belonged to a rebel tribe or joined the army of tribal guerillas, you were at the mercy of the infamous Roman legions which now swept north towards Leicester and the Midlands, and west to the Isle of Wight, Maiden Castle in Dorset and then to Exeter. This time, the legions were merciless rebel-hunters. Over the four years of Plautius's governorship they ripped through the new province, overpowering the tribal *oppida* and employing a scorched earth policy to those who still refused to submit. The evidence is all too clear: devastation from Roman missiles at tribal sites – and row upon row of Roman military forts along Britannia's new frontiers.

One leader who was definitely not submitting to the invading army was Caratacus. He had vowed to fight on after his assault against the Romans at the Battle of the Medway and the death of his brother, Togodumnus, at the hands of the Roman army. The story of his resistance soon became famous throughout the British Isles and even spread to Rome where he was later described by the historian, Tacitus, as "foremost amongst British chieftains". Having lost his own heartlands, Caratacus escaped to the almost wholly *un*-Romanised Silures people who lived in the mountainous regions of what is now South Wales; he also made contact with the Ordovices in the north of Wales who proffered some support. For a country filled with tribes for whom war was practically a pastime, it might seem odd that Caratacus was accepted into their lands, particularly when his arrival would mean nothing but trouble from the furious Romans. It has been suggested that the Druids may have played some part in his acceptance and it is certainly well known that they were influential across Britain from their base on the island of Mona, just off the coast of Wales, now Anglesey. There are also intriguing references in the ancient Welsh bardic poems, the Triads, that Caratacus and his father had strong dynastic links with Cornwall, just across the water to the south; if true, this could mean that this powerful noble also had family ties within Wales and the west that would guarantee at least a hospitable welcome, if not the support of kinship.

From his mountain hideout, Caratacus now gathered around him others who rejected the Roman occupation and by the winter of 47-48, they were ready to make their move. From his own intelligence and no doubt the divinations of the Druids from their base on Anglesey, he would have known the time was right: Plautius had already quit the province to receive his ovation in

Rome, and his successor – Pubius Ostorius Scapula – had yet to arrive. In the leadership vacuum this created, Caratacus launched his attack, descending from the mountains, across the River Severn and into the lands of the province where the Roman army had settled down for the winter, never dreaming that anyone would launch an assault during the closed season for warfare.

It is an interesting aside that during Plautius's governorship of Britain, he had brought his wife over to be with him – but it seems that Pomponia Graecina might have been rather too receptive to one feature of the Britons' culture that her husband was trying to expunge: some time after their return to Rome, it appears she was accused of practising a "foreign superstition". Was this the very Druidism that the Romans were trying to stamp out? It might just be that she brought more back home with her than just the experience of a foreign land.

Meanwhile, Ostorius Scapula arrived in Britannia in AD 47 and found himself immediately at war with Caratacus, who not only knew the ground better than Scapula did but who was mustering popular support as he went. Realising that he would have to work hard both militarily and in terms of stamping his authority on the tribes in the province, Scapula now employed a range of tactics that might have brought him temporary aid – but either through ignorance, carelessness or lack of any real choice in the matter, he merely shored up more problems for the future. To weed out those who were past their fighting best, he established a *colonia* at Camulodum (Colchester) where retired legionary veterans could live out their days as a kind of Dad's Army, ready to defend the ideas of Rome and protect the eastern flank of the new province. While it might have seemed sensible to establish a firm base of power, the taking of more and more land from the local Trinovantes tribe to give to the retired soldiers caused a great deal of local resentment, especially when the Trinovantes had been both the support for and one of the raisons d'être of the Roman invasion a few years earlier.

While trouble was brewing here in the east, over to the west, Scapula was employing every weapon in his military toolkit. He "occupied with encampments the entire country to the Avon and Severn" in readiness for the guerrilla attacks from Caratacus's bands of men; then, adding a final insult to injury, he also ordered even the friendliest of tribes including the client kingdoms to hand over all their weapons. To a proud warrior culture, this was the height of emasculation, especially when it was probably rudely enforced by detailed searches of farms and fields. In fact, the move not only made Scapula and his occupying forces deeply unpopular and thereby stirred up even more anti-Roman resentment, it even caused a small but significant revolt within the Iceni tribe that had thus far been totally compliant.

The Iceni king Prasutagus may have come to power around the time of the revolt but he cannot have been involved directly or he would have lost his "client" status. However, clearly some factions within the Iceni decided to go it alone and fight without the obvious support of their king – and they were soon joined by some of their neighbours among the Coritani and the Catuvellauni. Together, this composite army of Britons fought bravely from one of the Iceni hillforts but they were no match for the Romans, even though the enemy's army consisted of auxiliaries rather than legionaries. The revolt was soon put down, and the agitators presumably killed in the fighting, or executed shortly afterwards.

Having quickly extinguished the Iceni unrest, Scapula then headed north-west into what is now Cheshire in an attempt to drive a Roman wedge of power between Caratacus's bands of rebels. These were now moving among the nearby Deceangli tribe in the north-east corner of Wales – but just as important as the trouble in Wales was the potential danger of Caratacus gaining support from the large and worryingly unstable confederation of the Brigantes in the neighbouring swathes of northern England.

In retaliation against the Roman onslaught heading northwest, Caratacus and his "brothers" (whether literal or not is not known) launched parrying attacks at the Romans without much effect and then retreated back into the hostile highlands of Wales where the legions were loath to follow, at least for the moment. With him were the Silures people of central and south-east Wales whom Scapula had publicly vowed to exterminate down to the last man. Scapula's uncompromising attitude displays something of his temperament and mood against an enemy that was making a mockery of his command and his army, but it merely had the result of stirring up even more anti-Roman hatred.

Knowing that they were now fighting for the survival of their tribe, the Silures banded together in the territory of the Ordovices to avoid Roman incursions into their more accessible homelands. But things were going too slowly for Caratacus: without a significant win – and soon – he would doubtless begin to lose support for the rebellion, and as soon as their numbers dwindled, they would be doomed.

Girdled by a fast-flowing river, the hill rose proudly from the green-clothed landscaped. Its steep sides with their natural strategic advantages had been made even more impenetrable by man-made fortifications of tall stone ramparts built around its flanks: this fortress that now punctured the very sky stood as a symbol of free Britons – one that would teach the foreign army that the rebels were as embedded in this hostile landscape as the rocks that resisted the scouring wind.

Caratacus had used the detailed local knowledge of his guerrilla army to choose the perfect site for what was to become the decisive pitched battle against Scapula and his Roman army. Entombed in the defences – possibly the Iron Age hillfort on the limestone massif at Llanymynech near Wroxter in Shropshire – Caratacus's forces lay in wait, heavily armed with swords, spears and piles of stones to use as missiles against the enemy. But this hill was no Trojan horse: the Romans had been lured to the site and they knew perfectly well that the rebels were up there; the trick would be to get at them before they were slaughtered.

To the waiting rebels, the sound of the advancing Roman army was enough to warm the blood. Launching a furious attack on the legionaries wading through the river below, they now sent a deluge of missiles onto their heads that would surely wipe them out. But Caratacus had not reckoned on the sheer sticking power of the Roman army. With cool discipline even in the face of terrifying odds, the Romans kept up their attempts to scale the embankments, holding their famous "tortoise" formation with shields held over their heads until they reached the ramparts – then, as one soldier died, another one took his place at the front of the line in a relentless conveyor-belt of force until the Romans eventually inched up the slopes. Little by little, the army was gaining ground; soon they were at – and then spilling over – the defences with a roar, pushing the rebels backwards up the hill to the higher ground until there was nowhere left to go. Now the odds had changed as the fighting became the more familiar hand-to-hand combat at which the Romans ruled supreme. From this moment on, the outcome was almost inevitable: devoid of body armour and lacking their charioteers and cavalry, the Britons were outclassed – and those who could, fled.

Caratacus knew the game was up but he was not yet ready for death. In the mêlée of defeat, he escaped so quickly that he even left his wife, daughter and some of his "brothers" behind to be captured by the advancing Romans and kept as live bait for their rebellious kinsman. But where could he go? If he went south or east, he would be heading into the domain of the enemy, and westwards lay the barrier of Snowdonia. His fateful decision was to journey north-east to the land of the Brigantes – a choice that would transform not only his life but the shape of politics in northern Britain for decades to come.

The Brigantes ruled a vast tract of land that stretched the breadth of Britain from Carlisle to Newcastle down over the mountains of the Pennines to just north of Chester in the west to South Shields in the east. A vitally important buffer zone for the Romans – securing the north against incursion from the Caledonians of Scotland or eastwards from the rebellious Welsh tribes – it was ruled by the infamous Queen Cartimandua, a woman whose reputation far outstrips the hard facts about her life.

We know very little about this Iron Age ruler other than through the writings of classical authors, some sparse archaeology and perhaps the occasional coin; yet this woman would not only play a starring role in the story of Caratacus but also that of another rebel and high-profile British leader, Queen Boudica of the Iceni. Together with their male rebel counterpart, these women provide stark evidence of our desire to tell stories about long-dead characters, to lift them out of the dust of history and breathe new life into them – even if that life is gained at the expense of the truth. Picking through the debris of ascribed motives and historiography is a time-consuming and often frustrating task: the need for humans to communicate in stories is fundamental to the way we communicate and shape memories. As the British Museum's J D Hill repeatedly told me: "We actually need *more* stories in archaeology – but those stories must be based on real evidence." The trouble is that evidence is extremely thin on the ground.

Even though Cartimandua lived on his home patch, Richard Hingley at Durham is pragmatic: "I think it's unrealistic to hope to find much more than we have for Boudica and Cartimandua, which is essentially a few mentions in Tacitus and Cassius Dio, and some scant archaeology; after all, we don't even find much evidence for individual people in ancient Greece or Rome. Both women were living in a peripheral province and a *pre-literate* province. If the native Britons had been literate, we'd have had inscriptions on monuments and things like that but the ancient Britons just didn't *do* that so it's hard to attribute finds to her. However, that's not to say that much more work isn't needed. The north of England in particular has been ignored as there are relatively few universities here and there's far less development than in the south and east – and it's often developers who pay for digs on their sites. But things *are* changing, especially over the last five years or so, with a number of new and exciting finds turning up, including an early Roman villa at Piercebridge that dates from around the late first century. According to our existing theories, these shouldn't really be here as this area was meant to be more militarised than civil, but the more we learn, the more we have to refine our thinking about the north and far west of England in the early Roman period."

The Brigantes were a complex tribe. Though officially pro-Roman and a so-called client kingdom with some degree of self rule, they were a diverse band of peoples within a vast area – and were well-known to have both pro- and anti-Roman factions which occasionally bubbled up to the surface. As Caratacus raced north-east, fresh from his humiliation on the hilltop, he was clearly hoping that some of these bellicose people would offer him sanctuary like the Silures and Ordovices had done – and perhaps even join his cause. With the great numbers of tribespeople they possessed, this would give the rebellion a serious chance of defeating the Romans and driving them back down south, perhaps even back to Gaul.

But it was not to be. In a misjudgement that cost him his career and almost his life, as soon as he arrived at Cartimandua's court in AD 51/52, she had him promptly taken prisoner, clapped into chains – and then handed over to the Romans and the wrath of Ostorius Scapula. For this seasoned military leader, this must have been a moment of intense and satisfied joy: after no doubt savouring the catch, Caratacus was sent to Rome to be paraded in chains along with his family in front of Emperor Claudius himself.

Why did she act with what even the Roman historian, Tacitus, denounced as "treachery"? The truth will never be known but modern suggestions have included Cartimandua's fear that Caratacus's growing power and fame in uniting Britain against Rome was diminishing her own status. It is also likely that the ancient Britons would not have regarded her actions as treacherous at all, for how can you commit treachery against a rival tribe? Just because Caratacus and Cartimandua were both Britons, it didn't mean that they felt any form of bond as Tacitus may have assumed; in fact, it would take hundreds of years after the Romans had left the country before the native population had any sense of being from a nation of "British" people. Meantime, in the context of an ever-changing political landscape it would always have been a gamble to ask for help from another tribe – and Cartimandua had clearly already aligned her Brigantian kingdom with Rome. As for why Caratacus went to the Brigantian queen in the first place, we know that Cartimandua was associated with a personification of the goddess Brigantia so there might have been a religious reason why he sought sanctuary with her – and why she handed him over to the Romans. A final possibility comes from the ancient Welsh bardic poems, the Triads. These posit a genealogy through their fathers' line which makes Cartimandua and Caratacus second cousins – and therefore they would have regarded each other as "family". If true, this is one occasion where blood wasn't thicker than water; Cartimandua now regarded herself more closely connected to the Romans than to British rebel fighters.

Shortly after the capture of Caratacus, Scapula died – worn out by the tirelessly warring Britons and the constant pressure of life in one of Rome's newest but most troublesome provinces; if anything, losing their own leader merely invigorated the Britons who now flared up, like the multi-headed Cerberus guarding the gates of Hades. Wherever the Romans went they were dogged by the rebels' violent new lines of attack that snapped at their heels all over this marshy, cold and inhospitable country. Meanwhile, Scapula's death had taken Rome completely by surprise and it took until the end of the year AD 52 to find a suitable replacement. This finally came in the form of the elderly but experienced Didius Gallus who gradually, like the fabled hero, Hercules, finally managed to contain the vengeful British beast, or at least to give the appearance of containing it to the emperor back in Rome.

The sun streamed through the bright mountain air, hitting the water in a million shards of light; then slowly the glossy surface of the lake began to ripple, then shudder and then split open as a vast silver triton began rising from the centre of the lake, powered by some elaborate underwater machinery: this was the signal for an epic naval battle to start, in a bid to delight the crowds watching from behind a wooden barrier. But this was no real battle between the fleets of Sicily and Rhodes: this was a mock battle for the amusement of the emperor Claudius, even though it would involve the two sides fighting to the death. According to the classical biographer, Suetonius, there was nothing the emperor enjoyed more than a big, aggrandising public display. He would sit for hours at gladiatorial games and rejoice as he watched the death-throes of the defeated. Now, having decided to drain the vast Fucine Lake in the Apennines to make more land for agriculture, he marked the start of the work with the mock naval battle, reported to involve some nineteen thousand convicted criminals, specially saved up for the purpose.

> *"But when the combatants on the armadas cried out, 'Hail emperor! We who are about to die, salute you,' and he answered, 'Health attend you,' – they all refused to fight, arguing that with these words they had been pardoned. Upon this, he hesitated for a short while, deciding whether or not to kill them with fire or the sword but at last, leaping up from his throne and running along the shore of the lake in his risible tottering manner, he at last incited them to fight, by means of both threats and promises."*
>
> SUETONIUS: *"CLAUDIUS", 21*

Claudius would use any excuse for a spectacle – and the defeat of the Britons was the biggest feat of his reign, which is why the story of the native rebel leader, Caratacus, doesn't end with him being shipped off to the capital in captivity.

Having fought the Romans through every means possible for an incredible eight or nine years, Caratacus was now something of a celebrity, both in Britain and in Rome; on top of this, he was further built up to suit the Roman PR line that with his capture, the war was over and Britain had accepted its new rulers with good grace. There was now another chance for Claudius to win a major public relations coup. In front of a great audience gathered for the purpose of revelling in Rome's dominance over its empire, a procession of hostages was brought out, ending with Caratacus's family and then the man himself. But according to the historian Tacitus, whereas the others stood in mute deference with their heads bowed, when the rebel leader reached where Claudius was seated, Caratacus stood firmly upright and proclaimed:

> "Had my rank and ancestry been matched by my good luck then I would have come into this city as your friend instead of your captive ... My current fortune is as degrading to me as it is glorious to you. I had horses and men, arms and riches – small wonder that I was reluctant to give them up. Just because you Romans want to rule over the whole world, does that mean that the world has to accept slavery? If I had been immediately punished as a prisoner, neither my disgrace nor your triumph would have become famous. My punishment would now be followed by oblivion – but if you save me, then I will be an enduring memorial of your clemency."
>
> TACITUS: *ANNALS, XII, 37*

Claudius looked at the dignity of this rebellious Briton and gave him and all his relatives full pardons. After all, Caratacus had served his purpose well – firstly by providing Rome with a famous anti-hero to so visibly conquer, and then to illustrate the wonderful clemency of the emperor.

Tacitus makes one further comment about this curious spectacle: apparently, Caratacus and his family not only paid homage to Claudius – they also gave it to Agrippina, his infamously evil and much-hated wife. She was seated on her own throne nearby, no doubt further gaining the ire of the nobility who detested the way she had assumed an almost regal position alongside the emperor. The respect paid to Agrippina by the Britons may have seemed quite natural to people from a culture where having queens was nothing out of the ordinary, but to the Romans it was absolutely shocking. But while Caratacus and his family could be forgiven for being barbarian foreigners and thus ignorant of "civilised" Roman ways, the fact that Agrippina had actually *accepted* the honours doubled the insult and underlined a growing thirst for power by Claudius's new wife who would go on to become one of the most reviled women in the Roman empire. It is hard to overstate her role in the public perception of women rulers, and she proves a worthy focus for a study in her own right: the vile legacy of this hated woman pours through the pages of classical literature like the poison she seemed to favour as her murderous *modus operandi*. What's more, this poison was about to spill over into the Roman perception of two famous "queens" who were starting to flex their muscles thousands of miles away in the barbarian lands of Britannia.

Although much of the detail of Caratacus comes from Tacitus, it is Cassius Dio who adds the epilogue to his tale, writing that once pardoned and living out his days in Rome, Caratacus "wandered about the city … and after witnessing its splendour and its greatness he exclaimed: 'and can you, then, who have got such possessions and so many, covet our poor tents?' " In fact, nothing is known of the rest of the great rebel leader's life. In terms of Roman history, he had served his purpose: a rebel, brought to book, who revealed the mercy and greatness of an emperor. Undoubtedly, Caratacus would have been impressed by the city of Rome, and he would doubtless have also realised that while as a rebel standing in front of the emperor, he was one more icon of Rome's omnipotence, just like the grand buildings that now filled his eyes. He would also have known that once pardoned, he became a nobody.

As for Cartimandua, the quisling queen of the Brigantes, her story would serve as another morality tale in every sense of the word, and one that would act as the perfect foil to the tragic tale of Queen Boudica of the Iceni.

CHAPTER 7

"HYENAS IN PETTICOATS"

Agrippina the Younger and Cartimandua, the Client Queen

"…woman is a selfish creature and addicted to jealousy to a vast degree, and calculating enough to agitate and override the natural instincts of a man, and to mislead him by her continual designs. For she is always working upon dishonest speeches and other sorts of hypocrisy, like an actress on the stage, when she is seducing the eyes and ears of her husband…

Moreover, if there are children, she becomes proud and too free in her speech… And becoming utterly shameless, she proceeds to violence, and she performs numerous hostile acts. For the man who is caught by a woman's seductive charms… being won over by the impulses of love – is no longer the same person towards others; but he is completely transformed, becoming, without even suspecting it, a slave instead of a free man."

THE ALEXANDRIAN JEWISH PHILOSOPHER, PHILO (10 BC – C.AD 50),
HYPOTHETICA 11.14-17

Agrippina was the exact opposite of what a Roman wife should be: the most powerful woman in the Empire since her marriage to Claudius in AD 41, she poured scorn on the womanly ideal of chastity, piety and selflessness. To most Romans, women should be seen and not heard – and preferably only ever seen when being suitably deferential to their husbands and masters; Agrippina was one woman who was best not seen at all unless you had a death wish.

It was just two generations since the emperor Augustus had put in place his reactionary social reforms which carved a deep and stifling niche for women in Roman society – a niche into which the British queens Boudica and Cartimandua would soon be trapped by their Roman and Greek biographers. Like looking at a fly through the amber filter of an ancient resin, the culture of the classical world coloured the stories we have of both the British queens and other powerful women of the age – so to understand the versions of history that have been passed down to us, it's first necessary to explore the attitudes towards women in Ancient Rome.

Mediterranean society had, like many others in the classical world, a deep-rooted suspicion of women who got "above their station" and whether sirens or Amazons, their fundamental sexuality was perceived as a threat. However, if sex was indeed power then this could be used by women to their own ends, setting up a fierce but exciting frisson between a culture that decried women who dared to make themselves visible – and those who had the "audacity" to step into the limelight, such as Agrippina, Cleopatra, Cartimandua – and Boudica.

Fearing that a decline in Roman morality – and a decreasing birth rate among the nobility – were contributing to Rome's troubles at home and abroad, Augustus instituted new legislation that shackled women's liberty and made them subject to their husbands' and fathers' control, literally on pain of death. By law, all men and women now had to marry – and any woman found committing adultery could be legally killed; where death was avoided, divorce was now mandatory, along with a loss of her wealth and dowry. Women were even restricted from attending public spectacles; in fact, the only way that a woman could gain the approval of the state was by producing three or more children – whereby she got to wear a special garment and win extra freedoms including tax breaks on property.

Not only were these intrusions into the domestic sphere unwelcomed by the bulk of the population, they were flouted by the upper classes, including Augustus's own daughter, the sexually voracious Julia. By the time Agrippina reached adulthood, the existing laws and social mores had little meaning for the ambitiously minded young woman – and she became the embodiment of the very wanton, impious and ruthless behaviour that Augustus believed would cause the downfall of the state.

Agrippina loved power – and the more she tasted, the more she wanted. As the sister of Caligula, she had been raised to see what power could achieve and wasted no opportunity to go in pursuit of it. Having lost her first husband to a mystery ailment, she poisoned her second husband so that she could incestuously marry her uncle who was now Emperor Claudius. However, there was a slight problem: Claudius was already married to his current wife, Messalina but this presented no real barrier to such an experienced and wily murderer and the feat was achieved with ease in AD 48. From that moment onwards, Agrippina set about killing anyone who could not or would not help her achieve her plan – to make her son, Nero Claudius Caesar Augustus Germanicus, the next Emperor of all Rome. The tidal wave of murders masterminded and sometimes even carried out by Agrippina bordered on debauchery and yet no one dared act against Claudius's consort, even when rumours abounded that his own demise in AD 54 from what seemed to be poison had been effected by his less-than-loving wife.

Whatever the truth of the matter, in AD 54, Nero became Rome's fifth emperor at the tender age of just sixteen years old which – as everyone in the capital quickly realised – of course meant that he was still under the influence of his mother. It is hard from the surviving histories of the period to decide which of the mother-and-son combination was the more hated; most of the references were written from the safety of years after both their deaths when new political factors had come into play, so it is often hard to disentangle the disgust shown to these figures from the fawning attitudes towards the writer's latter-day, but often equally powerful, patrons.

Agrippina's lust for power had sickened the Romans and raised some uncomfortable memories of powerful women before her. The disruptive influence of Cleopatra was still keenly noted: her love affairs with Caesar and then Mark Antony had coincided with some of the bloodiest civil wars in the history of the republic and made her an obvious example of how things go wrong when a woman is allowed to rule. Her legacy now blended with Agrippina's to conjure up a witches' brew of sex and power that could bring down not only the greatest of men but great empires and even whole civilisations, too. The conclusion was obvious: women rulers were a corrupting force, a perversion of nature and a portent of inevitable doom.

It was during this time of Agrippina's reign of terror among the nobility that another woman was causing problems for the Romans at the periphery of their Empire. As with Agrippina, this was a woman who should have been fêted as a heroine by the Romans but instead had come to be regarded as a troublesome liability. We know very little about Cartimandua, whose name translates from the Celtic as "sleek pony"; there is no physical description of what she looked like other than an intriguing reference to her as a "false red-haired queen of the mists" but no other documentary evidence supports this assertion. Likewise, there is little background detail at all to illuminate her life but what we do know marks her out as an enigmatic and intoxicating character. Much more than that, however, she is important not only for being a female ruler among the very first rulers in the historical record for Britain, but also for the significant part she played in shaping the political landscape of Roman Britain. She may have been denounced by the Romans and perhaps even her own people for her treachery and overt sexuality (which would have been considered perfectly acceptable had she been a man) – but what scant facts there are speak for themselves: she was also an extremely clever politician who managed to stay in power and protect her people for around two decades in one of the most turbulent periods in British history.

"It's a beautiful part of the country in which to work," mused the archaeologist, Richard Hingley, as we walked across the campus at Durham University. I had made the three-hour journey to interview him by train, using the time to absorb the landscape of what once formed the home of the Brigantes. "There's a real sense of escaping into a wild and remote countryside – twenty minutes out of the city and you really feel like you've hit nature in the raw. And you get that sense from Tacitus's account of the Brigantes, that they were a people who fitted their lands."

The long rocky spine of the Pennines, cut deep with river valleys, dominates what was once the Brigantes' tribal lands. The Greek geographer Ptolemy described their domain as stretching "from sea to sea". It's a landscape that is Britain in microcosm: barren mountains, fertile valleys, wild moors and lush, wooded lowlands – and its conflicting geographies were mirrored in its people who held strong but diverse views on how they should be governed. The only part of the north of England that the Brigantes did not control was Yorkshire's East Riding which lay under the control of the Parisi tribe – the same name of tribe that occupied and gave its name to the area around the French capital.

The current ruler of the often loose confederation or hierarchy of Brigantian tribes was the infamous Queen Cartimandua. Archaeological evidence backs up the idea that the tribe was used to powerful women: an altar in Birrens, Dumfriesshire contains a relief carving of their patron goddess Brigantia – the Celtic word for High One. The carving shows the deity wearing a mural crown to denote prestige in battle and carrying a spear and the globe of victory. Not only was she a potent religious figure, this altar suggests that at times the tribal influence might have stretched even wider and the Brigantes name is certainly well-documented by a whole range of classical scholars including Tacitus, Juvenal, Seneca and Pausanias.

The Brigantes were distinct from their southern, more Romanised compatriots; at the time of the invasion of AD 43, these northerners were typically still an Iron Age community, with an economy based on agriculture, no apparent use of coin-mints (though some coins have been found here) and despite some skilled metalworkers, little in the way of material wealth and urbanity. However, it seems that their reverence of women ran deep throughout their lands and their culture: the rivers Braint and Brent were named after their patron goddess and she was also associated with sheep and cattle, the mainstay of the Brigantian economy; both the name of the goddess and the term, Brigantia, were enduring, lasting well beyond the period of Roman Britain and into the fifth century AD where they were embedded in oral folklore that was ultimately written down in the epic bardic poems such as *Y Gododdin* by the sixth-century Welsh poet, Aneirin.

But regard for individual women was not solely reserved for the gods; evidence from grave finds in the Brigantian areas suggests that women could – and did – rise up through the social hierarchy to achieve positions of respect and influence within the community. In Iron Age Britain it was relatively rare for people to be buried in graves although East Yorkshire seems to have bucked this trend by establishing whole cemeteries of them, and some of these contain burial goods such as pots or brooches. Since 1960, archaeologists have excavated over seven hundred graves in East Yorkshire and most contain simple burial goods or more usually none at all; however, of the graves found so far, seven contained chariots used as part of the funerary rites – and remarkably, two of these so-called chariot burials contain the bodies of women. High-status women might have been unusual but they were clearly not beyond the Britons' imagination.

One of the most impressive finds from the region is the chariot burial at Wetwang Slack, found about twenty miles to the east of modern-day York and dating to around 300 BC. In spring 2001, workmen on a building site for a new housing development discovered the grave located at the top of a hill, facing northwards in accordance with Iron Age tradition. Further examination revealed an incredible trove of detail: the woman was aged somewhere between thirty-five and forty-five – well beyond the Iron Age average – and even by modern standards she was incredibly tall, standing at five feet nine inches (1.75 metres). Most intriguing was the fact that she clearly suffered from some form of facial disfigurement on one of her cheeks like a large strawberry birthmark, giving her face an asymmetrical appearance and no doubt marking her out as "different". Was this why she was given a special burial? There are no weapons in the grave so she probably wasn't a warrior; the presence of a beautifully detailed iron mirror placed against her ankles may mean she was a queen or princess but it could just as likely be that she was a priestess (perhaps of a deity like Brigantia) or a seer and the mirror had some magical or religious significance.

Though nothing more about her is known, this high-status woman who has even been called a "queen" was delicately placed in the grave with her mirror, beads and food for the afterlife, surrounded by the ornately decorated and carefully dismantled chariot. Detailed investigation revealed that the chariot was probably one that was actually used rather than built specially for the funeral; it was then gently covered by the chariot platform before the earth was heaped in a mound over the woman's crouched body. The burial of such a fundamental and prestigious piece of equipment underscores the importance of the horse and chariot for these ancient people as you were only buried with your most precious or symbolic possessions. However, the gaps in this woman's story are as numerous as the voids left in the soil when the wood, leather and fabric rotted away to rejoin the cold earth – but here was a woman who was clearly valued by her community and buried with tenderness and respect. But what makes her more than just a curio is the fact that she's not alone. The other female grave is equally rich and interesting, and together they support the assertion made by classical and modern commentators alike that the British tribes were comfortable with the idea of powerful women – and it seems they revered them, even in death.

So what evidence do we have of Cartimandua? Is there a rich burial site or a material record of her life? My search for this almost-famous heroine from Britain's ancient past was proving increasingly frustrating as there appeared to be nothing that rooted her to the reports by Tacitus of her existence. And then I came across a reference not just to a Cartimandua coin that had been found but some that seemed to link her with her warrior-husband, Venutius. The legend on the coins read "Cart…" or sometimes "Cartive". In terms of hard evidence, it seemed too good to be true.

I immediately got on the phone to Philip de Jersey who looks after the Celtic Coin Index in Oxford and questioned him about the alleged finds. He groaned. "Yes, it would be very convenient, wouldn't it, and combining Cartimandua with Venutius would be an ingenious explanation of the 'Cartive' reading. Unfortunately, it's just not true. The coins are actually referring to a ruler

The infamous 'Cartive' coin, once thought to be that of Cartimandua and Venutius

called *Cartivellaunos*, and he was most likely a man! It's all a bit like the Boudica-face coins which turned out to sport a moustache: sometimes, we only see what we want to see, and I think that's the case with the Cartimanduan coins as well." It was yet another lesson in wanting something too much, although Philip did leave just a trace element of doubt: "Of course, it might perhaps be conceivable that 'Cartivellaunos' could have been miscopied as 'Cartimandua' – it does seem unlikely, but then so is the name Boudica being changed into Boadicea or Bonduca – and we know that this was the case." As it would so often prove in the search for the real story of Boudica's world, the best we could do was make an educated guess.

The beautiful but bleak landscape of the Brigantes, with its mountains, impenetrable moors and fast-flowing rivers, made access difficult and encouraged the development of discrete communities rather than one united people. The wild nature of the land, its vast size (it was the largest tribal region in Britain) and the challenges wrought by its difficult geography were further paralleled in the characteristics of its people: the Brigantes were reportedly proud and fierce, infamously unruly and prone to revolt. We don't know how or when Cartimandua came to power, though it is clear she was already queen within a few years of the Roman invasion. From the few coins that have been found within the Brigantes area and bearing the names Volisios, Dumnocoverus, Dumnovellaunos and Cartivellaunos, it has been suggested that she was part of that royal dynasty: Volisios may have been their father, whose rule passed to his "son" and then on his own death, to Cartimandua. This surmise fits neatly with Tacitus's comment that she was of "high birth" but is unlikely to be proved without doubt.

    She first comes to light in Tacitus's account of the year AD 51 – the first British woman to be mentioned by name – and it appears that this pro-Roman queen had already been in power for some time. Given Tacitus's reference to her noble ancestry, it is unlikely that the Romans put her on the Brigantian throne but if Cartimandua's rule did witness the arrival of the Romans, her motives for her early submission to the Emperor Claudius after his invasion are never mentioned in the original texts. Perhaps she reckoned that a strong Roman authority would make her own people easier to govern, perhaps she wanted the wealth and personal kudos that came along with collaboration – or perhaps she was playing a very canny game in realising that the best way to keep the Romans out of your lands was to give them some nominal sense of being in charge already. If Cartimandua was pursuing this last strategy, she played it to perfection: the Brigantes were among the very last peoples of England to be directly under Roman rule and with the help of the invaders, she grew even more wealthy and powerful.

Whatever her motives for submitting to Claudius, Cartimandua offered up her people and her lands as a "client kingdom" for the Romans, under her authority. Like the kingdom of Cogidubnus in the south of England, the client kingdoms of Britain provided taxation and support for the Romans in return for Roman protection and the absence of direct military rule; they also provided a cheap and easy buffer zone between lands under the absolute command of the provincial governor and the hitherto unconquered lands to the north and west. Cartimandua's kingdom was large but not cohesive, her terrain was frequently uninviting, and she controlled little in the way of plunderable resources; in other words – from the Roman point of view – she was welcome to it: they had little to lose by letting her remain a client queen and, just like Cartimandua herself, they had much to gain in return.

To the Roman way of thinking, although women rulers were a distasteful and dangerous phenomenon, it almost seemed to make sense that in this wild and savage country the barbarians would think nothing of having a queen rather than a king to rule over them. Even the salacious details of her personal life so pruriently detailed by Tacitus seemed to make sense in the context of Britain; after all, its people were hopelessly uncivilised and even Caesar had portrayed them as sexually incontinent, so what more could one expect? Cartimandua was tolerated because she was useful to the Romans and not much of threat to their stronghold in the province, but as far as they were concerned she was the very worst kind of ruler: female, foreign and visibly sexual.

As one of the only two client queens ever recognised by Rome and just like her predecessor, Cleopatra, it would be this carnal power that the Roman elite most feared and despised; what's more, to the Roman psyche at least, it was almost inevitable that history would repeat itself – and that her potent brew of sexual politics would ultimately bring her down – and possibly Roman control of Britannia as well.

Cartimandua did have a male consort in the shape of the high-born warrior, Venutius, and for the first few years of their appearance in the historical record, it seems they ruled their people together although Tacitus never gives him the title of "king", possibly because of his anti-Roman leanings. What the Brigantes people thought of their queen and the "client" status is anyone's guess as little is known of their attitudes and even less was written down. However, from the troubles and insurgencies that were noted by the Romans, it seems that the relationship between Rome and the Brigantes, between fellow Brigantes and even between Cartimandua and Venutius was as rocky as the scree slopes of the Pennines. The invaders might have had the support of Cartimandua but she didn't necessarily bring her people's or even her husband's support with her. However, the archaeology on the ground suggests that for a while, at least, she was able to rule without these.

Today, the small village of Stanwick-St-John lies to the west of Darlington in North Yorkshire's rolling, green countryside flanked by woodlands and farms. There is little here beyond some curiously undulating grasslands and stretches of stone rubble to suggest its former glory but this was a site of immense strategic importance for the Brigantes and, in particular, for their queen. Under the debris of almost two thousand years lie the secrets of its history which date back to around 400 BC; around AD 50, it was massively expanded to encompass around eight hundred acres and a "super-fort". This Iron Age tribal stronghold of the Brigantes – possibly even the first capital of Northern England – has long since been muffled by the smothering hand of Roman occupation; its boundary, marked out by large, broad ramparts, now silent under layers of vegetation.

The impressive buildings constructed here in the heart of Brigantian territory have been the source of speculation since the first major excavations by Sir Mortimer Wheeler in the middle of the last century. However, recent excavations near to where Richard Hingley works at Durham have challenged much of the previous thinking about the site as a focus in the battles between Cartimandua and Venutius. In fact, no major signs of attack have been found at Stanwick. So if it wasn't defensive, what *was* the function of this substantial set of structures? The answer seems to live in the material remains at the site. Although the houses were circular in the British tradition, there were Roman-style roof tiles – and when this evidence is combined with the exotic Continental imports such as glassware, large, earthenware amphorae and a metalwork hoard of one hundred and forty-six items (especially stylish horse and chariot gear), the weight of probability suggests that what the archaeologists have found is perhaps the most important settlement in the whole Brigantian kingdom.

Was this, then, the site of Cartimandua's royal seat? Although Aldborough and even York have been thrown into the frame, Stanwick certainly is a leading contender and the suggestion is supported by a range of luxuries imported from Gaul which show that the person who lived there was of high status and an unusual level of wealth – in fact, something akin to what was found at the presumed residence of Cunobelin in the far south of Britain from as early as AD 30.

Recent excavations have led archaeologists to the conclusion that the site was expanded to serve as a trading post, presumably taking advantage of the new routes being opened up by the military and their retinue of foreign traders. Tacitus comments that although Cartimandua was of noble ancestry much of her wealth came from the Romans – and whilst some of what he writes was undoubtedly to make Rome look benevolent, the experience of their other client ruler, Cogidubnus in the south, underlines the material gains of being one of the Empire's "favoured" tribes.

To begin with, then, the alliance with Rome worked in Cartimandua's favour: she grew richer and more powerful and – superficially at least – the Brigantes would have bathed in their new-found prestige. This is the period when exquisite pieces of Romano–British metalwork were created, some of which survive today such as the bronze mounting from Elmswell and the bronze horse-ring from Aldborough with its terrifying half-man half-god figure. The display culture so beloved of the Iron Age Britons was certainly alive and well in this period of Cartimanduan supremacy but internecine strife would soon bring the Brigante tribe – and the relative independence of the region – to its knees.

The first indication that all was not well with the Romans' critical northern "buffer zone" comes with Tacitus's report that around five years into the client relationship, in AD 48, a civil war broke out amongst the Brigantes which was serious enough to divert the new governor Ostorius Scapula from his efforts to bring the Welsh tribes under Roman control. The governor was now forced to head back to northern England to resolve the *discordiae* and to re-establish control of the client kingdom for Cartimandua which he did by executing the ringleaders of the uprising as an example of the stark choice facing the Britons under Roman rule. This was precisely the time that the Britons were becoming polarised as either *with* the Romans or *against* them, under the influence of the British rebel leader, Caratacus; for many, the decision was literally a matter of life or death. That Caratacus himself chose to seek sanctuary from Cartimandua in AD 51 suggests that a large body of her people remained unconvinced by Roman rule, for a leader like Caratacus would surely have had good reason to head into their lands for safety; that he was then handed over to his enemy by the very queen from whom he'd sought sanctuary says that while he might have correctly judged the mood of her people, he badly misjudged the mood of their ruler.

Cartimandua knew which side her bread was buttered on: handing over the head of the British resistance earned her the approval of the Romans which she clearly valued well above the approval of her own people. It might also have been payback for helping her retain her throne during the civil unrest around AD 48 and it certainly removed a threat to her power from a potential rival leader. However, when later reported by Tacitus, this whole episode of Briton-against-Briton shows just how factioned the indigenous population was at the time; it also shows the power of the Romans to destabilise tribal allegiances and – to the Roman reader at least – the power of queens to subvert both honour and integrity.

With the rebel leader now safely in chains and unable to stir up any more trouble, the Romans must have thought their battles for Britain were almost over; they certainly rewarded Cartimandua well for her loyalty. However, while they were concentrating on trying to consolidate their control over the remainder of the province, the loose confederation of the Brigantes reeled from stasis to crisis. There are hints within a poem written by Seneca that the early part of Nero's reign (from AD 54) was marked by unrest within the Brigantes and although the facts and chronology are less than clear, it seems that by AD 57, things had come to a head. The relationship between Cartimandua and her husband Venutius had broken down to such an extent that they not only split up but went to war against each other in a deeply personal way that set family against family. Underlying the split was probably Venutius's enmity for the Romans – and in the absence of Caratacus, it was now the queen's former consort who rose up and led the assault against the military occupation.

In Tacitus's account of what happened next, it isn't hard to see the Romans' admiration of male military might, and their deep-rooted hatred of powerful women – and, especially, of powerful women rulers:

"But after Caratacus, the capture of Venutius, a man outstanding in his knowledge of the warrior's art, from the tribe of the Brigantes…and long faithful and protected by Roman arms when he was married to Cartimandua the queen, was divorced from her and immediately went to war, entering into hostilities even against us. But at first the fighting was just between themselves, then Cartimandua, with cunning arts, seized Venutius's brothers and relations. This incensed her enemies and they were reeling in disgrace in case they would have to submit to the rule of a woman, and so warriors, strong and handpicked, invaded her kingdom. The affair had been foreseen by us, and cohorts sent to help fought a fierce battle, which had a hesitant start but a happier outcome."

TACITUS: *ANNALS, 12.40*

Even Venutius's treachery against his former allies pales into insignificance against Tacitus's loaded description of the queen's morality, which he variously describes in his writings as lustful, self-indulgent, treacherous and savage: her tactics of taking hostages (a normal course in the warfare of the time) are regarded as base and "cunning arts" – like those of a witch or a sorceress – in contrast with her husband's "outstanding … knowledge of the warrior's art"; likewise, her enemies were allegedly "reeling in disgrace" at the thought of having to "submit to the rule of a woman" – even though many had been her loyal subjects all the time she was married to Venutius. The only conclusion from the passage is that what we are reading is more about Tacitus's very Roman view that women were not fit to have power, rather than a genuinely factual account of what actually occurred.

Despite their disapproval, the Romans helped Cartimandua resist the attacks by her husband and win control of her lands once more. Again, the chronology of events has been the subject of much debate as the two versions of the story written down by Tacitus at different times seem to be at variance; however, the lack of any real archaeological evidence that the Romans had direct rule over the Brigantian lands at this time (as they did after AD 69 when Cartimandua had been deposed) would suggest that the queen was still in control of her client kingdom after the uprising.

The real dispute in her story's timeline emerges from around AD 57. Sometime between then and AD 69, she divorced her husband and then ruled the Brigantes with the support of her new lover, Vellocatus – her ex-husband's armour-bearer. To the Romans, this was a double outrage – a combination of the very worst kind of leadership that anyone could conceive: a female consorting with a subordinate in lieu of her brave warrior husband. It was almost as bad as letting a slave rule over freemen. To Tacitus's audience, this was the story of Cleopatra, Caesar and Mark Antony all over again – but at least they were high-born men who had proved their might: Vellocatus might well have had the rank of squire but to all Roman intents and purposes, he was a virtual unknown.

There is some doubt about the meaning of his name, translating as either "fighter of the good fight" or "better in battle" from the Celtic or from the Latin, "sly shaved one" or "clear-sighted fighter". Whatever his name, there was no doubt that Vellocatus had caught the eye of Cartimandua either through genuine desire or the political expediency of depriving her ex-husband of one of his closest supporters. She was not concerned with any nominal prestige or offence to Roman ideas on morality: she had made her choice – one which according to Tacitus, served only to inflame an already precarious relationship between queen and dominion:

"Her house was immediately shattered by this scandal: her husband had the support of the tribe, the adulterer had the queen's lust and savagery. So Venutius, having garnered support and with a revolt of the Brigantes themselves at the same time, took Cartimandua to the very edge of disaster. Then she sought help from the Romans, and our cohorts and cavalry, after uncertain battles, managed to rescue the queen from danger: the kingdom was left to Venutius, warfare to us."

TACITUS: *HISTORIES 3.45*

The final civil war which ended Cartimandua's reign appears to have occurred around AD 69 – the timing of which fits the general context of confusion and disarray in the whole of the Roman empire at the time, when the focus of both politicians and the military was on events in the capital rather than out in the peripheral provinces. Venutius had long declared his hand: by now, he was not only Cartimandua's fiercest enemy; as the leader of the anti-Roman faction in Britain he chose his moment to strike when the occupying army was at its weakest in an attempt to kill two birds with one stone, just as his rebel predecessor had done in his own fight against the Romans in the early years of occupation.

The seeds of Venutius's momentous rebellion had been already sown the previous year when, on June 9, AD 68, the emperor Nero had committed suicide. According to his biographer Suetonius, among the emperor's final words was his own humble epitaph, "What an artist is now about to die".

"He had an unquenchable thirst for immortality, and to acquire a reputation which should never fade; but it was whimsically directed...
He died in his thirty-second year...and the public joy was so great, that the common people ran about the city with the caps of freedom upon their heads."

C. SUETONIUS TRANQUILLUS: *THE LIVES OF THE CAESARS, 55-57*

Few would mourn his passing. He had certainly achieved infamy during his reign – from his political acts, to his turbulent relationship with his mother, to his public displays of his poetry and lyre-playing – and had lived by his own saying that "hidden talent counts for nothing". But his death now plunged the empire into the same turmoil and insecurity that had defined its birth.

Rome now became the centre of a power struggle which sapped the strength and army from its colonies while four successive emperors battled for survival in just one year. The Emperor Vespasian ultimately prevailed but while he fought to regain control of his provinces, Venutius used the power vacuum and redeployment of some eight thousand legionaries from their British base to launch the devastating attack on Cartimandua and her supporters. The new governor of Britain, Vettius Bolanus, tried his best to intervene but the Brigantian warrior doggedly fought Cartimandua's army and the Romans until both were seriously weakened. Although Cartimandua was saved (allegedly by Vettius Bolanus himself), this is tragically the last we hear of Rome's client queen or of Vellocatus, her lover. They both disappear from the historical and material record – perhaps even employing their likely "citizen" status to withdraw to Rome. It is an entertaining thought that the great capital city might even have played host to an uncomfortable reunion between the wily queen and the thwarted but now pardoned rebel leader she had handed over to her new political masters. If such a meeting ever took place, it's unlikely there would have been much of a rapprochement.

As for Brigantia itself, the kingdom was no longer under the control of the Romans but of the new rebel leader of Britain, Venutius. Free of Cartimandua and her imperial sympathies, the former consort and new ruler of the Brigantes fought a ferocious campaign against the Romans who desperately needed to regain their buffer zone to the north; Scotland was still full of unconquered barbarians and Wales was less than secure. Without the Brigantian lands soon back under Roman control they would have to face a shameful retreat into the southern half of Britain – hardly the most auspicious start for the new Emperor Vespasian who was in troubled times at home.

Venutius's strength lay in the tried and tested guerrilla tactics employed by the Celts of mainland Europe and for a while, he achieved and maintained some success against the Romans in a series of bloody battles. But ultimately his brave but old-fashioned warriors were no match for the tight discipline of the enemy: in AD 71, the governor Bolanus was replaced by Quintus Petillius Cerealis – an appointee of the new Emperor, Vespasian. Cerealis already had direct experience of fighting the British: a decade before, over a thousand of his men had been annihilated in the political insurgency thrown up by another British queen – the legendary Boudica – so when it came to rebellious Britons, he had a long memory and a short fuse. This time, he arrived in Britain with a new legion of soldiers which he installed in Lincoln, then he marched northwards with perhaps two more legions to wrest back control of the north. A series of forts, including a large military base at York and a series of wooden buildings around Carlisle gives testimony to his resolve: he wanted Brigantia back, and he was determined that he would get it.

There is no written or material evidence of the final battle between Venutius and Cerealis but it is clear that the British rebel was driven into submission by around AD 72 – leaving his precious kingdom once more under the control of his enemies. The process of Romanisation started by Cartimandua was now almost complete. Having hitherto mainly experienced the light touch of a client relationship with Rome, Brigantia was now heavily militarised with new roads, forts and a large occupying army – and it would stay this way for as long as the Roman Empire stretched to Britain. England had once again been subdued – and the groundwork was in place for Agricola's campaigns into the barbarian lands of Scotland.

Cartimandua might have gone but it seems she was not forgotten. Although there is no historical or archaeological record of her fate after that dramatic rescue by Bolanus, there is some slim but tantalising evidence that her life, her legend and her personification as the goddess Brigantia may have become so strongly imprinted on the Brigantes and their neighbours that she passed into oral history and then into the legend of King Arthur's erstwhile wife, Guinevere. Guinevere's story was first laid down by the one the earliest of all British historians, Geoffrey of Monmouth, who introduced the story of King Arthur to the literature of Europe. This twelfth-century bishop published the monumental *Historia regum Britanniae (History of the Kings of Britain)* around

1135–39 and although its factual content has been described by academics as being "almost nil", it is invaluable for giving a flavour of the medieval desire to compose an ancient ancestry of Britain and also for first laying down many of the "creation myths" that have helped shape the British consciousness for the next thousand years.

There are some striking similarities between the two stories of Cartimandua and Geoffrey's Guinevere (called Gwenhwyfar): both ditched their husbands for one of his subordinates (Vellocatus and Mordred); both Cartimandua and Mordred sought the help of the occupying armies; and in both cases, the end result was civil war and the loss of the kingdom. As for the queens themselves, both women survived the fighting – Cartimandua being rescued by Bolanus, and Guinevere fleeing to a convent. However, perhaps the most interesting connection is that Geoffrey of Monmouth locates the entire Guinevere story in what was the kingdom of the Brigantes: her base as co-ruler with Arthur was given as York while the death of Arthur has been recently posited as at Camboglanna (today's Castlesteads) on Hadrian's Wall – well within Brigantian lands.

So while Queen Cartimandua has faded from public consciousness, has her meme been passed down to us firstly via oral history until the alleged time of King Arthur, and then via the legend of Arthur and Guinevere which survives to the present day? There does appear to be an uncanny correspondence between the stories of the Brigantian queen and her Arthurian counterpart – not least in the fact that both women were portrayed as flagrantly and shamelessly complicit in their adultery and thus their tales became morality stories as much as "genuine" histories.

However, perhaps even without the moral aspect of their tale, it's likely that their stories might have endured. We have seen how the Brigantian people were noted for their independent spirit – and the loss of independence is not something that is easily forgotten by the proud people who stem from heroic, warrior times. Is it possible, therefore, that the stories of the final and pivotal battles by the Brigantes against the occupying armies of Rome – let alone the morality tales of the lustful queen – survive in their own very British, oral form, alongside the Roman written histories of Tacitus? Other cultures like the Maori or Hawaiians can take their detailed oral histories and genealogies back many hundreds of years – but these societies have only been literate for around three centuries whereas our oral traditions began to fade under the advent of the Romans some two thousand years ago. But this also means that some of our early oral histories might have been written down for posterity.

It's a hard case to call: during my search for Boudica time and time again I came into conflict with wishful thinking that had been reported as "fact" and it's enough to make one wary of even the most alluring "coincidences". But we're only just beginning to appreciate the importance of "soft" sources of historical data such as oral histories, literature and poetry, and they still sit uncomfortably on the traditional research table – I think much to the detriment of our broad-based scholarship. So when it comes to Cartimandua's story surviving in Guinevere's, it's unlikely that it could ever be proven but the thought is just about credible enough to make it enticing.

CHAPTER 8

THE DRUIDS OF MONA

"But why speak of these things when the craft [of Druidism] has even crossed the Ocean and reached the empty voids of Nature? Even today Britain practises magic with reverence and with such grand ritual it might seem that she gave it to the Persians."

PLINY THE ELDER: NATURAL HISTORY, XXX, 4

"We decided to go to the place on Ynys Môn where we believed the Romans landed and then talked together about where we had the most powerful experiences: and then we found it – this one spot, on the south-east coast, with the incredible power of the rocks behind us and in front of us the waves that were lapping the waters of the Menai Strait across to the mainland of Wales."

Emma Restall Orr's voice was soft but passionate, like a child describing something extraordinary with an urgency that spills out across the room. A Druid priestess known as Bobcat, she has spent her life exploring the "natural connection" between the landscape and spirituality, and now runs the Druid Network which organises Druidic events such as the "deep ceremony" at Stonehenge during midsummer's dawn.

"I think there's a profound connection between the human soul and the land, and that came across with such strength at Ynys Môn – the Golden Isle, the mother isle of Druidry, the land that gave birth to our spirituality and shamanic tradition. You can imagine what it was like two thousand years ago, travelling by foot or horse through the barren, rocky landscape of Snowdonia and then – in front of your eyes – unfurls this incredibly lush island, this barley basket, this jewel of fertility and serenity.

"I went down to the battle site with a colleague from the Anglesey Druidic Order to relive the Roman invasion, to make rituals to honour what had happened and explore the slaughter from every perspective – Roman, native, even from the land itself. What the ancient Druids had done was to close a gateway to the Isles of the Blessed during the massacre, to protect what they had, to protect the land; we wanted to open those doors to allow them to return, to offer some healing within the British Druidic tradition.

"There were such deep, powerful feelings in the place. Quite by chance, the date was September 11 – the same date as the terrorist attacks in America – and although it was coincidental, there was a strong sense of the *Pax Americana* connecting with the *Pax Romana*: both striving for peace through war and brutality.

"During the day, the reality of modern life had covered the whole area – you could see the built-up landscape across on the mainland, you could feel the modernity everywhere. The weather had also been wild and stormy, with thunder and lightning and an incredible noise on the roof of the roundhouse where we had been preparing for the ritual – but as soon as we reached the beach that night, it stopped and everything went silent. We were there with a group of about forty people, and the weather was absolutely still; not a whisper of wind and just the sound of our drums in the darkness – so it was incredibly easy for us to imagine that the lights of the buildings across the Menai Strait were the lights of the Roman campfires on the eve of battle. My overriding sense was one of pure inevitability as we fell into our trances, our meditations, our dancing, songs and stories. We called out to the wind, to the visions around us as we went through that battle. We saw women and children running around screaming, we saw people walking into the water to face their fate. Perhaps more than the loss of life, it felt like the loss of stories that was the most devastating. We had a feeling, as we relived those moments, of thousands of years of our heritage being destroyed. It was terrifying but there was also an extraordinary sense of grief, for when a people are so intimately connected with the land, you can't run away – there's nowhere else to go."

I let Emma talk, hearing her words but also the emotion bound up in her experiences at the beach. And when she had finished, I asked her what she felt was the significance of that day back in AD 60, when the Romans swept through the Druid seat of Ynys Môn, or what we call Anglesey. She paused for a while, and then continued: "I think that without that Roman attack on the Druids, their attempts to exterminate the whole Druid order, we wouldn't have so quickly lost our connection with the land. It really was one of the huge turning points in our native history, up there with Oliver Cromwell and moments like that. But we must remember that it was the Druids who invited the Romans into Britain, to help them win over other British tribes. The Druids got greedy for power and for possessions, and we must acknowledge and bear that responsibility – and for the material corruption of our culture and our disconnection from the land ever since.

"However, I do fully believe that the spiritual animism that existed within the land and the people survived elsewhere, in areas where Roman culture was slower to spread, even within Britain under Roman rule, where there was no wealth and mundane power to grasp. It continued within the women's traditions, the bardic traditions, as a spiritual strength: deep connection to the land, where the mud, the wind, the river, the rain are all gods to be honoured, celebrated … breathed."

Politics – even the sexual politics of queens – was one thing; the dark arts were something entirely different. For the Romans faced with bringing the wild landscape of Britannia to heel, they knew they were in a strange country with women rulers and blue-painted warriors but while these could be dismissed as just barbarians who would soon be fully conquered by Roman military might, the practitioners of the dark arts represented a terrifying level of danger that was physical, spiritual and magical. The warriors may take your life but the Druids would steal your soul. These priests, judges, bards and diviners controlled the minds of the Britons, inciting them to hatred of the Romans and fuelling them with ideas of resistance. If the land were ever to be fully conquered – both physically and emotionally – then this threat had to be neutralised.

The low, green Isle of Anglesey, or Ynys Môn, stands proudly from the swirling waters of the Menai Strait like a bold but ancient gesture of defiance. The largest island in England and Wales, it keeps a watchful distance from the mainland of North Wales, protected by the quicksands of a strait which ranges from two miles to just two hundred feet wide. The island's coastline is heavily indented with headlands that claw their gnarled fingers into the sea; but as you journey up from the beaches to the sweeps of heaths, bogs and copses of woodland that inhabit the interior, the sense of it being a truly magical, other-worldly place is as pertinent now as it was two thousand years ago when its very identity was defined by the supernatural to both British and Roman minds. For Anglesey, or Mona as the Romans called it, was the seat of the Druids.

The human history of the island dates back to well before the Romans had even contemplated invading Britain, when small groups of Neolithic islanders fished its waters and hunted on the low, wooded hills. These people set up standing stones and cairns and then slowly started to clear the unusually fertile land for agriculture until the island became well known for its quality cereals and cattle. Looking eastwards to the mainland and westwards to Ireland, its location meant that it was perfectly placed to play an active role in the prehistoric sea routes that connected northern Europe with the Mediterranean so although it was an island, it was far from cut off from contact with the wider world.

Intellectually, too, its connections with mainland Europe were surprisingly close – and far too close for the Roman way of thinking. Usually, the Romans were happy to embrace the native religions of the people they conquered but while they were prepared to take on the Celtic gods, they regarded the Celtic spiritual leaders as far too powerful and politicised. As the Druids of Gaul were gradually squeezed northwards by an advancing Roman culture that was often openly hostile to the native religious order, Mona grew in importance as a repository of the oral wisdom that had succoured the Celtic world for centuries. Much more than a seat of religious learning, Mona became a schooling ground for new recruits in the battle against Romanisation.

The Druids were drawn largely from the tribal aristocracies of Britain and Europe and had long since become almost a class of their own, not unlike the Hindu Brahmin caste in India. These were the men – *or women* – who could interpret the language and mood of the gods; and this meant they could also intercede on their people's behalf. Their power and influence is hard to overstate: in a time when inter-tribal warfare was a defining characteristic of Iron Age culture, Druids were perhaps the only group of people who could be guaranteed a warm welcome and safety in any household in the land, advising kings as easily as commoners. In fact, if Caesar's account of them is to be believed, they were perhaps the one unifying and unified force in the Celtic World, with an annual gathering at Chârtres attended by Druids from all over Europe.

While the first recorded use of the word *Druidae* was by the Greeks in the second century BC, its actual meaning is thought by many to derive from the Celtic words for oak (*dru*) or knowledge (*wid*). The basis of much of our knowledge about the Druids of classical times came originally from the Greek writer, Posidonius, who was a major influence on the later writings of Strabo, Diodorus Siculus and Caesar, while in his *Natural History*, Pliny also discusses the existence and function of the Druids. During his *Gallic Wars*, Caesar made careful note of his observations of the Gauls, dividing all men of high rank as either Druids or knights; he further claimed that the system of Druidic training was invented in Britain before spreading across Europe but this original seat of power was still the best place to go for learning. Although this elite band contained the most learned people in the land, it was reportedly proscribed to write any of their knowledge down – which, combined with their later suppression by the Romans, means that scholars today are restricted in their learning to what others wrote about the Druids, rather than hearing from them in their own words. They certainly bear little relation to the modern-day "Druids" who are an artificial construct from the eighteenth and nineteenth centuries; they have a fascinating story of their own, but that belongs to a later Britain.

According to Caesar, just to become a Druid was no mean feat: it required around twenty years of study to achieve a sufficient standard of learning, during which time an alleged minimum of three hundred and fifty histories and romance tales would have to be memorised until they were word-perfect; then, as well as their religious instruction, they also had to become experts in astronomy, astrology, medicine, the laws of the natural world and also the laws of the Celtic world. Having listened to the arguments, whatever a Druid decreed *had* to be obeyed; failure to comply simply was not tolerated and the punishment would be a total exclusion from sacrifices and thus society – to all intents and purposes, you would effectively cease to exist. In this respect, Druids were even more potent than kings – they had the power over life and death, the power to stop or start battles and the power to mediate with the gods themselves. Small wonder no Celt would ever dare to challenge them.

The beliefs of the Druids are difficult to gauge as we have little in the way of supporting archaeology or vestiges of their practices in our modern-day customs; we're therefore largely dependent upon the writings of the Greeks and Romans – and they were coloured by their own value-systems. Even harder than locating evidence from material remains is to identify the meanings of the objects, particularly when they are no longer in their true context. Perhaps the most illuminating surviving Druid artefact is the famous Coligny Calendar from north of Lyon, which dates back to the first century AD. This incomplete bronze sheet is a rare example of the nearest we have to a religious text: it is written in Gaulish using Latin script and lists the series of auspicious and inauspicious days for a five-year time period, no doubt used for making predictions and decisions over the most suitable timing of events. Other finds include a lead tablet known as the Larzac inscription, discovered in 1983, and the 1992 discovery of a bronze tablet in Northern Spain. Although both of these were written in the Celtic language, the actual script used was Greek.

According to the classical writers, Druids communed with the spirit world by means of divination and it was widely reported that this included the sacrifice of humans, often via the largely unsubstantiated device of the "wicker man" – a woven cage containing sacrificial victims that was locked shut and then set on fire. The outrage with which this was often discussed by the classical commentators is ironic coming from a culture that thought nothing of throwing men and women to the lions for entertainment. However, the general practice of Celtic head-hunting and human sacrifice made good travellers' tales and it does seem to be supported by both archaeology and depictions in Celtic art.

Both Strabo and Caesar make gruesome reference to the wicker man in their descriptions of the Gaulish Celts, and burning or fire was one of the four ways of ritual murder or human sacrifice which connected with the elements; also included in the grim list are hanging (air), stabbing (blood) and drowning (water).

Normally, it appears that criminals were used as the Druids' sacrificial victims but in his account of the Gallic War, Caesar recounts that when no criminals were available then the innocent would do just as well – the critical part was to use the victim's death-throes as a means of divining the will of the gods.

In Britain, the evidence on the ground certainly adds credence to the ancient assertions: on August 1, 1984, a peat-cutter named Andy Mould was loading blocks of peat onto an elevator from where they would be transported to a shredding mill. As he loaded on one block, he thought he saw a piece of wood in the fibrous soil and so threw the offending item on to the floor. When it struck, it crumbled to reveal its grisly and unmistakable contents: a human foot. Mould immediately called the police to report a suspected murder – but little did he know he was almost two thousand years too late. The police arrived and together they searched the peat bog for the rest of the body, still unsure if they were dealing with a crime. Eventually, a flap of darkened skin on the surface of the peat bog led to the remains of a well-preserved mummified human. Though clearly dead for some time, the body was taken to hospital for analysis and here it transpired that the authorities were not dealing with a modern murder at all – but a murder that had taken place between AD 50 and AD 100 in the wild and wet landscape of Cheshire's Lindow Moss.

The chilling story of the man was later unfurled by experts at the British Museum. Pete Marsh, as the mummified body was originally called, was a young, reasonably tall, well-nourished man around twenty-five years old when he was violently attacked with blows to the back of his head by what seemed to have been an axe. Stunned but still alive and breathing, the murderers took some twisted rope and wrapped it around his neck, pulling it tighter and tighter until he was on the verge of suffocating. The force of the strangulation broke two vertebrae and closed off his windpipe –and then, eyes bulging, he finally died, agonisingly choking for breath. But it seems that was not enough for the murderers: once he was dead, they took a knife and cut his throat, letting the blood drain out from his body before abandoning him in the boggy soil.

While the scientists could work out the pattern to his last grim moments on earth, when it came to finding a motive, they had to dig a little deeper. The first indication that they were dealing with some kind of ritual murder was in the "triple killing" – by blows, by strangulation and by having his throat cut – but there was more: the contents of his stomach revealed that he had eaten some burned bannock, or bun, just before his death and that this was made from a range of cereals. However, they also found evidence of pollen grains from mistletoe amongst the meagre contents of his stomach and it was this that suggested that Pete Marsh – or Lindow Man as he was by now more respectfully named – might in fact have been the victim of Druidic sacrifice. The links between Druids and mistletoe had been well known for thousands of years – but why would they be sacrificing a high-status man? Slowly, the jigsaw pieces all came together to present their desperate picture.

The true facts of the young man's death can never be known but one scenario goes as follows: Lindow Man, with his manicured fingernails, well-trimmed beard and uncalloused hands, was a young nobleman, aristocrat – or even a Druid himself, living at the time of the Roman invasion of Britain. With their traditional culture increasingly under threat, the Druids decreed that a powerful, high-level sacrifice was needed to appease the gods and drive the Romans out of their lands. On the day of the Celtic fire festival of Beltane that welcomed in the spring, a bannock was baked, a section of it charred, then broken into a bag. Whoever selected the burned section would give themselves up as human sacrifice to save their lands from the Roman threat. That piece was selected by Lindow Man and so – dressed in nothing but his fox-fur amulet, he submitted himself to the gods.

British Museum expert, J D Hill, wryly reflects on the dead man's significance: "I think he stands as the Everyman for prehistoric Britain. It's the closest we can get to meeting an ancient Briton, but the mystery that still surrounds who he was and his death also sums up the frustrations and joy of doing Iron Age archaeology!"

However, even an offering as potent as a young nobleman could not stop the tide of Romanisation and within a few years of his death, his lands were firmly under the control of an enemy which moved to enforce its own very different philosophy and world view on its newly subjugated province. On the whole, Druidic practices were much earthier than those of the Greeks and Romans – the

Celts had less need for grand marble temples and great memorials; the sacred places of the Druids tended to be the streams, marshes and wooded groves where they were closer to the nature, the spirits and the life-force that suckled the world. And in that world of constant warfare, life and death were an ever-present reality. The Celts fervently believed in the transmigration of the soul after death, so being killed, whether on the battlefield or as a human sacrifice, lost a little of its fear, if not its pain: your soul would merely pass on into the afterlife.

Ancient rites were reported to include the use of oak trees where the mistletoe grew, golden scythes to cut the mistletoe, the blood of white bulls and herbs and stones for healing. There was also talk of the "Druid's egg" – a powerful talisman, otherwise known in Scotland as the Druid's crystal, along with the shamanistic use of narcotics such as cannabis (evidence of this was found in an early Celtic grave in Hochdorf, Germany) and mushrooms to induce a trance-like state in order to commune with the spirits.

Rome's expansion into Europe and the lands of the Celts was like two worlds colliding and each must have felt bemusement at the strange practices of the other. Until the first century AD, much of the reportage was based on early ideas akin to the later concept of the "noble savage"; these were generally sympathetic and told of a whole panoply of Druidic skills and practices just as today's travel guide would discuss foreign cultural practices. However, over time and with the growing cultural confidence of the Roman empire, anything that wasn't Roman or Greek tended to be seen as "barbarian" or "savage" – that is, naturally inferior, and this attitude percolated from the periphery of the empire through conversation and literature to shape the attitudes of those back home. In order to conquer other peoples, it was first necessary to convert, or remove, the intelligentsia who controlled the mindset of the savage masses, yet the Druids proved hard to convert; the only way forward was therefore to remove them from power.

> "Druids were an absolute threat to the Roman State because their science and
> philosophy dangerously contradicted Roman orthodoxy. The Romans were
> materialistic, the Druids spiritual. For the Romans, the State was a monolithic

structure spread over territories and deliberately organised into a hierarchy;
with the Druids it was a freely consented moral order with an entirely mythical
central idea."

PROF. JEAN MARKALE: *LA FEMME CELTE*, 1972
TRANSLATED BY A MYGIND, C HAUCH AND P HENRY © 1975

The classical biographer, Suetonius, alludes to a ban by Augustus on Druidism amongst the citizens of the empire but with the succession of Tiberius, this ban was to change into something approaching genocide. Tiberius issued an edict to expunge the Druids "and that class of seers and doctors" altogether. However, it proved to be harder to kill ideas than people: the evidence from early Roman Britain and the classical texts proves that there were still significant numbers of Druids with tangible power at the time of the Boudican revolt.

Both Romans and Celts were pantheistic and the last thing the invaders wanted to do was stir up any resentment from the native gods so they were placated – even honoured – and welcomed into the fold.

While native gods didn't offer a threat to Rome's imperial control, the Druidic class of priests most certainly did. So was the existence of Druids in Britain a reason for invasion? Bringing this island race and the Druids under Roman control would have been of benefit to the Romans as they were well known for stirring up anti-Roman feeling both in Britain and across the whole of Gaul. However, some commentators believe that a more profound and fundamental change was afoot within the Druid order. J D Hill argues: "You only tend to get single, unified religions once you get it written down in a book – and we didn't become a literate society until well after the Druids' destruction. Even then, there are still variations in provincial religion and cult.

"I suspect that what was actually evolving was a great deal more complex, with variations around a theme that we or the Romans might call 'Druidry'. If the Druids were outlawed and suppressed and considered 'baddies' across the board, then why was the dominant shape of temples Romano–Celtic? Why did Roman Britons worship British gods? Why did Roman British priests wear regalia similar to that worn by earlier priests/Druids? I think that in reality some Druids were redefining themselves in a changing political context; in other words, there was a schism between the 'progressives' or 'quislings' as they might be regarded, who sided with the Romans to remain in power, and the 'traditionalist' Druids who wanted their autonomy, so withheld their support for the foreign invaders. After all, there were winners as well as losers when it came to the Romanisation of Iron Age Britain."

For both the Celts and the old-style Druids, it was impossible to draw a dividing line between religion and politics as both were intimately intertwined; the only boundary they accepted was between this world and the other-world – and even then it was possible for man and god to pass from one to the other. In the meantime, the Druids were defending a spiritual way of life that defined their politics – and their enemies.

It is likely that the Druids were behind the growing resistance to the Roman occupation of Britain after Caesar's conquests of 55 and 54 BC – and the reason why Aulus Plautius met with hostile forces along the southern coast in AD 43. After all, the Druids knew what was going on in continental Europe and hated the Romans as much as the Romans hated them. Even as late as AD 69, during the so-called "Year of the Four Emperors", Druids were actively encouraging Gaulish uprisings against the Romans. Ultimately, however, it would take the rise of a new superpower to finally drive Druidism from the cultural map of Europe – and this wouldn't be a political force but the rival philosophical and spiritual force of Christianity.

The rise of Christianity would not only extinguish Druidism as the prevailing ideology of the Celtic peoples, it would also have a profound effect on the balance of power between the sexes. Female Druids were reported or alluded to by many of the classical writers and later written about in the Irish vernacular myths. While it would be wrong to call the Celts or the Druids "matriarchal", there is evidence of a wide range of positions that women could hold throughout Iron Age Europe beyond that of wife and mother. As the Romans, and then Christianity, transformed these indigenous cultures, women's roles as seers, spiritual leaders, diplomats, ambassadors, poets, witches and even teachers of war-craft were driven underground or extinguished altogether under the heavy foot of a more patriarchal system of beliefs. The relative "freedom" women had experienced in these societies compared with their Greek or Roman peers was now being steadily eroded as their options were defined more closely around the home and family.

However, all that was centuries in the future. For the Britain conquered by the Romans following their invasion AD 43, the menacing terrain of mountains, fast-flowing rivers and treacherous bogs and swamps meant that campaigning was always bedevilled by the threat of guerrilla attacks from people that could be as hostile as their countryside. Here, having a little local knowledge was a distinct advantage and it quickly became evident to the outsiders that the Britons would prove to be tough adversaries. It is hardly surprising that given their experience in Gaul, the Romans were wary of the Druids of Britain: their European counterparts have proved themselves adroit at stirring up trouble and the Druidic base on the Island of Mona made a perfect training camp for those wishing to learn the art of guerrilla-style warfare. This was no paranoia on the part of the Romans: the Druids really did want them out of Britain; what's more, they had the power to influence tribal leaders and mobilise the masses to rise up in revolt.

There has recently been growing consensus among academics that it was the Druids of Anglesey who had given both credence and support to Caratacus's guerrilla army that became the scourge of the Romans in the years after the Claudian conquest until his capture in AD 51. Without doubt, the Druids did not shy away from politics and if they were unhappy with any situation, they would regard it as their duty to try to put things right. For Caratacus, receiving the blessing of the Druids would have given him enormous weight amongst the disparate and normally hostile tribes that he hoped to make his powerbase – and it's not beyond the realms of possibility that the closer the tribe to Anglesey, the more influence the Druids would have had.

While the support of the Druids may have given Caratacus both the moral backing and the tribal support he needed, it would have contributed to the growing Roman hatred of this "priestly class"; before long, the Druids would be viewed as the true enemy of the Empire. Even after the capture of Caratacus and the subsequent transfer of anti-Roman command to Cartimandua's ex-husband, Venutius, it is likely that the Druids still cast the war as a *spiritual* imperative while harbouring any rebels seeking refuge from the Romans.

However, as tribe after tribe of insurgents were suppressed by the military campaigns of the Governors Plautius (AD 43-47), Scapula (47-52), Didius Gallus (52-57), Veranius (c.57-58) and then Paulinus (58-61), the Romans drew ever closer to the crucible of resistance – the Druids of Anglesey. At last, it was time to take direct action to snuff out their insidious power once and for all and to free the Romans for the real "civilisation" of Britannia. What was needed was a decisive assault on Mona – a genocide that would extinguish the cauldron of Druidic malcontent.

While Veranius was regarded as a man of diplomacy, his successor was anything but. A military man through and through, Paulinus's goal was to extinguish all resistance and secure Britain for the Romans by whatever force was needed. His army pedigree was impressive: he made his name as a commander by taking his men up and over the Atlas mountains of North Africa – a landscape that rises up to four thousand metres in altitude; the mountains of Wales and of the Brigantian Pennines would be small fry in comparison.

By the winter of AD 59-60, the bellicose Silures of central and southeastern Wales had been, if not tamed, then contained; the Ordovices of the Welsh border country were by now firmly penned in; and to the north, the Deceangli of Flintshire were also under Roman control. As such, the field was wide open for an assault on the island the Romans called Mona, and the rest of the winter season was spent preparing for the land and sea campaign on the far western coast of Britain the following spring.

Everything was going smoothly for Paulinus and his men. They had secured their rear, were making good progress to the Menai Strait and beyond them the island of Mona was almost in sight. Loading up the flat-bottomed boats they had been building all winter, Paulinus and his men began to cross the water – the cavalry by fording and swimming, the infantry by boat.

Waiting on the other side of the water was a vast crowd of Druids and their followers who knew their time had finally arrived. One can only imagine how they had spent the past weeks and months, hearing the rumours, trying to divine the will of the gods and then seeing the steady march of Roman power across the land, edging ever closer to their sacred isle. It was not in their nature to run away; and anyway, there was nowhere left to go. Only Scotland and the far reaches of Cornwall were free from the harrying attacks of the Romans but for how much longer? The cold force of Empire was gathering in front of their eyes: they had no option but to trust in the gods and face their fate with fortitude.

There is, perhaps, a poignant legacy of those dark days of the winter of 59/60. During the Second World War, the Royal Air Force aerodrome at Valley on Anglesey needed to extend its runways for the American Flying Fortresses that would shortly be arriving at the base. Peat was required for sealing the landing strips and a source was located in a nearby bog at Llyn Cerrig Bach – Welsh for the "lake of the small stones". When the diggers moved in, the workmen started to see all manner of metalwork coming up with the deposits but to begin with they assumed they were merely pieces of scrap. The head groundsman was William Roberts, a local man with much experience of the soils in the area. His daughter, Evelyn, picks up the story:

> "The peaty material was lifted out by dredgers into a lorry but over the course of the day, the lorry began to get stuck in the mud. My father and the men tried to get it moving but the wire rope they were using broke. My dad looked around and noticed an old chain lying in the peat nearby. He picked it up, hooked it onto the lorry and then on to a tractor, which duly pulled the lorry free and they used it like that for the rest of the day."

Thinking it looked rather unusual, Mr Roberts took the chain back to his office where a friend commented that it looked so old they should phone the museum. When Mr Roberts explained what he had found, the museum's curator raced straight up to take a look at the curious object and then told its discoverer the shocking news: the chain that William Roberts had been using all day to haul several tons of lorry out the boggy ground was a chain from a slave gang and had been lying there for almost two thousand years.

At ten feet long with five hinged neck rings attached, the slave chain was originally manufactured around the middle of the first century AD by Belgic metalworkers. The Belgae were slave-traders, so this could well be a relic of their business, or just purely symbolic. Whatever its original use, it was an object of significant workmanship and value – so what was it doing in the bog?

For the ancient Britons and all Celtic peoples, water – and also streams, lakes or marshes – had strong links with the spirit world. They regarded the energy and strange reflectivity of water as something divine or supernatural and, as such, anywhere that had water was a place to connect with the gods. By these standards, Llyn Cerrig Bach was a truly special place. With its ethereal landscape of small lakes and rocky outcrops, it still evokes much the same feeling of "other-worldliness" that it would have done two thousand years ago when the Druids and natives of Anglesey regarded it as a special and powerful place.

At times of uncertainty or fear – or if there was a particular request for the gods – objects of real value to their owners would be cast into streams, lakes or marshes as so-called "votive offerings" to appease the gods and hopefully bring good fortune. Like throwing pennies into a fountain, the sacrifices to the gods would make them look kindly on the supplicants, and people would come from miles around to cast their precious possessions into the sacred waters, often ritually breaking or "killing" them before they threw them in. Over time, offerings made of wood, leather or bone would have rotted or dissolved away in the acid waters of the bog but the increasing use of bronze and iron meant the objects survived as silent witnesses to the island's troubled past until they were lifted out two millennia later by the wartime workers.

By the time the bog had been dredged by Mr Roberts's men, over one hundred and forty six objects had been retrieved – all metal and varying from decorative plaques to swords, spears, a shield, horse-bits and metalware from harnesses and chariots. What's more, their places of origin or manufacture point to a huge geographical area stretching from the south coast of England to the north country of the Brigantes and possibly beyond. Did this mean that Anglesey was attracting a vast influx of Britons around this time – and if so, why? Were the votive offerings from pious Celts so concerned about the Roman threat that they made the long journey to the sacred waters of Llyn Cerrig Bach – or were the objects cast into the lake by refugees from war-torn tribes? Frustratingly, all we can do is surmise. It's impossible to gauge the true meaning behind such a large hoard of votive offerings and there is no other supporting archaeology from the same period that can shed further light on the situation, but whatever the reason for the finds to be so rich, so plentiful and from such a wide area, the people making those deposits were deadly serious about wanting divine assistance: something major was threatening everything they held dear.

For the Romans, the scene awaiting them on the shores of Anglesey must have been an awesome sight, and it is worth quoting Tacitus, at length:

> *"On the beach stood the enemy forces with their dense ranks of armed warriors, while between the ranks darted women, dressed in black like the Furies with dishevelled hair and brandishing torches. At the same time, the Druids, raising their hands to the heavens and spewing dreadful imprecations, terrified our soldiers with the awesome sight so that they were paralysed with fear, standing motionless and exposing themselves to wounds. Then, buoyed up by their general and encouraging each other not to flinch before a troupe of frenzied women, they carried their standards forwards, cut through all resistance and torched the enemy with its own fire. Next, a garrison was set up among the vanquished population and their savage, sacred groves were destroyed, for they considered it their duty to cover their altars with the blood of captives and to consult their gods using human entrails."*

> TACITUS: *ANNALS XIV, 30*

Just like with Cartimandua, Tacitus uses the language of scorn to describe the women on the beach. He even has Paulinus goading his men for being scared of these "frenzied Furies"; clearly, when it came to describing British females, Tacitus preferred to drop the "noble" from any idea of the "noble savage".

The Romans might have hated the Druids but they still respected and feared their gods. To the common soldier, the thought of going into battle against an entire priesthood was a terrifying thought in itself, made a thousand times more so by the screams and cries and curses assailing their ears and the scene of horror in front of their eyes. Small wonder that they were rooted to the spot: this was like the first landing in Britain when row upon row of Britons lined up along the cliff tops and later swooped down onto the shoreline; the Roman nerves had failed then and they almost failed again.

But the clamour and curses were all that were left in the Druids' armoury. Once their enemy was propelled into action, the Druids would soon have known their fate without any recourse to augury. There is no mention of how long the battle took but the outcome is certain: the sacred sites of the Druids were destroyed with a brutal passion and the hated, priestly class on Mona was all but wiped out. Paulinus must have been pleased; he had done his job with ruthless efficiency.

Even now, the echoes of that day still have resonance along the coast of Anglesey – and not just for modern Druids like Emma Restall Orr: legend has it that Bryn-y-Beddau or the "Hill of Graves" is where the survivors of the slaughter buried their dead. In less than twenty years, the Romans would be back, this time subduing the island for good. Anglesey had been "civilised". But standing on the bloodied shoreline, watching his troops picking over the dead, even the Roman's battle-hardened general could not have anticipated what was about to come next.

CHAPTER 9
THE OUTRAGE AGAINST BOUDICA

"What better than a woman who stays at home, manages the house for you and raises your children; who gives you joy when you are healthy and comfort when you are sick; who shares your successes and consoles you for your failures…"

CASSIUS DIO'S REPORT ON THE EMPEROR AUGUSTUS'S SPEECH ABOUT FAMILY LIFE

While Suetonius Paulinus was heading west to tackle the Druids of Mona, over in the far east of Britain in what is now Norfolk, a tragedy was unfolding of Greek rather than Roman proportions. The Icenian King Prasutagus died after a long and prosperous reign of at least thirteen years. On his death, he left behind two daughters and a wife whose influence would be felt for the next two thousand years: her name was Boudica, queen of the Iceni.

By now, my search for Boudica had led me across the UK and Europe, through many hundreds of books and papers and scores of interviews – but finally I had arrived at the woman herself. As Philip de Jersey had warned me: "The more we learn, the less we often know" – and there was the inevitable tension that the queen's true story would not live up to my hopes or expectations. If my journey had taught me anything, it was to beware of sentiment and always look at the agenda behind the histories. But would this lead to rejecting the very elements of her story that had attracted me to it in the first place? Like a child letting go of a favourite blanket, it was time to leave behind our old school histories, our emotional connection with this icon from the past, and the cultural confusion that credited the Romans with bringing us civilisation – yet made their enemy a national heroine. One thing had become all too clear: the Boudica story is as much about *us* as about an Iron Age warrior queen.

King Prasutagus was a "client king" of the Romans; he was allowed to keep his kingdom as long as he maintained a pro-Roman stance and paid his dues to his conquerors. It is likely that the Iceni were one of the tribes (or a confederation of tribes) who submitted to Claudius after his invasion of Britain in AD 43 and the fact that they were still under indirect Roman rule by AD 60 suggests that the Iceni rulers maintained their friendly relations with the Romans ever since. As a client king, it is likely that Prasutagus was considered to be a full Roman citizen; he was certainly sufficiently Romanised to have left a will when he died which laid out his wishes for his lands and his family. The trouble was, while that may have been appropriate for a citizen in Rome, it was not deemed appropriate behaviour from someone who was to all intents and purposes a vanquished ruler of a barbarian tribe.

Prasutagus's will left half his estate to his offspring and the other half to the Roman Emperor, Nero. On the surface, the conditions of the will sound perfectly reasonable, for the Iceni had retained control of their kingdom following the Claudian conquest of Britain and had seen wealth (at least for some) and stability as a direct result. Undoubtedly, there had been those in the tribe who were against the political union but the ordinary people had no freedom to make their voices heard; the client relationship had been sealed and cemented shortly after the invasions, seemingly by Prasutagus's predecessor, King Antedios, who ruled from around AD 25 up to the time of the conquest and possibly until the first Icenian rebellion of AD 47. At the time, Britain was seething with native fury against the Roman invaders; Caratacus was still on the loose launching his guerrilla attacks on the anxious legions and the Britons were damaging the credibility of the supposedly invincible foreign army. This first revolt amongst the very tribe who should have been pro-Roman was reportedly triggered by some heavy-handed policy by the provincial Governor, Ostorius Scapula; he demanded that Iceni homes should be searched and all weapons confiscated to prevent them joining in with the general dissent that was bubbling up throughout Britain. The Icenian anger at being treated like enemies was enough to cause an uprising in the form of a battle, probably based around the Iron Age fort at Stonea Camp which was then an island in the Cambridgeshire fens. However, the warring Icenian factions did not stand a chance against the might of the Roman army, particularly when the latter would have been able to draw on loyal Britons to swell its ranks. The rebellion was quickly crushed and the insurgents annihilated; from then on, the Iceni may have still smouldered in resentment, but they did not let the Romans see it.

We know very little about Antedios: he comes to light only as a result of some gold and silver coins bearing his name, so we know nothing of his motive – if he did indeed sign the client treaty with the invading army. However, from the Roman point of view, the arrangement would have suited them well: a client relationship with the Iceni created a vital buffer zone to the north of Camulodunum (modern Colchester), the Romans' capital in their newly occupied territory. This provided the army with added protection against attack and cost very little in terms of military personnel, freeing soldiers to be deployed to the battle zones. Meanwhile, the client king would have been provided with privileges, wealth and the promise that they could continue in power on behalf of the Romans. In theory, at least, it was an arrangement that suited everyone.

The lands of the Iceni stretched across most of what is now East Anglia, covering today's Norfolk, north Suffolk and north-east Cambridgeshire. The tribe's origins were typical of many Iron Age groups in Britain at that time – an apparent amalgam of native Britons who had lived in the area since at least the Bronze Age together with some immigrants from the Belgic tribes of the Low Countries and then later, more aristocratic immigrants from the Marne valley in north-eastern France who brought with them their warrior skills, superior iron swords and also their speedy war chariots.

While the bulk of the tribespeople were subsistence farmers, there were also specialists in metalworking, pottery and other manual trades; the archaeology of the period discovered to date also suggests that the horse played a crucial role in society. The horses bred and broken by the tribe were much more than a means of transport or carriage; they were visible emblems of wealth and power in a culture already well known for its love of decoration and display. They were also intimately linked via the spirit world with the Celtic mother-goddess,

Epona, who embodies the earth's fertility and whose name derives from the word for horse. With its central role in both the practical and the spiritual worlds, it is unsurprising that the horse was a popular icon – but the Iceni take this a stage further: horses predominate on Icenian coins while the accoutrements of chariots and riding survive in archaeological finds. To have four legs or wheels was the ultimate status symbol – and the Iceni paraded their horses just as their modern neighbours, the so-called "Essex boys", do with their souped-up, alloy-wheeled, go-faster-striped cars today.

There is one intriguing piece of evidence from Iceni coins that sets them apart from every other tribe in Britain at the time: they minted the only coins that appear to bear the tribal, as well as their rulers', names. Were the Iceni, then, a people of uncommonly strong tribal pride? Did they have a level of political cohesion and identity unheard of in the rest of Iron Age Britain? When writing about the widespread revolts that bubbled up against the Romans, inspired by the actions of the rebel leader, Caratacus, Tacitus describes the Iceni as "a powerful tribe, which war had not weakened", so it is clear that they did have a strong identity not only among the British tribes but one that was apparent to the occupying Romans as well. It is just possible that their self-sufficiency and pride might be behind the widespread absence of any large amounts of Roman imports prior to the invasion of AD 43; in fact, notwithstanding their Romanised elite, some academics have gone as far as suggesting that the Iceni people actively

A silver unit bearing the inscription 'ECE' – an expression of pride in Icenian tribal identity?

resisted the dilution of their own culture by the Romanisation that was happening elsewhere in Ancient Britain and Gaul.

As for the tribe's political cohesion, evidence from coins marked AESV and SAENV – perhaps the names of other kings – along with evidence from Roman texts certainly hint that there might have been factions within the Iceni and that it might have been one of these factions that led the first revolt against the Romans in AD 47. However, there is a distinct lack of supporting evidence from the ground of any large-scale in-fighting between Iceni tribespeople or even between the Iceni and their neighbours. The local population appear to have lived in the traditional Iron Age roundhouses made of woven branches with watertight thatched roofs. These were clustered together in open and undefended settlements throughout their lands; hillforts, relatively common elsewhere in the southern half of Britain, are few and far between in the territory of the Iceni – though, admittedly, in this low, flat landscape, this might have had more to do with the local geography than politics. There was, however, a series of defended enclosures clustered in the west of the Iceni lands, presumably marking the area out as in some way special – and enclosures only need to be defended if there is a perceived threat. Ultimately, though, we can only speculate as to why what appear to be *tribal* coins were minted; they remain an interesting anomaly and a reminder that our understanding of this tribe and its people is very much incomplete.

What we do know is that not long after the Roman invasion of Britain by Claudius, and certainly after the revolt of AD 47, a king whom Tacitus called Prasutagus appears to have been on the throne. He may even have been minting his own coins (possibly the last Celtic coins ever minted in Britain) which bore the inscriptions merging both Latin and Celtic in the form of the words "SUB" the Latin for "under", "R" or "RI" symbolising the Celtic for "*Ricon*" or King, and "PRASTO" for Prasutagus. However, this reading of the inscription on this very rare coin has recently been challenged to give instead the name Esuprastus, apparently the name of a king from the neighbouring Corieltauvi tribe to the north-west. Did Tacitus (or the coin maker) get the Iceni king's name wrong? It cannot be denied that mistakes were made both by the people inscribing the coins and Romans correctly "hearing" British names. The coins might still relate to

Tacitus's "Prasutagus", but if it was someone completely different, then they were certainly active in producing coins from around the 30s AD to the end of the client kingdom and the revolt of Boudica.

On the reverse of one of the coins, the person who made it has left a note of his own name in the legend, "ESICO FECIT", which translates as "Esico made me". This boastfulness written in Latin makes a strong argument for the coins being made under the direction of the Romans in one of their client kingdoms. Shame, then, that poor old Esico left out the "R" of "PRASTO" and thereby made clear who had spelled the king's name incorrectly.

Meanwhile, it is hardly surprising that no coins have turned up for Boudica: her rule as the de facto leader of the Iceni tribe was probably less than a year, and much of that would be spent far away from her homeland.

According to Tacitus, King Prasutagus was "famed for his long prosperity" but all that came to an end with his death in AD 60. His final wishes over what should happen next were by no means outrageous: according to Caesar's observations on the Gaulish Celts, it was perfectly normal for a woman to inherit everything on the death of her spouse; however, on this occasion, Prasutagus decided to make his daughters his heirs in lieu of his wife. Perhaps they were still young enough to be under her guardianship or it could have been that by expressly dictating that they were his heirs, he shored up their rights to inherit and rule the kingdom on Boudica's death; later, when Roman Britain was more established, we see plenty of evidence from tombstones of fathers making daughters their heirs. There is also the chance that the Icenian King preferred his daughters to his wife – or was even doubtful of her continued loyalty to their Roman masters. Whatever Prasutagus's reasons, the fact remains that the will shows a certain degree of sexual equality in the indigenous culture.

However, the ways of the Britons were alien to Rome: to the emperor, governor and especially the procurator, Catus Decianus, it was entirely unacceptable of Prasutagus to assume that his estate was his to give away at all. As far as they were concerned, he was their *client* king – not a king in his own right; he ruled on behalf of Rome, was subordinate to it and had benefited handsomely because of this relationship. To their way of thinking, the relationship was with Prasutagus, not his royal line and certainly not his wife or daughters: once he was no longer king, the kingdom must pass back to the real power behind the throne where it would be completely absorbed into the Empire.

The "long prosperity" of Prasutagus was clearly too much for the Romans to resist: using the perceived sleight against Nero and the official inventory of the king's estate as their excuse, the reaction was extreme and decisive:

> "...his kingdom was looted by centurions, his house by slaves, as if they were the bounty of war...All the chief men of the Iceni, as if Rome had received the whole country as a gift, were stripped of their ancestral estates, and the king's relatives were made slaves."
>
> TACITUS: *ANNALS, XIV 31*

To Tacitus, and to any Romans reading his account, the behaviour of his fellow countrymen was shockingly brutal: the two things that "civilised" Romans hated was any corruption of the ideals of Roman society – and that included slaves getting above themselves or when those in positions of power abused their privileges with profligacy. The Annals would certainly have made good drama; however, Tacitus was playing a double game, not only giving the raw details of what happened to Prasutagus's kingdom but also doing so in a way that served to highlight the degenerate morality of the Empire under its hated emperor, Nero.

Another matter close to Roman hearts was sexual propriety – from both sides of the gender divide. While women were expected to behave demurely, men were also expected to behave with honour. And what was being meted out to the royal family in Nero's name was enough to shock Tacitus's audience to the core:

> "his wife Boudica was flogged, and his daughters raped."
>
> TACITUS: *ANNALS, XIV 31*

In that one short line lies the seeds of hatred. Suddenly, the Romans had gone from attacking royal property to violating the King's own kin – and the shame of this debasement would have been felt very, very deeply by Iceni and right-thinking Romans alike. The whole account is told with barely concealed bile towards his own countrymen who thereby heaped opprobrium on to the name of Rome. They had done more than "just" strip and then flog a wife and woman of the ruling nobility – and presumably by her rank of client queen she was also a Roman citizen; they had also gang-raped the two young princesses – who were probably both virgins. Such treatment of women was beyond belief: under Roman law, it was unlikely that any free women would ever be flogged even in punishment, while any man found guilty of rape would face execution; as a final insult to the Roman moral code, both the beating and the rape would have been regarded as particularly odious as they were perpetrated on members of the ruling class.

I discussed the significance of this sexual violence with Philip Crummy, a softly spoken Scottish archaeologist and the hugely respected director of the Colchester Archaeological Trust who has spent the last three decades scraping away two thousand years of earth to reveal the city's ancient stories. "I think the whole episode of the rapes is really interesting: we know that raping could sometimes be a prelude to an execution as it was against Roman law to execute a juvenile virgin. So is this what the Romans had in mind? Were the rapes only part of the intended punishments for Boudica's family? Of course, we just don't know – but I think you have to look at the *meaning* behind the Romans' actions to get to the truth of the matter."

If Tacitus and his Roman readers found the whole episode of the rapes and beatings utterly distasteful, then it doesn't require much imagination to work out the Icenian response. Virginity was highly respected throughout Iron Age cultures as it signified both purity and also powerful, latent sexual energy; to have it forcibly stolen was a double insult; the fact that it was the young princesses' maidenheads that were stolen trebled the insult. To the ancient Britons, the Romans had not only abused their queen and her daughters: with Boudica being the earthly representative, priestess or perhaps even the embodiment of the goddess, Andraste, they had desecrated the gods as well. For a people who would barely leave home without gauging the will of the gods, the crimes were an assault on their whole system of beliefs and they would not – could not – be tolerated.

Surprisingly for a writer who tends towards the graphic, Dio Cassius makes no mention of the rapes or the beatings and instead puts his focus on a financial cause to the ensuing troubles. He describes a situation whereby Claudius had given money to the high-ranking Britons who had supported the Romans in their invasion – but then the procurator of the island, Catus Decianus, had insisted it was paid back immediately. This would have been troublesome enough in itself but was compounded when the statesman and philosopher, Seneca, who had lent the Britons forty million sesterces – worth about £50 million today – at a good rate of interest then demanded repayment in full and, if necessary, by force. The Britons, and especially the less-Romanised tribes, were not as familiar with money-culture as their invaders. Although coins had been in circulation for well over a century, theirs was a still largely a culture of barter and gift-giving, and you would never ask someone to give a gift back. The Romans' demand for "repayment" of the loans would have left the Britons facing serious financial hardship and genuine confusion and anger, not least at the humiliation caused to such a proud people.

Wounded pride, shame and humiliation make uneasy bedfellows with peace. Even Tacitus is fairly unequivocal in placing much of the blame on the Romans but no one, probably not even Boudica herself, could have guessed what would happen next. What started as an upwelling of anger against the way the occupying army had treated the royal family grew into something that transcended any personal motive; the violation of their queen and her daughters was now just the touch-paper to a volatile situation that had been building in might ever since the Roman invasion. For seventeen years, the Iceni had suffered at the hands of their supposed allies: their people had been taxed to pay for the costs of being invaded, the young men had been taken to serve in the foreign army, their rulers had been emasculated and their warriors had even been deprived of their weapons by a people who were meant to be their allies. Any dissent had been put down with brutal force but while the Romans could beat the Britons in battle, they failed to win their wholehearted support – and the Romans knew this only too well:

"The Britons themselves submit to the levy, pay tribute and the other charges of government, provided that there is no abuse. That they bitterly resent: for they are broken in to obedience, not slavery."

TACITUS: *AGRICOLA, 13*

The slow burn of resentment was now ignited by the ultimate insult to their royal family, their gods and status of the whole tribe. The Iceni had the cause; what they needed next was a leader. And into the limelight stepped their outraged queen who now stood before them as a living metaphor that the tribe could be badly bruised and abused but it still had its dignity – and that dignity was saying that it was time to fight back.

John Davies took me around his new Boudica Gallery at Norwich Castle Museum – an impressive space that tells the story of the Roman conquest, occupation and Boudica's rebellion – in a touchingly human way. As chief curator for the museum, he selected the very best pieces to bring her story to life: on show are some of the artefacts from her day – humble brooches and pots from the common man and woman contrasting with some magnificent golden torcs. Roman and Briton, rich or poor, he has tried to capture the diversity of life in the first few decades following the Claudian invasion. "Boudica is such an important figure as well as being a world-famous name, so she has a central role in international history, too," he said. "Think of the famous names from the Roman period and you're likely to come up with Julius Caesar, Jesus Christ – and Boudica. Yet, like Jesus, she was only in her early thirties when she died. But despite that, it's reassuring to think that some of this material might even have been seen by her. It's that intimate connection with the past that has brought visitors here in their tens of thousands – sometimes from overseas or other parts of Britain but a lot of them from Norfolk itself. There's still a lot to learn, though, and we're continually having to update the gallery as new information comes in from archaeologists and metal-detectorists but it really is worthwhile: here in Norfolk she's *our* personality – and we're immensely proud of that."

It's typical of how the legend of Boudica has outstripped the facts that we cannot even be certain what the queen of the Iceni was really called. Boudica comes from the Celtic word *bouda* meaning victory, so she was either called the Iron Age equivalent of Victoria or that name was a title she assumed either when she first became queen or after the war against the Romans. In the absence of any definitive archaeological proof – her name on coins, a palace or relics that link her to the right time and place, all we have to go by are the words of Tacitus, who was writing between fifteen and sixty years after the event and then of Cassius Dio some hundred years after the revolt. One name she was never called was Boadicea which has been erroneously passed down to us after a medieval scribe made a copying error: he mistook the "u" for an "a" and the final "c" for an "e", changing Tacitus's "Boudicca" to "Boadicea" – and as this seemed to make sense and sounded suitably Roman, this was the version that eventually stuck.

Assuming that Tacitus was broadly telling the truth, Boudica not only existed, but she was the wife of the king. This would make her a consort rather than a queen by rights but here other documentary support comes into the realm: the experience of Cartimandua proves that it was not beyond the realms of the Iron Age imagination to have a woman serving as an independent ruler. And it seems from the classical writers and the Celtic legends that women could not only hold powerful positions within society, they could also transcend more modern gender roles in taking their people to war. Women had a close connection with warfare in a range of different guises as spectators at the edge of the battlefield, instructors for warriors, war-goddesses and even as warriors themselves. Romans and Celts feared and venerated the awesome power of the warrior queen: to both cultures she represented the human and the divine that connected heaven with earth; she symbolised the beginning and end of life and also the personification of fertility and death – and thus she assumed a potency unattainable by warrior men.

The goddess most closely associated with Boudica was Andraste who could well be the same goddess as the Gaulish Andarta, whose name translates as "unconquerable" – and there are certainly parallels between Andraste, Andarte and the earthly queen named Boudica or Victory. It further seems that Brigantia, the goddess of the Brigantes tribe that was ruled by Queen Cartimandua, was linked with Minerva, the Roman goddess of war. The connection between these warring goddesses and the two warring queens is highlighted by the relief found at the Chedworth Roman villa museum which depicts a goddess with a halo of hair above her head, carrying a spear in her hand, together with the legend, "Dea Regina" or "Queen Goddess". This expression is almost tautologous: to the Ancient Britons, both words meant women who ruled with divine powers.

If the only surviving description of Boudica's appearance is anything to go by, it was perfectly believable that Prasutagus's queen could call on divine and well as earthly powers. Cassius Dio's account is the stuff of legend and while it closely parallels the common themes from previous Greek and Roman writers, his is the only reference to Boudica's infamous red hair that has defined her image for the last two thousand years. His classic lines go as follows:

> "In build she was very tall, in her demeanour most terrifying, in the glint of her eye most fierce, and her voice was harsh; a great mound of the tawniest hair fell to her hips; around her neck was a large golden torc; and she wore a tunic of many colours upon which a thick cloak was fastened with a brooch. This was her general attire."

CASSIUS DIO: ROMAN HISTORY, BOOK 62

The idea of the ancient Britons as tall is rarely borne out by examination of the few available skeletons from the period but there is much documentary evidence from classical scholars that the whole panoply of Celtic-speaking peoples in Europe were perceived as of unusually great height. As for being "terrifying", it was commonplace for warriors to paint or decorate their bodies with blue pigment in what seems to have been some semi-religious pre-battle rite but the effect would also have been dramatic on the enemy. To see not only a blue-painted warrior but a *naked* blue warrior would have been quite startling. However, in this case the indication is that she remained fully clothed

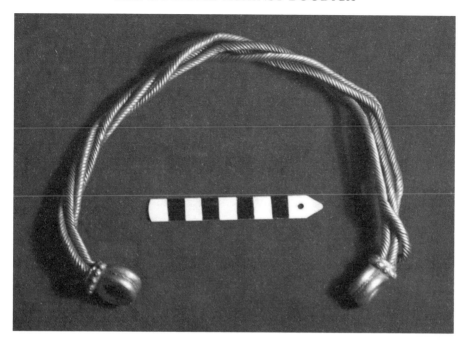

One of the finest examples of a torc found in the UK. Made in the 1st century BC and worn by the highest status members of society. Could this have been worn by Boudica? Discovered in SW Norfolk in 2003 and now on display in Norwich Castle Museum

and it was more her demeanour that struck fear into the beholder.

The harshness of her voice as described by Dio probably had more to do with painting her as unfeminine than any real vocal characteristic. There is certainly no suggestion that the Celtic language sounded hard upon the ear but with Dio being the only commentator to mention her appearance, this assertion is impossible to confirm or deny.

Along with body paints, another tactic used by the image-conscious ancient Celts was to coat their hair in lime to stiffen it. This would have the effect of lightening it in colour and also making the warrior look even more terrifying in appearance – but again, there is no suggestion that Boudica followed this trend as her hair "fell to her hips" in a manner equally fashionable amongst Celtic people. However, as already discussed, the symbolic power of the redhead was apparent even from early classical times: as well as being visibly different and therefore "strange" or "other", there is a suggestion that red hair signified high status in Mediterranean and North African societies, presumably because it would take both time and money to achieve this effect in naturally dark hair. Furthermore, the royal line of the Egyptians stemmed from Macedonia, where natural red hair was not uncommon, and this would also confirm the status of the bearer. Luckily for Boudica, Christianity had yet to penetrate British and even mainstream Roman attitudes at this point, for Judas was said to have had red hair and thus the rise of Christianity is mirrored by a decline in both the status and appeal of the redhead, so that by the middle ages, a redheaded female was in danger of being heralded a witch.

There is good archaeological evidence to back up Dio's assertion that Boudica wore a golden necklace: torcs have been found in buried hoards including the remarkable Snettisham hoards which contained a variety of styles, sizes and dates of deposit, from the mid-first century BC to the first century AD. These magnificent pieces of jewellery have been found in iron, bronze or gold and can be seriously impressive; they were worn by high-status individuals such as kings, queens, battle champions or nobility, and even though the larger ones were often hollow they still would have been far too heavy for general wear, leaving their use for display, ritual or religious ceremony.

As for Boudica's dress, we know from the classical texts as well as archaeological discoveries that the ancient Celts certainly had a love of brightly coloured clothing. Bodies found in the boglands of Denmark show the remains of a woven fabric similar to modern Scottish tartan in its use of different colours on the warp and weft to make a chequered design. The heavy woollen cloaks made by the Gauls were famous in Rome in much the same way as Indian *pashminas* are nowadays; with different weights of fabric to match the requirements of the seasons, they were high-value objects of status for the wearer as well as being remarkably warm, durable and weatherproof with all the natural lanolin contained in the wools. The tunic would have been a standard item of clothing, secured at the shoulders with a number of straps that might have varied according to whether the woman was married or not; certainly, the style of clothing with its fastenings at the shoulder would have enabled ease of access to breastfeeding mothers who would have represented a significant proportion of female society.

The final piece of Dio's description focuses on Boudica's brooch. The Britons were renowned for their love of decoration and while the popularity of brooches was partly functional as they held together two ends of a cloak, they also gave the opportunity to display both wealth and status. The standard design had a pin at the back which functioned a little like a modern kilt or safety-pin, though there were variations using safety-chains as well. Brooches would have been worn by both men and women and were frequently made of iron and highly decorated with inlaid enamel, precious stones or intricate metalwork designs.

Of all types of jewellery that survive today, brooches are among the most numerous as they had to endure the rough and tumble of everyday life and so were in constant danger of falling off and being lost. It is no surprise that forty-seven brooches are amongst the finds discovered at the religious Icenian site at Thetford where hundreds if not thousands of people would have jostled together in the arena: these are precisely the moments when precious jewellery is lost.

But if Boudica's clothes were standard dress among the ancient Britons, there was something else about her that set her apart. According to Dio, Boudica was also "possessed of greater intelligence than often is found in women"; while this might have well been the case, it was no doubt too unsettling to Dio and his Roman audience to contemplate the fact that Boudica was in any way ordinary; she *had* to be viewed as abnormal as she had taken it upon herself to defy Rome. To even entertain the thought that she was nothing special and that other women could do the same would have been too unnerving, too threatening for the mindset of the great invincible Empire.

Despite being told so much of her appearance, it is hard not to yearn for real depth in the classical texts to help Boudica appear as a fully rounded person and not just a character in history. Particularly frustrating is that neither of the classical commentators gives us an intimate window into Boudica's home – the alleged scene of the Romans' brutal domestic violence. Even archaeology, which can normally provide the touching details of human life, has only provided us with four possible options for this seat of royal power. The Iceni sites notable for having a mint are Saham Toney, West Stow, Needham and Thetford – but these options are important in their own right: this is the largest number of sites of any contemporary tribe and makes the Iceni unique in Britain; it also adds weight to the idea that power within the tribe might well have been *de*centralised amongst a number of factions.

Around AD 50, a vast rectangular structure some thirty-two thousand square metres was rebuilt at Thetford and, in its heyday, it would have been an impressive sight: the size of five football pitches, the whole area was bounded by two ditches separated by nine fences laid out in a series of concentric boundaries around the perimeter but its purpose seems to have been as a key religious or ceremonial site as there is little in the way of domestic or defensive archaeology. There was only one entrance into the inner enclosure and that was through a corridor of large posts on the eastern side of the structure that led to a great timber gateway; once inside, there was a wide open area a little larger than a football pitch that would have been perfect for public gatherings, overlooked by a two-storey wooden building left over from the site's previous incarnation.

Norfolk Museum archaeologist, the late Tony Gregory, suggested that the site was in fact the royal palace of Boudica but there is no supporting evidence for this, although she might well have used the site. However, additional evidence that this was a meeting place comes from the discovery of those forty-seven brooches that could easily have fallen off the owners' clothing as people jostled together in a crowd. Was this perhaps the site where the Iceni people massed when they decided to wreak their revenge on the occupying Roman forces? Does the evidence on the ground point to this being the rallying site for the new Iceni army? The evidence is circumstantial but the timing makes it likely that it bore witness to some part of the revolt.

As the news spread of Boudica's flogging and the princesses' rape, the Iceni tribespeople left their fields and homesteads and began to gather en masse near to the royal residence. Showing their support for their queen and their hatred of the Romans, the disorganised rabble quickly started to gain a focus and gather a momentum that had been suppressed since the revolt of AD 47. The crushing of that Iceni revolt was followed by thirteen years of relative peace when any background resentment towards the occupying force had been capped by King Prasutagus's pro-Roman stance. But no longer. Like a bottle of slowly fermenting beer, the pressure had been building up and was now ready to explode. The Iceni had good grievance to go to war once more – and this time nothing and no one stood in their way.

More surprising was that the Iceni were now joined by their southern neighbours, the Trinovantes, who were also close to bursting with their own unvented anger against the occupying army. They had been the first native Britons to sign up to a treaty with the Romans way back in 54 BC when Julius Caesar had made his second attempt at invading the island. But a century of supposed friendship with the occupying army was about to come to an end.

For the Trinovantes, the cause was one of almost total emasculation: in AD 49, land in the former Trinovantian capital of Camulodunum had been taken by the Romans to make a new *colonia* – somewhere retired soldiers could live. Then the Trinovantes nobles were hit with all manner of taxes and ex gratia payments to pay for the construction and running costs of a gigantic new temple to honour the dead but deified emperor, Claudius. The Britons were even expected to work at the temple, taking them from their usual labours and forcing them to pay homage to a foreign god and the very man who brought them into servitude.

These moves were almost guaranteed to rub dirt in the faces of the conquered Britons and at the first sign of uniting behind a strong leader, the Trinovantes put aside any petty tribal jealousies and flocked to join Boudica's army.

For the watching queen, seeing the crowds building up before her eyes, it would have been like seeing her future roll out in front of her: there was only one response, only one plan of action – and that was to wipe out all trace of the Romans' polluting culture and their gross abuse of every man, woman and child in the conquered territories. Since the arrival of the Trinovantes, this was no longer simply a tribal matter: this was serious; this was all-out war.

"I definitely think there *was* someone out there called Boudica," mused Philip Crummy in one of our long phone conversations, "though it's hazy as to what she was actually doing. There really is the tiniest, tiniest amount of evidence but I still believe she existed." So how did he envisage this woman? "Well…" He let out the word as if he were exhaling thoughts. "I see her as head of the army but the rebellion was a much bigger thing that spread across the whole province. To my mind, she was more a figurehead rather than a heroic or a Winston Churchill war leader. I suspect that she was actually part of a big group of leaders but the other names haven't survived – probably because the Romans over-focused on the fact that she was a woman, which all added to the disgrace of her rebellion. As for the Britons, I would imagine the individual tribes would have their own leaders so it would be more a confederate army – after all, the British were not exactly known for working together. But I really don't think that she could have been acting on her own: the revolt was too big, too widespread to be managed by one person. The warriors would not have been acting as one single army but as a collection of loose tribal groups under a party of war-leaders in which Boudica was key – but, no, she couldn't have been alone."

Farmers told their neighbours, who told their kinsmen who told their neighbours: the tribes were rising up against the invaders and the locals hurried to leave their farmsteads and get ready for battle. In a mounting flurry of industry, new weapons were smelted – particularly the spears favoured by the native fighters – and old ones taken out of hiding and cleaned, the horses were made ready with all their finery and the fields prepared for their departure. The East Anglian countryside began to empty and spill out on to the roads and tracks heading south toward Camulodunum.

The timing of the revolt could not have been better, at least for the British: the campaigning season of AD 60 saw the main Roman forces busy with their efforts to wipe out the Druids' cauldron of political mischief in Anglesey over in the far west of Britain – just about as far away as they could be from the Britons who were now massing under Boudica in the east. Whether or not the Druids had sent word of their impending fate to stir up revolt as a distraction in the east – or whether the Britons just seized the best opportunity to wrong-foot the enemy – can't ever be proven but by the time the Romans got to hear of Boudica's revolt, they were up to their eyes in the ethnic cleansing of Anglesey: the Druids were being slaughtered and their religious sites desecrated beyond repair. But while the threat from the so-called Isle of Mona might have been neutralised, it left the bulk of the Roman forces hundreds of miles away from the new threat that had risen in the east.

Tacitus calls the British uprising a "sudden revolt", suggesting that it caught the Romans unawares. And so it might: the Iceni had been allies of Rome for the past seventeen years while the relationship between Rome and the Trinovantes went back even further, to the time of Julius Caesar. Roman military action might have been almost invincible but their intelligence had failed badly – Suetonius Paulinus had been too tied up with the warring factions in Wales and the despised Roman procurator, Catus Decianus, had been concentrating too hard on how much he could screw out of Prasutagus's kingdom to consider the political ramifications of his actions. In a bid to assess the damage and come up with a rapid plan, Paulinus grabbed a small contingent of men and made an immediate move back east; Catus Decianus just panicked. Though the citizens of Camulodunum pleaded with him for support in the knowledge that they would be Boudica's number one target for attack, he barely managed to scrabble together a couple of hundred poorly armed troops to help defend them. He now knew that both sides would want his neck on the block and he ungallantly abandoned the sinking ship and fled in fear to Gaul. While he had escaped with his life, his fellow Romans would not be so lucky.

CHAPTER 10

BOUDICA'S ATTACK ON COLCHESTER

Fifty, forty, then thirty miles from Boudica's massing army, Camulodunum was holding its breath. Its wide, gravelled streets that would normally have crunched with the busy feet of residents, traders and animals now rested in eerie silence in the summer sun. Every once in a while, a door would have opened in from one of the rows of white-plastered buildings flanking the street and a family would stumble out, weighed down with their possessions, before melting down one of the side-streets, out of the town and into the shadows of the countryside. Those who could were already boarding boats on the nearby River Colne and sailing south through the marshy lands into the safety of open water. Not even years of training could steady the pulse of the soldiers and veterans who were taking anxious turns to be on watch for the natives on the warpath. The town which, a few days earlier, had been the proud showpiece of the Roman administration now shuddered in all its conspicuous urbanity; it could do nothing but believe in the power of its own magic and hunker down in a vain attempt to merge back into the British soil.

Driving into the sprawling modern town today, Colchester has the feeling of a town on the periphery. Road signs direct you to the "town centre" or "London"; at the railway station, commuter crowds are flocking to the capital in their daily journey to work. But two thousand years ago, Colchester *was* the capital – the most important site of early Roman Britain and the nerve centre of foreign occupation. Occasionally, as you drive around the ring-roads you can still see vestiges of its grand historical past in the snatches of rocky wall that once bounded the settlement but now sit silent and uncomfortable against the concrete and brick like a deaf, elderly grandparent at a child's party. However, for those prepared to get out of their car and walk, there's an almost magical network of ancient narrow streets and alleyways flanked by buildings whose basements dig down through time as well as soil, and some of which – like The George Hotel – even sport a resident ghost or two as a wispy connection to days gone by. Beyond the town centre, in the wide green space of the park and gardens stands a magnificent castle which serves as a remarkable testament to how we have continually refashioned the buildings of our ancestors. Two thousand years on, there is still also a thriving garrison at the town, though the military presence is fairly discreet: Colchester is now a place for shoppers and workers, cars and buses.

Originally named for Camulos, the Celtic god of war, Camulodunum had already borne witness to several reincarnations but none would be as bloody as the one it was to face. What was now a Roman town had started life as a native British settlement, largely agricultural in feel but with increasing amounts of Roman imports as a preface to the actual military invasions of Julius Caesar and then Claudius. Shortly after this second major invasion of AD 43, Camulodunum began to change from being a settlement where residents were linked together by family, kinship or tribal bonds to somewhere that showed the first real vestiges of being a proper town with a diverse range of people with many different backgrounds coming to live, work and trade.

Under the rule of the wealthy Catuvellaunian King Cunobelin (c.AD 10-42) who either took over the former land of the Trinovantes or occupied a Catuvellaunian enclave within his neighbour's territory, Camulodunum became the largest settlement in south-east Britain at around ten square miles in area, with a series of protective dykes for defence. Although essentially not much more than a large farm with some specialist zoned areas, the settlement had an importance that was political, religious and economic in nature with its own burial grounds and a mint producing a range of coins. The remains of the actual homestead of the powerful king survive today in the form of cropmarks in the fields at Gosbecks, sadly only clearly visible from aerial photographs. These show the dark lines that were the boundaries of his immediate domain which would have consisted of the classic Iron Age defences of ditches or dykes with steep ramparts laid out strategically to prevent attacks from the war chariots.

However, even with its grand status during the reign of Cunobelin, Camulodunum would have seemed most bizarre to a modern visitor: far from being urban, with streets and shops and a metropolitan buzz, the pace would have been almost pastoral with the dominant sounds emanating from the grazing cattle, sheep and goats with the snuffling of pigs and the snorts of the horses as a gentle background rhythm, accompanied by the sounds of humans working in the surrounding fields, the thatched houses and nearby workshops. The only available transport links were the crude but extensive drove roads and rivers navigable to shallow-bottomed boats and while the archaeology of the site shows these were effective enough in getting foreign goods into Camulodunum and presumably local exports out again, this was a culture of haves and have-nots. While the chiefs and their sons might have travelled to Gaul and even been educated in Rome, most ordinary people would barely have ranged more than a dozen or so miles from their lands.

It has been estimated that Cunobelin – whom the Roman historian, Suetonius, described as King of the Britons – minted something like a million gold coins during his reign and won control over the bulk of south-east England. But for all his power and wealth, he died shortly before the Claudian invasion and the town site was taken personally by the emperor in AD 43 to become the base of the Roman military and administrative rule, with much-improved transport links inland by means of new roads and also the sea routes to the continent.

Slowly but surely, Camulodunum became a typically Roman town. However, rather than erase all signs of its British past and start the town from scratch, the Romans built their legionary fortress and a number of other military buildings but left intact many of the key features of the Iron Age settlement, some of which are still visible today. Although relatively few of the invaders would actually have come from Italy, let alone Rome itself, the "Romans" were essentially an urban people with cosmopolitan ideas. On top of that, they were a people who were used to colonising new frontiers: almost like "painting by numbers", they had a well-established culture of town-planning with many provincial settlements following a basic plan involving a mix of military, economic, social and religious functions.

But much more important than just creating the *look* of a Roman town was creating the *idea* of one. Out would go the old ways of bartering, tribal obligations and local fiefdoms; in would come denominational coinage, a capitalist economy and loyalty to a distant emperor. The key to Romanising the new provinces, however, was in designating towns as *coloniae,* a place for retired soldiers who were given (or just took) parcels of land for housing and allotments for subsistence. This was far more than mere land grabbing or imperial largesse: by establishing a *colonia,* the authorities knew they were deliberately spreading Roman ideas like a virus throughout the body of Britain. Though the initial invasion may have been violent, the cells would slowly breed and spawn Roman culture throughout the land until the host country was completely overtaken. Once the new province had been sufficiently Romanised, there was little, if any, need for continued military action within its lands, freeing up the army to keep expanding ever-outwards the frontiers of the empire. This Roman "civilisation" was therefore by no means an innocent or accidental by-product of the invasion: it was a critical part of a process of wealth extraction that began with informal Romanisation, progressed to military rule and was completed with political, economic and cultural domination.

Camulodunum was typical of a native settlement undergoing this process. During the AD 40s and 50s, it went through a period of increasing industrial activity with the new economy stimulated by the needs of the occupying Roman army and its new status as the Colonia Victricensis (City of Victory) of Camulodunum, from around AD 50. Evidence remains of the metalworkers, potters, tile-makers (for the Romans preferred their roofs to be tiled, not thatched) and while little proof of masonry or carpentry survives, these construction skills would certainly have been among those which were firmly in demand. However, even in this "urban" environment, the backbone would still have been agriculture: after all, the thousands of incomers needed to be fed.

For the first seventeen years of its new life, Camulodunum had grown in size and complexity until it felt like a more organised, regimented version of a modern country town today. Girdled by the swathes of farmlands appropriated from the Britons and now owned by the soldiers and their families, the town itself displayed the grid-like system that the Romans loved so well, in this case probably around seven blocks wide and four blocks long, filled with the characteristic white-painted rectangular buildings with their pitched red-tiled roofs similar to those that litter the Mediterranean today. Gone were the traditional thatched, circular homes and workshops of Cunobelin's time: now the town sported all the set pieces of Roman urban life including houses, shops, a marketplace, baths, a 3,000-seat theatre and the temple dedicated to Claudius. Surprisingly, the one thing that the town didn't have was any defences. The Iron Age earthworks that surrounded the old settlement had been filled in and built over as the new town expanded and either through over-confidence or apathy, they had never been replaced. This was unusual for a Roman settlement – particularly a military one in a newly conquered land – and their absence would play a significant role in the town's destruction in AD 60/61.

There is evidence, however, that there was some resistance to the developing new town: in the early 1970s, archaeological excavations in the city made the chilling discovery of six human skulls in the ditch of the legionary fortress that was meant to protect Camulodunum from outside enemies. The skulls were sent to Cambridge University for forensic analysis: one had a serious fracture like a deep thumbprint on the back of its head, caused by being hit with a blunt instrument like a sword pommel; another had a deep gash at the base of the skull from being struck by a sword or axe in a botched first attempt at beheading the victim – a double chop so graphic that it gave the expert who was examining it "quite a turn". Though there is no way of telling to whom the heads belonged or the reasons for their execution, the fate and location of the decapitated skulls suggest a macabre sequence of events: six men – perhaps local Trinovantes – executed around AD 55 for some violation or rebellion against the Roman authority. They were decapitated and their heads presumably displayed on poles at the town gate as a graphic warning to their comrades not to resist the might of Rome. Over time the skulls made their way off the poles and on to the ground and then into the ditch which was filled shortly afterwards; they lay in their makeshift grave for almost two thousand years, silent witnesses to the fact that perhaps all was not quite as well in Rome's newest province as the dispatches home might suggest.

Any "little local difficulty" in Camulodunum was to be overtaken by a holocaust of unimaginable scale as Boudica's army swept the forty miles from the tribal lands of the Iceni, gathering momentum and recruits as it went. From the classical texts and the archaeological remains in modern-day Colchester, it is possible to piece together a reasonably detailed picture of what happened next, though the story makes grim telling. For the few thousand soldiers and their dependents and slaves, the entrepreneurial traders who had moved into the developing town and the British sympathisers-cum-collaborators with Rome, military action was something that happened elsewhere – on the provincial frontiers to the north and west of Britain, particularly in the borderlands and highlands of Wales. They could never have guessed what would be their fate – or that the might of Rome would fail to protect them. Despite its veneer of sophistication, the supposedly settled world of Camulodunum was about to be turned upside down.

According to the graphic accounts of Tacitus and Dio, a number of strange portents at this time added to the sense that something catastrophic was about to befall the new province. The statue of Victory at Camulodunum mysteriously fell down, its back to the enemy as if it were fleeing in a bid to escape its fate; meanwhile, women "excited to frenzy" prophesied the impending destruction of the town. In the Senate House at night there were reports of ghostly laughter and "ravings in a strange language" while the town's theatre resounded with howling and wailing. As if this wasn't bad enough, over in the Thames estuary the waters gave off a reflection of an overthrown town while the sea turned to the colour of blood and the ebbing tide left debris that took the form of human bodies washed up on the shore. For the superstitious Romans who knew that their governor was hundreds of miles away fighting the rebels in the west of the province, these were the omens of certain doom, and no doubt their anxieties were whipped up further by the pro-British insurgents who, according to the classical historians, were filtering through the town's population.

The people of Camulodunum knew they were exposed but must have been almost paralysed with fear. The procurator's dispatch of two hundred soldiers would do little against the tens if not hundreds of thousands allegedly in Boudica's army who were heading straight for the town. They had no Roman legions, no governor, no procurator – not even a city wall or basic defences.

One can only imagine the frantic last few hours as pure fear and disbelief washed through the remaining townspeople of Camulodunum. Many of the veterans would have spent years trying to subdue the Britons – it was only a decade since the rebel army of Caratacus had ruled the western fringe: surely they could now resist the rebel army of a mere woman who sought to threaten everything they had fought for? And now, after twenty-five years of fighting, twenty-five years on the move, they had nowhere else to go: this was their reward; this was home; they may have driven the natives out but this was all they had. The foreigners took a final look at the empty dream they had tried to build on British soil.

For the Iceni, Trinovantes and their fellow Britons who had joined the rebel forces as they made their way to Camulodunum, this was going to be their first real taste of blood since the Roman invasion in AD 43. Since then, other than a few skirmishes and petty uprisings, their whole warring culture had been suppressed by the foreigners' military powers. Now, as more and more of their countrymen swelled their ranks, there was a growing excitement that they could at last reclaim their lands and revert to the glory days of their former existence. Having Roman imports was one thing; having the actual army threaten and demean them was another. For these farmers, carpenters, metal workers and labourers, this was an opportunity to regain their sense of self-respect and also an opportunity to put their world back into its proper order of gods and chiefs, war and peace, for how could they serve both the spirit world *and* their new foreign overlords? Something had to give – and the gods would surely protect them.

There was no dishonour in being led by a woman, for the queen now heading their army was a link between the earth and the heavens, and Boudica knew how to divine the will of the gods through her relationship with Andraste. There was also no dishonour in uniting with men who were previously their enemy, for not only had the Druids ordained that resistance to the Romans was the right path for all the people of their land, there was also a precedent:

Britons had united under both Caratacus and Cassivellaunus against the Roman threat. What was more, the time was right for rising up against the invaders: they had abused a royal household, insulted the gods, treated warriors like common slaves and then, in their arrogance, had assumed the tribes were so accepting of the new order that they could even take back the money they had been given without any kind of backlash. Well, the Britons were about to teach the Romans a lesson they would never forget.

By now the army of tribespeople had swollen into a torrent that flooded off the roads and into the surrounding countryside where it swept up yet more recruits as it continued south. With the men came their families, their children, animals and their wagons – no point in leaving them behind at the mercy of a vengeful enemy – this was the way they used to fight – whole communities staking everything they had on victory. Under the leadership of their queen and her daughters, the mood of the army was buoyant and daring: here was an opportunity to relive the old days of ritual warfare, where each warrior had a status and pride that had been denied him for the last seventeen years. With each step that they took, the old feelings flooded back. Warriors traded their boasts of deeds and bravery – and their distant glorious past seemed once more within reach.

As Boudica and her forces drew closer to the seat of their enemy, they paused for a while to take in the symbols of foreign rule, from the rigid grid patterns of the streets, to the red-tiled roofs of the block-style houses and the gigantic temple of the Roman emperor who thought he was a god. Everything they saw before them evoked the heavy hand of Rome that had debased their honour; and everything would now be sacrificed to the gods in order to get their old world back again. As they looked ahead at the alien townscape laid out before them, the hushed silence was little more than a prayer for the dead.

And then – at Boudica's command – a cacophony of battlecries, horns and hoofs announced the warrior queen's arrival, and hell was unleashed on the Roman town of Camulodunum. The Iron Age army exploded across the outlying fields of the settlement, across the shallow ditches that were once defensive earthworks and into long wide streets that led to the buildings and back courts. They burst through each and every room seeking out the enemy and smashing anything that couldn't be looted – amphorae of olive oil, shops full of clay pots, warehouses packed with government-issue kitchen supplies – anything that had been abandoned to their merciless tribal wrath.

There are no details of what happened that day other than the scant reports of Tacitus and Dio and the evidence burned into the ground but the words and the fire combine to suggest a tsunami of vengeful Britons sweeping through the town, the orderly grid-pattern of the Roman streets now playing to Boudica's advantage: for anyone trying to make their escape, there would have been little in the way of twisting lanes or alleyways in which try to hide.

For the British, there was nothing sweet about their revenge: if the gods needed blood, they would get it; they would stop at nothing to vent their fury, avenge their queen and win back their freedom. The attack would have been like a violent blood-letting; all the evils and pent-up frustrations of the past seventeen years were now being cleansed by the sword, the spear and fire. It didn't matter that their weapons were old, or were the weapons of the field: hunting spears, scythes, stones and knives were all used to stab and hack and slice their way through anyone who resisted. Behind the front line of warriors, whole families would have torn through the buildings to catch any stragglers and strip them of loot before stacking brushwood inside the bare rooms to transform Camulodunum into its own funeral pyre.

Grossly outnumbered and realising they were beaten, the Romans knew there was only one hope of sanctuary in the smoking, screaming town: the Temple of Claudius offered refuge for those who were quick enough: the thick stone walls and solid brass doors would provide all protection they needed against the raging tumult of Britons until they could be liberated by the military back-up which must surely now be on its way. Hundreds of Roman men, women and children ran for their lives to the far corner of town and up the steps of the grand temple entrance, slamming the heavy doors shut behind them.

To the jeering Britons outside, the temple was the most grotesque piece of architecture that summed up Roman rule. Still under construction, the giant edifice dominated the townscape of Camulodunum and drained the local people of their money, time and effort as the costs of building it were heaped upon their shoulders. The temple represented the arrogant excesses of a Roman culture which had stolen their lands, taken their wealth and insulted their own gods. It is painfully ironic that the half-built temple now became the final refuge of the surviving townspeople who barricaded themselves inside and prayed for help.

As the Romans huddled inside the temple with only the flickering light of their lamps, they would first have heard the screams of Boudica's army outside, then the thunder of missiles on the doors and walls and then the sounds of the walls being scaled and the roof tiles being removed to gain access to the huddled masses below. One can only begin to imagine the mounting horror of those inside as they realised that no help was going to arrive.

Unbeknown to the terrified Romans cowering in the temple, their forces had already made a disastrous attempt at rescuing their beleaguered countryfolk. Commanding the Ninth Legion was Petilius Cerealis, by many accounts an impetuous man but one who would rise over the next decade to become governor of Britain. When he heard that Boudica had raised an army and was heading south in the direction of Camulodunum, he quickly gathered together a detachment of his legion and raced down towards the town from his base in the east Midlands. It should have been no more than a hard three-day march but Boudica's forces were ready for them: en route to Camulodunum, he was ambushed – probably by a separate band of rebels – and around fifteen hundred out of his two thousand best infantrymen and horsemen were annihilated in a brutal and well-orchestrated attack. This was a total disaster for the Romans; Cerealis had little option but to head back with what was left of his cavalry to his fort at modern Longthorpe in Peterborough where he did his best to protect his force by building a smaller, more easily defended fort and then holing up until some kind of calm returned to this hostile land. His efforts at rescuing Camulodunum had not only failed dismally, but just like his fellow Romans to the south, Cerealis and his surviving men were now themselves under threat from the warring Britons.

Meanwhile, for the men, women and children holding out in the temple, it was the beginning of the end. They had been inside the cold, dark emptiness of the vast structure for two whole days – but no imperial god could save them now. As the last of their lamps flickered and died, so all their hopes were extinguished. Outside were possibly tens of thousands of Britons, baying for blood, looting the buildings and transforming their proud town to ashes; inside were all that remained of the doomed Romans of Cumulodunum. They had tried to defend themselves with no leader, no battle plan and a mere seven hundred or so soldiers most of whom had already been pensioned off; but now they knew they had failed. Although the walls were made of thick stone and plaster, the Achilles' heel of the temple was its tiled roof. When the Romans heard the Britons scrabbling on to the tiles, then smashing them like the shell of a giant egg, they knew that it was over: with the final defences breached, the victorious natives rained down on their helpless enemy and everyone inside – men, women and children, Romans or their British sympathisers – were butchered.

The last vestiges of Camulodunum had now been annihilated. Around ten thousand people are estimated to have died during the sacking of the town, with all its buildings destroyed in a holocaust of fire and hatred. As the tribes of Britons celebrated their glorious victory with feasting and thanksgivings to the gods, the acrid smoke of the devastated town hung on their clothes and in their hair and dimmed the light for miles around. Wearing the smell of death like a badge of honour, they collected their loot, loaded up their carts – and planned their next target.

CHAPTER 11
THE EVIDENCE ON THE GROUND

For almost two millennia, the story of the assault on Colchester was just that – a story written down by the classical authors. During the nineteenth century, there was still argument over whether or not the modern town of Colchester was really the Camulodunum of Tacitus and Dio. The favoured alternative was Maldon, based almost solely on the fact that the name sounded more like Camulodunum than Colchester. It was only in the early years of the twentieth century that the cold, hard evidence of the brutal attack was revealed in the ground. During their work in Essex around 1919-1920, the archaeologist, Sir Mortimer Wheeler, and his colleague, Dr Philip G Laver, investigated the "vaults" of the city's castle and realised that they were not vaults at all but part of the foundations of an ancient classical temple. But which temple was it? Could it really be the infamous Temple of Claudius mentioned by Tacitus and Dio? With each new discovery in the 1920s – and particularly the discoveries by Rex Hull of some ancient pottery shops in 1927 – the documentary and material records of the Boudican revolt at last began to coincide. The interest generated by each new discovery spurred many other archaeologists to take a renewed interest in what lay beneath the surface of the modern town of Colchester.

Like taking a spoonful of trifle, it was possible to dig down through the layers of time back to the early Romano-British period – and there it was: the definitive evidence that Tacitus and Dio were (broadly) telling the truth. The Boudican destruction horizon is a layer of burned red earth at a uniform level in the soil that corresponds with the period around AD 60/61. Varying in depth from half a metre or more to just a few centimetres and containing a range of deposits including fragments of pottery, tiles and other building debris, it provides a fascinating slice in time and a crucial marker for archaeologists. The pinky-red horizon is still clearly visible in the basement storeroom of Colchester's George Hotel .

Like a poor man's Pompeii, the destruction horizon has preserved some of the more intimate details of everyday life in early Roman Camulodunum which have allowed archaeologists to reconstruct glimpses of what it must have been like to live in the town around the time of Boudica's rebellion. The depth and spread of the layer also underlines just how intent on destruction Boudica's forces really were: it was no mean feat to turn Camulodunum into a raging inferno as most of the buildings were made of plaster walls and tiled roofs that were not easily combustible. Far from their traditional image of being chaotic, undisciplined fighters, the Britons must therefore have made a very deliberate, well-planned and systematic effort to set the buildings on fire to ensure the maximum amount of destruction.

It is hard to get a sense of the devastation Boudica's army wreaked on the Roman township; while some commentators use words like "holocaust" to describe what occurred, Philip Crummy, head archaeologist of the Colchester Archaeological Trust, which organises all excavations in the modern town, dislikes the term, considering it "too emotive" and also inappropriate as this wasn't ethnic cleansing but total annihilation of Romans *and* their British collaborators, "who were considered part of the problem, too". Instead, he prefers to call the sack of Camulodunum "another Dresden". "In terms of its physical appearance, this would have been a far more accurate description," he said. "The settlement would have borne all the hallmarks of a heavily shelled city – there would have been walls left standing for sure but the roofs would have completely caved in with the fire, creating the feel of a deserted, destroyed townscape. In other words, it was a merciless piece of total annihilation of both people *and* buildings by the British rebels, all wrought in the name of war."

From analysing the deposits in the burned layer, it is possible to work out what kind of buildings were present, how they were made and sometimes even the way in which they collapsed in the fire. Archaeologists have been able to identify a whole range of shops selling a variety of products: there were at least two pottery shops on the High Street which sold Samian ware – the characteristic red-glazed pottery from Gaul – though there are suggestions that one of the shops may have been destroyed in a previous fire; one building at North Hill is thought to have been a government store and contained over thirty identical and unused culinary mortar bowls whilst a nearby room and corridor threw up over eighty storage flagons; next door to these there were twenty amphorae, sadly smashed but which once contained olive oil that had come all the way from southern Spain. Colchester may have been at the "ends of the known world", but the Romans still demanded their traditional foods.

The level of detail thrown up by the excavations is astounding: in 1971, archaeologists digging away in the corner of a room in what is now Lion Walk unearthed the remains of what seemed to be a couch – about the size of a single bed – with a pair of wool-stuffed mattresses as the upholstery. From the imprint left on the remains, it was possible to work out that the fabric was a piece of twill with a diamond pattern woven into it. So why wasn't the upholstered couch taken by its original owners or by the looters? Surely such a good-looking piece of furniture would have been rescued before the room was set on fire? Once again, archaeology has been able to provide forensic evidence which might provide the answer: underneath the mattresses was the impression of a piece of rope in the floor beneath the couch – perhaps some broken webbing – suggesting that rather than being a luxury object, this was actually a rather tired, decrepit couch that was too old and broken for the inhabitants to try to save at the time of the attack. When the Britons swept through the town, they clearly considered it not worth the bother of looting, preferring to be more selective in what they took.

Finds from other buildings were a mixture of the practical and the decorative, as one might expect from everyday life in a high-status town: a complete semi-circular gridiron for cooking, a leaded bronze dice-shaker with two dice, a leaded gunmetal stamp for embossing leather and a glass cameo with a design of a sea-nymph.

The intensity of the fire also had another unexpected effect that allows us to see a snapshot of the types of food and drink the people of Camulodunum ate: rather than consuming everything in its midst, the intense heat dried out organic matter that would otherwise have decomposed while the lack of oxygen meant that other items turned to carbon and thus kept their original form. The variety of foods is surprisingly broad and exotic for a northern European town, demonstrating that many in Camulodunum were reluctant to give up their traditional Mediterranean diets. Finds have included olives, a bag of twenty-three dates, a plum, figs, lentils, beans and coriander. Flax seeds were also found at the site of the Cups Hotel in today's High Street and these would have been used to make linseed oil or cloth. Meanwhile, the discovery of more carbonised seeds, including grains of wheat, shows us that these were a large part of the Romans' staple diet – but just in case it all seems too healthy, finds also included the earliest recorded discovery in Britain of the sprouted barley/wheat mix that was used for making ale.

However, it is not just the discoveries, whether pottery, food, buildings or a whole range of metalwork brooches, latches and other metal fragments, which can tell us what was going on at the time of the Boudican revolt; what is equally telling is the *lack* of certain artefacts from the sacked town – especially the lack of gold and silver objects. This points towards a remarkably thorough looting by the rebel forces who seem to have taken anything of value other than the occasional gold coin that was clearly missed; of course, any survivors of the sacked town would also have made a detailed search for any materials that were still usable after the fire and some of these, for example some burned roof tiles, have been found recycled in the town that grew up from the ashes after the assault of AD 60/61. Archaeologists found three hoards of relatively low-value coins over a forty-year period from 1926 to 1965 but from the signs of burning on some of them, instead of them having been buried to keep them safe, they seem to have been just lying around in purses or boxes at the time of the attack rather than having been buried to keep them safe, and therefore missed by both looters and survivors alike.

While plenty of Roman–British evidence has been found, there is surprisingly little in the material record from the time that proves a link between the destruction of Camulodunum and Boudica's Iceni tribe. Only a set of bronze rings, or terets, which were used as part of horse reins, point towards the involvement of the tribe as the rings are decorated in a distinctive

Bronze head of the Emperor Claudius

style from Norfolk and North Suffolk. While this wouldn't win the case in a court of law, it is the best supporting evidence that we have from the ground as to who was behind the revolt.

More circumstantial evidence comes from the discovery of what seems to be material looted from Camulodunum, found up to sixty kilometres away. The most famous discovery is the head of Claudius. This magnificent piece of sculpture was found in the River Alde at Rendham in Suffolk by a young boy who was swimming there in 1907 and saw it lying on the riverbed. He took it home, gave it a coat of whitewash and displayed it in his garden where it was fortunately recognised for what it was – the severed head of the statue of Claudius from Camulodunum. That the statue met with a violent end is beyond doubt as the blow to the back of the head and the jagged edge where the head was ripped off the body will both testify. It would make perfect sense that the ancient head-hunters of Britain would have treasured the head of the enemy leader's statue as an object of immense symbolic and even religious value. After a violent life, its final resting place is the British Museum, which bought it for a bargain five shillings some years after its discovery.

Gravestone of Longinus Sdapeze

The violence wrought on Camulodunum was reserved not just for the town itself but spilled over in the surrounding settlements. Like the urban dwellings, these homesteads were also plundered then set on fire and their populations killed or driven away, leaving the Boudican destruction horizon to spread its red fingers out into the Essex countryside.

In terms of corroborating evidence for a motive, the discovery of two Roman gravestones has long been cited as a key illustration of just how much the Britons hated Rome. The first of the gravestones belonged to a soldier named Longinus Sdapeze who originally came from Sarfica in Thrace (what is now Sofia in Bulgaria). According to the stone's inscription, he was part of the First Squadron of the Thracian Cavalry who died aged forty with fifteen years' service and clearly much respect under his belt. The stunning artwork carved out above the engraved, square base depicts Longinus in full regalia on his decorated horse – and underneath him cowers the crouched and naked figure of a Celtic warrior. However, when he was first discovered in 1928 in a garden in Lexden Road by some workmen lowering the level of the ground, poor Longinus had no face, foot or hand; his tombstone was face-down with a large crack in the base where it had snapped.

The obvious interpretation was that Longinus's gravestone had borne the brunt of the British anger against the Romans and his stone desecrated as a result. Similarly, the magnificently carved stone of his fellow soldier, Marcus Favonius Facilis, who was a centurion of the Twentieth Legion, was also found face down and smashed. Was Facilis yet another victim of the explosion of anti-Roman feeling by the British? The lack of weathering on the fronts of each of the memorial stones indicated that they had been face down for a great many years – perhaps since the time of Boudica's revolt.

However, in 1996, the archaeologist James Fawn went back to the Lexden Road site and found not only many stone chippings but a slice of stone that contained the whole of Longinus's face, along with some other missing bodyparts. On close examination, rather than these being chopped off two

Memorial Stone of Marcus Favonius Facilis

thousand years ago, it now seems more likely that they were detached from the soldier during the building works that led to its "discovery" in 1928. As for Facilis, it seems that the base of his stone merely snapped off and ignominiously fell face-down into the dirt. Which just goes to show the dangers of trying to make the facts fit a nice, neat storyline.

There is, however, one final curious piece of evidence from the archaeology of Camulodunum which points to another worrying contradiction with the historical record. According to Tacitus and Dio, Boudica's army slaughtered anyone and everyone who crossed their path in a violent bloodbath that shocked Rome to the core. Executions were rife – and they were carried out in the cruellest and most obscene fashion. The trouble is, if that was the case then where are all the bodies?

Not a single body or even a single vestige of human remains has been found in the debris of Camulodunum despite over more than eight decades of meticulous archaeological excavation. Nor have any mass graves been found lying outside the town in the surrounding countryside. The thousands who were allegedly slaughtered seemed to have simply disappeared without trace. So – were the ancient historians lying or did they just get their facts wrong? In fact, argues Norfolk's Dr John Davies, there is very little skeletal evidence from the Iron Age in general: "It's a tough question what people were doing with their dead bodies: we think that they were normally undertaking "exposure", that is, leaving them in the open air, perhaps on platforms, like the native Americans did. However, this wouldn't have been a quick process and it's unlikely to have been undertaken for the hundreds or thousands of massacred victims from the sacked Roman towns. Are we then awaiting the discovery of grisly mass graves from the period? We just can't say."

Without the existence of a body, it is hard to prove in a court of law that a murder actually took place – and so it seems for the Colchester of AD 60/61. Documentary evidence may be there from Tacitus and Dio, but while we have graphic evidence from the ground that a catastrophic fire swept through the town around this time, we have no hard evidence at all that Boudica was to blame or that her forces killed anyone in the town.

The only body found to date in over eighty years of archaeological excavations was that found on North Hill back in 1965. Here, some charred bones – a jawbone, a piece of shoulder bone and others – were found on the clay floor of a veranda in a house outside the main focus of the town. The body – such as it was – had been much disturbed and was really not much more than a few carbonised human bones. Could the picture of mass-slaughter painted by the classical commentators therefore be overplayed? The answer is almost certainly, yes. It is clear from the evidence of the texts themselves that the population of Camulodunum had sufficient warning of the attack for Catus Decianus to send his paltry band of reinforcements; moreover, Cerealis had enough forewarning to get his troops on the move towards the beleaguered city before they were cut down in the British ambush.

More evidence comes from the archaeology itself: we can see that the houses were relatively empty of possessions – so much so, in fact, that they had to be deliberately set on fire *and then deliberately kept* on fire which was no mean feat when they were built of materials that were poor combustibles. This was no fire of London, spontaneously jumping from house to house: the houses had already been stripped bare – either by their owners or the rebel army – but both options would require time that isn't alluded to in the classical texts, time that might also have allowed for the occupants to make their escape.

This option is supported by the lack of human remains, suggesting that many of the townspeople did indeed manage to escape along with many of their possessions – either that, or the tidy-up after the holocaust was unusually thorough. In all then, it appears that while the town was indeed devastated in the attack, many of the people who lived there did survive and may even have been able to filter back to the smoking remains once Boudica moved on to her next target. But while their homes and businesses could be rebuilt and Camulodunum could rise up from the ashes, it would take much longer to dispel the awful memories of that day when the vengeful army of Britons rained down upon their heads.

The most likely suggestion is that the population who had the money and the means to escape did so. The town's residents were largely drawn from across the whole of Europe so were already well used to travelling – either from their days in the army or in their jobs as traders and workmen. They were experienced and resourceful, with a world view that stretched far beyond their back yards. They would also have had the time: unlike their Roman counterparts who could manage a forced march of twenty-five miles a day, Boudica's army would be travelling at a painfully slow pace – probably no more than around ten miles a day on the rough tracks and lanes. Even travelling flat out, it would have taken around a week to make the journey from Norfolk to Essex. What's more, the rebel army contained whole families of women and children, together with their belongings piled into wagons or carts – and these would have slowed them down even further. The people of Camulodunum would also have had the mode of escape – along the main road to London or via the River Colne to the Thames or eastwards to mainland Europe. Looking at Colchester today, it's all too easy to forget that this was once a major node of communications, both in the late Iron Age and early Roman period: without good transport links by land and water, the town would never have achieved its status as a Roman *colonia* and the seat of Roman administration. It is therefore highly unlikely that the population would just sit around and wait for death.

However, the case for the mass-slaughter of the people of Camulodunum is not entirely beyond belief. One final explanation for the lack of bodies comes from the words of Dio. He describes how the townspeople were taken away to sacred groves where they were then executed in the foulest of manners. This could certainly account for the lack of bodies found in the town itself. While the thought of Boudica's army dragging their victims off for execution might sound savage, it's important to remember that these were not just a bellicose mob on the warpath, they were a profoundly religious people who believed in gods that demanded blood sacrifice. Head-hunting had long been a part of the culture of the Celtic-speaking world, as was blood-sacrifice to propitiate the gods. It is just possible, therefore, that the mass graves from the Boudica revolt are still lying somewhere under the cold, wet earth, as yet to be uncovered. But one thing is certain: the Camulodunum that was rebuilt *after* the revolt was nowhere near as large or as crowded as the town that was the Romans' showcase in Britain up until Boudica rode into town. Something happened to make those people disappear – and the answer to that question is still out there, waiting to be revealed.

CHAPTER 12
BOUDICA'S ASSAULT ON LONDON

News of Boudica's attack on Colchester shocked the Romans to the core. When he learned the full horror of the disaster that had befallen the town, the immediate problem for governor Suetonius Paulinus was to get back from the North Wales coast as quickly as possible to meet the rebels in battle and redeem the honour of the empire. Camulodunum was not just the home of the legionary veterans, it was the showcase of Roman Britain so any attack on the town was an affront to the achievements of Caesar, Claudius and now the Emperor Nero – and imperial insults were not to be tolerated. There was also the small matter of Paulinus's personal reputation which was something he took very seriously: being known as that governor who lost Rome its northernmost province was not a title he particularly craved.

London (Londinium) at the time of Boudica's revolt in AD 60.
Note the difference in settlements between the grid-like Roman town
and the more organic development of the Ancient Britons

However, having just launched the attack on the Druids of Anglesey, he and the bulk of his men were three hundred miles from the enemy who were by now undoubtedly swaggering with the victory of their first successful assault against Rome. So far, the Britons had travelled south from the lands of the Iceni to those of their new Trinovantes allies and now it seemed they were all headed towards the trading port of Londinium which nestled on the banks of the River Thames. Londinium was a relatively new town, set up by the Romans to serve as a good centre for trade to the Continent and also inland to the rest of Britannia – and as a town based on trade, it offered relatively rich pickings for the rebel army. It was also poorly defended; in other words, it was an obvious target for their next attack.

Prior to the invasion of AD 43, there were Iron Age people living around Southwark and the rest of the Thames Valley in isolated homesteads on the higher, less marshy lands that otherwise dominated the local landscape, but within a few years of the Claudian conquest, the landscape was already beginning to change. Compared with its modern descendent, the Thames of early Roman Britain was a broad, slow-flowing tidal river some three hundred metres wide at low tide and over a thousand metres wide at high tide, with a vertical rise and fall of no less than a metre and a half at the site of the now-developing settlement. Before the advent of a bridge and to a lesser extent even after its construction, it would have been a familiar sight to see small ferry boats shuttling merchants and the town's inhabitants back and forth between the north and south banks to the small clusters of buildings that were starting to grow up there.

The Thames offered a natural barrier between the increasingly Romanised lands to the south and east and the more traditional cultures of the north and west. However, in terms of development, the north bank offered the best opportunities for settlement, being higher in elevation with hills and definite watercourses like the Walbrook Stream; its southern partner was characterised by the marshy, flood-prone land that had caused such problems for both Caesar and Claudius.

Although its name was given by the Romans, the word Londinium appears to be ancient British in origin and was first applied to the small settlement that grew up on the north bank of the Thames from around AD 50, seven years after the Claudian invasion. The first few buildings were located on the raised ground at what is now Cornhill, east of the Walbrook stream; this was also the intersection where the road from the crossing point of the River Thames bisected the road that ran in an east-west direction between the Roman towns of Verulamium (modern St Albans), about twenty-five miles away to the north-west and Camulodunum, around forty miles to the north-east.

Strategically, the siting of Londinium was an inspired choice offering facilities for sea-faring ships to sail right up the Thames estuary to deliver their cargoes and then reload with all the desirable British goods listed by Strabo: hunting dogs, slaves, iron, tin, gold and silver. Londinium also offered a suitable location from which the new Roman overlords could administer both the north and south of the new province.

This proto-town was centred about twenty metres downstream of the current London Bridge where two Roman roads were re-routed to converge. Around this crossing point, strange new buildings of wood, clay, timber and mudbrick began to grow up on the horizon – buildings that would have seemed most foreign to the indigenous population. Although the Ancient Britons were curious enough and canny enough to know that here was a way to improve their lot – to begin with at least, they preferred to stay living in their traditional roundhouses around the town's periphery.

It did not take long for the first new shops to start appearing though they tended to be small affairs with the shop or workshop at the front and the living quarters at the back. One of the craftsmen who had set up shop in the growing settlement was Caius Albucius from western Switzerland, who was an entrepreneurial potter; he set up a workshop in London, stamping his name on the neck of a flagon which survived the Boudican assault, to be discovered by archaeologists two thousand years later. He would have been typical of the geographical range of immigrants, relatively few of whom would have been from Rome or even Italy. We also know of a manufacturer of blown glass and a cutter or engraver of precious stones that were used to make personal seals but there would have been hundreds of others – craftspeople, artisans, financiers and merchants – whose personal stories of how they came to be

Typical Iron Age roundhouse, Butser Ancient Farm, Hampshire

in Londinium have long since faded into oblivion.

The Roman culture was much more cosmopolitan and mercantile than that of the Iron Age Britons who had got by for centuries on occasional trade along the old drove roads and pathways. Now, aided by the beginnings of a road network and the growing use of the Thames for organised trade, Londinium was poised to take off for a glorious two thousand years of history making. Although it was not clearly state-sponsored like the prestigious Camulodunum, there was a definite sense of order behind the chaotic façade of the new town that points to the development of some form of town council, with tell-tale signs of the characteristic planned grid system of streets and rectangular buildings, some of which were provided with water from wooden pipes.

Within a few years of its development, buildings had sprawled southwards to the suburb at Southwark suggesting some kind of bridge or ferry crossing; they had also encroached westwards across the Walbrook stream towards Ludgate Hill; to the north of the growing settlement, around modern Gracechurch Street, a small forum or market square was also constructed with a gravelled floor to keep off the worst of the mud from the goods that were bought and sold. Londinium was most certainly a town that was on the up; through it were filtered all the products (and profits) of the new province: slaves from Scotland, jet from Whitby, lead from the Midlands, gold from Wales, marble from the Isle of Wight, and corn, wool, pottery, cattle and oysters from East Anglia. Britain was now part of a major trading empire.

And it was to this bastion of Roman culture that Boudica was now headed. Unlike Camulodunum, Londinium was purely a trading town; it had no major fort, no colony of veterans, no real military status at all, though it does seem to have already positioned itself as a centre of administration as the procurator Catus Decianus appears to have based himself here, albeit unofficially, before his rapid departure to Gaul. It was also from here that Decianus was seemingly able to drum up the two hundred poorly armed troops to send to Camulodunum's aid. But despite its lack of imperial patronage, Londinium was truly and undoubtedly a Roman creation – and that meant it had immense symbolism as a target. In terms of the feel of the new town, it would have had the same buzz as the colonial towns of New York or Chicago, Sydney or Wellington at the start of the nineteenth century – a constant clatter of cartwheels on stony roads, the smell of strange foods cooking, the square sails flapping on ships and boats in the docks and all manner of different accents and languages as the multicultural population plied their trades in a bid to make their fortunes.

With its prime location as the centre of the communications hub of the new province, it would not have taken long for word to filter back to Londinium's population that there was trouble brewing among the Iceni, and with Camulodunum just forty miles away, it would only have taken little more than a full day for news of the *colonia*'s demise to reach the town by horseback.

One can only imagine the growing feeling of anxiety among a population of around thirty thousand people who were so conspicuously foreign and who so symbolised the new ways of the occupying Roman forces. Even more anxious must have been the Britons who had cast in their lot with the immigrants; they would have known only too well what a warring army of Iceni, Trinovantes and all manner of other tribes would think of those who had gone over to the side of the Romans: by colluding with the enemy, they would share in their fate – just as the native Britons had done in the destruction of Camulodunum. Jenny Hall, Roman curator at the Museum of London, goes one step further: "I think that Boudica's army would have wreaked even *more* vengeance on anyone who collaborated with the Romans, and this ties in with the reports of the atrocities in the classical texts. There was quite a substantial number of native Britons who had thrown in their lot with the Romans, especially women who had married or set up home with those involved in the Roman army and administration. Of course many of those would have been evacuated before Boudica's army arrived as there would have been plenty of warning for the attack; but those who remained would have come off even worse than the Romans."

But it wasn't just the town's obvious Romanisation that put people under threat. In terms of defence, the population of Londinium knew that they were seriously vulnerable. In all likelihood, Catus Decianus had sent any spare troops to the bloodbath at Camulodunum and it's doubtful that many, if any, could have returned; what's more, the procurator who was meant to offer some leadership to the province had now fled to Gaul, leaving the Londoners to try to save themselves. With Paulinus and the main bulk of the Roman Army over in Wales – and the absence of any large structural defences even if they had the manpower and arms to hold them – there was no real hope that they could put up a fight. Their only chance was that Paulinus would be able to race to Londinium in time to help them, but with every hour that passed without the sound of the returning governor and his troops, the despair grew into terror.

The adage that you can win the battle but lose the war, can be proved by what happened next with the two respective armies. While Boudica's army was celebrating their victory over the Romans in Camulodunum, Paulinus was already working out his battle strategy. Camulodunum to Londinium was just over two days' hard march for a Roman soldier but for Boudica's army, it would have taken much longer. Unlike Paulinus, Boudica did not have the advantage of unquestioned leadership: as more and more warriors of neighbouring tribes swelled their ranks on their journey south to Londinium, her army grew larger – and more unwieldy. Separate tribal and regional factions were as much used to fighting each other as fighting the Romans; they now jostled and boasted about who were the better warriors, who had the best loot, who had the better weapons; after all, theirs was a display culture where bravery and bravado went very much hand in hand.

Meanwhile, Paulinus knew that an army was judged by the end result – not by how they got there. Leaving the main bulk of his forces to finish off their work in Anglesey, he took a small detachment of cavalry and raced to the great mercantile town on the Thames where he could clearly assess the mounting military crisis. Once his troops were finished with the Druids, they would have to follow on as best they could in a forced march down what would later be called Watling Street.

Paulinus's route to London is the subject of much debate: did he head overland through Wales and then directly to the south-east – or did he take advantage of the westerly winds and sail in a fast galley to Chester before proceeding by horse to the beleaguered town? Whichever route he took, he arrived in Londinium before Boudica and quickly took stock of his options. With the British army heading towards their next target, he knew his own men would never beat them to defend the town. He had only managed his own speedy arrival by bringing with him only a small unit of cavalry and there was no way he could take on Boudica's forces with so few men. As he looked around at the abandoned streets, the whole place must have had an air of impending doom about it. Many of the young and useful people in the town had already made their escape, taking with them as many of their wares as they could find transport for; others had shut up shop and headed into the outlying settlements.

Unusually for such a hardened military man, Tacitus reports that Paulinus suffered some uncertainty about what his next course of action should be. Should he stay and defend the town or use the time and distraction of abandoning it to Boudica's army to get his troops into shape for the kind of battle the Romans liked best? He no doubt met with the civic leaders and surveyed the hushed streets and lack of defences; he knew there was only one answer: it may have seemed heartless to some and profligate to others, but Paulinus was governor and his decision was final: he gave the command to gather together as many of the population who were willing and able to leave – and then ordered his men to get out of Londinium as quickly as possible before the hordes of angry tribes descended and wreaked devastation on the town.

For the stunned population, the truth was hard to swallow. Many refused to believe that the mightiest nation on earth was not prepared to defend its own people and they pleaded with the governor to change his mind and save them. No doubt had the town had some kind of imperial status, the decision would have been harder, though the end result might still not have changed. Instead, Paulinus held his ground: he could not risk the same annihilation that the veterans and Cerealis's men had suffered in order to save what was little more than a shanty town with a few key public buildings. It may have been a thriving model of entrepreneurship but whereas houses, shops, docks and public buildings can go on to have a second lease of life, humans can't rise from the ashes and start themselves again.

Those who were able to escape with the cavalry could be offered some protection by the army; some preferred to make their own way along the extensive network of routes to the military areas a few days' walk or cart ride away. Some may have even headed out to the well-defended and "safe" kingdom of Cogidubnus where they would have been assured of a friendly reception. However, for the others, their only recourse was to try and hold themselves together and convince themselves that all would be well – even though the experience of Camulodunum had proved that this was now beyond the realms of possibility. Roman London was left to the vengeance of the British.

The sight of Paulinus, his cavalry and the rabble of refugees leaving the town must have been a hideous experience for those who, in the words of Tacitus, were too "tied to the place by the weakness of their sex, or the infirmity of age, or the attractions of the area". Once the bulk of the population had gone, the normally bustling streets would have had an eerie silence. However, the moment the silence finally broke in all its terrifying clamour, the noise was only part of a general precipitation of violence that rained down on the town.

There are few human details in any of the classical accounts of the uprising which tell just how Boudica's army actually descended on Londinium but the version given by Dio is almost beyond imagination in its level of horror. What

Tacitus refers to as being "cut off", Dio regards as being "indescribable slaughter"; the fact that Dio then goes on to describe the slaughter in such gross detail gives the modern audience the initial impression that they are surely just reading an "urban myth". The salacious descriptions were no doubt included as much for their dramatic effect as any real claim to truth: these "histories" were designed to be spoken out loud as entertainment as much as read silently to oneself. However, even if they contained just a smidgen of truth, they would still offend every shred of sentiment known to humankind. He writes:

> "The most vile and inhuman atrocity committed by their captors was the following. They strung up naked the noblest and most refined women and then cut off their breasts which they sewed into their mouths, in order to make the victims appear to be eating them; afterwards they skewered the women on sharp sticks run lengthwise through the entire body."
>
> CASSIUS DIO: HISTORIES, BOOK 62

The crimes of barbarity are heaped upon the Britons: not only do they strip high-status women naked when those women come from a society that deems married women should even cover their heads out of piety and modesty, this act is compounded by them slicing off the very symbols of their sexuality and then abusing the flesh by sewing it into their mouths to "shut them up". If true, were the Britons suggesting that the Romans "eat their words" having ordered a similar sexual humiliation of their queen and her daughters? Was this some deeply spiritual act that the gods demanded as a type of payment? The simulated raping of the women by impaling them lengthways on wooden skewers has a clear meaning in terms of it sexual violence – but was this a religious act or merely revenge for the abuse of the princesses that married crucifixion and execution with the most hideous form of counter-rape?

There are no human bodies which serve as witness to the testimony of Dio and no supporting evidence from the material remains of the town. The hundred or so "Walbrook skulls" that were found in the Walbrook stream and which were for long linked with the Boudican uprising have also now been cleared of any involvement. Not only do they fail to show any signs of violence which would surely be evident if the people died in a bloody battle, most of the skulls are those of young men – precisely the type of people who would have been willing and able to flee the town in advance of the British army. Furthermore, the lack of jawbones on the skulls is a sign that they lay around decomposing for perhaps months before being deposited in the water when the jawbones fell off. Although the find was impressive, the facts cannot be made to fit the Boudica storyline.

As for the descriptions so graphically told by Dio, if the historian was trying to shock his audience then even in that culture of gladiatorial games, he must have succeeded, for barbaric behaviour is necessarily the work of barbarians or "foreigners" who would fight like animals when they are cornered. If anyone in the empire doubted that the provinces needed the civilising force of Rome then surely this was the proof, for what we have in Dio is a two-thousand-year-old snuff movie. But he doesn't stop there:

> *"They did all this accompanied by sacrifices, banquets, and lewd behaviour, not only in all their other sacred places, but especially in the grove of Andate. This was their goddess of Victory, and they regarded her with most exceptional reverence."*
>
> CASSIUS DIO: *HISTORIES, BOOK 62*

Suddenly, what first appeared to be no more than a dramatic "urban myth" begins to gain a macabre ring of truth. The religious underpinnings of the gruesome rites laid out in this passage by Dio cleverly evoke a barbaric bloodfest that is only stopped from being totally bestial by the reference to their "exceptional reverence"; in every other way, the Britons have no more morals than a pack of wild animals that will kill, gorge themselves and fornicate without compunction. However, in a culture that buried its dead with their weapons and most prized possessions, it would be fitting that high-status human female sacrifices should be given to propitiate a war-goddess and seek her benevolence in a revolution against the enemy. Leading archaeologist Philip Crummy bears witness to the fact that to the ancient Britons, as to many cultures, it was unthinkable to execute a virgin. The solution? "You would rape her first, then kill her." It might seem shocking today, but it would have been entirely coherent with an ancient moral code.

As for the goddess referred to as Andate – or Andraste as she is called by Tacitus – her name bears a striking resemblance to Andarte, a goddess worshipped by the Vocontii of Gaul. Some have also commented on possible links with Andred, a lunar mother-goddess of fertility. There is not enough evidence to say beyond doubt whether or not they are one and the same but there is certainly no doubt that Celtic people throughout Europe worshipped goddesses of war. What's more, we know that women were intimately associated with the battlefield, either in the role of goddess, Druidess priestess or warriors, or as wives, mothers and daughters who would frequently position themselves at the edge of the battlefield to spur on their men to feats of heroism and keep themselves out of harm's way from a marauding enemy.

Meanwhile, what Tacitus and Dio fail to tell us about the sack of London, we can see to some extent from the archaeology. The Boudican destruction horizon is almost as evident here as it is in Colchester but it appears to be more patchy and less intense. However, any reference to intensity is strictly relative: the molten glass and level of destruction found still point to temperatures in the region of a thousand degrees – hot enough not to want to be around. The red layer of burned daub from the buildings is typically around twenty-five to sixty centimetres deep, indicating that the crumbling buildings were only a single storey high, just like the majority of buildings in Camulodunum and Verulamium; another similarity between the three towns is that the buildings appear to have been largely empty.

There have been some interesting and poignant discoveries from the destruction layer, such as the four sealstones hidden from view in a pot in what appears to be a jewellery shop in Eastcheap, while in King William Street a hoard of seventeen burned bronze coins from the reign of the Emperor Claudius was discovered. Their owner had never returned to retrieve them: was this an indication of his fate?

Other discoveries have also shed light on the Londinium of AD 60/61. When digging underneath what is now Fenchurch Steet in the City, archaeologists found a store room containing dark beads that turned out to be cereal that had been burned in the Boudican fire of London. Closer investigation began to tell a more fascinating story: the grains included einkorn which was cultivated further south in Europe rather than in Britain itself. This showed that some of the grain had been imported into Britain from overseas – but why should Britain be importing grain when it should have been producing enough to meet its own needs? One possible answer is that there had been something of a bad harvest or famine in the province during the previous season and so the traders had started to buy in grain. Could this have been an additional cause of the general unrest amongst the Britons that was so troubling to the Romans at the time? Given that the native population had to pay some of their taxes in the form of grain, it is quite possible that the Romans would have given them the choice to either pay their taxes and go hungry – or face the consequences. Perhaps this time the ancient Britons had simply had enough: they decided to take matters into their own hands, brokering their own kind of violent resolution.

Two of the largest towns in Roman Britain now lay in ashes; Boudica's army had done its job well. But the thirst for revenge had not yet been slaked: to the north-west lay another symbol of the hated foreign rule – this time, not a Roman town *per se* but a town of British collaborators who appeared to glory in everything Roman-style. And for Boudica's army, this was a cultural insult too graphic to bear. Slowly gathering their people around them, the tribes began their next journey north-west.

CHAPTER 13
BOUDICA'S ASSAULT ON ST ALBANS

The Roman town of Verulamium was not really Roman at all. Nestling in the gently undulating landscape of what's now Hertfordshire, it had its roots in the Iron Age settlement of Verlamion, ruled by the Catuvellauni tribe. Verlamion was not only well established, it was well defended by the traditional series of earthworks such as dykes and ramparts which extended around farmsteads and areas of open countryside. Its Catuvellauni leaders were originally of Belgic extraction and they now ruled over one of the most powerful and prosperous tribes in the whole of Britain. At the time of invasion by Julius Caesar in 54 BC, their warrior-king Cassivellaunus had his base at what had been the tribal stronghold of Wheathampstead, a few miles to the north-east of Verlamion. However, following his defeat by the Romans, the tribe had expanded north and west while transferring their base to Verlamion, near to modern-day St Albans. Their enormous wealth seems to have come largely from agriculture and this is certainly supported by evidence from the pollen record around Verlamion showing that vast swathes of landscape had been cleared for livestock and arable production which would have been capable of supporting the high-status – therefore non-productive – members of the ruling elite.

The name Verlamion comes to us from the coin record of the later Catuvellauni ruler, Tasciovanus, who reigned in the area from around 15 BC to c.AD 10. From the number of coin-moulds found at the site – and particularly in one small area under what was to become the forum and basilica complex – it seems he had a mint at Verlamion and therefore it was possibly also the site of his royal residence. There is certainly archaeological evidence of a large cremation cemetery in use from around AD 1 to 60 at what is now King Harry Lane. The wealth and geographical spread of the burial goods suggests that the inhabitants of Verlamion were far from being country bumpkins – they were high-status individuals with strong connections to the major trading areas of Europe and further afield. Equally remarkable for a modern audience is the fragment of human skull from Folly Lane in the town that grew up after the Roman conquest. The possibility that they had kept this fragment as a trophy or religious object perhaps stands as testament to the enduring significance of head-hunting in Iron Age Britain; clearly, this was an item of such high value that it could not be thrown away even when fashions changed.

When Tasciovanus died at the start of the new millennium, he was succeeded by the powerful King Cunobelin and the new leader of the Catuvellauni seems to have increased the tribe's wealth and status. It was Cunobelin who went on to defeat the neighbouring Trinovantes tribe in Essex, developing the Iron Age fortified settlement at Camulodunum which was taken over by the Romans to become the effective capital of the whole new province of Britannia. Under Roman rule, the old enmity between the Trinovantes and the Catuvellauni tribes had been forcibly suppressed but now the cork was out of the bottle: this time it was the Trinovantes who were riding high on their new-found independence as part of Boudica's rebel army – and they were longing to settle old scores.

Perhaps because they were already such a progressive and relatively wealthy people, after Claudius's invasion of AD 43, the Catuvellauni population of Iron Age Verlamion rapidly took up new Roman styles and ideas and soon they were calling the settlement by the Romanised name of Verulamium. Without any real imperial assistance, they now shook off their agricultural mantle and started building an unashamedly Romano–British town – the third largest in the province. The Romans were so impressed by the attitude and achievements of the population that they not only routed one of their most important roads – later called Watling Street – through Verulamium, the town also won the Roman privilege of being classed as a *municipium*, just one step down from a *colonia* like Camulodunum. As the only site awarded this honour, the impact was enormous;

it meant that the local magistrates and their families could effectively become Roman citizens, with all the privileges that citizenship afforded.

Although we might not recognise it as something we would call a town today, from what is left in the archaeological record of the old town of Verulamium in its pre-Boudica days one gets the feeling that there was an enormous sense of civic pride. They had no large Roman forts or garrisons, no Roman governors or procurators directing the town's development, no one telling them what to do. The local Iron Age population had built upon the strengths of their native settlement and developed the town *by* themselves and *for* themselves; as well as all the traditional features of their pre-conquest lives, they could now look upon the rows of rectangular and sometimes even stone houses, shops and buildings festooned with grand colonnaded walkways and know that they had built their new "townscape" in the very latest fashion.

By the summer of AD 60/61 as rumours of Boudica's attacks turned into eyewitness accounts, the Catuvellauni of Verulamium also knew that their town was the next in line to face the wrath of Boudica's army. This time, there were few amongst the population who would wrap themselves in denial: by now, word of the destruction of the Romans' base at Camulodunum and the similar fate of their trading port at London had spread across much of the province. If the Romans were unable to defend the former and unwilling to even try to save the latter, what hope did the largely British population have of help from their foreign overlords? The answer was clear: it was time to move out.

While the buildings and streets of Verulamium were slowly emptying of both people and possessions, the smouldering remains of Roman Londinium were also being abandoned – but this time by the ecstatic army of rebel Britons. With their plunder-lust sated, it was time for the great army to head north-west. With two major victories under their belts, the Iceni and their comrades were riding high on a wave of glory with an orgy of feasting, drinking and celebrating to honour their success. For Boudica and her chiefs, it must have been hard to re-kindle the momentum they needed to continue their assault against the Romans but they knew that Suetonius Paulinus and the main bulk of the Roman army were not far away: they may have won two battles but as for the war itself – that was far from being over.

Slowly the vast, cumbersome rebel army began to get underway, wagons groaning under the weight of their proud families and their plundered loot. Imagine a massive football stadium spilling out its crowds, the hordes spreading further and further afield. The Britons were slowly slithering their way north, leaving a trail of destruction behind them. As for a strategy, it is not clear that they had much of one beyond sacking any settlements that were home to their enemies and ultimately trying to free Britain from the tyranny of their Roman masters. Other than a few elderly former mercenaries who had fought against Rome in Gaul or maybe the lands around the Rhine, they had little knowledge of dealing with an organised enemy; most of their own battles had been against their neighbours and even these were sometimes fought by single champions in hand-to-hand combat, so organising a major war against a powerful military machine such as the Roman army and outside their own lands was completely beyond their experience.

To modern eyes, the obvious thing to do would have been to try to intercept Paulinus before he could re-join his legions, leaving the soldiers rudderless and the province without either governor or procurator. Such ambushes played to the Britons' strength: they had already done this with deadly effect to the forces of Cerealis and in theory they could do it again. It would then be a matter of routing the military bases around the country to show the Romans that their precious province was no more than a piece of imperial arrogance. But what then? Before the Roman invasion, there was no such concept as "Britain" from within the island and no sense of the people being one nation, just a host of warring tribes. And as the Catevellauni were about to discover, those ancient tribal enmities ran very deep indeed.

At Boudica's signal, the Britons exploded into the enemy town and soon got to work, killing any inhabitants who had failed to escape, looting what remained of the town's possessions and then setting on fire what was left. It didn't take long to rip through the settlement, but it seemed that, for the first time since they launched the uprising, their luck was beginning to change. The winds were now blowing against their advance, making it harder to get the buildings to burn with the intensity they needed to completely destroy all vestiges of the town. It could also have been that by now, the rebel forces were growing tired of burning empty buildings which had been stripped bare by their owners.

There is still the same thick layer of burned, red earth as testimony to the ferocity of the fire and the havoc it wreaked on the daub buildings. Evidence remains, too, of the same Samian pottery with its red slip glaze blackened by burning and the stumps of blackened wall that are all that was left of the grandiose buildings at the heart of the town. However, as the winds changed direction and the consuming fires lost their teeth, some of the buildings in the south-west corner of one block of buildings known as *insula XVII* managed to remain intact; likewise some outbuildings to the shops in the north-east corner of the same *insula* similarly escaped the torchings, while thirty-seven unused Samian pots also escaped being looted though when they were found they were spilling out across the veranda as if the shop itself has been thoroughly vandalised. Other finds include two complete pots that filled up with burned daub as the building surrounding them went up in flames; the remains of a burned wooden water tub have also been found, still full of burned material from the walls and ceilings of the room but a nearby pit bears witness that the linen chest inside it failed to make it through the firestorm.

The most striking difference between the remains from Verulamium and the other sacked towns is that here not a single hoard of coins has been found, nor has any grain been discovered. This can only point to one thing – that the population had time to make a thorough evacuation of the town and left nothing of real value to the advancing rebels. If nothing else, that would have left the Catuvellauni with some small sense of satisfaction over their old rivals.

For the warring Britons, without much in the way of killing and looting to fuel their passion, sacking a town was a lacklustre task compared to the richer pickings of both London and Colchester. They finished their business as quickly as they could and then moved on to find more and perhaps better-equipped targets elsewhere.

As the tidal wave of violence crashed out into the surrounding lands, outlying farms and wealthy Romanised homesteads fell prey to the advancing mob. Evidence of the destruction horizon extends well beyond the town itself, showing that the rebels burned anything they could get their hands on. Five kilometres from the town centre, the mob destroyed a house that lay just to the east of Watling Street in modern Park Street; this was burned down to its clay floors. And to slake their thirst for revenge, two kilometres north-west of Verulamium, Boudica's army laid waste to another farmstead even though this was defended by the traditional earthworks of a ditch and neighbouring rampart. There is little doubt that the family it contained were Britons, not Romans: although there were rectangular outbuildings, the house itself was a native roundhouse. It seems the rebels were now reverting to their former days of internecine warfare – and all the while, the greater enemy under the ruthless command of Suetonius Paulinus was regaining its strength and devising its plan for what would become the ultimate battle of Britain.

CHAPTER 14
THE FINAL BATTLE

Three towns now lay in smouldering ruins: three towns, and according to Tacitus, some seventy thousand "citizens and allies" had been killed, plus the fifteen hundred or so crack troops of Cerealis. This level of devastation gave Suetonius Paulinus a problem: these were not the kind of numbers that he would want to be sending in his dispatches back to Rome. Even though the figures quoted by Tacitus are almost certainly exaggerated, there is no doubt that substantial proportions of Romans and Roman sympathisers had been wiped out by Boudica's army. This not only physically loosened the Romans' hold on the territory, it also weakened their intellectual capital in terms of "Romanising" those parts of Britain that the military could not reach. To lose a province would be unfortunate in the extreme; to lose it to a woman would just be sheer recklessness. While the later reports of the number of casualties enhanced the reputation and threat of the warrior queen – and in turn, the reputation of anyone who could defeat her – even half the reported seventy thousand dead would have represented a serious disaster in the eyes of the emperor and Nero was not a man that anyone in their right mind would want to upset.

The little that we know of Paulinus's career suggests that he was reasonably experienced in dealing with revolts and uprisings: twenty years ealier he had been sent to Mauretania to quash the trouble there; and, according to Pliny the Elder, he had conquered the Atlas mountains of North Africa in just ten days, but even that feat must have seemed ancient history when faced with the challenge ahead of him in the form of Boudica and her victorious army.

After he had abandoned Londinium to the devastation of her forces, he and his men rode hard to get back along Watling Street to regroup his main forces. According to Dio's account of the rebellion, Paulinus would have liked more time to delay the confrontation – possibly even until the following season – but his men were growing short of rations and he was forced to take some definitive action. As for Tacitus, he makes no mention of this and instead prefers to concentrate on the more constructive, positive tale of a governor he clearly respects.

For their part, the British were buoyed up by the successes of the last three battles. Having wiped out the three largest towns in Roman Britain, they had every right to feel elated by their achievements but this was no time to rest on their laurels. Boudica would have known that Paulinus was north-west of the smouldering remains of Verulamium; and she would know that *he* would know where she was now – and that she was coming after him. Traditionally, the British tribes had always had their greatest successes in the type of guerrilla warfare fought by leaders like Caratacus when they could catch the Romans off guard and unawares. Boudica had already witnessed the brutal success of her warriors cutting down the soldiers of Cerealis in this way. The problems came when the enemy had a chance to organise itself and set in motion the devastating killing machine that had made the Romans first masters of the Mediterranean and then masters of Europe. Pitched battles were not the Britons' forte but perhaps – just perhaps – things were now beginning to change.

The gods had looked favourably upon her army in the last three battles where not even the pride of the Romans in their capital town could resist the bravery and sheer numbers of her warriors. She had honoured Andraste with the blood of her victims in the sacred groves and that would surely make them pleased with her actions. The only problem was now her army itself: it had grown so large with its success that her warriors were becoming impossible to co-ordinate; what's more, the old habit of fighting each other rather than uniting against a common enemy was beginning to rear its ugly head. Boudica's success now rested on keeping her army focused and being able to use the sheer numbers of warriors to overwhelm an entire Roman army if – and when – it came to battle.

Few details are known of the movements of both armies between the sacking of Verulamium and the final battle; even less is known about the location of where they met. Arguments about the actual site abound, from Surrey to Birmingham to Towcester but what is almost certain is that

Paulinus would have tried to keep as many details as possible on his terms, not Boudica's. And in many ways, he still had some advantages on his side. He would have known that her numbers totally outstripped his own but her army was untrained, so he had to use skill to outwit the greater army; he would also have realised that his strength lay in forcing the British into a pitched battle that was fought at a time and in a place and manner that he could control; he might also have guessed that his local knowledge could well have been better than hers, for the Iceni had generally stayed within their tribal lands over in the far east. He also had the benefit of having spent at least three seasons fighting in the hilly areas of western Britannia so his men not only had the experience, he knew how to pick an advantageous site for the battle.

Dio alleges that Boudica had an army of two hundred and thirty thousand people and even though this is probably grossly inflated, even half of this number would have looked invincible; Suetonius Paulinus had assembled around ten thousand men from parts of his Twentieth Legion, the Fourteenth Legion and various local auxiliaries. He had previously sent for the Second Legion Augusta, founded by the former Emperor Augustus, but its commander, Poenius Postumus, had failed to deliver the necessary men. It is highly unlikely that Postumus would have actively disobeyed a command from the governor himself; what is more likely is that he was genuinely unable to spare the men due to some trouble near his own base in Exeter, and there is some evidence of a rebellion in Somerset around this period. However impossible it might have seemed to respond at the time, it was a decision that would cost him his life.

It is unclear whether Paulinus ever received word from the Second Augusta that they were not going to arrive, but he was not able to wait much longer. Boudica's forces were steadily advancing and gearing themselves up for more glorious battles that would rid their lands of the foreigners who dared to make them slaves. It is likely that the Britons would have followed Paulinus north-west along Watling Street. As for the location of where they finally met, all we have to go on is a brief description by Tacitus which, although it sounds vague, may well have drawn on the eyewitness account of his father-in-law, Agricola, who at that time was fighting under Paulinus as an officer in the Twentieth Legion:

> *"[Suetonius Paulinus] chose a position approached by a narrow defile, shut*
> *off at the rear by a forest, having first ensured that there were no enemy soldiers*
> *except at his front, where an open plain extended without any threat of*
> *ambush.".*

TACITUS: ANNALS, XIV. 34

It is not hard to see why Paulinus chose this spot: the narrow defile or steep-side gorge would have shoehorned Boudica's troops into a funnel so instead of the Romans having to face a giant bloc of marauding warriors, their flow would be regulated by the physical geography of the site, giving the Romans much more in the way of control. By choosing this site, Paulinus had also protected himself from being attacked from the rear as no chariot and few warriors could effectively fight from within a forest. And in front of the Romans was a plain – a wide open space where the Britons would not only be completely exposed but the manoeuvres of both sides would be clearly visible to the commander of the troops who would then be able to orchestrate the best tactics on the day.

But where exactly is this final, infamous battlefield? It's a question that has kept both academics and pundits entertained for generations since the idea first arose of matching the classical texts with a host of British antiquarian "discoveries". An early favourite from the eighteenth century was Primrose Hill in north London – largely because it was a "sacred" site for the recently re-formed Order of Druids so it accrued some mythical connections to the past. Another north London possibility has been mooted as Battlebridge Road – largely because of its name though there is no mention of a bridge in any of the classical accounts.

The trouble is that while Tacitus's description may be tantalisingly detailed, it is almost meaningless in its lack of context and the changes wrought on the landscape of Britain over the last two thousand years. Not only do we not have the site itself, we don't even know the Romans' route from Anglesey to London and then westwards. But perhaps this misses the point: this lack of clarity is another key factor in keeping the appetite for the Boudica story whetted; in the absence of some definitive archaeological discovery, arguments will just keep on running.

The leading favourite of recent years has been Mancetter in Warwickshire in the West Midlands, north-west of Verulamium along Watling Street. Unlike some of the other more ludicrous suggestions, this had the ardent support of the late archaeologist and Boudica expert Graham Webster along with Dr Paul Sealey and Jenny Hall – and it makes logical sense in terms of Paulinus's movements and Boudica's likely response, although it does take both armies reasonably far north. Moreover, there are nice geographical features which seem to fit with Tacitus's description of where the battle took place: bisecting Watling Street near Atherstone lies a ridge of old, hard rock running north-west to south-east that could fit with the description of the landscape. Was the "open plain" that this ridge overlooks really the flood plain of the modern-day River Anker? Topographically, the area seems to match quite well and although the ridge itself has been extensively quarried for gravel over the past few hundred years, it is still possible to see some narrow defiles along its length which equate to that described by the Roman historian. Other pieces of circumstantial evidence come from the archaeology itself: a series of infilled ditches have been excavated here since the 1950s, throwing up pottery from the reign of Nero, and the trench for a new drain at the local manor house revealed a small hoard of bronze and coppper Claudian military coins – likely to have been some small change buried by a soldier. A final discovery adds more weight to Webster's choice of battlesite: whilst digging in his garden, a near-neighbour of the Manor House uncovered three complete amphorae on top of a clay floor. Further investigation revealed an entire military site lying deep under the village at Mancetter but until this is fully investigated, the likelihood that Mancetter is the battlefield remains open to question.

A more recent suggestion for the battlefield is just north of Verulamium along Watling Street. The site around Cuttle Mill, near the Roman town of Towcester, has long been the origin of much local folklore about buried treasure and ancient battles. Its Northamptonshire location puts it potentially right on track for a meeting point between the advancing British army and the Legions heading back south from Anglesey, in what would be a twelve-day march. Like Mancetter, its geography seems to fit neatly with the description and logic of Tacitus: there is indeed an open plain near to the river that leads to a narrow valley that would have almost certainly been bounded by woods. So was *this* the site of the famous last battle? The British Museum's Iron Age expert, J D Hill, thinks that it's feasible: "I don't think Boudica got as far as the Midlands as some people assume, so would lay my bet around the Chilterns to the north-west of St Albans, although if further north then not as far as the Fosse Way. The Romans would want to retreat to Gloucester or Exeter if they lost, which is why Towcester seems a good idea."

Towcester would certainly have made a strategically sensible rallying point for the Roman troops that were meant to be coming from Exeter, Peterborough and Anglesey and would also have offered better protection from Boudica's chariots due to the indented geography of the area. But, as with all enduring legends, the simple answer is that there is not enough detail to be sure.

For Philip Crummy, director of the Colchester Archaeological Trust that has done so much to transform our understanding of Boudica's rebellion, one has to be pragmatic about the lack of a definite battle site: "My personal guess would be to place it somewhere in the Chilterns as the landscape feels right for the description but it really could be anywhere. Something might turn up someday but in the meantime, it's a favourite hot potato for pundits – and it all keeps the interest in Boudica's revolt against the Romans alive as a matter for debate amongst historians and archaeologists. Life would be a bit dull for us if we knew every detail about everything."

Jenny Hall, Roman curator at the Museum of London, agrees: "It's probably somewhere in the sweep up the road from St Albans around the Mancetter region but we just don't know. Boudica's army wasn't organised and they certainly had nothing like a clearly laid-out strategy like the Romans did; they were just a rabble really – and in fact, that was their undoing in the end."

Whatever the eventual meeting point, one can only imagine the cocktail of anticipation, fear and excitement that ran through both armies in intoxicating quantities. The Romans stood out in their silver and red blocks against the hillsides: dressed in their battle-gear with their helmets and armour gleaming in the strong, summer light, the glint from their weapons sent Morse flashes of warning to the enemy that needed no decoding. Both sides knew how Romans were armed – with javelins, daggers and the characteristic *gladii*, the short, double-edge sword that would stab, slice and twist in enemy flesh when used in close combat. Precision trained and experienced, they now stood rigid in their assigned positions, silent and motionless, watching the hordes of Britons jeering at them, waving their weapons in defiance. The Britons had armed themselves with anything they could lay their hands on: there were large numbers of hunting spears and knives and, for the privileged, swords and shields. They had waited seventeen long years to put right the defeat that had left them subjects of a foreign land; for their part, the Romans knew they had seventeen years of investment and their reputations on the line. Each soldier and warrior knew that this was effectively a fight to the death.

Paulinus had drawn up his men according to his battle plan: his cavalry at the flanks, his trusty legionaries in the centre and the light infantry and auxiliaries in between; facing them was the bulging wall of Britons who outnumbered the enemy by a ratio of around ten to one, grouped together in tribal bands by their leaders or chiefs who now raced up and down in their chariots relaying the orders of Boudica's council of war; and behind the massing warriors sprawled a huge assemblage of wives, children, sisters and mothers, all gathered together with their possessions, their bounty and their loaded wagons to watch the spectacle for themselves.

For the legions, the sight of the Britons' families clustered around the edge of the battlefield would have been strange but not exceptional: they had witnessed the same scenes in their wars in Gaul – and while it struck them as somewhat gory if not a foolhardy thing to do in case the enemy needed a speedy retreat, that was the Britons' choice. But for the Britons – like their comrades across the water – this was no pleasure trip for their wives and children: better to bring your family with you than leave them to the mercy of detachments of enemy soldiers who would rob, rape and murder anyone left at home. And what better way to propel a husband, brother or father to fight with true bravery than to have him watched by his own community? With everyone here at the same time, the women were protected and the men dared not shirk their duty on the battlefield. But on this occasion, the Britons' strategy was about to backfire on them with an almost unimaginable horror.

With both armies poised, there was no longer any turning back for either Boudica or Suetonius Paulinus. As the din of British battlecries was hushed to a low but threatening rumble, it was now the turn of the commanders to rally their troops to the point of selfless bravery and try to focus their attention on the deadly task ahead. Boudica mounted her chariot, drove to the front line and surveyed her army – then spoke to her warriors for the very last time.

Her clarion call is lost to history; the stirring words recounted by Tacitus and Dio owe more to dramatic tension and historical tradition than they do to the actuality of what Boudica and Suetonius Paulinus would have said – but for all their often ham-fisted hyperbole, the monologues offer the student of language some interesting insights to the minds of the authors whose work the speeches almost certainly are. It is worth giving the two versions: first, Tacitus, in full:

> "Boudica in her chariot with her daughters in front of her, rode up to tribe after tribe, arguing that it was perfectly normal for Britons to fight under women leaders. 'But now it is not as a woman descended from illustrious ancestry, but as one of the people that I am avenging my lost freedom, my lashed body, the outraged honour of my daughters. Roman greed has developed to such an extent that not even our persons, nor even our age or our virginity are left unpolluted. But heaven is on the side of just vengeance: one legion which dared to fight has been destroyed; the rest are cowering in their camps or anxiously seeking a means of escape. They will not stand even din and shout of so many thousands, let alone our attack and our weapons. If you balance the strength of our armies and the reasons for this war, then you must conquer or die. This is a woman's decision: as for men, they can live and become slaves.'"

> TACITUS: *ANNALS, XIV. 35*

The speech, which finishes in the Latin with a series of spittingly alliterative v-sounds, is a clever piece of oratory which draws out the favourite Roman themes of the perversity of women rulers, freemen becoming slaves and the dangers of moral degeneration – all subjects which would have stirred the Roman audience's heart. Interestingly, and at face value, Tacitus seems to de-feminise Boudica by saying that she does not speak "as a woman": this has the no doubt intended effect of initially giving her *more* credibility amongst an audience where powerful women were distrusted. Likewise, he strips away her status, saying that she is acting not as someone "from illustrious ancestry" but "as one of the people" – a faux piece of humble camaraderie that is a thinly disguised reference back to the (perceived) halcyon democracy of the Roman republic. Yet here Tacitus is playing a clever game: by so blatantly saying that Boudica is *not* talking as a female and *not* as someone of high status, he protests too much: such a skilled orator would have known that the denials only served to emphasise that she was very much a woman *and* a queen, and it is precisely these facts which makes her so captivating a character for his history.

Other tricks of rhetoric – something any well-educated Roman man would have to have studied – include the use of "triplets" to add dramatic effect: expressions such as "lost freedom", "lashed body" and "outraged honour" are followed by "our persons", "our age or our virginity" and – in just one paragraph of Boudica's speech – they are used no less than four times. Tacitus then makes the mood even more pointed as he slows down the rhythm for maximum effect: using the analogy of a set of weighing scales, the triplets become pairs of opposites (e.g., "conquer or die") – with the very last pair flagging up once more the incongruous sexuality of the speaker that has previously been denied. The final phrase sums up Tacitus's whole system of beliefs on the rightful structure of power: in the topsy-turvy world where women take control as the true moral leaders, even freemen will be treated like slaves.

This theme of slavery and men allowing themselves the humiliation of being ruled by women is picked up and echoed by Dio. Although he positions his great Boudica speech before the sacking of the cities, its tenor uses the same rhetoric and ideas as Tacitus's pre-battle speech – once more put into the mouth of Boudica as she raises a spear in her hand and addresses the masses:

> *"You have realised through experience how different liberty is from slavery; therefore, while some of you may have believed the enticing promises of the Romans through sheer ignorance, now that you've tasted both you'll understand how wrong you were in choosing foreign oppression to your ancient way of life – and you'll have come to learn that it is better to have poverty with freedom than wealth with servitude. For what can be worse than the treatment we have suffered since these men came over to Britain?"*
>
> CASSIUS DIO: *HISTORIES, BOOK 62*

Boudica-cum-Dio then continues for a while with a tirade on the injustices of the Romans' taxation policy towards the Britons before berating her people by saying it is actually all their own fault: they allowed the Romans to successfully invade in the first place. With enough over-egging to make the speech a verbal soufflé, Boudica then goes on to philosophise about Britain's place in the world and the Roman perception that Britons dwelt on a "different earth and under a different sky". While this is true, its purpose here is more to reiterate to Dio's audience that we are dealing with exotic creatures – like the strange beasts and ethereal land in the travellers' tales of Germanicus's fleet when they were stranded in Britain just half a century before. Complaining that Britons are misunderstood, Boudica then tries to unite the disparate tribes in her ranks by referring to their home "on one island" and their "one common name" despite the fact that there is no evidence that the Britons of the period ever fought with a common "British" consciousness.

The next section of Boudica's protracted monologue deals with the differences in bravery between the Romans who arm themselves to the hilt and hide out in forts and the Britons who fight with just a shield for protection and then blend seamlessly back into the landscape for protection. Once more, Dio portrays the Britons as almost romantic and magical creatures of nature; just like the noble savage, they are uncorrupted by the artifices of civilisation, and instead slink around in the shadows until bursting forth like barbaric woodland elves or nymphs:

> *"We have such an excess of bravery that we consider our tents to be safer than their walls and our shields better at protecting us than their whole suits of armour. Because of this, when we win we capture them and should they overpower us we can still escape — and if we decide to retreat somewhere, we can melt away into swamps and mountains so that they can never find us…unlike us, they fall prey to hunger, thirst, cold or heat; they need shade and shelter, they need leaven bread, wine and oil — and without these they die, whereas we have grasses and roots for bread, the sap of any plant for oil, water for wine and trees as houses. What's more, we know this landscape as a friend but to them it is strange and dangerous. As for the rivers, we can cross them naked whereas they find them hard to cross even in boats. So — let us prove to them that they are hares and foxes trying to rule over dogs and wolves."*
>
> CASSIUS DIO: *HISTORIES, BOOK 62*

When she finishes this part of epic monologue, Dio further reinforces the magical nature of the Britons by the description of Boudica releasing a hare "from the fold of her dress" (as opposed to plucking a rabbit from out of her sleeve) to divine the will of the gods. According to Dio, the hare ran in an auspicious direction and the crowds went wild with delight at the support of the heavens for their cause.

Someone as educated and erudite as Dio would have been well aware of the symbolism of the hare to the Britons, as it was an established part of the classical writings on Britain. In his *Gallic War*, Julius Caesar commented that hares, along with the cockerel and the goose, were never eaten, while Boudica's reference to the hare in her speech — and then one's use in divination — seems to fit with what we know about the animals from British and European archaeology. Hares stood out as strange and unpredictable beings, much like the gods themselves; their habit of darting around as ghostly figures of the night — precisely the time when the spirit world would be most feared — merely added to their mystery while their violent "boxing" each spring earned them a special resonance in the warrior culture of Britain. Their spiritual significance is clear from the remains that have been found layered in ritual burial pits in Ewell in Surrey, Jordan Hill in Weymouth and even in the Icenian territory itself at Ipswich. They have also been represented in Romano–British art and sculpture, particularly in relation to the hunter-gods of Britain and Gaul, where they were frequently depicted as quarry.

Boudica's reference to the Britons as dogs and wolves played on a pre-eminence of these creatures in the Celtic cultures of Europe which is well recorded in both classical writings and the archaeology from the ground. Dogs had a duality that made them intriguing: regarded as hunters – literally dogs of war – they were also loyal guardians or protectors. Having both these attributes, they could represent the spirit world as well as the physical world itself. This is shown in both art and actuality, with the remains of dogs in numerous burial pits and wells around Britain. Dogs were such a central part of Celtic life that the name "dog" or "hound" itself was transferred to a wide range of great war-heroes, including the Irish *Cú* Chulainn, the sorcerer *Cú* Roi mac Dairi and even the powerful Catuvellauni King *Cuno*belin. Interestingly, though, the idea of a "hare" trying to rule over a "dog" is nothing more than a zoomorphism of the old Roman theme of slaves upsetting the natural order of life by trying to rule their masters.

The final piece of rhetoric put into Boudica's mouth by Dio demonstrates the writer at his least subtle. Whereas until now it has been just about possible to suspend disbelief and imagine the warrior queen using Dio's words to address her army, he now indulges in a rant against Nero that is blatantly Roman in origin, rampantly sexist in its tenor and overtly biased in its politics:

> *"Raising her hand up to heaven, Boudica cried: 'I thank you, Andraste, and talk to you woman to woman, for I don't rule over any burden-bearing Egyptians like Nicrotis did, nor over the trading Assyrians like Semiramis (we have learned something from the Romans), and we certainly don't rule over the Romans themselves as Messalina used to do, then Agrippina and now Nero. He may call himself a man but in reality he's a woman, playing his lyre, singing*

and trying to make himself look beautiful. No — I rule over Britons: men who might not know how to work the soil or have a trade but who excel in the art of war and share everything, including their children and wives, so that the latter are as brave as their men. Therefore, as the queen of such men and women, I humbly pray for victory, that we should live and have our freedom against these people who have warm baths, eat fussy foods, drink unmixed wine, anoint themselves with myrrh, sleep on soft chairs with withered boys, and who are slaves to a musician — and a bad one at that! Don't allow this Mistress Domita-Nero to lord it over me or you men: let her sing and lord it over the Romans for they are the ones who deserve to be her slaves, having given in to her for so long. But you, Mistress, you alone will always be our ruler.' Having concluded her address to her people in such a manner, Boudica led her army against the Romans."

CASSIUS DIO: *HISTORIES, BOOK 62*

Like a student cramming every example into the last few minutes of an exam paper, Dio goes completely overboard in dredging up every single example of powerful, evil or misguided women rulers that he can think of and turned it into a speech. It was almost as if he had lifted the list of dangerous women from Propertius's Elegy on the enslaving power of love and placed it in the mouth of the Iron Age queen. Nitocris was the first queen to exercise political power over Egypt but had the cunning to allegedly trick one of her successors into revealing his greed; Semiramis was rumoured to have had an insatiable sexual appetite whereby she seduced the most handsome of her soldiers and then would have them killed in the most ruthless abuse of sexual power; Messalina may not have been a queen in her own right, but she used the power behind the imperial throne to murder anyone who stood against her or tried to diminish her influence. As for Agrippina, her reign of terror even caught her own son, the Emperor Nero, in its violent grasp until he finally managed to summon up the courage to have her murdered. Although at face value, Boudica is raised up to the pantheon of the known-world's hall of fame for queens, the list of women rulers would do little to enhance her reputation; to Dio's educated Roman audience, she would be damned by association.

Whereas Tacitus gives Boudica a powerfully emotive monologue, his pre-battle speech from Suetonius Paulinus is almost perfunctory in its commands as he reminds his soldiers that they are highly trained and disciplined professionals:

> "'Before you,' he said, 'you can see more women than warriors. Cowardly, unarmed, they will give up the moment they see the weapons and bravery of their conquerors who have given them such a drubbing so many times before. Despite your many legions, it will be the few who decide the true outcome of the battle, and it will add to their glory that so small a force have won the respect of a whole army. Keep your ranks tight, and once you've discharged your javelins, then continue the slaughter and devastation with shields and swords, never stopping to think about plunder: when you've won yourselves a victory, you can have it all.'"
>
> TACITUS: *ANNALS, XIV. 36*

Typically, Dio's version of Paulinus's speech is considerably more florid, referring to the threats of "entrails sliced from our bodies" or being "spitted on red-hot skewers" and other gruesome fates that would be suffered should they lose to the Britons. Addressing each of his three divisions in turn, his words are less convincing as those of such a seasoned military man as he tees up the drama and jeopardy the soldiers now face:

> "Choose, therefore, whether you would prefer to get the same treatment as some of our comrades and be driven out of Britain altogether, or by winning, to gain revenge for your friends who have fallen — and at the same time give humanity an example not just of benevolent clemency towards the loyal but inevitable severity towards the rebellious."

He finishes with a theme that resonates with Tacitus's speech for Boudica:

> "Let us, therefore win a victory over them — or die right here. Britain will be a fitting monumnet for us, even if every other Roman should be driven out: no matter, our bodies will possess this land for all time."
>
> CASSIUS DIO: *HISTORIES, BOOK 62*

For the women and children craning their necks at the edge of the battlefield, half excited, half terrified, this was probably the largest crowd of people they had ever seen; in fact, it was probably the largest number of people ever to have gathered in one place in the whole history of ancient Britain. Yet despite the masses, one can picture the families desperately searching for the faces of their husbands, sons, fathers, brothers and perhaps even mothers and sisters in the hordes of warriors in front of them. But the amorphous crowds would have blotted out their view like the rising sea as it builds to the crescendo of a wave: now everyone was poised; everyone was ready.

In the last few moments before war commenced, chariots raced along the British lines, whipping their warriors into an ecstasy of hatred that had already been fuelled by large quantities of ale; the Romans, meanwhile, stood square in their clean, shining lines showing little of the terror they must have been feeling. Then, at Boudica's command the battle horns sounded and the warriors unleashed their fury; one can barely imagine the cacophony that exploded from the Britons as they roared towards the Roman front line with a seismic wave of thundering energy. This was the moment that both sides had feared and lusted after – raw and naked passion against cold, military steel.

In the ordered rows of Romans, every sinew would have strained to hold their position against the basic human instinct for fight or flight. But they had their orders – no man was to discharge his javelin until Paulinus gave his signal. Five hundred yards, four hundred yards, three hundred yards and closing; the Britons charged across the open plain, into the jaws of the funnel-shaped defile that led to the waiting legions; two hundred yards, one hundred yards – then as the Britons made their final race towards the disciplined blocks of Romans, Paulinus gave his command: the air screamed with flying javelins followed by the muffled thuds of around seven thousand long, barbed tips connecting with the dull resistance of earth, shield – and human tissue. But still the Britons kept on coming. Like the heads of Hydra, as soon as one warrior fell, another would rise up in his place in a nightmare of mythical proportions. A second deluge of javelins rained down on Boudica's army and as they struck home on the unprotected flesh, a defensive rampart of thousands of bodies began to block the warriors' path.

Once their missiles were all discharged, it was time for stage two: a lightning flash of steel announced that the Roman legionaries had drawn their short swords from their scabbards as they now raced down the slope in their deadly wedge-shaped formation towards the enemy. The clash, when it came, was electric – a fusion of light, sound and white hot energy as the leading soldiers cut a gash through the mass of British warriors, dividing them, annihilating them with the cold, relentless butchery of a professional strategy of death. The blunt shunt of the shield partnered the swift, stabbing twist of the sword; and still the Britons kept on coming. But like a tug of war in reverse, the Romans now pushed forwards, cutting down all who fought before them. The Britons would not even have had the room to raise their swords as they were shoehorned together by the sides of the valley, the wedge-formation of Roman soldiers and the crowds of their own warriors racing up behind them. Crushed together, their strength in numbers now became a weakness in contrast with the organised blocks of well-spaced Romans.

Amidst the bloody chaos, little by little, both sides would have sensed that the advantage was turning. In the mêlée of the hand-to-hand combat where you were close enough to feel the gush of your enemy's breath as you stabbed the life from him, the Romans would have realised that the war cries of the Britons were slurring into the agonised screams of the dying. And yet Boudica's army fought on with the knowledge that the die had been cast and until it stopped rolling, so would they keep on moving forward until faced with their destiny.

From his position on the slope overlooking the battlefield, Suetonius Paulinus would have seen the subtle but growing signs of a glorious victory playing out on the field before him. As his cavalry swept down in a steady pincer movement that trapped all before it in a giant claw of death, the tumult of Britons began to lose its fervour: it was now battling for survival in a writhing sea of blood and body-parts where it was hard to tell the living from the dead. And then the flood of warriors slowed, halted and reversed. In a tangle of desperation, anger and fear, the Britons now began to flee, pursued by the cavalry and the flanks of roaring, bloodied legionaries but the warriors were trapped by their own wagons that sealed the edge of the battlefield. Women, children, animals and carts piled high with the trophies of a war: nothing was spared the wrath of the Romans who carried their orders through to the end.

And then it was over. As the light faded and the soldiers sifted through the piles of steaming corpses searching for fallen comrades, possible bounty or any as yet un-dead enemies, their officers counted the grim tally. Tacitus reports the numbers of dead as eighty thousand Britons and just four hundred Romans – a sum that would put it in the record books for the number killed in just one day until the advent of World War One; Dio says only that "many" were slain. Allowing for the usual levels of exaggeration, the truth has been estimated at closer to forty thousand Britons and around a thousand Romans but to put this into context, a death toll of fifty thousand is equivalent to the number of people killed when the Americans dropped the atomic bomb on the Japanese city of Nagasaki.

As for Boudica, we have no record of when she knew she had lost the battle for Britain, or even if she survived to see the tide turning. There are two versions of her death: Tacitus says she ended her own life with poison; Dio that she fell ill and died. Both amount to the same effect – that in losing the battle, she surrendered her life. It would certainly not have been regarded as "womanly" by the Romans to die on the battlefield or by her own sword; poison was regarded as a particularly female way to commit suicide and would have been well-known to classical audiences as the way the Egyptian queen, Cleopatra, chose to escape the humiliation of defeat. However, Boudica did not play by Roman rules: as a British warrior queen she may well have chosen to die by the sword. The fate of Boudica's two daughters is not mentioned by either writer and nor is there a clue in any material remains: they disappear from the record along with all reference to the actual site of the battle, two more nameless victims of the Roman conquest of Britain.

The death of Boudica was also the death knell for her rebellion. Dio claims that following their defeat, the Britons had tried to keep up the resistance but without her, it too faded away and died. Tacitus merely tells us that the Roman army had to spend the winter "under leather" – camping in leather tents that would have provided scant comfort for the victorious soldiers and little shelter from the cold, hard rain and snow. Small wonder, then, that their reprisals against the natives were so vicious.

There were other casualties – and not all in terms of revenge. When he heard word of the resounding victory of his comrades, Poenius Postumus, the camp prefect of the Second Legion who had failed to send his troops to aid the Governor, fell on his sword with the shame of depriving his men of their part in the glory. His was a personal tragedy, played out in all its agonising regret, hundreds of miles from the killing-fields that put an end to British hopes of freedom from Rome for the next three hundred and fifty years.

Boudica may have died and, with her, any hope of freedom from the iron yoke of Rome but what she had achieved in the battles and the purging fires ensured that she would reside in the memories of both the Romans and the Britons for at least the next fifty years. And then, just as the last embers of resistance were starting to fade, she rose from the ashes like the phoenix of mythology in the writings of Tacitus and, later, of Dio. The first stage of her life may have been over – but the larger part of her story had only just begun.

CHAPTER 15
THE AFTERMATH

"We should have lost our memories and our tongues had it been as easy to forget as to be silent."

Tacitus: Agricola, 2

I had talked to the experts, read all the books and papers; I had seen the remnants of her material world – the weapons, the coins, the structures and also the intimate domestic details of everyday life. But had it been possible to truly peel back two thousand years of distance to get close to the woman who had so instilled me with curiosity? It could be my background as a geographer but it was only when I walked through the *landscapes* of Boudica, from her homeland in Norfolk to the battlegrounds of Colchester, London and St Albans, and finally to the countryside of the Midlands where her mortal story supposedly ends, that I felt any strong sense of connection with the Iron Age warrior queen. I spent many days and hours walking along country lanes through the flat, open farmscapes of East Anglia, hoping that the fresh air and gentle winds would blow away the confusion of myth and legend from the kernel of her true existence. So what had I learned? Sitting on a tree stump, eating a packed lunch by a field of cut corn, I played with a stray stalk in the dusty earth.

Just as the Iron Age Britons expressed themselves by painting their bodies and decorating their world with their trademark swirling designs, we have a fundamental need to make our own pictures with words, to tell stories that make sense of our reality, almost as though we were camped around a fire with our comrades-in-arms, en route to fight the Romans. There may be precious little evidence of Boudica herself but there's a huge abundance of material from her world, if only we care to look; and an almost unlimited amount of understanding about ourselves. Just like that tripartite belt-mount found by John Wells, the

Norfolk metal detectorist, these are the three legs that keep the story moving, and we must never forget that our interests, our insights and our system of beliefs become part of the story – whether it's Tacitus's feelings about women and power or our own confused relationship with our Romanised past.

Perhaps even more than discovering about our Iron Age roots, it's the influence of the Romans on our psyche even today that had been the biggest lesson. Much of the ancient history is taught and displayed as "What the Romans did for us", as if civilisation began with the conquests of Julius Caesar, and then the Emperor Claudius. I've read book after book that takes AD 43 as the starting point of our true history. But where does that leave Boudica and her Iron Age people? If we venerate the Romans to such a degree, surely that leaves the Iceni queen with a stain across her name. Boudica can only become an icon if she's removed from her true history and set apart from the real landscapes of her life – landscapes that were complex and changing and hard to pigeonhole. Once stripped of her native clothing, she can be dressed up in whatever guise most suits our purpose, a multipurpose heroine. The trouble is, when we try to set her back in her proper context, we realise that she's still naked.

There is so much that has been lost about this most influential figure from our past – and much of that is lost forever. But there are whole landscapes of learning that can still be explored, and can still throw up treasure in terms of nuggets of understanding. And these may be of more value than any gold torc or royal palace.

Benevolent clemency towards the loyal, inevitable severity toward the rebellious: that was the promise put into the mouth of the British governor in his great pre-battle speech. Of course, Cassius Dio was able to write this with the benefit of hindsight and there is little doubt that the sentiment was followed through to its harshest extremes but in the days and weeks after the battle, the whole province of Britannia must have reeled with the impact and implications of what had just happened. For the Romans, they had won a glorious victory fighting against the odds and hopelessly outnumbered – but the enormity of what had been at stake would now be hitting home to their commanders. Three towns lost and at least two thousand soldiers – that was no minor uprising. One can imagine them now seeing a potential rebel in every British face, a potential ambush behind every quivering branch, and all the while the blank stare of hatred in the eyes of the newly re-subjugated peoples of Britain. Rome had taken a kicking but now it was the turn of the Britons.

For all his lurid details and flowery prose, Cassius Dio finishes his account of the revolt with the peremptory comment that realising they were thoroughly defeated, the Britons "scattered to their homes. So much for affairs in Britain". However, Tacitus takes a more analytical approach and give us some insight into the days and weeks that followed the quashing of British resistance to Rome.

Still shaken from being so hopelessly wrong-footed by Boudica, Paulinus now brought his army together and kept them in their temporary camps until he was confident the situation was under control – even though that meant they had to keep living in tents and campaigning outdoors over the cruel winter months. Although underplayed by the classical authors, their own losses must have been significant as seven thousand new men – two thousand legionaries, eight cohorts of auxiliaries and a thousand cavalry – were sent over from Germany to help get the province, and Roman authority, back on its feet. One can imagine the tales told during the long nights of darkness as the victorious soldiers recounted the horror and then the glory of the final battle to their new comrades, for such was the stuff of legends. Meanwhile, the cramped conditions in the cold, wet tents must have added to the resentment of an army that would normally retire to the safety and relative comfort of their forts for the winter.

By day, however, they would have had plenty of time to exercise their hatred as the troops swept through the British countryside seeking retribution for the uprising, setting fire to farmsteads and foodstores and putting the local tribespeople to the sword. It was not enough of a defence merely not to have taken part, to the Romans that still made you complicit in the revolt. Only the client kingdoms such as those of Cogidubnus and Cartimandua escaped the widespread retribution, for they had been amongst the few who had remained steadfast in their loyalty. Had they joined with Boudica, the potential for removing the Romans from Britain once and for all would have been almost boundless, for the rebels would then have had both the manpower and the money to keep the resistance fighting for years. However, both British rulers had taken the Roman shilling and remained solidly pro-Roman, regardless of their people's desires. In return, their power, their lands and their fortunes were spared and doubtless increased as an example to others to back the winning side.

For the losers, the devastation on the battlefield was nothing compared to that which was now wrought across the remainder of the Province, and nowhere more so than in the lands of the Iceni and Trinovantes. All vestiges of Prasutagus's client kingdom were systematically stripped away: his lands, and those of Boudica, were now under direct and unforgiving military control. Forts were built all over East Anglia in the aftermath of the uprising – as much to serve as commanding iconography of the new foreign rule as to impose its will. The Iceni were either killed, forced out of their homes or sold into slavery in a genocidal revenge that devastated an entire people.

Few material remains stand witness to the rampaging hatred and ethnic cleansing that was now sweeping through the land; the native settlements used little in the way of enduring stone or brick that would survive the onslaught, let alone the ravages of the following twenty centuries, and even Roman remains are thinner on the ground than logic would lead us to expect. The brutal truth of what happened to those who had answered Boudica's call – and even those who had stayed – has meanwhile been muffled by two millennia of changes in the landscape that have hidden or destroyed much evidence of those terror years of Paulinus's revenge.

However, some clues to the mood of the time might just be found in the buried hoards of coins and other treasures that have come to light in the East Anglian soil. Although these can be difficult to date, the general theme appears to be that they were either deliberately buried as some form of votive offering to the gods or hidden to keep them safe from threat or danger. In the case of the Boudican uprising and aftermath, the number of hoards, their content and their geographical distribution makes it credible that desperate people hid what wealth they had (or had looted) to save it from being plundered by either warring Britons or vengeful Romans; the fact that they never returned to collect their possessions points a silent finger at their fate. Some of the more spectacular hoards have contained coins, richly decorated metalware – particularly for horses

– and also jewellery but while it is easy to be carried away with the objects themselves, it's important to bear in mind the human price attached to them: a large proportion of the buried treasure once belonged to very real people who were scared enough to leave their ancestral lands and their most prized possessions in a futile bid to save their lives.

Tracing the people who owned or commissioned the artefacts is notoriously difficult, especially if the goods are found by themselves so cannot be placed in any kind of context. However, there are generally clues in the different types of styles and design in the discoveries which can help archaeologists try to identify something of their origin and perhaps then suggest the likely stories behind their burial. Whereas Romans favoured geometrical or symmetrical designs such as chequerboard patterns picked out in coloured enamel, Iron Age tastes eschewed any form of symmetry, preferring instead the more organic, flowing patterns characteristic of much European Celtic art. But sadly it's not always that simple: the general rules are complicated by cultural assimilation and also the inclusion of vast numbers of Gauls in the Roman army and entourage who would have brought their own local styles and tastes to foreign lands.

Meanwhile, there has always been a problem in understanding the past: how to actually *find* the objects and structures from the relevant period in history – and then, how to *interpret* them in order to learn more about the objects along with their historical context. The most radical leaps forward in piecing together the material artefacts from periods like Boudica's have only occurred in the last two hundred years. While intriguing discoveries have been made by accident over the two millennia since her revolt, it is only with the advances of the last two hundred years that we have been released from the tyranny of reliance on myth and the classical writings of Tacitus and Dio to tell the stories of the late Iron Age and early decades of Roman Britain.

The foundations for this progress in understanding the past were laid down in the nineteenth century when a range of quantum shifts occurred in our understanding of how the earth and humans had developed: firstly, the rise of geological science brought with it a realisation that the earth, and therefore civilisation, was much older than previously thought. This idea was compounded by Darwin's theory of evolution which again required a vastly longer history than had ever been accepted. New evidence started to appear – and that evidence has shone a light into the darkness of Iron Age and early Roman history. Finally, a breakthrough in antiquarian thinking occurred around 1819 when a Danish museum curator, C J Thomsen, devised the concept of successive stages of technological innovation, naming them the Stone Age, Bronze Age and Iron Age. This launched a more systematic approach for the study of early man that could at last provide an intellectual framework for the assortment of finds that the antiquarians were producing. By the end of the nineteenth century, General A H Pitt-Rivers had developed a more methodical approach for fieldwork, and the new discipline of "scientific" archaeology was born.

But it wasn't just the academics who had the copyright on science. Arguably the greatest advance in modern archaeology was being developed not in offices or museums but on the oil-stained wooden benches of an inventor's workshop. With every wire that was positioned, every connection that was made, a burst of energy surged forth that would illuminate even the darkest recesses of our past.

In the last decades of the nineteenth century, a machine was being designed that would turn the world of archaeology upside down – and drag it out of the hands of museums and academics in a turf war that would rival some of the great battles of Boudica. The humble metal detector has its origins in a cautionary tale of scientific blunders, insanity and professional arrogance. On March 4, 1881, James Abram Garfield was elected as the twentieth President of the United States – the first left-hander to be elected to office and someone who could allegedly write Latin with one hand and Greek simultaneously with the other. Despite these impressive talents, his period in office was to last just seven months after he fell prey to the delusions of an American lawyer named Charles Guiteau. Guiteau had suffered from bouts of mental illness for some years and had drifted from strange religious cults to the Republican party. Thinking that politics was now his true vocation, he grew desperate to be selected as a foreign consul and when his application was denied, he took the rejection to heart. After a dream in which he thought God had told him to kill the president, he purchased a .44 pearl-handled revolver for fifteen dollars and proceeded to stalk the president; on July 2, 1881, Guiteau found Garfield boarding a train at a Washington railroad depot and shot him twice in the back.

One of the bullets just grazed his skin; the other penetrated deep into the president's body but miraculously did not kill him – that was left to the doctors, who spent the next three months probing his flesh to find the bullet with unsterilised fingers and instruments. When they still failed to find the offending bullet, the White House called Alexander Graham Bell – the inventor of the telephone and great friend of the administration ever since the first phones were installed there. He was now invited to try out his latest invention – a simple and crudely built metal detector – but even though the theory behind the machine was sound enough, the experiment failed dismally. The signal Bell had been receiving during his examination of the President was not only confusing, it resulted in even more unclean and unnecessary surgery for the ailing leader because the so-called "bullet" Bell had discovered was nothing more than the metal bedframe on which the President was lying. However, by now it was too late: weakened by probable blood poisoning and with a raging fever, James A Garfield suffered a fatal heart attack and died on September 19, 1881. As the medics presented their bill for $85,000, an autopsy finally revealed the position of the second bullet – safely lodged in a protective cyst some four inches from the President's spine; what's more, the pathologist's report concluded that without the invasive treatment, the President would actually have survived.

After this somewhat ignominious start, metal detectors slowly improved their success rate and following an improved model designed by Dr Gerhard Fisher in 1931, they became an essential aid to the army during the Second World War when they were used to locate buried weaponry and wires. Following the war, they continued to be used to find buried mines and other materials and gradually they became a trusty gadget of the common man in his hunt for buried treasure. However, despite the fact that they were undoubtedly good at their job, to some professional archaeologists their users were simply treasure hunters who raped the nation's material heritage. The 1980s saw the launch of the British Council for Archaeology's "Stop!" campaign; its mood was echoed by local archaeology groups, some of which accused the people who used metal detectors as being nothing more than selfish – often even criminal – hobby-hunters. The charge was that these people ripped precious clues about our past out of their contexts that could otherwise tell us so much – and then either sold the artefacts for profit or hid them away in private collections so that they were lost to history. In return, the metal-detectorists argued the archaeologists were just being protectionistic, trying to hold on to their monopoly – and as long as the hobbyists didn't break the law, they had every right to indulge their pastime.

There has, however, have been a suggestion that there was a less worthy reason for the growing polarisation between the two camps – that there might have been more to the archaeologists' prejudice than simple professional interest. Along with the highly reasonable concerns over the loss of both artefacts and knowledge, a growing number of detectorists and some archaeologists posited that a class factor was involved: while archaeologists

Poster produced and distributed by the Council for Kentish Archaeology during the "troubles" of the 1970s and 1980s

are highly educated professionals, metal detectorists tend to be working- or lower middle-class, relatively uneducated (at least formally) – and the victims of professional snobbery.

Trevor Austin, general secretary of the National Council for Metal Detecting, remembers only too well the animosities of the time: "We could never understand it – we had so much material but the professional archaeologists just didn't want to know. Ninety per cent of the metal detectorists were behaving themselves; just that small minority of nighthawks were abusing the system – well, we call them 'nighthawks' but really they were just thieves with metal detectors. As for the rest of us, we knew that we were totally reliant on the goodwill of the landowners so we always tried to treat them with respect. The point is, we go where archaeologists don't go – and that's why we find things like the Baldock Hoard, a Roman votive offering to a new goddess called Thenua, which the professionals had missed. We also *rescue* a lot of material that would otherwise be destroyed, like the Winchester Torcs that had already been carried down the field by the plough. I would say that in the twenty-five years or so that I've been detecting, archaeology has been transformed by the likes of us."

Norfolk Museums' curator, Dr John Davies, has much sympathy with the metal detectorists' plight. "I think it's quite bold to suggest it was a class issue, though there may be some truth in that, but there was certainly a process of professionalisation happening within archaeology at the time, and that made it harder for amateurs to get officially involved. Along with that, this was a period when the university archaeology departments were growing and jostling with each other for position and status – and it was against this background that amateur metal detectorists began to emerge. And of course, what they stood for could be perceived as being in quite the opposite direction to that of the professionals."

The stand-off was doing no one any good but much more than that, it was actually inhibiting our understanding of the past. The amateurs had the time and equipment to go out looking for artefacts but not necessarily the specialist knowledge of how to extract the maximum learning value from what they found; meanwhile, the professionals had the knowledge but neither the time, the manpower nor the financial resources to survey the countryside for interesting discoveries. The late Tony Gregory, then the deputy director of the Norfolk Archaeological Unit, realised that the status quo could not continue. Crucially, he had never subscribed to the idea that metal detectorists did more harm than good to archaeological remains, believing instead that they were doing nothing more than a form of "controlled sampling" in layers of earth that normally had been already disturbed by ploughing or other activities; in other words, they were not doing any harm but were often doing much good. And so he came up with a radical solution.

What Tony did was to encourage his staff to work *with* the metal detectorists to the mutual benefit of both sides – a simple but effective answer that quickly won the support of not only his colleagues but also the local metal detecting clubs as well. By sharing their respective skills, both sides realised that they could gain enormously from the relationship – and ever since that time, the metal detectorists of Norfolk have turned up more finds than anywhere else in the country, deepening our understanding of the region in the Iron Age and providing a wealth of material in exchange for archaeological information and help in identifying some of their more unusual discoveries. In fact, so much material has come to light as a result of his legacy that in 2001, Norfolk Museums opened a brand new Boudica Gallery that is now one of the region's main tourist attractions. In the words of the chief curator, John Davies: "Boudica has come home."

In 1962, at Hockwold-cum-Wilton in Norfolk, on the edge of the Fens, Mr W F Curtis was doing some fieldwork when he came upon a cache of fine Roman silverware. It was a hoard of remarkable beauty: although broken and crushed for recycling by the time it was discovered, it contained five double-handed wine cups and two bowls which would have been spectacular in their day. As for their origin, they clearly did not come from the house of an ordinary Iron Age family as they would not have had the money or connections to obtain the valuable pieces, let alone the taste for exotic wines; the best guesses are that they were either the prized possessions of a wealthy colonist – perhaps looted from the sacked town of Camulodunum – or they might have belonged to a high-status Roman sympathiser who obtained them as gifts or via trade. Some commentators have even alluded to them possibly coming from the royal household of Boudica herself, being buried for safe-keeping when the Romans were raiding her palace. Whether loot or genuine possessions, the owner never came back to claim them.

More drinking vessels were found in two other hoards, at Crownthorpe in Norfolk – discovered by metal detectorist Derek Woollestone and dated to around AD 60 – and at Brandon in Suffolk; meanwhile the hoard found nearer the coast at Westhall stands as testimony to the high regard in which the Iceni held their horses and also their chariots. The harness mounts, decorated terret rings (the loops or rings on a horse's harness pad for the driving reins to pass through) and the linchpin terminals would have made a magnificent show on the two-horse chariot for which they were intended; likewise, the smaller hoard of brightly decorated terrets and harness mount found at Saham Toney attest to the pride of the Iceni in their horse culture at a time when many of the other British tribes were abandoning their chariots.

The largest of the hoards – and the one that can be most confidently dated to the years of Boudican revolt and its aftermath – is that found at Santon Downham in Suffolk. An iron knife and set of smith's tongs indicate that this could well be the hoard of a metalworker caught up in the revolt. Was he busy making weapons and horse tack for Boudica's revolt? Perhaps he even accompanied the army in their assault on Roman Britain; unfortunately, there is not enough evidence to give us his story but we can tell from the other items in the hoard that he was living at the time of much cross-over in Roman and native styles. The complex assortment of artefacts contained in the hoard neatly sums up the state of culture in Britain at the time of the rebellion when, even in the proud lands of the Iceni, Roman influences were beginning to show. However, the horse gear in the hoard is unashamedly native with the classic curvilinear designs of the Celtic world while the ducks portrayed on a beautiful spouted strainer bowl are classic Iceni motifs. Our metalsmith clearly had an eye for the designs of the Iron Age past as well as the Romanised future.

In terms of its archaeological importance, what makes the Santon hoard more precious than even its intrinsic or cultural value is that it contains brooches and pieces of Roman military armour that mean the hoard can be fairly reliably dated – back to the Boudican period. This opens up a range of scenarios for the burial of the hoard: was this the loot from the metalsmith's moment of rebellion? If so, the presence of Roman armour would have sealed his fate during the savage witch-hunt by Paulinus's men. Small wonder, then, that their owner would try to keep the dangerous loot hidden – and no surprise that a metalworker would be damned by his trade as guilty of complicity by the vengeful Roman army.

With each new discovery, whether common or rare, another small piece of knowledge can be added to the jigsaw of understanding for Britain around the time of Boudica's revolt. However, occasionally an object appears that is so rare and so remarkable, it is almost as if a whole new landscape is revealed before our eyes – a landscape that has the power not only to surprise but also to remind us that Britain was now part of the greatest empire on earth.

Such an object is the so-called Hawkedon helmet – possibly another piece of loot from Camulodunum. The bronze, wide-necked helmet was discovered in April, 1965, by a farmer ploughing his field at Hawkedon in southern Suffolk – but this was no ordinary helmet: it was more than double the weight of a legionary model so was unlikely to have been used by the military. Instead came the intriguing possibility that what the farmer had found was the practice helmet of a gladiator, weighing some five and a half pounds with traces of tin on the surface that would, in its prime, have made it shone like silver. The helmet – still in remarkable shape – is stunning even today, though it must have been incredibly uncomfortable to wear. Top heavy with its fin-like structure, the helmet is designed for safety; a broad visor juts out above the eyes with another at chin level – both front and back – to protect the wearer's neck, and in between these two collars of metal lies a grid covering the eyes and nose.

Similar gladiatorial helmets from the same period have been found in Italy with a particularly interesting one in Pompeii – roughly the same size and shape as the Hawkedon helmet but much more finely decorated. So, was its British counterpart stolen from the colonia stores by one of Boudica's army? Camulodunum is certainly the only Roman town in the vicinity of the farm. And whoever took it from its original location made the journey back to

Reconstructed Gladiatorial Helmet

Suffolk, so if it was one of Boudica's rebel warriors, the likelihood is that he, she – or at least one of their comrades or family – survived long enough to bring the treasure home. Meanwhile, the find has raised more questions about its origin and life in early Roman Britain than it can answer; and the story behind the helmet's burial in the Hawkedon field remains a tantalising mystery.

But it's not just the hoards themselves that can give us information about life in Roman Britain. Although there is little in the archaeological record from the period immediately after the revolt to rival the Boudican destruction horizon for sheer drama, the geographical pattern of the distribution for the hoards and other rich finds from the lands of the Iceni and their compatriots tells us that there was widespread uncertainty around the time of the rebellion. John Davies, Boudica expert at Norfolk Museums, is convinced these hoards tell a powerful tale: "I know that some scholars have suggested that these twenty-five or so hoards of silver coins of the Iceni weren't all buried in response to Boudica and that they were deposited over a longer period. However, there's recently been some remarkable work by a Cambridge coin enthusiast and scholar that is again suggesting the opposite – that they were in fact all deposited over a relatively short period of time, that is, probably in response to the unrest at the time of Boudica."

And it seems that their owners may well have been justified: there are glimpses of possible violence that followed Boudica's defeat as the Romans wreaked revenge on the lands of the guilty. Reference has been made to a pit at Baldock in Hertfordshire that was found to contain the remains of ninety-eight sheep, dated to around AD 50-70. Could these have been confiscated and butchered by the Roman army as they marched towards East Anglia the winter after the revolt? The flock would certainly have provided a substantial amount of meat and possibly even fleeces to help keep out the unwelcome cold of living outdoors in a British winter.

A more poignant tale is that of the Icenian farmstead on the edge of the sandy Breckland at West Stow: this was occupied up to the middle of the first century when all signs of habitation suddenly stop, only to reappear some ten or twenty years later in a much more sophisticated form. There is no direct evidence but it is tempting from the timing to assert that the people who lived here in their traditional roundhouses went off to fight in Boudica's army – and never made it home.

However, one clear-cut expression of Roman vengeance against the Iceni appears to be at the very seat of Boudica herself, at the religious complex at Thetford. This imposing site could well have been where Boudica held her council of war with her people and those of the neighbouring tribes at the start of the revolt. However, as with the farmstead at West Stow, the site was abandoned after the revolt and this time it was not re-used for around two hundred years. Curiously, though, its demise was not through any purging flames of fire; instead, it appears to have been systematically dismantled with posts rocked in their sockets to loosen them at the base, or holes dug alongside to aid their removal. Even the ditches were partially filled in with the earth from the neighbouring ramparts. There is no direct evidence as to who were the culprits but five pieces of Roman military equipment were found at the site, dating to around the time of the rebellion and the Roman reprisals.

★

Meanwhile, the Roman backlash wasn't just reserved for the Icenian rebels; to the south, in what is now south Suffolk and Essex, the Trinovantes were also experiencing the wrath of Roman revenge for the destruction of Camulodunum and the near-drubbing they had received at the native army's hands. As ever, the evidence is fragmentary and hard to find on the ground but just occasionally there are sufficient pieces of the jigsaw to try to build a better picture of what happened in the period after AD 60/61.

One possible supporting story comes from the remains of an old fortified enclosure at Burgh near Woodbridge in Suffolk. The defences here had been upgraded just before the Roman invasion, but around AD 60 these improvements had been destroyed. A used javelin head and an artillery bolt found on the site have been identified as Roman, and suggest that the site came under Roman attack, but there is not enough evidence to judge whether these were lost during the invasion or around AD 60 when the new defences were destroyed. However, circumstantially, a good case could be put for the weaponry being discharged in the period after the Boudican uprising when the Romans were venting their anger against the Trinovantes who collaborated with the Iceni queen's army.

But it wasn't just those who had fought against Boudica who toured the land looking for revenge. Around seven thousand new soldiers were transferred to Britain from their base in Germania. Such an influx of new troops – and the relocation of existing ones to the rebellious regions – would have transformed the landscape of the less secure parts of the country, changes that would leave their imprint in the soil. And sure enough, with the advent of new technology such as aerial photography and geophysics for surveying, we can now see patterns in the land that were not clearly visible before. What is emerging is a network of forts, roads and military buildings springing up all over the conflict zones in the years immediately after the Boudican revolt.

In the territory of the Iceni, aerial photography has highlighted a series of presumed early Roman forts or marching camps at Caistor St Edmund, Swanton Morley, Threxton, Ashill and Barton Bendish. John Davies is again pragmatic: "It's difficult to date these sites precisely but they probably date to the Boudican

*Bronze statuette of the Emperor Nero, decorated with silver and neillo inlay,
and standing in the guise of Alexander the Great.*

period." What's more, in the tribal lands of the Trinovantes in Essex, there appears
to be at least one Roman fort at Chelmsford which is dated as being constructed
during this volatile period; a much larger military base discovered at Great
Chesterford would have had a more significant role in maintaining the uneasy
peace. In fact, spread over the entire region are remains that can be fitted into the
general picture of destruction and domination: there is a possible marching camp
at Horstead near Norwich, while a school archaeological dig in 1950 found
evidence of military activity on the old road to Caistor, the capital of the Icenian
lands. Also found at the Coddenham site was a great deal of burned and broken
material up to a metre deep, including building debris and Samian pottery, which
encouraged a local antiquarian to suggest as far back as 1825 that this was the
remnants of a villa or farmstead destroyed along with its inhabitants by the
warring and merciless army of Queen Boudica.

It is no surprise that this final location was the cause of so much excitement and hypothesising: along with the layer of broken and burned debris were found a Roman funerary urn, a number of Roman coins and also a beautifully worked circular bronze box containing some exquisitely decorated silverware. However, the *pièce de résistance* from the nearby lands of the Earl of Ashburnham was a bronze statuette of the Emperor Nero, found a few years beforehand and donated by the Earl to the British Museum. Highly decorated with much fine detail, the statue is clearly from a period when Nero was highly regarded, as he appears to be standing in the guise of Alexander the Great, with his foot on a globe (now missing) and a sceptre of office in his hand. Given that he was hated by the time of his death, this statue must date from his actual reign. When the figure was found back in 1795, it was missing an arm which had led to the suggestion that it was possibly deliberately pulled off and the statue thrown away when the Emperor died in AD 68.

Elsewhere in the region, Roman forts have been identified like the large one at Pakenham and perhaps also at Stuston in Suffolk. A spectacular discovery from the garrison at the fort at Coddenham included a soldier's grave: inside lay a stunning mirror-case with a decorated lid showing Nero addressing his troops; not only was this beautiful, it also was useful in dating the discoveries. Much of this evidence comes from aerial photographs and far more work is needed on the ground to say conclusively whether many of these sites really are from the post-Boudican period.

The Roman fort at Lunt in the Midlands provides a fascinating story that illustrates something of the aftermath to the uprising. First identified in 1960 by a local archaeologist, Brian Stanley, excavations six years later confirmed his theories and revealed a major Roman fort complex overlooking the modern city of Coventry. With each subsequent investigation, more of the complex picture has come to light, illustrating the constantly changing demands placed on the military in the years following Boudica's rebellion. After the quelling of the revolt, the location of the fort in the Midlands meant it was perfectly positioned to become a major supply base for Paulinus's policy of systematic retribution against the Britons and over the next few years it underwent an incredible amount of rebuilding, firstly relating to the time when the Roman troops were flooding back into the area in the immediate aftermath of the war and culminating in the site being largely abandoned around fifteen years later when troops were redistributed for Agricola's campaigns in the north.

Around AD 63 a large circular compound was added to the grounds, levelled and re-surfaced with sand and gravel and surrounded by a wooden wall around eight feet tall. Though rare, this appears to be something called a *gyras* – a training ring or arena used for breaking horses – perhaps the very horses that were confiscated from the Iceni and the other warring tribes who had used the creatures to such devastating effect in their chariots. For the Romans, this would have been a precious windfall: horses were hard to come by, particularly the valuable and often highly trained creatures of the Iceni. For the Britons, depriving the tribespeople of their horses would have been like forcibly removing someone's pride-and-joy car: not only would they have been an invaluable means of transport, they were also part of the very spirit of the people – a form of conspicuous wealth, a means of display and a boast of status. To lose all this would have been to break the very soul of the horse-culture of Britain, and the loss would have been felt particularly acutely among the Iceni who so loved and revered their horses. In the years following the revolt, the wild grazing lands of the Iceni were forcibly drained and turned over to agriculture; like the animals they adored, their people had now been broken into servitude.

Some tribes did try to fight on but the heart and soul had gone out of the British resistance to Roman rule. And if the savage military response was not disincentive enough, the famine that now gripped Britain crushed the lifeblood out of the surviving Britons. Tacitus blithely puts this down to the tribes being rash in choosing to wage war rather than plant their crops for the coming year but there is no doubt that the loss of manpower and the scorched-earth policy employed by the vengeful Romans had much to do with the mass starvation that followed. There is also little doubt that the Romans continued to extract their taxes and food supplies from the famine-stricken Britons, considering it their just deserts for the all the trouble the uprising had caused. Finally, there is that evidence from the Boudican destruction layer of the burned but *imported* grain containing weeds from the Mediterranean: perhaps famine was gripping the province *before* the revolt of AD 60/61 as well as after – and this would go a long way to explaining the Britons' dissatisfaction with life under their Roman overlords.

It seems, however, that ill-feeling washing through Britannia wasn't just reserved for the Britons; Tacitus reports the growing dispute between the governor and his new procurator, Julius Classicianus, who had been sent as the successor to Catus Decianus. Unlike Decianus, who was blamed for contributing to the rebellion by his heavy-handed treatment of the Icenian royal household and generally callous greed, Tacitus portrays Classicianus as a spineless administrator who wanted peace at any cost. What Classicianus now wanted was to remove the ruthless Suetonius Paulinus and replace him with a new governor less interested in revenge and more interested not just in appeasement, but also wealth extraction. To the new procurator's way of thinking, the brutal response of Paulinus was actually prolonging tension in the province and doing more bad than good for Romano–British relations, let alone for his own provincial revenues which had taken a distinct turn for the worse since the genocide. However, while the argument between governor and procurator raged on, it left a vacuum in real leadership that would have offered the Britons little incentive to give up the fight for freedom. The "little local difficulty" between governor and procurator continued until the constant stream of bitchy dispatches to Rome eventually forced Nero to send an ambassador to try to sort things out.

Polyclitus was an imperial freedman, sent by the emperor to survey the state of Britain – and resolve the tensions between the warring governor and his new procurator, and the Romans and their vanquished subjects. As told by Tacitus, this powerful favourite of Nero instilled fear into the legionary soldiers and their officers but the tribespeople (and no doubt Tacitus's classical audience) merely found it risible that a former slave should try telling Roman leaders what to do. Whether or not the British reaction is true is hard to substantiate but the whole situation must have been chaotic as the Roman factions fought each other as well as the Britons. One suspects that it was just as well that Nero never discovered what was going on or he might have signed up to the British head-hunting tradition.

Eventually things began to improve for the British: Suetonius Paulinus was replaced as governor by the former consul, Petronius Turpilianus, who took a much more conciliatory line towards his new subjects. As a huge fan of the ruthless Paulinus, Tacitus does not let the opportunity pass to make a snide comment at his successor, commenting that he "neither challenged the enemy nor was troubled himself, and disguised this tame inaction with the honourable name of peace". However, both the Romans and the Britons doubtless welcomed the dawn of a new era in imperial politics and after two decades of fighting, the province of Britannia reluctantly took some respite in a period of relative calm.

There is one postscript from the archaeology of Boudica's revolt that offers a known ending to a real human story: this is the tombstone found in London of the man who had run Britannia while Suetonius Paulinus was off getting his *triumph* in Rome – the erstwhile procurator, Julius Classicianus, or to give him his full Roman name, Gaius Julius Alpinus Classicianus. Part of this was found in 1852 when workmen were removing rubble from excavations to make a cellar for a house in London's Trinity Place. The house backed on to the old Roman wall and amongst the forty cartloads of stone that were taken away for dumping was a first-century tombstone for an old Athenian and a large slab engraved with the words DIS MANIBVS (to the Shades of the Underworld) along with the name of Classicianus. This could only be one thing: the memorial monument of Julius Classicianus, and this was further confirmed when a fragment of the supporting bolster for the dish at the top of an altar was also found in the rubble, giving vital clues to the shape of the procurator's monument.

In 1882, another large stretch of the Roman wall was destroyed to make way for London's Inner Circle Railway but no more of Classicianus's tomb was found and it was feared that the remainder was lost; then, in 1935, during the construction of what is now Tower Hill station, yet more of the inscription was found lying upside-down as part of the bottom course of the Roman wall. This contained the critical three lines of letters from the base of the inscription that proved beyond doubt that the Classicianus mentioned was indeed the same man that had taken over from the much-hated Catus Decianus, and who in turn had been scorned by Tacitus for disagreeing with the harsh reprisals of Governor Suetonius Paulinus. Although the middle two lines or so are missing, it is possible to read the legend:

DIS

MANIBVS

C.IVL.C.F.FAB.ALPINI.CLASSICIANI

....

....

PROC.PROVINC.BRITANNIAE

IVLIA.INDI.FILIA. PACATA. INDIANA

VXOR F

Although on his death his wife, Julia Pacata Indiana, may have sent Classicianus "into the shades of the underworld", his impressive monument has survived the two thousand years since Boudica's revolt first brought him to the province of Britannia; it has now been restored to some of its former glory and is on public display in the British Museum as a permanent and poignant memorial to the war-torn days of AD 60/61.

Antiquarians, archaeologists, amateur metal detectorists – and pure accident: all of these have added their parts to the story of Classicianus's famous predecessor, the warring Queen Boudica. The last two centuries of technological and intellectual advance has revolutionised our understanding of her rebellion's impact on both the people and the landscape of Britain. However, this does not mean that she was forgotten for the two thousand years that separated her death and the re-discovery of her material legacy. Long before the debris of her revolt worked its way to the surface, the Iron Age warrior queen was starting her bumpy ride into the limelight of British history, as either hero or heretic.

CHAPTER 16

UP FROM THE ASHES...

Roman Britain after AD 60/61

"Her death it brought us bitter woe
Yes, to the heart it wrung us,
And all because she didn't know
A mushroom from a fungus."

ELIZABETH NEWBERY: *THE LOOKOUT GUIDE TO THE QUARRELLING CELTS*

"No one can deny that she had a huge impact long after her day," muses archaeologist Philip Crummy in an office groaning under the weight of work in progress. We were discussing the legacy of Boudica and her revolt for the Roman Empire. "After all, when the Romans rebuilt Camulodunum, they added a city wall and a large defensive ditch – what's now called Gryme's Dyke – as they weren't going to be caught out in the same way twice. But much more than that, it became increasingly common for them to build defensive earth ditches at a whole range of new settlements that were springing up after the revolt. I think the *lack* of defences at Camulodunum in AD 60 must have been viewed as less of an oversight and more of an outright scandal."

It seems the Boudica effect was felt not just in the burned red layer of soil: her revolt had changed not only the landscape but the psyche of the Romans from an almost arrogant confidence to an anxious paranoia. Clearly, Tacitus and Dio were *not* exaggerating the significance of her story: Britannia was now transformed into a new mental and physical space – and the story of the next four hundred years of Roman occupation bears all the hallmarks of a warrior queen's fiery fingerprint.

It was as if the province was holding its breath: an anxious peace now settled over the province of Britannia under the rule of its new governor, Petronius Turpilianus. Boudica might have been dead, along with her cause, but the debris of her uprising festered in every strategic decision the Romans now made. The drubbing she had given to military rule in Britain – and just as importantly to imperial confidence – reverberated in provincial policy for at least the next decade. The Romans stopped trying to expand their British frontiers and just concentrated on consolidating what they had already got. Financially, militarily and politically, they could not afford to have another rebellion in the province.

Turpilianus knew his job was now one of reconciliation and relationship-building with the Britons; there were to be no new military operations under his command, and the same would be true for his successor, Marcus Trebellius Maximus, who ruled Britannia from AD 63 to AD 69. It was only with the appointment of Petillius Cerealis in AD 71 that the old days of conquest and frontier-chasing came back into vogue – an attempt for total domination of the island that would eventually see the Romans being driven back by the Caledonian tribes in AD 117 to the eventual northern border of Hadrian's Wall, near to the modern border between England and Scotland. However, all that was half a century ahead; for now, Cerealis had his own reasons for reasserting Roman dominance over the Britons: he had been the commander of the detachment of soldiers marching down from Peterborough who had been so severely routed by Boudica's army. His new appointment as governor of the province was the perfect opportunity to exact some personal revenge for his dented pride – and for his thousand men who had been cut to pieces.

But if the mood was tense in Britain in the post-Boudican era, it was even worse in Rome. Since his murder of his mother in AD 58 and then of his wife, Octavia, in AD 62, the Emperor Nero was realising that he could behave exactly how he liked without fear of public or even private censure. While Paulinus and his army in the province were trying to defeat Boudica's warring rebels, the emperor was giving performances of his lyre-playing and when this didn't satisfy his artistic pretensions, he took to the stage as well – little realising how embarrassing he was to himself and those who were forced to watch.

By AD 63, his grip on reality was becoming ever more tenuous as he signed his heart over to new religious cults in a bid to find some meaning to his life or, perhaps, just more power. Unfortunately for the Christians, their fledgling religion wasn't one of his chosen few and following the great fire of Rome in AD 64, Nero placed the blame for the inferno squarely on their shoulders. While he set about rebuilding the city in the imposing style of the Greeks, he continued to kindle a Roman hatred of the faith that would last for three hundred years until the conversion of the Emperor Constantine in the fourth century AD. By then, not even a new faith would be enough to save the unwieldy Roman megastate from its inevitable implosion. By AD 410, time achieved what Boudica never could: the end of Roman rule in Britain.

Meantime, in the absence of strong political leadership from Rome, the whole of the empire was growing uneasy. It wasn't just Britain that was rocked by civil unrest; trouble was brewing in both Gaul and Spain, which had the potential to jeopardise the entire Empire. On the June 9, AD 68, after singing, playing and murdering his way into a corner, Nero finally ended the misrule of Rome by committing suicide by putting a dagger to his throat. He knew that he had squandered a fortune, alienated his people and, critically, lost the support of the army – but now it was too late. His death was not the focus for much genuine grief and misery, though Nero had the last laugh: with no clear successor, the empire was plunged even further into despair and civil war.

Against this background, it is small wonder that after Boudica's uprising the policy in Britain was strictly one of trying to repair and maintain the status quo. With the rest of the empire suffering uncertainty and strife, the dwindling revenues from taxation in the provinces were becoming a growing cause for alarm, particularly when Nero had been squandering his way through the coffers in Rome. At last, after what has been known as the "year of the four Emperors" in AD 68-9, Caesar Vespasianus Augustus finally took the throne and brought about the first period of stability for almost a generation. Vespasian's background was suitably impressive and not without some personal colour: he had already won notoriety for allegedly being pelted with turnips during his pro-consulship of Africa and then – more dangerously though not unsurprisingly – for falling asleep during one of Nero's artistic performances. The ten-year reign of this experienced and able politician was marked by a restoration in the fortunes of the empire and a renewal of the expansionist policies in the province of Britannia.

Immediately after the revolt, the Romans had set about rebuilding their prized capital at Camulodunum, with renovation works also taking place shortly afterwards in both Londinium and Verulamium. The need to rebuild was emotional as well as administrative – the province could not be without its *colonia* and its increasingly urban population could not live without their towns. This is clearly borne out by the archaeology in Colchester which shows that there was barely enough time for the top layer of the Boudican destruction horizon to have weathered before reconstruction began again, while the pottery record shows barely a break in its two-thousand-year continuity. Although Camulodunum had been the worst affected of the three sacked towns, this was the settlement that now had to be raised back up as quickly as possible and although the new town was on a smaller scale, there seem to have been enough survivors to effect some kind of "business as normal" policy once the debris had been cleared away. Within a few years, a new *Colonia Victricensis* had risen from the ashes to parade its renewed glory – only this time with the addition of a substantial defensive wall to protect it from any future attacks. That the protective wall largely achieved its goal is beyond any argument: about half the original structure can still be seen today.

As for the second target of Boudica's wrath, Londinium was already a *de facto* place of provincial administration at the time of the revolt and its influence grew even stronger in the years after the uprising and attack. Jenny Hall, Roman curator at the Museum of London, picks up the story: "There is little doubt that the new procurator, Classicianus, based himself here in the early AD Sixties and although there are hints from the archaeological record that it took some time for the pace and volume of trade to fully recover, we can see from the pottery record – and the development of the quayside – that just like Camulodunum, the settlement quickly got back onto its feet. I think it had probably had the biggest buzz of any of the early Roman settlements so it's hardly surprising that it took over the role as the major town in Britain."

For London, the major phase of re-birth was under Vespasian. During this time, the town became a key supply base for the growing demands of the military and also – now that they knew the army wouldn't be withdrawing from the province – for the increasingly Romanised population who decided that the Romans were here to stay. The superior port facilities over its rival settlement at Colchester meant that the town became even more strategically important, with larger ships able to sail from Europe right up the Thames to the heart of the developing city. Throughout the Seventies and Eighties, the facilities were improved even further by the construction of a substantial new quay, some six hundred and twenty metres long. This was lined with wood specially selected for the purpose in a major construction project with wharves, warehouses and jetties that made the docks the envy of the entire province and laid the foundations for its evolution into a world city over the next two thousand years.

From merely "scraping by", Londinium now grew into a self-confident and sophisticated settlement with all the accoutrements of Roman life, including a timber amphitheatre for gladiatorial games which was built around AD 70 at Guildhall, a vast new forum replete with outbuildings for provincial officers and staff and – the *pièce de résistance* of any Roman town – the public baths, built around AD 80 at Huggin Hill. The wonderful discovery of some skimpy leather women's knickers at Queen Street in London caused much speculation: normally, Roman women would wear a strip of cloth to support the breasts and another piece of cloth, like a loin cloth, called a *subligar* or *subligaculum*, meaning "little binding underneath" on their lower halves. However, these tiny leather briefs were well made with hemming all the way around the hourglass shape and there were laces at the sides for fasting the underwear to a snug fit. But what on earth were women doing in the years following the Boudica revolt that required leather underwear? Jenny Hall looks after the discovery: "Suggestions have included their use by women who were menstruating but the most likely answer is that they were worn as part of the costume of female acrobats or performers where they would be neat-fitting with a bit of 'give'. And from the pictorial evidence that we have from elsewhere in the empire, that would have been just about all that they were wearing, except for kneepads." Whatever their use, well-worn and with a hip measurement of just thirty-one inches, their owner was certainly someone in good physical shape.

As well as entertainment, it seems that tourism, or at least travel, was also on

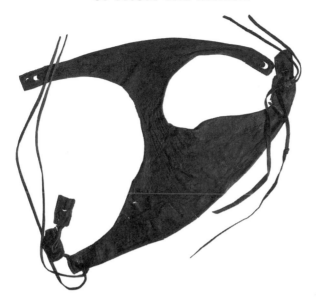

Leather briefs found in Queen Street, London,
possibly belonging to female acrobat or performer

the rise. On the south bank of the Thames, the destroyed suburb at Southwark was experiencing its own reincarnation with the construction of a large stone building in the early AD Seventies which appears to have been some kind of hotel for all the provincial bureaucrats that were now employed in keeping the country running.

At some point during the reconstruction of Londinium and the growing confidence across the entire province, it must have been realised that the former trading settlement was beginning to overshadow the political centre of Roman power at Camulodunum. From the scale of investment in the rebuilding, it seems most unlikely that the town's renaissance could have been achieved by private money alone. It is unclear precisely when, but at some point around this time, the provincial administrators made London the new capital of Britain.

Meanwhile, thirty miles north-west in the sacked town of Verulamium, it was an altogether very different story. Unlike in Colchester and London, this time there was no phoenix rising rapidly from the ashes of Boudica's destruction and no surge of renewed confidence from the population that they could rebuild their homes and businesses even better than before. For the Britons who had made Verulamium their home, there was no great tradition of urbanity and its fragile hold had been shattered by the events of AD 60/61. From the archaeological record, it appears that the thick layer of burned material was barely touched in the years following the uprising; in fact, it would take almost two decades for the town to get back on its feet and raise itself up to some of its former glory. If the original Roman town was incomplete at the time of the uprising, it remained so for a long while after Boudica had left the town. The forum and basilica were only finally completed around AD 79 and progress appears to have been slow, either through lack of funds, lack of manpower or lack of motivation. Rosalind Niblett is unequivocal: "I think that Boudica really did devastate the population. Verulamium was just on the cusp of becoming a sort of 'show town' when she and her army tore through it. For the ten or fifteen years after her uprising, the wealthy Catuvellaunian elite clearly decided it was safer to hoard their money rather than invest it in ostentatious buildings that could be burned down – we know they *had* the money as it's turned up in the form of buried gold and silver coins; they just chose to keep it for themselves or their gods."

There is, however, evidence from the writings of Tacitus that the Romans actively encouraged the rebuilding of their cultural centres after the uprising. In his biography of his father-in-law, the celebrated Roman general Agricola, Tacitus makes reference to the fact that during the winter of AD 79-80, a few years after his appointment as the new British governor, Agricola poured himself into the drive to make Britons more "Roman" by adopting urban lifestyles centred around all the trappings of cosmopolitan life. It was seen as a mark of status and largesse to fund the building of iconic buildings, such as a forum or temple, and the state was not beyond giving whole communities a helping hand towards both self and civic improvement if it served the purpose of spreading Roman civilisation to the masses. After all, the more *Roman* the population, the less likely it was that another Boudica would rise up from the ashes and again destroy their hard work.

The renaissance of Verulamium was aided by its proximity to the by-now flourishing Londinium – another indirect impact of how the Iceni queen forever changed the geography of Britain. Whereas in pre-Roman times, and to some extent even up to the revolt itself, Verulamium was marginal to the main trading centres, the massive growth of London now had a profound effect on its smaller partner. Just a day's march away for the army, or a day's ride for a cartload of goods, Verulamium was now within striking distance of the new capital's "suburban effect" and its location on Watling Steet, the main route out to the north-west and Chester, assured that it could get a free ride on London's coat-tails. And the rapidly developing town made good use of it: by AD 100, Verulamium had an extensive Roman grid system of metalled and stony streets with their attendant shops, workshops and houses, along with a forum/basilica and all the paraphernalia of cosmopolitan life. At the heart of the new town was a strong commercial and administrative area, and at its centre was the large forum complex covering an area of more than two thousand square metres with some often magnificently carved Purbeck marble stonework. The forum would have had the traditional large, colonnaded courtyard and an outlying piazza, and its stature would have continued to grow with the whole area being improved right through to the late second century.

The feel of the new town would have been unashamedly Roman, with impressive stone buildings, Mediterranean-style shops and houses, and wide, cambered streets. Temples grew up to support the new faiths and beliefs of the population that were melding with the long-held traditional ideas about the spirit world. As well as the physical infrastructure, there were all the services of urban Roman life such as water channelled right across the town and probably even fountains as well. And for relaxation, there was of course the grandiose baths complex, with its warming hot air piped from the central heating system. By the end of the first century, the urban landscape of Verulamium was exotic, imperial and decadent; Boudica's army would have spun in their graves to see all their hard work of destruction obliterated by the shiny, new settlement that announced in a clear voice that Britain was now, truly, a Roman province.

As for the Britons in the re-invigorated province, the uprising had removed whole swathes of the active labour force from the areas of the Iceni and its fellow tribes and this undoubtedly had a serious effect on the landscape of eastern Britain after the revolt. Along with the swingeing reprisals came widespread famine that would have done much to reduce not only the numbers in the rural population but also their anti-Roman spirit. To the north, in the lands of the Brigantes, the bellicose Britons still had some stomach for revolt and demonstrated this during the final years of Queen Cartimandua's rule and beyond, but south of their lands, the Iceni and the Trinovantes were crushed into submission.

There is one final irony in the landscape of Roman Britain in the years after Boudica's uprising: the scorched earth policy of Suetonius Paulinus had left a blank canvas in the tribal lands of the Iceni which the Romans were now determined to fill with their own designs. With the vast bulk of the troublemakers killed and their kinsmen enslaved or forced to migrate, the provincial administration could unleash their long revenge. This came in the form of a new Roman town called Venta Icenorum – laid out in all its organised glory near an old military fort by modern Caistor St Edmund. The relics of the town can still be seen today, from the large amphitheatre to the grid-like streets which show clearly on aerial photographs. Built around AD 70, Venta Icenorum, or "market place of the Iceni", was the administrative seat for the region – and the beating heart of Romanisation that would feed the surrounding areas with the gospel of true civilisation. From its humble beginnings in wattle and daub and wood, the town developed into a full-scale Roman town with stone temples, vaulted baths with central heating and a piped water supply.

For a people who had lost their soul, compensation could be found in the baths, forum, shops and theatres of the smart new town; certainly the bulk of the town's population appear to have been native Britons who gradually came to join the urban lifestyle of their new overlords. In its heyday, Venta probably had somewhere in the region of three to five thousand people living in its Mediterranean-style houses; gone were the thatched roofs and circular layouts of their previous homes. The town had a sewerage system to keep the smell down during the hot summer months, and it was now possible to pop out to the shops to buy their daily bread.

But it seems that for all its magnificence and urban sophistication, the descendents of Boudica's warriors never really felt at home here. The population actually seems to have declined as the town became more established, and after the fall of the Roman empire and the rise of the Saxons, the people of

Venta abandoned this landscape of Roman artifice and melted back into the flat plains of the Norfolk landscape. For almost fifteen hundred years, the ruins of the town lay largely forgotten under fields until an RAF flight in 1928 took the remarkable photographs that brought it back to the fore. An archaeological dig followed and the layers of neglect were peeled back from the town to reveal the neat and ordered settlement that tried, and in the long run failed, to convert the Iceni from the proud rural warriors of Boudica into true Roman citizens, in heart, mind and soul.

However, against the backdrop of the continually changing tribal fortunes in the pre-conquest era, the period after Boudica's rebellion had become a time of relative peace for the majority of Britons. Within a decade, martial law had softened into civil administration: politically, the ground rules of governance had been set – and they would stay that way for most of England for the next three hundred years until the decline of the Roman empire. By AD 78, the fierce guerrilla resistance by the Welsh would finally be subdued while the rebellious Brigantes were being controlled by the networks of Roman forts and military bases. The growing political strength in the province meant that the Roman army could now re-distribute itself to start expanding the frontiers even further to the north, leaving the lands of the south to be controlled by civilian administrators in the new *civitates* across the country. No new Boudicas emerged to trouble the Roman mind: Britannia and the Britons now effectively belonged to them. Confident that their rear was free from the threat of uprising, the Romans started their push north into Scotland where they reached as far as the Highlands with their glorious victory against the Picts at Mons Graupius in c.AD 84 before lack of manpower forced their reluctant retreat back to the permanent boundary at Hadrian's Wall in the first half of the second century.

Nevertheless, the mere fact that the governor, Agricola, would even contemplate his push north into Scotland is testament to the belief that the province of Britannia was now safely Romanised with enough people buying into the new culture to guarantee its maintenance even without the bulk of the army or the direct presence of the governor. The threat of uprising had been extinguished, its tribal aristocracy transformed from warriors to civilians. Status was no longer achieved by fighting and feasting, it was down to money and influence – much as it is two thousand years on, in a modern Britain that still bears witness in both landscape and culture to almost five hundred years of Roman imperial rule.

CHAPTER 17
REBIRTH
& REVIVAL
Making History into Herstory

"…rather than any dishonour should grow by me, I myself will take up arms
– I myself will be your general, judge, and rewarder of every one of your virtues
in the field…[B]y your obedience to my General, by your concord in the camp,
and your valour in the field, we shall shortly have a famous victory over these
enemies of my God, of my kingdom and of my people."

ELIZABETH I, SPEECH TO THE TROOPS AT TILBURY
ON THE EVE OF THE BATTLE OF THE ARMADA, JULY, 1588

The queen knew that everyone was watching her, sitting atop her magnificent steed, her trademark red hair glowing like fire in the sunlight and clothed in a dazzling white dress and silver breastplate; in fact, she had made sure she was the centre of attention, parading her great horse throughout the vast, sprawling squadrons of her army. Now, though, she stilled the beast, sat high in her saddle and addressed the troops like a shimmering apparition:

"I am come amongst you as you see at this time, not for my recreation and
disport, but being resolved, in the midst and heat of battle, to live or die amongst
you all – to lay down for my God, and for my kingdoms, and for my people,
my honour and my blood even in the dust. I know I have the body of a weak,
feeble woman; but I have the heart and stomach of a king – and of a king of
England too."

But this wasn't Boudica – she had been dead for almost fifteen hundred years. This was Boudica incarnate: Elizabeth I of England, addressing her troops at Tilbury in July 1588. Instead of Rome and its empire, this time the queen's enemy was the new megastate of the Mediterranean: Spain, with its armada of battleships now lined up for war just off the coast of Britain. The two women may have been divided by a millennium and a half of history, but together they were transforming the image of women in power and shaping a compelling legacy that would root the idea of the warrior queen firmly in the public imagination right up to the modern day.

Elizabeth's accession to the throne in November, 1558, had been marked by a gloriously triumphant procession into the city of London amid demonstrations of patriotic fervour, peeling church bells and public jubilation. This was a time of severe religious schism between holders of the Catholic and Protestant faiths – and under her predecessor, Mary Tudor, the young Elizabeth proved herself adroit in manoeuvring between the two opposing factions. Her upbringing had required a skilful *pavane* of stepping between the two faiths – at least in terms of outward appearances; however, she had been born and raised a Protestant by her father and despite her relative conservatism (compared with the last few years of Bloody Mary's reign), she was now welcomed as the saviour of England's independence from the Holy Roman Empire – the last vestiges of Roman control over Britain.

Elizabeth may have been of the right faith at the right time, but as far as many were concerned, she was the *wrong* sex. This was far more than just a conundrum: it was deeply troubling to a nation that had lost its self-assurance and now looked for strong leadership. Under Mary Tudor, England had been forced to give up Calais, its last stronghold on the continent; the country was now politically isolated, its economy was in freefall and its society riven by the religious divide. Both England and Scotland had been under the control of a "monstrous regiment of women" – and for both countries the result was considered a cultural calamity. Clearly, little had changed since the views of Tacitus and Dio on the fitness of women to rule over a nation. Elizabeth's reign would thus not only require a remodelling of church, state and international geopolitics, it needed a complete makeover of women and power.

The basic problem for church and state was this: in the Bible, God commanded Eve that "Your desire shall be for your husband and he shall rule over you". This meant that in His Divine Plan, women were subordinate to men – but if you had a Queen Regnate, she would inevitably challenge God's commands by ruling over her husband, her parliament and her people: ergo, queens were anathema to the Christian faith. But after the death of Henry VIII's only son, Edward VI, there *was* no male heir to the throne – only Henry's two daughters remained – and many argued that both of those were illegitimate in the eyes of God: Mary, because of the "incestuous illegality" of her parents' marriage (Catherine of Aragon had married Henry's brother, then Henry – an act proscribed in the Bible); and Elizabeth, as she was born after Henry's self-proclaimed divorce.

With England facing a monarchical crisis, the crown lawyers invoked a philosophical precedent which – in theory at least – allowed for the possibility of a woman becoming queen, not just by marriage but in her own right. The monarch was said to have "two bodies" – one human and mortal, the other political and immortal. If the human flesh was weak, through youth, old age or infirmity, then the Privy Council and Parliament could act under "God's will" to ensure the survival of the body of the state. And if this could be done for a sick or senile king, it could also be done for a woman.

The next problem to be addressed regarded succession: it was hard enough for the nation to accept a female head of state – but with both of Henry's daughters considered by many to be illegitimate, their claim to the throne was even more tenuous. Mary Tudor avoided the moral question of her illegitimacy by neatly arguing that she claimed the throne by right of law rather than inheritance: Parliament had passed the Third Act of Succession in 1544 which allowed for Henry's daughters to become queen after his death, and he had confirmed his wishes in his will of 1546. As the older daughter, the death of Edward VI meant that she was now first in line to the throne and in 1553, Mary was crowned Queen Mary I of England and Wales.

There was still, however, the issue of queens and marriage: what would happen if the Queen chose to marry a foreign king – would he have dominion over England? Even though he signed a marriage treaty preventing him from claiming the English throne for himself, Mary's controversial marriage to Philip of Spain caused extreme anxiety throughout the land. Philip was despised – but the blame was put squarely on Mary for putting the country in such a vulnerable position in the first place. When she died childless in 1557, the relief at her passing was muted by the dread of having yet another troublesome queen with all the problems they inevitably brought along with them.

Despite the outward displays of jubilation for her entry into London, Elizabeth knew she would have to work hard to convince her new dominion – let alone the rest of Europe – that she was fit to govern. The first years of her rule were set against the same rampant misogyny her sister had faced, shored up by selective use of "God's Word" in the Bible and chauvinistic classical thinkers such as Aristotle and Aristophanes who were even now fresh and exciting after their rediscovery in the Renaissance. Across the length and breadth of Britain, people were still struggling to come to terms with its raft of female monarchs whose very existence challenged not only religious doctrine but social and political convention – the very pillars of sixteenth-century society. The result was an outpouring of bile against any woman who did not know her place – which in the Divine Plan, according to the German priest Martin Luther, God had decreed as "Kinder, Kirche und Kuche", i.e. "children, church and kitchen".

The debate about women's proper role in society was given some encouragement from an unlikely source; the typographic printing press. This had been invented around a hundred years before, apparently by Johannes Gutenberg in 1450, but it had taken a further twenty-five years for the writer and translator William Caxton to publish the first book in English. He set up his Westminster press in 1476 and it wasn't long before the public realised that printed material could reach more people more quickly than scribes or orators could ever achieve: in other words, the medium was perfect for the spread of religious ideas, chief among which was the new religious orthodoxy of Protestantism. Luther's writings were now joined by those of his Scottish contemporary, John Knox who published his infamous book, *The First Blast of the Trumpet Against the Monstrous Regiment of Women* in 1558 – the year of Elizabeth's accession. His tirade may have been directed against Mary Tudor, "that Jezebel of England" as well as the queens governing France and Scotland, but his viewpoint was general and dogmatic:

> "To promote a woman to bear rule, superiority, dominion or empire above any realm, nation or city is repugnant to nature, contumely to God, and the subversion of good order, of all equity and justice."

Knox might have been at the more extreme end of public opinion – and he was certainly embarrassed by the fact that a *Protestant* queen was on the English throne by the time his words were published, but he was far from being alone in his views: this was the era of the so-called "pamphlet wars" where claim and counterclaim about the nature and aptitudes of women flew hot off the press. Often anonymous or published under pseudonyms, *The Schoolhouse of Women* (1541) is typical of the genre, denouncing women as nothing but gossips whose powers of reasoning are "not worth a turd". However, earthy humour was not solely confined to the literate classes: a popular joke in the sixteenth century ran as follows:

> *Man 1: Why did you marry such a small woman?*
> *Man 2: Because she was the least of all the evils.*

Against this background, Elizabeth knew she was doubly vulnerable, both from those who reviled her religion and those who denigrated her sex. She therefore spent the first part of her reign gradually neutralising the Catholic threat to her throne by quietly removing any Catholic from positions of power. But her greatest coup was in helping to stage-manage one of the most extreme *volte-face* that public opinion has ever made: converting misogyny into the cult of courtly love – and queens from harbingers of inevitable doom into the "mother of the nation".

Elizabeth had learned from her sister's example: she had watched Mary trying to convince a sceptical public and had seen what worked and what did not. Like Mary, Elizabeth now started employing language as weapons against misogyny: if

Elizabeth I: "The Sieve Portrait"
c1583, by Quentin Metsys the Younger

Elizabeth is shown carrying a sieve as a symbol of her chastity as England's Virgin Queen, emulating the Vestal Virgin of the story by the humanist scholar, Petrarch: such was the virgin's virtue, she was able to carry water in a sieve without spilling a drop.

she was not respected as a woman then she would simply become one of the men. She began to play down her refined femininity, and talked instead of being a "prince" or of having "the heart and stomach of a king, and of a king of England, too". The body natural might have been a woman in all the fine dress of a queen but the body politic was transforming herself into a man.

Having reassured her subjects that, appearances aside, a queen was no different from a king, her next coup was to remove the anxiety over queenly marriage by almost certainly making the deliberate choice to stay chastely single. Of course, there was a precedent for this in history, too – the Amazons were said to have refused the bond of marriage as it would bring them under a man's control and they were not prepared to give up their awesome power. The classical myth played well with Elizabethan audiences nervous about any dilution of England's autonomy; it also added even more weight to the stately image of their monarch – an image she worked hard to foster. This "virgin queen" – unblemished by carnal distractions – began to assure her people that "there is no prince that loveth his subjects better" and to convince them that their love of her was more precious "than … any treasure or riches". To her courtiers and her people, this moral and disciplined leader had eschewed sexual love for courtly love – the purest, most perfect expression of utter devotion.

Courtly love was more than just an idea; fuelled by a promise that could never be resolved, it was a powerful mechanism for binding queen and subject together in a dynamic, enduring relationship that guaranteed Elizabeth's supreme position in the country's affection. Its inherent contradictions gave it perpetual motion: while offering as its prize the chance of unfettered intimacy, courtly love also kept Elizabeth at a distance from her subjects as it was by its very nature unrequited – and by making sure it stayed unrequited, she emasculated the very men who could have used their sex against her. This *coup de maître* not only increased the queen's allure: as a "weak, feeble woman" who ruled over powerful men it crucially narrowed the gender divide that had left her so exposed.

Elizabeth had now achieved a remarkable transformation of her public image but there was one aspect of her role as queen that was especially problematic – so much so that she would have to draw upon the help of other sources of support. It was safe enough for Elizabeth to be "wed" to her subjects or to be the "mother" of the nation: it was expected that women should be good wives, lovers or mothers and the "servile" role hardly taxed the public imagination. However, the problem lay with a queen acting outside the domestic sphere in what was perceived as the ultimate male domain: warfare. Mary Tudor had gained bitter experience in trying to convince her peers that she was fit to fight: in 1557 she had challenged the King of France to battle in Rheims – but he merely laughed at her and sent her envoy back, saying he could not take the threat seriously "when a woman sends to defy me to war".

Women and war: it's a theme that perplexed both Tacitus and Dio in the years after Boudica's death and has troubled people for the next two thousand years.

Elizabeth I: "The Pelican Portrait"
c1574, attributed to Nicholas Hilliard
Here, Elizabeth is shown with a pelican pendant on her breast to symbolise
charity, redemption and the selfless love of her subjects. According to
legend, the pelican pricked its own breast to feed its children with its
blood. The pelican jewel was a favourite of Elizabeth's when she was being
painted - and selfless love was one of the Queen's favourite themes.

In January, 2005, Condoleezza Rice was interrogated before the American senate
as President George W Bush's nomination for Secretary of State: the questioning
lasted an incredible nine hours and from the news coverage it seemed that one
main question was on everyone's mind – was she tough enough to take America
to war? I found myself glued to the broadcasts, unable to believe the poorly
disguised sexism in some of the reports, for the issue was less about her politics
or the policies of the Bush administration; it was the fact that she was taking
on the role *as a woman*. Small wonder, then, that the warrior queen has an ageless
fascination.

★

With England's power in Europe destroyed by the military defeats of Mary's reign, Elizabeth could not afford to be regarded politically as the weaker vessel. Like the Roman Emperor Claudius invading Britain, she had to prove herself in the theatre of war for the sake of her status at home and abroad. And her opportunity came in 1588 when Philip II of Spain was massing his naval fleet to mount his invasion of England. His motives were simple: to restore the Roman Catholic faith to England, to punish England for its pirates and the harrying attacks by Sir Francis Drake and to teach England a lesson after it sided with the Dutch against rule by Spain.

For Elizabeth, this challenge to her authority was deeply personal: as her former brother-in-law, Philip was now at risk of regaining the English throne – a thought which Elizabeth refused to countenance both for her nation's and her own sake. Philip may have had the bigger army – but Elizabeth had the faster ships and better guns. And, like her passionate admirers, she also had the resourcefulness to draw upon the theme that had given immortality to another British monarch: the warrior queen, Boudica.

There is no hard evidence that Elizabeth and her advisers drew directly on this infamous queen from Britain's past to legitimise the role of the female fighter in her speech to her troops at Tilbury; there is even the strong probability that the queen's reported speech and apparel were much later fabrications – part of the cult of Elizabethan hero-worship – but however they came to public attention, it cannot be denied that the parallels between Elizabeth and Boudica do bear an uncanny correspondence, not only in the images created to depict the two women but in the very language used in their epic pre-battle speeches. It is almost certain that Elizabeth knew of her infamous predecessor: Polydore Vergil had written his radical "new" history of Britain around 1512-13, borrowing heavily from Tacitus as a source of information; this was published in 1546, and by 1582 had so impressed the Privy Council that it became required reading in all English schools.

However, as one of the educated elite of Europe, Elizabeth would already have been familiar with the famous authors of antiquity; she had in the words of her tutor, Roger Ascham, a "perfect readiness in Latin" and the classics that would have included Tacitus. Since his rediscovery in the fifteenth century he had become one of the best-sellers of the Renaissance and was now considered to be essential reading; in fact, Tacitus was later translated into English by Sir Henry Savile, who tutored Elizabeth in Greek. With few heroic warrior queens available to history, Elizabeth – or her chroniclers – would have sought inspiration from every one they could find, and then poured it into the dramatic address to her troops.

Both women's speeches have them claiming to be acting as "one of the people", both talk of facing the enemy threat with the support of their god(s), and both vow to "take up arms" to restore their people's freedom and their own damaged "honour". What is more, both women say they are well-prepared to die for their cause. But perhaps most interesting of all, both women make a special feature of their gender, laying male and female stereotypes side by side – and then confounding them by standing as the exception to the rule. Even the iconography of them addressing their soldiers in the very field of battle is a shocking image for the times – and it's a powerful image that's made all the stronger by Elizabeth's protestations that she is "a weak, feeble woman" when in fact she is majestic on her white horse, a singular woman directly addressing the thousands of men in front of her. Small wonder, then, that in the glory of victory over the Armada of Europe's dominant empire, Elizabeth became the reincarnation of the Iron Age warrior queen.

Within a decade or so of victory over the Armada, Elizabeth's transformation from monstrous woman to virgin queen was complete and she reached the apotheosis of her cult worship. Superficially, at least, she had presided over the expansion of the British empire in North America (the colony of "Virginia" being even named after her), the amassing of embarrassing amounts of Spanish gold by Drake and the defeat of Spain's navy that, until then, had dominated the world's oceans. Domestically, she had brought political stability to her nation and achieved the remarkable feat of stabilising the debased coinage of the realm. Both at home and increasingly abroad, she was revered as a world-class leader and something close to a goddess. But much more than that – she had transcended her earthly embodiment to become a moral idea.

The move had begun around 1559 which saw the publication of John Aylmer's *An Harborowe for Faithfull and trewe Subjectes*; this rigorous defence of female government firmly connected the female monarch with "some secret purpose" of God's will. By the 1580s and 1590s, the idea of Elizabeth as God's proxy was now firmly rooted in English society, with the queen portrayed as the epitome of achievement in the life-long moral struggle. These years marked a flurry of fawning celebration in art, literature and the stage typified by Edmund Spenser's epic poem, *The Faerie Queen* – a public tribute to Elizabeth. The poet's heroine was "Gloriana" – the Faerie Queen herself and an unashamed representation of Glory and the real Virgin Queen. However, in a neat duplication of the "monarch's two bodies", the other strong female character in the poem is Britomart, the female knight-cum-warrior who represents the moral virtue of Chastity. In this literary *tour de force*, Spenser therefore manages to conflate the often conflicting faces of Elizabeth – as virgin and warrior – and unite them in a tale of a queen in her magical kingdom.

But the rebirth of the warrior queen wasn't merely left to Elizabeth I or Spenser's Britomart: the sixteenth century bore witness to an emerging corpus of literature that featured that first British warrior queen herself – Queen Boudica of the Iceni.

Until now, Boudica had had a bumpy journey throughout the centuries, being either traduced or ignored altogether. Her main raft of survival as a meme in public consciousness was through copies of Tacitus and Dio that lingered in monasterial libraries after the collapse of the Roman Empire. In AD 410, with the empire in tatters, the province of Britannia had pleaded for military support in the fight against Pictish and Saxon invaders; the request was refused, and although Roman culture lasted for another two hundred years, this effectively marked the end of Roman rule in Britain and the beginning of the so-called Dark Ages.

The term Dark Ages is itself a clear indication about how the period was later viewed by historians: this was a time when barbarism once more rose to the surface and the glory of Roman civilisation was lost. In this light, when Boudica was mentioned as a barbarian queen who had fought against the Romans she was unlikely to win much in the way of reverence. Her first extant appearance (though not by name) is in the work of Gildas, a sixth-century historian who chronicled the story of Britain from the Romans to around AD 547 when he finished his *magnum opus*. Written in fine Latin, *De Excidio Britanniae* is an important and scholarly text for the period in which Gildas reveals a profound despair at the ungodliness of his contemporaries. He was probably taught in one of the Romano–British schools that still survived at this time – a fact that would help to explain his mastery of Latin and his pro-Roman perspective. Even the title clearly lays out his angle: it translates as "On the Ruin of Britain".

In his "history" (which actually contains very few names or even dates), kings are "tyrants" and priests are "fools" but the passage attributed to Boudica's rebellion also sets it in a most unfavourable light:

> *"that treacherous Lioness, who murdered the Rulers who were left behind...to show the enterprises of the Romane Empire..."*

In this savage account of how Britain degenerated from the "manners and lawes" of Rome, even his own countrymen get short shrift: when the Romans sought revenge for the rebellion, these "crafty fox cubbes" failed to continue the fight for freedom:

> *"...backs in place of shields were turned to the pursuing foes, necks subjected to the conquering swords, cold fear invading all their limbs, and suppliant hands stretched out woman-like to be bound; so that it was said far and near, as a proverb and scornful reproach, that Britain was neither valiant in war nor faithful in peace."*

> GILDAS: *"DE EXCIDIO BRITANNIAE"* TRANSL. 1652,
> JOHN HANCOCK, (SPELLING MODERNISED FOR CLARITY)

Boudica next comes to light via the Northumbrian priest and chronicler, the Venerable Bede (c. 673-735) but his account of her rebellion in his *"Historia Ecclesiastica Gentis Anglorum"* (finished in 731) is just as vague, largely because he was drawing on Gildas for his own information rather than any classical sources or archaeology. Boudica aside, his work is more interesting for highlighting the concept of a single "gens Anglorum" – the English – instead of the many kingdoms that until now had characterised the country; and with the idea of an "English" Christian identity comes a stronger desire to find the origins of that island race.

This was the challenge picked up in the late eighth or early ninth century by the Welsh antiquary, Nennius. We know very little about the man himself but his lasting contribution to the canon of British literature is that he is the first recorded person to mention the infamous King Arthur in his *Historia Brittonum* – a history of England which he either wrote or edited – but like his predecessors, his treatment of Boudica's rebellion is scant in the extreme: her battle against the Romans is reduced to just a passing mention, although he claims to have drawn his materials from a wide range of sources, including "the annals of the Romans".

With Arthur now emerging as the dominant heroic figure of the early modern age, Boudica is squeezed completely from the history of Britain and essentially disappears, not even re-appearing in the mythical "history" of Geoffrey of Monmouth (d. 1155). Monmouth's *Historia Regum Britanniae*, or "History of the Kings of Britain", is a curious assemblage of stories, published some time between 1135 and 1139. He claimed it was translated from "a very old book in the English tongue" brought over from Brittany by Walter, Archdeacon of Oxford. Variously dismissed in the modern era as "spurious hokum" and "creative imagination" with a historical content of "almost nil", his work is more interesting for revealing something of the mindset of previous generations of Britons in how they manufacture their histories. He makes no mention at all of Boudica, preferring to focus on how Britain was founded by Brutus, the descendent of Aeneas, and Britons are thus intimately connected with the Romans who stem from a line spawned by Aeneas after his escape from Troy.

For almost four hundred years, Britain languished under this Romanised foundation myth; meanwhile, Boudica had been forgotten – at best reduced to a passing footnote in history. She neither fitted the kind of past the Britons now wanted for themselves, nor had she any relevance in their medieval society. This was a time when the church and state were extending their monopoly over the lives and even the thoughts of the people; there was certainly no room for a rebellious warrior queen who challenged the authority or ideology of "legitimate" government.

And then, in the dawn of the Renaissance, as the ancient classical texts were rediscovered and harvested for their information and new ideas, it became impossible to reconcile known fact with the pseudohistories that had sustained for centuries. With science, religion – even the arts being challenged by new twists on ancient ideas, the old historical myths were no longer convincing. While the original writings of Tacitus had long since been lost, copies of the first six books of his annals had been made around AD 850, with books 11 to 16 found in a separate, single manuscript dating from the eleventh century. In the days before printing transformed the availability of the texts, these manuscripts were as precious as gold: copying then by hand could take years, with each successive version introducing more errors and "improvements" – but to the rich and powerful, books were not only a store of knowledge, they were a symbol of wealth and prestige, and a key into the inner circle of the intellectual elite that was driving European politics and ideas.

The story of the *Annales 11-16* is typical of its day and especially typical of the Tacitus texts: like many of these literary treasures, it was stored in the famous monastery on the summit of Monte Cassino, some 120 kilometres/87 miles south-east of Rome. This manuscript, written in the hard-to-decipher Beneventan hand that characterised the monastery's work, is believed by many scholars to be only one step removed from the original text – a fact that enhanced its value inordinately and made it a prime target for book collectors who operated in the twilight zone of legality. There is documentary evidence that the *Annales* manuscript was used by a visiting bishop at Monte Cassino some time between 1331 and 1344, but it next comes to light some thirty years later in a list of books bequeathed to Florence's Santo Spirito monastery by the eminent Italian poet and scholar, Giovanni Boccaccio. Boccaccio died on December 21, 1375 leaving his vast library of works that had helped to ignite the humanist movement of the Renaissance; how he came to "acquire" the prized Monte Cassino manuscript is still the subject of much intrigue and suspicion: despite him being one of the leading figures of the early Renaissance, it seems that he wasn't above "liberating" it from the monastery shelves.

Such skulduggery was nothing in the book world – and more was to be added to the manuscript's secrets. It next comes to light in the hands of the

Renaissance intellectual and wealthy book collector, Niccolò Niccoli (1364-1437). His private library was the best and most extensive in the whole of Florence and it seems he would stop at nothing to enhance it. A letter from a friend begging to see the manuscript in around 1427 proves that it was then in Niccoli's possession, while the promise to keep its existence under wraps strongly suggests that it should never have been in Niccoli's hands at all. At his death, some ten years later, the treasured text was amongst those passed to the nearby monastery at San Marco, where it was copied and sold to an elite band of Renaissance humanist thinkers, and from then on was made available to a much broader section of the public following the development of the printing press in 1450.

Although only half of his *Annals* and *Histories* had survived, the works of Tacitus became required reading for anyone in the fifteenth and sixteenth centuries wanting to be considered well-read. Latin and Greek were still the *lingua franca* of the intelligentsia and no classical education was complete without a thorough knowledge of the ancient world and its histories. The fact that they were used in Britain by writers such as Polydore Vergil and his contemporary the Scottish humanist and historian, Hector Boece, to turn *national* histories on their head just made it even more important to know and understand what Tacitus and his contemporaries were alleging. Now, every assumption was ripe for challenge – the era of critical thinking had dawned.

By the time that Elizabeth was captivating her loyal subjects, the legend of Boudica was stumbling out of the pages of Tacitus and then Dio like a hedgehog from its winter nest of leaves – blinking into daylight and then looking around at a changed world. In the eight hundred years her story had slept since Nennius's *Historia Brittonum*, England had been transformed: the Romans were still respected but this was done against the context of a new and developing pride from the country's growing *English* identity, drawn from the achievements of the present day and the dynasties of *English* monarchs stretching back for hundreds of years. Now with a heritage of its own, England had less need to glorify a foreign past – and in particular a foreign past that battled against powerful women leaders like its current queen.

Boudica's story was now conflated with that of the queen and the two women mutually reinforced one another's public image. The timing was critical: women rulers were in desperate need of some good publicity – and now Elizabeth gave her citizens the perfect motive for revering powerful women and keeping them, literally, centre stage. Courtly plays, epic poems and even masqued balls were commissioned and stage-managed throughout her reign to celebrate great women from history and by inference, Elizabeth herself. Writers fell on any characters they could find who could illustrate the glory of women: from the Old Testament, the judge and prophetess, Deborah, and also Jael (who saved her people by hammering a tent peg through the enemy king's head) or warrior queens from classical antiquity like Pentheselia and her tribe of Amazons. One notable *masque* in 1579 – laid on to entertain the agent of a suitor for the queen – left little doubt about the kind of image Elizabeth wanted to put forth to the world at large: in an echo of the classical Amazonians, the actors played out an imitation of a tournament whereby six men were "defeated" by six ladies and had to offer their total surrender. Although portrayed through the genteel tableau of theatre, the message was clear: women could – and sometimes did – rule over men.

This was an environment into which Boudica could step cautiously into the open: though still regarded with suspicion over her prickly and aggressive behaviour towards the establishment, by the late Renaissance there were more spaces or niches available where she could feel at home. Her cause was given a boost in 1590 when, in the face of growing religious tension, playwrights were forbidden from dramatising religion and therefore turned instead to heroic and allegorical tales from history and mythology. From now on, Boudica was welcomed back into the sphere of public life, and people were soon watching her "story" in the new inn yard and playhouse theatres for a penny up to sixpence a time.

Boudica's rehabilitation had got off to a promising start: from her secure base as *Voadicia* in Virgil's history, Boudica had increased her heroic realm to include Boece's *Chronicles of Scotland*, published two years before Elizabeth's accession of 1533. Strong but essentially feminine, Boece creates his own image of Boudica which draws upon Tacitus and, according to some modern scholars, perhaps even indigenous narrative: now called *Voada*, she is the sister of Caratak (Caratacus) and Corbreid – both kings of Scotland – and has not only two daughters but a son whom her husband tries to disinherit in his will, in favour of the girls. Following the beatings and rape of Voada and her daughters by the Romans, the queen leads an army of five thousand British ladies who have been similarly dishonoured; they vow to fight to the death to "vindicate their injuries". When faced with defeat, Voada kills herself while her daughters survive – the elder being married to the Roman who raped her, the younger continuing the fight against the enemy with "manly courage" until captured and executed for being unrepentant in her role as a warrior woman.

As Elizabeth's reign progressed, Boudica's story was developed, refined and recycled: Virgil's Voadicia was picked up by Raphael Holinshed to help create his "Voadicia, alias Bonduica" in the *Chronicles of England, Scotland and Ireland* (published 1577 as two volumes) – which in turn was plundered by Shakespeare as a source of information for his historical plays. In the continual evolution of the story, the manifold themes of gender, war, religion and the monarchy were also adapted to suit the mood of the day: Queen Boudica of England might sometimes beat the Roman enemy who would frequently become the proxy for the Roman Catholic church; in other accounts, the rape of her daughters might be edited out if the idea of rape was unseemly to an Elizabethan audience, or Boudica's daughters might be expunged from the record altogether as they did not "fit" the comparisons between Boudica and a "Virgin Queen".

But whatever the formulation of this cultural pick-and-mix, its basic character was pleasing to Elizabeth's tastebuds. As Boudica's story became redrafted to match her own, the two queens became almost interchangeable so that when Spenser proclaimed "Bonduca" – "O famous monument of women's prayse", he could have used either woman's name: just like the concept of the monarch's two bodies, when it came to heroic and legendary women, the nation of Elizabethan England was getting two in one.

Boudica's reputation may have been shored up by helping to legitimise her sixteenth-century "counterpart" in her guise as warrior queen but by the last decade of Elizabeth's reign, it was growing hard to romanticise a crabbit old woman through the charade of courtly love. Elizabeth-the-idea was becoming more and more polarised from the Elizabeth-the-reality, now overly made-up with a white face and heavy red wig and short-tempered to boot. With the economy beleaguered by inflation, unemployment and a series of bad harvests, Good Queen Bess seemed to be losing her legendary grip over England; across the water, rebellions in Ireland were challenging her image as a warrior queen, while even her most loyal subjects at home were growing tired of the behaviour of her "favourites" who seemed to add nothing to the nation except greed and corruption. In the words of Sir Walter Raleigh, the queen was now "a lady surprised by time". With failing health and humour, she was manoeuvred into proclaiming James VI of Scotland as her successor – and then, on March 24 1603, in her seventieth year, Elizabeth I of England quietly died.

Conjoined to her royal alter-ego, Boudica could have suffered the same fate, disappearing once more into the silence of history. But after almost half a century of her reign, Elizabeth was too strong a brand to merely fade away and Boudica was too firmly rooted in the public imagination to drift once more into obscurity. However, while it could have been deemed disloyal to muddy the name of England's former sovereign, there was no such problem with a queen from the time of antiquity: like the Ugly Sister to James VI's male Cinderella, Boudica now became the focus of an attempt by playwrights and authors to reclaim the monarchy for men and put women back in their rightful realm of powerlessness.

On his triumphant journey south to London in 1603, James VI of Scotland scattered royal largesse over his new English subjects, showering them with bounty and titles in a move that won him both friends and favours. Already King of Scotland, he now became James I, the self-styled "King of Great Britain": England's most experienced monarch since William the Conqueror five hundred years before. He brought with him a reputation as a learned philosopher – astute, able and thoroughly commanding. And to begin with, his reign in England was marked by a popular sigh of relief: here was a real king – a man with a wife and children to provide stability for a royal line; Elizabeth may have been a fine queen in her day, but as a woman she was inevitably problematic: she had not been able to *sustain* her greatness like the *inherent* greatness of a man.

The patriarchal reassurance of the people was reflected in a swing in the tone of dramatic writing: within a few years of James acceding to the throne, English playwrights were not only facing more censorship than ever before, they were also penning a very different tale of the warrior queen Boudica, the former heroine of all England. Gone was her primal strength and courage – and in its place were the stereotypes that have been used to demean women for the last three millennia of recorded history: mental and physical inferiority, craftiness and petulance.

The new, darker and more misogynistic tone was ably demonstrated by one of the most popular playwrights of the day: John Fletcher was born in Sussex in 1579 and his childhood was steeped in the cult of Elizabeth. His own father had been a chief tormentor of Mary, Queen of Scots and had even officiated as the chaplain at her execution. But it seems that the younger Fletcher inherited little of his father's religious prejudice; he went up to Cambridge where he became a Bible Clerk and then re-emerges in the public record as a fully-fledged dramatist, writing his own scripts or co-writing or contributing to plays by all the major playwrights of the period, including Ben Jonson, Francis Beaumont, Philip Massinger and even William Shakespeare.

A flavour of the time came in Fletcher's first collaboration with Beaumont in a 1606 play called *The Woman-Hater* which was followed over the next few years by *The Maides Tragedy*, *Cupid's Revenge* and *The Woman's Prize*. Then, sometime between 1611 and 1614, Fletcher began writing a manuscript for a play based on the ancient queen who had almost driven the Romans out of Britain. Performed on numerous occasions throughout his career and after his death, *Bonduca* is a slim play that has undergone some considerable revision, from Boudica having a son, Hengo, to him being her "nephew". Fletcher seems to have drawn his information from Holinshed's *Chronicles*, though his styling of her name as Bonduca appears to be original while her two daughters are either un-named (the elder) or Bonvica (the younger). Once again, Caratacus appears as the mighty British warrior, Caratack, who commands Queen Bonduca's army of Britons and is the real seat of military and authoritative power.

To a modern audience, even in the play's early published form, *Bonduca* does not make easy reading as a piece of dramatic narrative but its language and symbolism are absolutely riveting. Rather than being a hero in her own right, Bonduca has evolved into a cantankerous, "meddling" "virago" who interferes with the campaign of Caratack and ultimately helps lose him the war. True to Tacitus's account, the daughters are raped by the Romans – but the audience's sympathy is in no way directed towards them as the young women then seek revenge by capturing and torturing their rapists until the men are released by a furious Caratack:

> Caratack: *A Woman's Wisdom in our Triumphs? Out, ye sluts, ye*
> *Follies; from our Swords Filch our Revenges basely? Arm*
> *again, Gentlemen: soldiers, I charge ye, help 'em.*
> Daughter 2: *By ————-, Uncle, we will have vengeance for our Rapes.*
> Caratack: *By ————-, You should have kept your Legs close then.*

The rampant misogyny expressed in the play continues when the daughters argue with their uncle over his release of the men who raped them; but he gives them short shrift, ordering them out of the room and back to their mother's side:

> Caratack: *Learn to Spin And cure your knotted Hemp.*
> JOHN FLETCHER: *BONDUCA – A TRAGEDY,* WRITTEN 1611-1614

Not only are women thus ordered back to their "natural" sphere – as opposed to being *un*naturally in the military domain of men, they are stripped of their power to think or act independently of men's authority. This was a favourite concept of Jacobite England: King James famously dismissing one "learned Maid" who could allegedly read and speak Latin, Greek and Hebrew with the simple question, "But can she spin?"! The comparisons in Caratack's sneering humour and spinning quip would not have been lost on a contemporary audience.

But under the humour lies a more serious threat for the power that women had expressed throughout the reigns of Elizabeth and the two Marys. The Scottish humanist and scholar, George Buchanan, was a bitter enemy of Mary,

Queen of Scots and had been one of those responsible for preparing the prosecution that ultimately led to her execution. He became the young James's tutor when he was still King of Scotland, and schooled him in the ideology of "proper" government, as written down in his *History of Scotland* of 1582:

> *"'Tis no less unbecoming [in] a Woman to pronounce Judgement, to levy Forces, to conduct an Army, to give a Signal to the Battle, than it is for a man to tease Wool, to handle the Distaff, to Spin or Card, and to perform the Services of the Weaker Sex. For that which was reckoned 'Fortitude and Severity' in a man turned to 'Madness and Cruelty' in a woman."*

In the absence of any real mass media or widespread literacy, Jacobite society learned its values from proclamations from the pulpit, from the king and from performances such as the raft of early seventeenth-century plays. Drama was *necessarily* male-dominated in terms of any storyline because the stage was deemed inappropriate for women until 1660 and the reign of Charles II; this meant that even a play which should have focused on a central female character like Boudica would inevitably have more men than women leading the action – women could give their name or appearances, but they could do so as boys or young men dressed up to suit the role. As well as banning women from the stage, Jacobite theatre was even more heavily censored by the Lord Chamberlain than it had been during Elizabeth's reign. Theatre wasn't just mere frivolous recreation, it could also function as the Soviet state television of its day – didactic and propagandist (both in terms of religion and politics) but with the message broadcast through the medium of entertainment, so what might seem a casual use of leisure time to a modern audience was hugely significant in terms of shaping public opinion.

Fletcher understood this all too well: his characters are a clear expression of the need for theatre to make moral judgements. Far from being believable as human individuals, the roles become allegories for male and female "virtues": women are therefore "whores", meddlers, commanded by the Devil, "sluts" and "follies" who betray "a strong man's valour to Fury" while the male characters are "worthy", brave, natural-born leaders and soldiers – regardless of whether they are British or Roman. The play concludes with Caratack fighting the Roman commander, Swetonius, but eventually ceding defeat:

> *Swetonius: Thus I embrace thee, And let it be no flattery that I tell thee Thou art the only soldier.*
>
> *Caratack: How to thank ye. I must hereafter find upon your usage. I am for Rome.*
>
> *Swetonius: Ye must.*
>
> *Caratack: Then Rome shall know The Man that makes her Spring of Glory grow.*
>
> *(they continue to talk, resolving their differences and forming a common bond)*
>
> *Swetonius: Ye shew a Friend's Soul. March on, and through the camp in Every Tongue, The Virtues of Great Caratack be Sung.*

For Fletcher, it was clearly easier for a man to love and respect his enemy if they were both soldiers, than to love and respect a woman with power. Boudica was back on the wrong side of the gender divide – too useful to be discarded into the midden of history, but her sole purpose was now reduced to an exemplar of how things go wrong when society lets a woman be in charge. According to Caratack, Bonduca had left nothing but a "wilderness of wretches", despoiling the very kingdom she had sought to save. Female rule might have made good theatre but its inevitable result was poor government.

After a successful career in British theatre, John Fletcher died in the London plague of 1625 along with some forty thousand of his neighbours in the capital, after giving up his chance of escaping to the countryside in order to be measured up for a new suit. Having helped to shape the cultural fashions of the seventeenth century, it is no small irony that he ended up one of its victims.

But when it comes to roles and rules for men and women, Fletcher's work – and Jacobite theatre – aren't quite as clear cut as they might first appear. A ribald undercurrent throughout the reign of James I was his effeminacy and rumoured bisexuality (he had fathered several children with his wife, Anne of Denmark). If the people of England wanted a forthright and macho patriarch for a leader, what they got was an ageing and effete philosophical dandy, who openly kissed other men in public, proclaiming his love and calling them his "wife" and himself, the "husband". In fact, it is alleged that the favoured joke from the city taverns to the Privy Council when James arrived to take up the throne in London was that "Elizabeth was King: now James is Queen!". It was hardly the shining example of traditional masculinity for which they had been praying.

While his rule in Scotland had been broadly welcomed as successful, James was growing increasingly unpopular with the English parliament and its people. There was now the mounting feeling that as well as inheriting a sexual changeling, they had been given a religious Janus too. In a move that was deeply troubling to English contemporary society, their allegedly Protestant king was now displaying pro-Catholic sensibilities by flirting politically with the Holy Roman Empire. Small wonder, then, that Fletcher alluded to Caratack's eventual submission to "Rome", while Bonduca for all her faults died loyal, never veering from her nationalist and *Protestant* path. It was a reminder after all the anxiety over female rule that it wasn't just queens who could prove problematic.

In an unwitting parody of his predecessor's Armada speech, the image of James passed down through history was of a weak, feeble *man*, fiddling with his codpiece, slobbering with his tongue too big for his mouth – and filling his court with young boys and male "favourites". In his own way, he *did* manage to exclude women from the political arena but he did not do this to expand a militaristic sphere; instead he pursued his divine right to behave – and to spend the nation's wealth – exactly as he pleased. By the end of his reign, he had managed to alienate both Houses of Parliament along with the nation, and to more than double the large debt left by Elizabeth.

On March 27, 1625, James I died of gout and senility at his favourite country residence at Theobalds in Hertfordshire. He was just a few months short of his fifty-ninth birthday and had been a king – firstly of Scotland, then of "Great Britain" – for all but one year of his long and eventful life. He was succeeded by his second son, Charles, who inherited the kingdom, a fervent distrust of the monarchy among the population and a debt of around a million pounds.

Charles I may have been born into royalty, but he was not born to be king. Small in stature, quiet in character with a dreadful stammer, and married to the hated French Catholic, Henrietta Maria, he was never going to be a popular choice. Under his reign the fundamentalist Puritans grew ever more reactionary and alienated from the king who clung onto his high church ideology; with parliament also moving further and further away from the monarch, the inevitable result was complete social breakdown – and in 1642, Britain descended into civil war. For the ordinary people trying to go about their daily business, this was a time of religious extremism, violence and savage tale-telling. After a promising start by the Royalists, the king's forces suffered a string of humiliating defeats against Cromwell and his New Model Army. Soon the country was polarised and treachery seemed to be around every corner. Leisure was now the recruiting ground of the devil: theatres were banned, witch-hunts were rife and any frivolity was interpreted as intolerable ungodliness. On January 30, 1649, following his capture and trial for treason, Charles I went to the executioner's block, still refusing to acknowledge the judgement of an earthly court over a divine king – but his death solved few of the country's political or social neuroses. Mid-seventeenth century England must have been a very dark place indeed.

The snakes and ladders of popularity that Boudica had been experiencing over the previous centuries was about to take another turn – and again, it would be due to external forces. In the era following Charles's execution, with no market for plays and little demand for anything that wasn't weightily religious and self-improving, the story of the warrior queen was once more largely hidden from view. For eighteen years, the theatres were silent, gagged by the laws of a land that lurched from the battles between king and country to the instabilities of parliamentary rule under Oliver Cromwell. The England that emerged under the restoration of the monarchy was chastened, exhausted and ready for social change. Charles I's oldest surviving son, now proclaimed Charles II, returned from political exile in Europe to the white cliffs of Dover on May 25, 1660, arriving in London amidst jubilant celebrations on May 29 – the day of his thirtieth birthday. He would earn his popular moniker of "the Merry Monarch" of Great Britain and Ireland, raising the curtain for British theatre almost as soon as he reached the capital.

In an atmosphere of improved religious tolerance and weary of civil strife, Britain could at last begin to relax under its playboy king. The resurgence of the arts led to an explosion of playhouses across London and the provinces, showing all manner of works from refined dramas and the ever-popular Shakespeare to the witty, clever comedies of England's first known professional female writer, Aphra Behn. Meanwhile, not long after Charles's arrival in London, and to celebrate its new freedoms, the Vere Street Theatre put on a production of *Othello* which starred an actor called Margaret Hughes, believed to be the first woman ever to appear professionally on the stage. Her performance was clearly received with much satisfaction: shortly afterwards, the Royalist impresario Sir William Davenant (believed by some to be Shakespeare's son) signed up eight actresses of his own for his brand new theatre company at Lincoln's Inn Fields. Women could now feature not only in the script – but treading the boards as well.

With theatres now employing men and women, the tone of the plays began to change. Love was in the air, with all its twists and turns and heartfelt intimacies; but while female roles became more numerous and with more in the way of lines, their roles were rarely weighty – and even heroic historical figures like Boudica had to conform to the moralities and stereotypes of the day. In effect, the warrior queen of the seventeenth century was little more than a genteel Restoration woman transported back in time.

A clear example of this re-versioning of Boudica can be seen in the work of the renowned English poet and humanist, John Milton (1608-1674). In his search for true godliness and meaningful morality, he had conducted a tour not only through the literary works of the ancient classical writers but also to Italy, where he met humanist Renaissance thinkers and the aged astronomer, Galileo Galilei, under house arrest for his heretical views on the nature of the universe. Likewise, Milton's own controversial views on democracy and the fallibility of kings landed him in custody under threat of execution. But his strong feelings about democracy and his devout religious philosophy could not be reconciled with the spectre of powerful, independent women in the shape of Queen Boudica and also Cartimandua. In his *History of Britain*, written in the final years before his death, he chastises the classical authors for using the story of Boudica to demean the virtues of his country, arguing that "out of vanity" they seek to

> *"embellish and set out their History with the strangeness of our manners, not caring in the mean while to brand us with the rankest note of Barbarism, as if in Britain Women were Men, and Men Women".*

The echoes with George Buchanan's treatise about men spinning and women ruling ring loud and clear despite the two men being on opposite sides of the politico-religious divide; Royalist or Parliamentarian, it seemed that neither side was prepared to espouse the concept of women warriors – even if a whole army of women would help them win their cause. Whereas Milton describes "Cassibelan, Togadumnus, Venusius and Caractacus" as "full of magnanimitie, soberness and martial skill", Boudica's battle against the Romans was, indeed, barbarous – and not so much a war but "the wild hurrey of a distracted Woeman, with as mad a Crew at her heeles". Milton was even unhappy with Boudica voicing her grievances about the beating and rapes, considering it to be unbecoming in a lady to even speak of such matters, let alone in the company of men; to his way of thinking, the queen should have put up and shut up like a good Puritan Englishwoman. However, with forthright women and effete kings blurring the strict boundaries that made Britain what it was, this strait-laced poet must have found seventeenth-century England a morally bankrupt place.

Milton never got to see Charles Hopkins's new tragedy *Boadicea, Queen of Britain*. It was performed in London at the theatre in Lincoln's Inn Fields in 1697, almost quarter of a century after the poet's death, and although it used real women actresses which would doubtless have left him most uneasy, it did build upon his views of women's suitability for war and power. The title role was given to Mrs Barry – one of the leading actresses of the period and a popular successor to Nell Gwyn, the actress-turned-mistress of Charles II – but despite the star-studded cast of male and female actors, the plotline was far from balanced in its gender roles: just like in John Fletcher's *Bonduca*, Hopkins's *Boadicea* could not be seen to rule alone; instead she had a dominant male commander (this time not *Caratack* but *Cassibelan*) who stole the mantle of "warrior" from the "warrior queen". Women might have made it onto the stage and gained the possibility for their economic independence but their roles were still governed by the social mores of the day.

In compensation for this loss of power, the monarch's realm was boosted from being queen of the Iceni to queen of the whole of Britain. However, Boudica was now little more than a feisty female figurehead: instead of fighting (and losing) military battles on the field, she fought (and lost) domestic ones at home, struggling to keep a rein on the very complicated love life of her elder daughter and the rebellious behaviour of her younger one. With its love of manners and complex plotlines, grand gestures and noble death, Restoration theatre was not yet ready to allow its queen to mire her hands in the real blood of conflict; it would take another century or more before Boudica would win back some of the darker powers of a true warrior queen under poets like Tennyson – and only then would she use them to claw at the terrified flesh of that insolent foreign army who dared to oppose her might.

CHAPTER 18
CELTOMANIA
The Founding of a New Ethnicity

"Rise from the dust, ye relicks of the dead, whose noble deeds our holy Druids sing, Oh rise, ye valiant bones, let not base earth Opresse your honours, whilest the pride of Rome Treads on your Stocks, and wipes out all your stories."

JOHN FLETCHER: *BONDUCA*, PUBLISHED 1647

As the actors were taking their places for the opening scene of Charles Hopkins's *Boadicea*, nearby in the streets of a London remodelled by Sir Christopher Wren, a small volume of travel writing was being laid out in booksellers' windows. *A New Voyage around the World* contained the thoughts and experiences of a pirate-turned-respectable explorer, William Dampier. Orphaned at sixteen, he had taken to the seas in search of his fortune and when piracy failed to provide anything but the chance to be captured and executed, he changed tack and sailed under the flag of the British Admiralty in search of new lands ripe for colonisation and plunder. The journal of his travels around the Americas and Indies became one of Britain's most popular books and the talk of the new coffee and chocolate houses that were springing up all over the capital. Dampier's writing was a window into another world, of Native Americans, runaway slaves and sun-drenched lands. Like some exotic alien fantasy, it fired the imagination of a people who had rarely travelled beyond their own shores and were struggling to make sense of their own identity and place in the new world order; within a few years the new genre of travel-writing would be outselling even the Bible.

The impact of Dampier's voyages is hard to overstate: as well as gaining vast sums of foreign money and information for the British Government, his work gave concrete and colourful examples of what the brilliant English poet and historian John Dryden had termed "the noble savage". Then, on a voyage in 1703, his crewmember Alexander Selkirk asked to be put off the ship in the Juan Fernandez islands, four hundred miles west of Chile in the South Pacific Ocean; he was rescued by Dampier on his final voyage of discovery, and the experiences of the adventurous Britain-turned-native was later written up by Daniel Defoe to become one of the best-loved books of all time – *Robinson Crusoe*, published 1717.

Dampier also wrote a graphic and approving description of his time amongst the Miskito Indians of the Darien coast in Panama – an account that was seized upon by investors in the scheme to set up a Scottish colony and lucrative trading base in the region. This settlement was Scotland's great bid for an empire, with all the wealth, power and prestige that went along with it, let alone the trading opportunities possible from a base in the Americas that could bridge the Atlantic and Pacific Oceans. However, in their fervent desire to build a dream, the Scots had seriously over-invested. When the colony was established in 1698 (much to the chagrin of both the Spanish and the English), it proved an unmitigated disaster: beaten by an oppressively tropical climate, the antagonised local Indians and rampant international hostility, its settlers either died of disease or were killed in the ensuing fighting, and the few who returned to Scotland face the opprobrium of a nation now on the verge of bankruptcy.

Hopelessly in debt, Scotland was propelled into accepting the 1707 Act of Union which bound it permanently and politically to its dominant southern neighbour. The effect of the Act was not merely administrative: an unanticipated result of the Union was the cultural fall-out across the whole of the British Isles. While a badly shaken Scotland struggled to recover its national pride and confidence, the merger also had a huge impact on England's other neighbouring nation of Wales, which had been forced to concede its own independence in the Union of 1536. With England the undoubted leader in the new state of Great Britain, both Scotland and Wales tried their hardest to assert a strong, new national identity to distinguish themselves from the English.

The early eighteenth century became a bubbling cauldron of politics, ethnic identity, national pride and colonial power; what's more, all this was mixed together with a strong stock of new intellectual ideas about the origins of civilisation and Great Britain's place in the new world order. The resultant brew was the Enlightenment with emphasis on reason, deduction and thoughtful extrapolation which were used to try and explain the confusion that pervaded every aspect of existence, from the restructuring of agriculture, revolutionary politics in neighbouring France to Sir Isaac Newton's scientific ideas and the burning question of why women were wearing "panier" skirts up to five metres wide. But rationalist philosophies, laws of motion and "universal gravitation" were not to everyone's taste. Throughout the eighteenth century, there was also a growing desire to balance the scientific view of life with something a little less detached, something that respected the emotional world in which people lived – a world that was being despoiled by the industrial revolution and the loss of that primal link between humans and the land.

Slowly throughout the eighteenth century the great new era of Romanticism was fermenting and gaining strength, often tied in with the growing popularity of antiquarianism which strove to explain the material relics of the past. The trend of antiquarian pursuits was matched by an intense desire by intellectuals to "read" the landscape in order to learn about the ancestral past of Britain – yet in the absence of any notion of the real age of the earth, much of the theorising was heavily laced with romantic or wishful thinking. And there was nothing the Romantics liked better than a savage, heroic Briton who could stir the passions and remind us of our glorious and fundamental nature: it was time to call upon Boudica once more.

Boudica grew in popularity throughout the eighteenth century because her "story" could be made to fit as an allegory or celebration of British (that is, largely *English*) nationalism, while the background of Roman imperialism fitted nicely with Britain's own expanding empire in the Americas. Together, the two ancient cultures of Britain and Rome gave strength and depth to a developing pride in modern English culture. Having survived the rebellions and revolutions of the seventeenth century, Great Britain was (at least ostensibly) united geographically and in terms of its politics and leadership; and after years of having to focus on its domestic troubles, once the "small" matter of the Scottish Jacobite threat had been resolved, it could now concentrate on looking outwards to an exciting world of opportunity.

Exploration in the Americas – firstly by the Spanish and Portuguese, then latterly by the French and English – had revealed vast continents of people who still lived a "traditional" lifestyle. While the merchants and developers used the so-called Indians' ignorance of western ways to their own financial and territorial advantage, back home the philosophers pondered on who these "barbarians" really were and what they represented. Clearly, they reasoned, there must be a continuum of development – from "primitive" to "cultured" (that is, like the learned philosophers themselves) and from "innocence" to the corruption that marked modern society. But were the differences between the two inherent and immutable? And if not, what propelled a people to "progress" (as it was regarded) from their natural state to a state of degenerate sophistication? While the moral, scientific and religious arguments raged on about the primitive condition and the effect of cross-cultural contact, there was little compunction about exploiting the situation for the benefit of "civilised" mankind; after all, what would the natives want with land rights and material possessions anyway?

However, for the intelligentsia at least, it was not so easy to disassociate the "barbarians" from the civilised societies of Europe. The descriptions of Britons as savages and barbarians by the great classical writers such as Tacitus and Dio were a disturbing ancient parallel to the modern world of imperial expansion and the new peoples being encountered. Could it be that Europeans were now experiencing what the Romans had done two thousand years before? Were Britons such as Caratacus, Cartimandua and Boudica once like the native Americans – or the poor wretched aborigines of New Holland? In a desperate need to make sense of a world thrown into moral and intellectual turmoil, scholars began to delve into the deep history of their own land, hoping that the old stones, the heroic legends and the writings of the Greeks and Romans would shed some light on the darkness of time.

As far back as the mid-seventeenth century, a pioneering band of antiquarians had started to dig down into the further reaches of Britain's material and literary background in an effort to compose a British chronology from its "primitive" past to the present day – a chronology that was based on reality rather than myth. One such antiquarian was the writer and historian, John Aubrey (1626-1697); growing up in Wiltshire, he had become fascinated by the large monolithic stones at nearby Avebury and spent much of his life in dialogue about their origin. Classically educated, he knew all about the Roman invasions of Britain and about Boudica's revolt when Suetonius Paulinus was attending to the Druids of Mona. Caesar had explained about the priestly caste of Druids and its strong links to Britain – so could it be that Avebury's giant stones were some kind of Druidic temple dating back to the period just before the Roman invasion? After all, it made rational sense that the early ancestors of the British would want to build temples to celebrate their gods, just like the cathedrals and churches of his own day; not only that, it was a sign of some sort of cultural sophistication – a glint of promise in an otherwise barbaric people.

However likely it seemed that Avebury was indeed the work of the Druids, in the absence of not only scientific dating but a coherent archaeological record, about the most that Aubrey could achieve was to speculate within an artificial timeframe: he therefore proposed that the monument was around two thousand years old; after all, the religious dogma of the day asserted that the Creation had taken place in 4004 BC with Noah's Deluge in 2348 (working back by genealogical reckoning from the number of "begats" in the Bible) so the "Druids' temple" could not be older than that.

Aubrey's ideas were picked up and developed by the next generation of gentlemen antiquarians, chief amongst whom was William Stukeley, a Lincolnshire physician and writer. In 1717, Stukeley came across a copy of Aubrey's unpublished manuscript on Druid temples which so impressed him that he devoted his life to exploring the British and European countryside in order to make a full record of antiquarian discoveries. This was published in 1724 as the *Itinerarium Curiosum*, or *Observant Itinerary* – a work not only phenomenally influential in his day but long after his death in 1765 at the grand age of seventy-seven.

While antiquarians like Aubrey and Stukeley developed their theories on the material legacy of the Druids and their ancient subjects, eighteenth-century intellectuals were finding their own ways to make sense of the past. Early linguists such as Breton monk, Paul-Yves Pezron, and the Welsh patriot and scholar, Edward Lhuyd in Oxford were building on ideas about national origins and noble savages within their own cultures and developing theories based on the panoply of European languages to explain their ancestral links and pedigrees. In the late 1500s, Scottish humanist George Buchanan had highlighted the similarities between Gaulish and Scots Gaelic, suggesting that his countrymen were descended from the Gauls. Now, over a century on, over half the population of the Scottish highlands, Wales and southern Ireland were still speaking their ancestral tongue, while on the Continent, the same was true in Brittany.

After years of detailed and painstaking research, Lhuyd and his contemporaries realised that there were indeed similarities between all these languages – in Lhuyd's case, between ancient Gaulish and his native Welsh, plus Cornish, Breton and Gaelic. Lhuyd was fascinated by the similar conclusions of his French colleague and after reportedly pushing hard for the English and Welsh translations of Pezron's study in 1706, he published his own groundbreaking work a year later. In the magnificent *Archaeologia Britannica*, he implies all of these languages are "Celtic" – a hugely significant step for although he never extended the concept to the people themselves this was the first time the *idea* of "Celticism" had been extended across the Channel to Britain. In the writings of classical authors, the word "Celt" had only ever been used to describe the people living in continental Europe; not only did the Greeks and Romans call the British people "Britons", they reported that when questioned, this is exactly what the indigenous population of Britannia called themselves.

Despite Lhuyd's rigour in using the word "Celtic" solely for the ancient language itself, within a few years the people of eighteenth-century Wales had started to use the word to describe themselves: in other words, for the first time in history, a Celtic identity had been created in Britain. However, the reason for this move has more to do with politics than history, genealogy or linguistics: traditionally, Wales had been one of the last preserves of the ancient Britons who were pushed back into the less-accessible western fringes of the island by the Anglo-Saxon invasions of the eighth century – yet three weeks after *Archaeologia Britannica* was published, the Act of Union was passed between Scotland and

Ireland and the word 'Briton' was adopted as the identity of the people of this new superstate. This left the Welsh with an identity crisis on their hands: in a period of growing interest in national roots, the Welsh were keen to disassociate themselves from the English-cum-British – and Lhuyd's work gave them the perfect new moniker. By calling themselves Celtic, they were adopting more than just a new name; they were aligning and validating themselves with an entire ethnicity and ancient tradition. The new Celts now had a distinct identity *and* a classical pedigree.

Regardless of the fact that their ancestors had never described themselves as Celts, over the next three centuries the idea of a special, antique identity would be developed even further, acquiring its own unique culture and politics and links with Ireland and the other *non-English* parts of Great Britain. And where there were no historical or cultural precedents to draw upon, sometimes Celtic "traditions" were simply made up.

The castle was set back from the road on a grassy hill that overlooked a series of roundabouts and an artificial duck pond; its squat, square nature defied you to gain entrance against its will, and the giant wooden door required a two-handed effort to pull it open. I had gone along with friends who had seen the property come up for sale and they thought it sounded eccentric enough to be worth a viewing. Dating back to the Middle Ages, it *was* a genuine Scottish castle, albeit now surrounded by a modern housing estate. But what assailed our eyes as we climbed up the stone staircase was a frenzy of *Scottishness*: everything was tartan, from the chairs to the drapes to the rugs on the floor. The heavy iron candlesticks and fireguard were of Celtic designs, as were the mirrors which swirled in a riot of strange beasts and birds in front of your very eyes, and the owner had the music of Enya and Clannad piped as Muzak into every room. It was, quite simply, a torrent of "culture" that fulfilled every cliché in the book. Trying to be tactful, we questioned the owner to see if this really was her style – or whether she had decorated it specially for the market. "Oh no, I don't live here," she replied, "I just rent it out to Americans. They love all that Scottish history."

The whole package of Scottishness was up for sale: for just over three hundred thousand pounds plus a lifetime of repairs, you could buy yourself a whole identity. But if that's what sells, then who can knock it? What is widely called "kilts and kitsch" brings in millions each year to the Scottish economy. Never mind that modern kilts were invented in the nineteenth century by an English factory manager, and that Scots had only been calling themselves "Celts" for a little over two hundred years. Gaelic is regarded as a national language of Scotland but it was only ever really spoken by the highlanders and those living in the western isles. The northern isles had "Norn", the north-east had "Doric" and the lowlanders had "Scots" – all far removed from any Celtic language. So what does it say about us that we crave such artificial associations for our own identities? They may be a superficial, materialist expression but the central idea must represent some modern desire to be part of a tribal grouping. Two thousand years on, are we still struggling to define ourselves, relying on what we're *not* (Roman/English/French), rather than who we really are? But if you pile the shallow cultural symbols deeply enough and stand them in opposition to anything "foreign", will that give our nationalism meaning?

The movement that had started as a scholarly, academic pursuit meanwhile developed into what is now widely called "Celtomania". Within a century, the word Celt would become accepted, common parlance for describing the peoples of Great Britain. The Scots, Irish, Welsh – even the English – seized upon the new connection to a Celtic past and gloried in everything that came along with it, including a love of "savage nature" and "natural" religion, especially that of the Druids and ancient Britons.

If anyone kickstarted the wave of popular Celtic passion then the accolade must be given to James MacPherson from Badenoch in the highlands of Scotland. Born into a family of farmers in 1736, he showed enough early promise to win a place at Aberdeen and Edinburgh Universities before returning home as the village teacher. However, James was both romantic and fiercely ambitious – and his aspirations ran much higher than mere teaching. At the age of twenty-two, he moved to Edinburgh to pursue his dream to be a poet. His first work, *The Highlander*, was a long and largely unsuccessful piece but this was blown away by his next major work – *Fragments of Ancient Poetry Collected in the Highlands of Scotland and Translated from the Gallic or Erse Language* – published in the Scottish capital in 1760. This book was an instant success, not so much for what it was, but for what it seemed to promise: a hidden treasure-trove of third-century classical literature from a forgotten Gaelic bard named Ossian (Oisín), akin to a Scottish Homer. At a time of a cautiously growing Scottish identity to replace the traditional one polarised between highlanders and lowlanders, MacPherson gave his country exactly what it was looking for: a grand, unifying and classical status along with an ancient oral and literary tradition that, critically, was older than that of England. Within months, MacPherson was being paid to go poetry-hunting among the Gaelic speakers of the Highlands and Islands – and while he did uncover some short manuscripts, it seems that where he couldn't find worthy literature he merely fabricated it, passing it off as traditional, and from the ancient canon of the Celts.

By 1761, his poem, *Fingal*, was an instant hit, full of wild, savage romance from the songs of the Blind Bard Ossian. The impact of the work was astonishing, inspiring poets like Goethe and drawing comparisons not only with Homer but with Virgil and Milton, too. In fact, so strongly did it stir the Romantic heart that it's alleged that Napoleon even carried a copy of the poem into battle. Two more "ancient" poems followed in 1763 and 1765 but by now his critics were demanding the young man reveal his sources. He could not, largely because there were no ancient Homeric epics in Gaelic – and certainly none older than the tenth century; good though they were, he had simply used the occasional piece of genuine Gaelic poetry and then made the rest up.

At the age of twenty-seven, wealthy and bathed in popular acclaim, he moved to Florida to work as secretary to the Governor which at least kept him apart from his detractors. Many of these were Irish scholars, angry at the clear mixing by MacPherson of Fenian and Ulster legends and then – as if this wasn't heinous enough – his appropriation of traditional *Irish* heroes, insisting that they were, in fact, *Caledonians*. Another non-believer was the great diarist, Samuel Johnson, who made his own tour of Scotland in 1773; he searched long and hard for the original Gaelic manuscripts purportedly used by MacPherson and, when he was sure they could not be found, accused the young poet of being a fraud. In the bitter exchange that followed, Johnson was at his irascible best:

CELTOMANIA

February 7, 1775

Mr James Macpherson, —

I received your foolish and impudent letter. Any violence offered me I shall do my best to repel and what I cannot do for myself, the law shall do for me. I hope I shall not be deterred from detecting what I think a cheat by the menaces of a ruffian.

Would you have me retract? I thought your book an imposture; I think it is an imposture still. For this opinion I have given my reasons to the public, which I here dare you to refute. Your rage I defy. Your abilities, since your Homer, are not so formidable: and what I hear of your morals inclines me to pay regard, not to what you shall say, but to what you shall prove. You may print this if you will.

SAM. JOHNSON

JAMES BOSWELL: THE LIFE OF SAMUEL JOHNSON, 1791

Completely and utterly unrepentant, MacPherson returned from America to London where he took up a post as a government lobbyist, making full use of his abilities to "spin" snippets into weighty yarns; he later bought a private country estate back in Badenoch where he eventually retired. Until the day he died, MacPherson refused to divulge his sources, leaving the arguments over the poems' veracity to continue well into the nineteenth century.

However, the fact that he knew his best chance of success was by forging a work of "Scottish" history makes the point about a developing Celtic Romanticism even more clearly: MacPherson had both spotted the trend *and* filled the gap in the market. The fact that he also succeeded in inspiring some of the most influential poets of the age such as Goethe and Thomas Gray is testament to the power of his work in helping to satisfy an emotional yearning for a heroic and mystical past. In the meantime, MacPherson had added momentum to the wave of Celtic nationalistic passion; he also played a fundamental role in the "Highlandification" of Scotland so revered by future writers such as Sir Walter Scott (1771-1832) and championed by the next queen of Britain.

But it wasn't just Celtic peoples who were embracing rampant Celtomania: the Welsh, Scottish and Irish may have been reacting against the tyranny of Anglicisation but that didn't stop the English from becoming some of the most fervent Celtomaniacs around. As well as feeling a kinship of their own to their barbarian ancestors – after all, Boudica came from Norfolk – they claimed a spiritual connection through the ancient caste of Druids. In an era where the church still exerted a firm control over religious worship (and gender roles), the idea of a more organic religion, expressed through works of nature rather than the constructs of man, found mounting appeal throughout the eighteenth century and beyond.

The ancient Druids of Britain had managed to survive the suppression of the Roman years, particularly in the less Romanised fringes of the country where they were eventually incorporated, transformed or annihilated by the more persistent ideology of Christianity. However, Druids retained an important place in folklore (normally in the role of the symbolic anti-Christian) and even in some folk practices, such as the sacrifice of white bulls in Wales which died out only in the sixteenth century – and the marking of Hallowe'en, a terrifying Celtic New Year's Eve, elements of which continue to this day.

However, the first known appearance of the Druids themselves in early modern British culture was in John Fletcher's play, *Bonduca* in the first decades of the seventeenth century. This was followed in 1624 by the historian and antiquarian Edmund Bolton's assertion that "Bonduca" had been behind the building of Stonehenge. However, the work that established Druids as a part of the fabric of British cultural life was Michael Drayton's *Poly-Olbion* (1612-1622) which sang of the Druidical wonders of England's romantic countryside. Milton, Thomas Smith, Edmund Dickenson – all followed in writing about Druids in hushed and reverent terms.

A blip in their popularity occurred during the time of Oliver Cromwell's assault against the Irish in the middle of the seventeenth century; around the same time the famous English architect, Inigo Jones, scathingly commented that

Stonehenge could not have been the work of Druids as these "savage and barbarous people" were not "studious in architecture ... or skilful in any thing else conducing thereunto"; meanwhile, Jones bet his money on the Romans having built the ancient monument instead.

Despite some limited opposition from the likes of Inigo Jones, Druids became the darlings of many in the upper classes, combing a classical pedigree with a more natural form of religion. In a time of rapid social and political change where many people were feeling dislocated and redefining their identities, Druidism offered a sense of belonging set within an ancient, moral framework. By the start of the eighteenth century, it was already making the giant leap from being an abstract concept in literature to being an increasingly popular movement for the educated elite. Unlike the freemasons, who were similarly mystical but who "only" dated back to the Middle Ages and were originally for "trade", and the middle classes, Druidism offered landed intellectuals a new sense of ancestral and spiritual belonging.

John Toland (1670-1722) was a leading apostle of this new Druidism. Although born and brought up as a Catholic in Northern Ireland, he converted to Anglicanism before leaving Ireland altogether to attend many of the leading universities of Scotland and England. Regarded as something of a firebrand, he embarked on a career as a moral philosopher and writer. It was while in England that he came into contact with the antiquarian John Aubrey and became fascinated by the ideas of a priestly class for the ancient Britons. In an eighteenth-century parallel to the grand conferences of Druids in Caesar's day – and in the same year the first Masonic Grand Lodge was formed, Toland allegedly founded a "Mother Grove" during a gathering at the Apple Tree Tavern in London in 1717. Attended by "Druids" and bards from across Great Britain and Brittany, this first meeting spawned a formal Druidic Order called the *Universal Druidic Bond (UDB)*; this was apparently followed at the autumn equinox by another meeting in Primrose Hill where Toland was elected as "Chief Druid". Although he later pulled back from some of his earlier ideas, along with Stukeley and Aubrey, his influence guided much of the Druidic expansion throughout the eighteenth century.

★

Druidism was now taking the so-called Celtic world by storm. In 1723, the Reverend Henry Rowlands published his *Mona Antiqua Restaurata* which reconciled Druidic beliefs with Christianity by claiming that Druids were actually descended from Noah. This was nothing new – William Stukeley had already made the same grand claim but now the idea was taking a firm hold and validating the "new" set of beliefs which could comfortably lie alongside Christianity. More interestingly, as a vicar on Anglesey and also an antiquarian, Rowlands made the connection between the classical "Mona" and the island on which he lived as the base of the Druids at the time of Boudica's revolt. This gave both the Druids and the Iron Age queen the legitimacy of a very real and grounded place in history; by making this breakthrough, Rowlands encouraged his peers to try to root the national mythology in physical geography.

Another of Rowlands's innovations was to scale down the idea of Druidic temples to mere Druidic stone altars in sacred groves, which were then "found" all over Britain wherever there were cairns and ancient gravestones. As for the Druids themselves, these were portrayed by the reverend in his own likeness – as patriarchal priests in the manner of the traditional Christian church.

By 1781, the allure of mystical movements such as Druidism and Freemasonry prompted a raft of formal and informal groups not only in Great Britain and Brittany but also in the expanding colonies of America; in some cases, members signed up as both Druids *and* Freemasons, as well as being members of mainstream Christian churches. More than any other period in history, the eighteenth century was an era of fashions – and this applied equally to one's identity and culture as well as the cut of your clothes or the width of your skirt. Religion, it seems, was just another way to express yourself and find your tribe.

On November 29, 1781, Henry Hurle – a carpenter and builder – set up the Ancient Order of Druids (AOD) which he based on Masonic lines: not only was it a secret society, it had its own lodges and was as much an organisation for like-minded people as a celebration of Druidism. Hurle spoke a great deal about the need for an organisation to promote the idea of "brotherhood" and "brotherly love" which descended from the teachings of the "learned men". As such (and ignoring the reams of folklore which talk of female Druids), he recommended that members of the Druidic Order should call themselves "brothers".

However, all was not well in this family of Druids: a schism soon developed between those who regarded the Order as a largely charitable organisation and those who considered it a mystical society. By 1833, the two factions accepted they could no longer continue under the same roof so while the mystics continued to call themselves the AOD, the group who championed Druidism as a charitable society voted to change its name to the United Ancient Order of Druids (UAOD) and it continues to function under that name to the present day.

But what exactly *were* the beliefs and practices of these various groups of Druids? The trouble was, no one really knew. There were no literary sources from the priests themselves, laying out what the classical Druids actually believed, let alone the details of their rituals. There had been Greek and Roman references to white robes, golden sickles, mistletoe and oak trees but all of these were scant in the extreme. What's more, they had been made by foreigners who were often deeply suspicious of the religious order and so they should have been regarded as of questionable integrity. Over a thousand years had passed since the last scattering of comments about Druids had been made and beyond the stone altars and temples that were now being spuriously claimed in their name, there was actually no *material* evidence that they had ever existed at all!

However, as with the "epic poems" of James MacPherson, all that was merely an inconvenience to the eighteenth-century mind. Just because no evidence remained, it didn't mean that it could not be "re-created"...or more accurately, reimagined. It seems bizarre now to look back on the flagrant concocting from scratch of a new spiritual dogma but much in the way that American prophet Joseph Smith would later claim he had been "guided" by divine revelation to write the *Book of Mormon*, the early Druids claimed they were merely writing down ancient beliefs and traditions that were conceived before the dawn of literacy. The point was that, origins aside, Druidism offered its subscribers a meaningful and convincing paradigm on which to base their lives – and that was enough to validate their membership in the growing number of Druidical orders.

As the movement gathered pace over the eighteenth and into the early years of the nineteenth century, there were different strengths and flavours of Druidism to appeal to the needs of those seeking a mystical alternative to conventional religion and philosophy. Respected intellectuals and even royalty were among those who dressed up as Druids, built "ruined temples" in their gardens, acted out "Druidic" rituals and even gave themselves Druid names. The fact that all this was based almost entirely on fantasy is quite stunning to a modern audience but it clearly underlines just how important it was for its subscribers to connect with a mythical, mystical past.

Perhaps the great example of an entire institution shored up by imagined histories is the modern Welsh Eisteddfod. Of all the countries that were now defining themselves as "Celtic", Wales had maintained some of the strongest traditions associated with the Druids, though mitigated through the less threatening (to Christianity) persona of the "bard". Bardic and musical gatherings known as eisteddfods were a regular feature of Welsh culture from the Middle Ages up to the early modern period, with recitals and awards for the finest contributions. A gathering in the twelfth century is even on record as featuring bards from other nations but by the sixteenth century, as England reinforced its political dominance over its smaller, weaker neighbour, eisteddfods were deemed too politically dangerous to put on as they involved mass gatherings of potential rebels. As such, the movement slipped into more informal settings though it still managed to attract some of the finest talents of the day.

Under characters like Edward Lhuyd and the poet, Goronwy Owen (credited with reviving the bardic tradition of Welsh poetry), the late seventeenth and eighteenth century was a time of Celtic revelation. Welsh scholars were hard at work devising new myths of origin for the Welsh people – and central to their work was the resurgence of traditional practices such as the eisteddfod which could take advantage of the new revival of Welsh literature and make it a nationalist showcase. But these new eisteddfods were not the simple gatherings that had characterised the previous centuries: this was a new blend of bardic competition and a celebration of the new Celticity, and while there were still many ordinary farmers and workmen who were skilled in the old styles of poetry, much of the new classical material came not from Wales at all but from émigrés now living in London and attending the Welsh Cultural Societies that flourished there.

Poets like Evan Evans and Edward Jones became bardic phenomena and cultural icons while writers like John Cleland, author of the "pornographic" novel about the prostitute, Fanny Hill, wrote more rarefied texts in 1766 and 1768 detailing the origins of the Celtic language and the dissemination through the Druids of a natural, primal wisdom.

However, one of the strongest expressions of ancient "Welshness" was orchestrated by the renowned forger and impresario, Edward Williams (1747–1826). Williams, who styled himself Iolo Morgannwg or Ned of Glamorgan, was the son of a stonemason who fell in love with medieval Welsh literature and historic artefacts which he started collecting avidly. Inspired by the French Revolution, he began to formulate his own brand of nationalist politics which in turn inspired many who read his works and heard him talk; however, in a re-run of the James MacPherson story in Scotland, fearing that the Welsh were losing their heritage and sense of identity, he built his collection into an entire intellectual thesis that went way beyond both fact and credibility. His undoing came when he claimed that he had manuscripts which "proved" that the ancient bardic tradition and Druidism had survived both the Romans and Christianity, flourishing intact in its integrity to his own day.

Williams had forged poems which he attributed to the great Welsh bards Iolo Goch and Dafydd ap Gwillim, along with major additions to the epic Welsh triads. In fact, the earliest document in his collection which is still the subject of much suspicion dates only as far back as the sixth century – two centuries after the Romans had left the country. Although much of his poetry is now respected by some scholars in its own right, the fact that he tried to pass it off as ancient has damaged much of its credibility; and though he became hugely influential in terms of a developing political Welsh consciousness, in the long run, the forgeries have done his personal reputation more harm than good.

However, a more welcome legacy left by Edward Williams to Welsh culture was in the form of the Gorsedd and National Eisteddfod. In 1792, on the green sweep of Primrose Hill in London, Williams called together the first assembly of

Welsh poets which he termed the *Gorsedd*, or Guild of Bards. The event was reported in the *Gentleman's Magazine*:

> *"This being the day on which the autumn equinox occurred, some Welsh bards, resident in London, assembled in congress on Primrose Hill, according to ancient usage."*

In fact, the claim to "ancient usage" was entirely man-made: the elaborate and stirring ceremony Williams had concocted borrowed heavily from rituals of Freemasonry, descriptions of Druids from the ancient Greeks and Romans (especially Pliny the Elder) – and healthy doses of his own imagination. The Primrose Hill *Gorsedd* featured the poets dressed up as "Druids" in long and flowing white robes while the leaders gave impassioned speeches aimed at rebuilding Welsh national pride. In the role of president was Edward Jones, a musician and antiquary who also believed in the need for the Welsh to celebrate and retain their traditional culture; it was Jones who had revived the eisteddfods a few years earlier which built in strength and popularity to become the huge National Eisteddfod of today and which, in 1819, went on to incorporate Williams's *Gorsedd*. Thus a genuine desire for a strong Welsh identity was served up with all the pomp and ceremony that gave it authority and credibility: this time, Williams and Jones had created a work of cultural genius.

The colourful and ceremonial event still figures strongly in the modern eisteddfod, with the Druidic order divided into three groups (à la Strabo): Druids (moral philosophers and priests) dressed in white, bards (singers and poets) in blue and ovates (diviners and natural philosophers) in green. And the Eisteddfod continues to use Williams's rousing cry, repeated three times for maximum effect:

Archdruid: *A oes heddwch? (Is there peace?)*
Audience: *Heddwch! (Peace!)*

Despite the fact that its rituals and dress are entirely fabricated from Williams's imagination and selections from the biased writings of ancient foreign authors, it remains both incredibly popular *and* respectable: current membership of the *Gorsedd* includes not only the Queen but the Archibishop of Canterbury – a sure sign that Williams was, for once, speaking a demonstrable truth when he claimed, "a man is no less a Christian for being a Druid, or a Druid for being a Christian" – as long as the "Druids" in question are the modern inventions and not the priests and bards of classical antiquity. It seems as though the title of Druid is irresistibly alluring to those seeking or already in the high offices of power: on August 15, 1908, the future prime minister, Winston Churchill, added his own name to a long and noble list in the United Ancient Order of Druids.

Talking to a group of modern, mainly female, Druids today I was surprised at the strong attitudes against the "boys' clubs" of the stereotypical "man with a long grey beard". They more closely aligned themselves with the ecological movement than any formally ritualised groups, eschewing "structures" for a more organic relationship with the natural/spirit world. Emma Restall Orr, leader of the Druid Network, draws upon many of the same themes: "To me, this is pure poetry – I don't have to base my spiritual tradition on facts: it's more about personal perception." We talked about how she had spent fifteen years of her spiritual journey combating patriarchy and was now a firm believer in the shamanic, polytheistic Mother Tradition. Then, as we said goodbye, she wished me well with the book, inviting me to let her know when it was due out because "many people in our network are fascinated by Boudica".

Award-winning author Manda Scott also explored Druidism as a university student. Though she now practises and teaches shamanic dreaming and spirituality, she is also famous for her series of fictional books about the Iron Age Queen – a subject she firmly believes was given to her by the spirits: "I asked them, 'What do you want of me?' and the answer I received was specifically to write these books about Boudica. They're about the whole culture and the spirit of the late Iron Age which must represent the apex of British indigenous spirituality as it then stopped with the Romans; they're not some kind of spiritual textbook, but they do offer the reader some guiding exploration if you want to read them at that level." However, it was Manda's next comment that really surprised me, particularly as by now she was on her fourth Boudica book: "I don't have as much of an affinity with the historical character as I do with my fictional characters who share the same narrative, though I certainly know more now about her life and times and have enormous respect for what she did. I think she's also important for us as she's one of the first Britons ever heard of and actually named – and she was almost victorious as an army leader *and* a woman. All these things make her an important character in our past as well as a good peg for my writing." She was absolutely right: her part-fiction/part-fantasy books have been compared to Mary Renault's *Alexander* trilogy which has kept the author in the bestsellers' list for years.

"With [a] voice that can weave a spell of magic about the plainest word" the great Italian soprano, Giuditta Pasta, held the audience completely under her power; looking out from the stage to the darkness of the auditorium of Milan's *La Scala* theatre, she knew from the way the hushed reverence of the first-night crowd had exploded into an appreciative roar, that both she and the opera were going to be a success. This was Boxing Day, 1831, and the curtain had lifted two hours earlier on the debut performance of Vincenzo Bellini's new and transcendental opera, *Norma*. Its leading ladies were two of the most famous sopranos in the world – Giuditta Pasta as Norma, the Druid high priestess, and Giulia Grisi as Adalgisa, a temple priestess and Norma's rival in love. However, unlike the audience who sat in silent amazement, the composer thought that the first production had been a total disaster ("Fiasco!!! Fiasco!!! Solemn fiasco!!!" he wrote immediately afterwards) yet its first run stretched to forty performances before going on to tour the rest of Italy and then London in 1833, where it was directed by Bellini himself, to the audience's wild delight.

That this story of forbidden and doomed love between Druids and Romans was filling some of the greatest opera houses in the world is testament to how deeply Celtomania had permeated the mainstream both in Britain and on the Continent. The idea for the opera was taken from the storyline of Alexandre Soumet's five-act verse tragedy of the same title which had been performed at the Odéon in Paris earlier that year; now with a moving libretto by Felice Romani, it rode high on the obsession for all things Celtic and inspired both

Brahms and Verdi with its passionate melodies. In an 1837 review, Wagner himself called it "genius" and "a great score that speaks to the heart".

The imagery of *Norma* is laid out in the opening scene where Norma's father, the high priest Oroveso, awaits the new moon to conduct sacred rites and dialogue with the gods. It's a dramatic start, using the classic stereotype of Druids as strange but powerful mystical priests, working with nature to commune with the spirit world. The Druid temples of the opera's scenery were well-known to the contemporary audience in Britain: large, mysterious stones were littered throughout the British countryside − and where they weren't, they could be "created" as part of the eighteenth-century craze for follies and ruins as a badge of ancestral honour. Of course, the small fact that there *is* no real archaeological or documentary evidence to support the existence of grand Druid temples made from stone (or anything else for that matter) was conveniently ignored in the myth-making eighteenth and nineteenth centuries. In fact, everything we know about the ancient practices and beliefs of the Celts and Druids (which is flimsy in the extreme) seems to militate against even the basic concept of grand built structures in favour of more natural, elemental places such as bogs and springs and wooded groves.

However, none of these facts was enough to dampen the Druidic enthusiasm of the age. One of the earliest follies was the "Druidic temple" that was found in Jersey and gifted to the statesman and military commander, Field Marshall Henry Seymour Conway in the 1780s in appreciation for his assistance against the military invasion of Jersey by the French. The Neolithic burial chamber − some twenty metres/sixty-five feet in diameter with a circle of forty-five large granite stones − was re-erected in his home at Park Place in Henley, Oxfordshire, where according to onlookers, it furnished the area with a deep sense of grandeur. Writing to the Countess of Ossory in August, 1785, Hugh Walpole recounted:

> "*I have been to Park Place on a pilgrimage to Little Master Stonehenge, alias the Druids Temple from Jersey, which is now erected on the bank of an eminent hill, with two wings of fir groves a small distance away, and is seen from the garden over a long ridge of firs that shoot up from the side of the beautiful*

descending valley seen in the horizon, it looks very high-priestly, and in that broken country may easily be taken for respectable ruins of an ancient castle or Caratacus' own summer-house. Park Place is now one of the spots most deserving to be visited in our island."

Meanwhile, the inscription on the stone circle tells nothing of the four ships that were reportedly used to bring the present across:

"For ages hidden from all mortal eye, this ancient Druid pile did hidden lie, oft did the priest to these rude Altar lead, the trembling human victim doomed to bleed, but here, this Temple will in future show, the grateful love with which our bosoms glow, that Caesen Father, and her chief, brave and attentive came to her relief! Therefore, oh! Conway, to record that day, and wishing thy great valour repay. She caused this ancient fabric to be sent, as a just tribute to that great event."

Other so-called temples were built or discovered, such as the magnificent "stone henge" constructed by William Danby (1753-1833) and set in the wild landscape of the moors on his estate near Ilton, North Yorkshire. Rumour has it that he even went as far as to offer an annuity to any hermit who would take up residence in his folly – with one candidate surviving there for an incredible four and a half years. With antiquarianism becoming a national obsession and the earth's history only believed to date back some six thousand years, "Druid temples" became an almost generic term given to anything that looked mysterious or romantic and pre-dated the dawn of Roman civilisation.

However, the "classic" seat of Druidical worship was – and still is for many – Stonehenge. From the late eighteenth, and especially during the nineteenth, century, this became popular as the focal point for ceremonies for the growing band of neo-Druids. The real age of the stones (around five thousand years old) would have been beyond the conception of the earliest pilgrims to the site, along with current ideas that the stones were hewn using picks made of reindeer antlers – but even when the archaeological facts have been laid out in modern times, this has done little to dent Stonehenge's popularity as a symbolic centre of Druidic worship. Reality, it seems, is not as persuasive a cultural force as myth.

As Great Britain embraced both the "Celts" and the "Druids" of its ancient past, a springboard was now in place to propel an ancient hero to the stratospheric heights of an international icon. The Age of Reason, with its deep-seated desire to catalogue and explain the real origins of Britain, had now passed over to the Age of Romance with its love of dramatic personalities. And with an expanding empire, the culture of Britain was now poised to take on the rest of the world. All it needed was someone to act as the trigger – and that came in the early hours of June 20, 1837, when Princess Alexandrina Victoria received word from the Archbishop of Canterbury and the Lord Chamberlain that her uncle, King William IV, had died – and she was now Queen of the United Kingdom of Great Britain and Ireland.

And along with the throne, the eighteen-year-old Victoria had inherited a culture rich in nationalism, patriotism and romance; in other words, a culture looking for a queen it could love.

CHAPTER 19
A QUEEN FOR ALL SEASONS
Boudica's Enduring Iconography

By now, Boudica had experienced almost every shade of public emotion, from adoration to outright hatred. But the machinations of the next century would carve her place irrevocably into the national consciousness – and prepare her for use as an international icon in the expanding British empire. If ever there was a time to try to reconcile the confusion of Britain's role in its own imperial history as the *defeated* nation – and the role of a native queen in almost driving the venerated Romans from our shores, then that time had arrived. Whether or not we have ever managed to reconcile these contradictions of our past, I would argue, is still open to question.

In the eighteenth century, Great Britain had transformed itself. Gone was the vulnerable, politically weakened country of old, exhausted from decades of civil war, rebellion and internecine strife; the 1700s had seen a settling of domestic boundaries. With England no longer needing to worry about an "enemy" on its doorstep, there was a steady growth of domestic confidence and nationalistic pride under more stable central governance. The landscape was also changing, though that change was often painful: the old feudal strip fields were being consigned to the past as the enclosure movement took hold; whole areas in England and Scotland were cleared of their inhabitants to make way for open sweeps of fields containing sheep, cattle or crops. Rampant rural distress provided a constant supply of labour for the developing industries of coal, iron and manufacturing which would help Britannia fuel the world; it also helped to shake up the inertia of the population. Whereas once you would live and die in your set stratum of society, there were now opportunities for social and economic mobility: Britain was gaining its nouveau riche. And alongside the new rich was the new power of a country that had won the Seven Years' War, "winning" North America and India from Spain and France and asserting its dominance in the new world order. Small wonder, then, that Britain could now afford the luxury of a little romance in its cultural life.

The rise of the Age of Romance with its love of mysticism and wild nature is clearly expressed through the developing poetry of the age – and often through the backgrounds of the poets themselves. On Boxing Day, 1716, Thomas Gray was born into a privileged but violent household. His escape to Eton at the age of eight gave this small, withdrawn and pensive child the stability he needed to make lifelong friends and his group – Horace Walpole, son of the prime minister, Thomas Ashton and the young poet Richard West and Gray – became known as the "Quadruple Alliance". Together they gloried in the opportunity to skip the playing fields in favour of poetry and the classics, where they refined their immense literary skills.

After a period at Cambridge University where he distinguished himself more in his personal writings than his qualifications, he embarked on a career as a largely unsuccessful poet until his "Elegy written in a Country Church yard" was published in 1751. Suddenly, the thirty-five year old was propelled to fame and it was during this period that he penned "The Bard" – a long, dark and difficult poem about a Druid who throws himself off a Welsh mountain rather than face a future under English rule. The poem invokes King Arthur as a romantic hero, along with a "form divine":

"Her eye proclaims her of the Briton-line;
Her lion-port, her awe-commanding face,
Attemper'd to sweet virgin-grace."

THOMAS GRAY: *THE BARD*, 1757

This powerful queenly vision breathes new soul into the spirit of Taliesin – the mystical poet of sixth-century Wales whose works had inspired Nennius in his

Historia Britonnum. Of course, the *Historia* which introduced King Arthur to the canon of heroes made only a brief passing reference to the warrior queen of the ancient Britons – and it appears that in "The Bard", Gray might have taken the same approach.

But if Boudica was edging back into the mainstream, another famous British female was riding a wave of popularity. A favourite song at the time of Gray's writing was Thomas Arne's *Rule Britannia*, taken from the masque, *Alfred*, and given its first London performance in 1745. Arne was more popular in his day than even Henry Purcell: his masques, operas and songs filled the nation's theatres and some were even adapted to serve as anthems for the Jacobite cause. However, without doubt the most enduring of his works was *Rule Britannia* which has been Britain's unofficial national anthem ever since it was first performed with its rousing refrain:

> *Rule Britannia! Britain rule the waves;*
> *Britons never never never shall be slaves.*

Mentioned in the full text, itself a close adaptation of a poem by James Thompson (1700-1748), is the reference to "Britain's native oak":

> *Still more majestic shalt thou rise, More dreadful from each foreign stroke; As*
> *the loud blast that tears the skies, Serves but to root thy native oak.*

The image of the oak is a traditional symbol of Britain's deep and enduring connection with the past; doubtless related to this is the fact that "Britain's native oak" is also the most sacred symbol of Celtic and Druidic lore, where it represents longevity, tradition and wisdom. It is no surprise, therefore, to hear echoes of Arne's imagery in another poem written when *Rule Britannia* was still the anthem of choice in the theatres and concert halls of Britain.

The famous poem – which contains a seamless blend of Arne's imperialist pride and Gray's mystical Druidism – was developed by William Cowper when he emerged from a period of religious fervency. Born in 1731 as the son of an

Anglican clergyman, he battled against misfortune and insanity throughout his life, finding solace in the English landscape, religion and the classics. However, for all his personal troubles, he enjoyed incredible public acclaim, becoming the most widely read poet of his day and the inspiration for future "nature" poets such as Burns, Wordsworth and Coleridge. Following an attempt at suicide when he was in his late twenties, he sought comfort in evangelical Calvinism but when he lost his passion for that fiery brand of religion following another breakdown, he turned back to writing the poetry that had given him so much pleasure. The result was his *Boadicea: An Ode* in 1780, a poem imbued with mysticism and nationalistic pride.

The work itself is a fascinating insight into Boudica's changing meaning to the people of Britain. In the eighteenth century, when Cowper was summoning her ghost, she is almost little more than a device or leitmotif for introducing the more important themes of romantic Druidism and Britain's glorious empire. Like in Nennius's *History*, Boudica is unnamed in the actual text and her presence is subsumed by — and in the end subservient to — the philosophising of the Druid Chief. The first two stanzas clearly lay out Cowper's beliefs about the relative importance of the two characters:

When the British warrior queen
Bleeding from the Roman rods,
Sought, with an indignant mien,
Counsel of her country's gods,

Sage beneath a spreading oak
Sat the Druid, hoary chief;
Every burning word he spoke
Full of rage and full of grief.

Compared to Boudica's wounded and emotional "indignant mien", the "sage" Druid has the more commanding presence. He even goes on to call her "Princess" as if she were a child instead of a "British queen" before giving her his prophecy of the future where Rome's pride will ultimately trigger its downfall by the resurgence of the Celtish "Gauls", and Britain (though not Boudica) will instead rule the world:

> *"Then the progeny that springs*
> *From the forests of our land,*
> *Armed with thunder, clad with wings,*
> *Shall a wider world command.*
>
> *"Regions Caesar never knew*
> *Thy posterity shall sway,*
> *Where his eagles never flew,*
> *None invincible as they."*
>
> *Such the bard's prophetic words,*
> *Pregnant with celestial fire,*
> *Bending, as he swept the chords*
> *Of his sweet but awful lyre.*
>
> *She, with all a monarch's pride,*
> *Felt them in her bosom glow;*
> *Rushed to battle, fought, and died;*
> *Dying, hurled them at the foe.*
>
> *"Ruffians, pitiless as proud,*
> *Heaven awards the vengeance due:*
> *Empire is on us bestowed,*
> *Shame and ruin wait for you."*

WILLIAM COWPER: BOADICEA: AN ODE, 1780

The political context for the poem, with all its proclamations of international glory, is interesting in the light of what was going on in Britain's colonies at the time: having seen victory in the Seven Years' War of 1758-63 which gave Britain control over North America, it was now in the process of losing it in the

American War of Independence (1775-1783). Notwithstanding this irony, *Boadicea* would be learned and recited by schoolchildren across the British Empire for the next two hundred years.

Unlike Gray, Arne and Cowper, the poet and artist William Blake (1757-1827) achieved no fame or fortune in his own lifetime but his legacy is probably the strongest of them all. Now considered to be a pioneer of Romanticism in western culture, in his own day his mystical visions merely singled him out as profoundly disturbed. Blake wrote "*The Voice of the Ancient Bard*" as part of his epic *Songs of Experience*, published in 1794. Blake, who readily identified himself as a Druid (and is claimed as a member by at least two Druidic orders), uses Druidic imagery in both his paintings and his poetry; in *Songs of Experience*, his great counterpart to the earlier *Songs of Innocence* (1789), Blake has the "Bard" as a central character, while in his later "*Prophetic Books*" his Druids take many guises of good and evil representing the tension in his own mind and his lifelong concern with the soul's struggle to free itself from reason and organised religion.

> *Hear the voice of the Bard!*
> *Who Present, Past, & Future, sees;*
> *Whose ears have heard*
> *The Holy Word*
> *That walk'd among the ancient trees.*
>
> WILLIAM BLAKE: *INTRODUCTION TO SONGS OF EXPERIENCE*, 1794

In many ways, his classic paintings with their mystical patriarchs – long grey-white hair and beards blowing in the wind – are the graphic equivalent of the Bard in Gray's poem:

> *Loose his beard, and hoary hair*
> *Streamed, like a meteor, to the troubled air.*

While Blake wrote of "Albion's Ancient Druid Rocky Shore", like his contemporary Wordsworth who focused on the darker side of Druidism (eg, human sacrifice), he never wrote of the warrior queen whose story brought the

British Druids into the limelight via the classical texts. In fact, since the days of Cowper, Boudica had taken a back seat to her patriarchal priests – but all that was about to change with the accession of Queen Victoria to the throne in 1837.

As the monarchy was passing into the hands of a young but stubborn eighteen-year-old, Britain was entering the Age of Steam with the building of Stephenson's *Rocket* almost a decade before and new railway lines now spidering their way across the country carrying people at the unprecedented speed of around thirty-six miles an hour. It must have seemed as though the pastoral tranquillity of John Constable's English landscape had died with the artist earlier that year. In the white heat of industrialisation, the working classes were joining the new trade unions that succeeded where the Tolpuddle martyrs had failed; in the busy towns with their growing throng of middle classes, angry women were invoking the name of Boadicea to write anonymous letters to *The Times* to defend their patriotism and the honour of their sex; and in Parliament, the newly elected Tory MP for Maidstone, Benjamin Disraeli, was booed down from his maiden speech, defiantly proclaiming, "I will sit down now, but the time will come when you will hear me." It was to prove a prophetic warning to his political opponents.

The young Victoria had survived a strict policy of isolation by her mother and rejoiced at her new-found freedom. At her very first meeting with the Privy Council the morning after becoming queen, she impressed its members with her self-assured performance and grace. Though short and slight, she had an engaging nature which many at court found utterly charming, not least Franz Albrecht August Karl Emmanuel, the German Prince of Saxe-Coburg-Gotha who arrived at Windsor on October 10, 1839 and was engaged to the Queen of England just five days later. Victoria had fallen instantly in love with her imposing royal cousin, in a passion that would border on obsession until the day she died, and the couple were married on February 10, 1840. But while the handsome prince may have won the heart of a queen, he was considered dangerously "foreign" and it would take the rest of his life – and indeed Victoria's – to convince the British public of his worth; so intense was the public's dislike of Albert that even his "English" queen was damned by association and the royal couple were regarded with deep suspicion for the first decades of her reign.

There was little in her early years to suggest that Victoria would be one of the most iconic rulers this country has ever seen. The new queen had inherited a monarchy that was more powerful than popular and highly unstable; the irony is that by the end of her vast reign, while she had ensured that the monarchy would remain a feature of British constitutional life with the Royal Family in the bosom of the people's affection, she had presided over a radical diminution in the monarch's personal power. No longer with any vestige of divine right, Victoria would become a thoroughly *representational* monarch – both politically and culturally. And she would achieve this feat by becoming embodied in the potent new symbols of empire: Britannia and Boadicea.

For years the monarchy had floundered in its credibility, initially due to the madness of King George III and then made worse by the playboy antics of the Prince Regent who would become George IV. After the death of George's only child, his brother William became next in line to the throne, being crowned King William IV for the last seven years of his life – but when he, too, died without a legitimate heir, the crown had passed to his niece, Victoria. Now, just as with the accession of Elizabeth, the crowning of Victoria as Queen of the United Kingdom of Great Britain and Ireland caused a mixture of national emotions: relief at some eventual stability in the monarchy and concern that the power of the crown now rested with a woman.

The new queen's initial lack of popularity (already evident in the political cartoons of the day) is borne out by an unconventional source: the naming of naval vessels in the nineteenth century. This list is a fascinating potential barometer of social and cultural change, particularly as ships tend to be regarded as being female; so, while it might not be terribly scientific, it certainly reflects the broad sweep of who is "in" and who is "out" of the establishment's affection. Taking five names – *Boadicea*, *Britannia*, *Britomart* (Spenser's Elizabethan warrior queen), *Victoria* and *Victoria and Albert*, the early favourite is *Britannia* with its first citation in 1762 – around a hundred years after she first appeared on British (as opposed to Roman) coinage – and then remaining popular with four more citations until the last in 1904; next to appear in the list of names is *Boadicea* who has three citations in 1797, 1875 and 1908; surprisingly, *Britomart* is also used five times between 1808 and 1898, making this fictional character a strong and perennial favourite; but far and away the most popular name is *Victoria* with eight citations. While naming ships after the queen is to be expected, the first of these citations is not until *eight years* into her reign in 1845 which supports the assertion that she was viewed with some scepticism in the opening years of her monarchy – a period when pamphlets circulating London asked what she did with all her money. As for *Victoria and Albert*, this was used only twice – in 1843, the year Princess Alice was born, and 1855 – right in the middle of the Crimean War. If the evidence of the ships can be believed, it seems that while Victoria managed to change her public image, Albert was never really welcomed in to the bosom of the British nation.

Two of the major turning points in Victoria's popularity were the Great Exhibition of 1851, followed by the Crimean War of 1853-86. The wondrous exhibition was a showcase for how Britain ruled the world – from its inventions and products to its administrative "genius" in managing its empire which was not only larger but also better-run than the Romans had ever achieved (or so the popular mythology ran). The cultural *tour de force* was centred on the magnificent Crystal Palace in Hyde Park and it played a huge role in firmly planting the proud idea of a glorious "mother country" amongst the people of the empire – a concept that was compounded by the expression that described the people of the colonies as the "children of the empire". Being not only female but a prodigious producer of children herself, Victoria almost unwittingly absorbed and then radiated back out this image of being the imperial mother lode – the source of all the greatness that Britain scattered with largesse across the rest of her world. Even if Victoria had broadcast her real views that childbearing was "the shadow-side of marriage", reducing women to the status of "a cow or a dog … when our poor nature becomes so very animal and unecstatic", it is unlikely that the public would have wanted to hear them; for the people of Britain, their queen was a good mother and a good wife and for the moment, that was enough.

The mother-role was not only useful for Victoria; it was also vital for her expanding empire which was now seen as benign and nurturing rather than domineering and forceful; and, as if to prove this point, in an innovation by the British cartographer Henry Teesdale, maps of the realm were no longer coloured their original strong red but were softened to the famous "Empire Pink" which was far more "fitting" for a female domain. Matriarchy, muliebrity and imperial munificence – it was getting harder to work out where Victoria stopped and her empire began.

But the growing public ease with this new maternal role was punctured by the Crimean War. The rocky experience of Boudica's legend after her death shows how hard it is to reconcile a mother-figure with a warrior queen – and so it proved for Victoria. Victoria was now *too much* defined as the mother of the nation to become a convincing war leader: it was surely against the laws of nature for women to give life on one hand and then take it away with the other. Britain was perceived as a rudderless ship blundering into the war: Victoria was not a convincing commander and her husband was rumoured to be trying to take the helm. The first years of the war were marked by a significant dip in her popularity; since her unpopular marriage and her subsequent wifely deference to the German prince, the British public worried that Victoria would not be able to stand up to Albert's feared pro-Russian sympathies. The queen and her consort were savagely lampooned in the weekly magazine, *Punch*, which became essential reading for anyone interested in the cultural and political life of Britain. However, while *Punch* was no friend of the monarchy, it was passionate about British interests; and if the queen couldn't lead the nation into battle then someone else would have to instead.

Victoria was not as skilled or as interested as Elizabeth I in managing the imagery of her reign. As a young woman married to a foreigner, she did not have the undying love of her people and wouldn't earn it until much later in her long reign by which time – by sheer dint of service – she had become part of the British way of life. Unable to adopt Elizabeth's mantle of warrior queen during the difficult years of the Crimean War, the queen and the whole idea of monarchy was floundering. But while she was damned by her sex in some ways, she was now able to use a gender stereotype to her advantage – to regain her pole position as leader of the nation.

Her masterstroke was to appeal to the morality and sense of duty of Britain's middle classes – a class that worshipped the idea of a mother's central role in the moral upbringing of her family. While Elizabeth may have had courtly love, Victoria had the equally powerful mother-love – which could now be expanded to a direct nurturing role to her "children". In the latter part of the Crimean War, Victoria connected with her public for what was probably the first time in her twenty-year reign. Now, getting actively involved with the "ladies' committees" for war relief, she visited wounded soldiers in hospital, became an ardent supporter of that bastion of female virtue, Florence Nightingale, and instituted the new Victoria Cross for extreme bravery in the face of the enemy. This was not paternalism: this was maternalism *in extremis* – and the public loved it.

But by choosing this path, Victoria had unwittingly caused herself a long-term problem. By casting herself in the caring role of mother, she had abdicated the monarch's role as a potent – if representative – war leader. However, by good fortune and clever allegory in the making of Britain's history, there was another character who could fit the role of warrior queen almost perfectly. Not only was she already much-loved by the public, she had the credibility for people to follow her into conflict of a military or even political nature; but best of all – she was pliant to the whims of whoever controlled her, whether that was the government of Britain or the popular press. Now the monarch and the warrior queen linked hands to lead the nation – and "Britannia" took up her throne once more. Britannia was the warrior-queen-cum-guardian-goddess who stood as the enduring personification of "Britishness". Both protector and inspiration, she was already a favourite nationalist character in magazines like *Punch*; now her image was reproduced in posters, prose and newspapers – and while individually Victoria and Britannia had significant roles to play, together they formed an unbeatable cultural force, for in this union resided a complete armoury of control. Victoria could now deploy the emotional power of a parent over a child in the domestic sphere, while Britannia could mobilise her army to conquer a new supply of children in the outside world. Britannia and Victoria now became one of the most successful double acts in modern history; and it wouldn't be long before the two women became imagined as one. As for the British people, they could finally ease up on hating Albert: their queen had at last made the Royal Marriage they desired.

Claudius striking down Britannia, depicted as an Amazon.
Marble relief c. AD 50s at Aphrodisias in south-west Turkey

Ironically for someone portrayed as the staunch defender of the nation, Britannia isn't really British at all but a figment of Roman imagination conflated with their own warrior goddess, Minerva, the Greek Athena. Her first known depiction as the embodiment of British fighting spirit was found as recently as 1980 in the ruins of the ancient city of Aphrodisias in Turkey – a favourite location of both Caesar and Augustus that was famed for its exquisite buildings and sculptures from the local white and blue-grey marble. Here, during excavations on the Temple of Aphrodite (c. AD 20-60), archaeologists uncovered a dramatic relief carved into a block of marble. The image, entitled "Claudius Conquers Britannia" shows a near-naked emperor (save for his flowing cape, helmet and sword) preparing to slay the fallen figure of Britannia on whom he is half-kneeling to restrain her. Bare-breasted like an Amazon, she remains frozen in the pose of supplication, twisting up in a final plea for mercy. The dramatic scene would have broadcast news of Britain's subjugation even to the illiterate masses who could not have failed to heed its graphic meaning.

Almost a century later, well after the Boudica revolt against imperial Rome, the Emperor Hadrian used Britannia for his own symbol of "domination" over the Britons on his coins. The image shows a seated woman in Roman clothes with a spear across her left arm and a shield under her other elbow – the classic accoutrements of Athena – but her pose and expression do not display the pride of the victor but the dejection of the vanquished: here she is representing the conquered nation which she embodies.

The Romano–British symbol of Britannia continued to be used throughout the Roman Empire on other coins, buildings and memorials but when the empire collapsed, Britannia seemed to disappear with it in a long sleep that lasted some fifteen hundred years. She was wakened in the Renaissance when the classics of Greece and Rome were brought once more to light and was quickly adopted to suit the purposes of Britain's first independent queen, Elizabeth I, where she fitted with the growing desire to connect the new nationalism of England with an ancient genealogical pedigree. However, just like the re-workings of Boudica, Britannia had been transformed in millennia away from the public gaze. No longer downtrodden and dejected, she held her head high with the resurgent pride of a country growing in confidence.

In the year of Elizabeth's death in 1603, the writer Henry Peacham published his *Minerva Britannia* – a so-called "emblem book" which sought to illustrate morality and virtuous behaviour. Among its illustrations was a print of Britannia in classical dress with an armoured breastplate, striding confidently towards a ship in what could be the walled city of London. Still clearly identified with the goddess of war in the book's title, Britannia is now as much queen as warrior, her spear replaced by the sceptre of the monarchy. While the ship probably represents the strong navy which Elizabeth and her father had bequeathed to the nation, it also makes an interesting connection with the mighty river god, *Ocean*, whom Caesar and Claudius both had to conquer before they could reach her shores, and may even have echoes back to Athena's battle with the sea god, Poseidon, for the suzerainty of Athens.

Britannia, Athena, Boudica, Gloriana and Britomart – when a queen was on the throne, they were all summoned up to enhance her glory. And even after Elizabeth's death, her influence pervaded the national consciousness: in 1610, the English chronicler and historian, William Camden used an image of Britannia at the top of his title page for *Britain, or a Chorographicall Description of the Flourishing Kingdomes of England, Scotland and Ireland and the Islands Adjacent.* Although seated and in the traditional pose of the Roman depictions, with a spear and shield, she again has her head held high and carries the sceptre of statehood.

However, just two years later, on the frontispiece of Michael Drayton's 1612 *Poly-Olbion*, Britannia is no longer a warrior queen but the bountiful goddess, carrying a horn of plenty instead of her traditional weapons. The folds of her classical robes now reveal a detailed map so that she has *literally* become the conflation of queen and country. While two cherubs place a wreath on her head, her "court" of historical British men, from Aeneas and Julius Caesar to a medieval king and an explorer tell the reader that *men* are the ones who play the active role in war and governance: Britain has now been conquered and tamed; to Drayton, there is no more need for a warrior queen.

Just like in ancient Rome, these images contained powerful messages for the predominantly illiterate population of Britain, for while they might not have been able to read, they had been brought up on the imagery of church and state: coded messages and allegory were their daily tutors. But if Britannia had become a graphic symbol for Elizabeth's nation state, it was still restricted to those who had access to books and art, and therefore, relatively elite. It would take another half a century before the warrior queen achieved her hegemony over the broader English sense of national identity by her first appearance on a mass-produced British coin. In 1672, Britannia became available to *all* her people in the form of the halfpenny and other copper coins. Still seated in the manner of Hadrian's Britannia, she this time looks out defiantly and bears her old spear plus a Union Jack on her shield. Writing around this time, Samuel Pepys commented that she also bore a striking resemblance to the King's mistress, Mrs Frances Stewart, the Duchess of Richmond and Lennox. He drew attention to:

"the King's new medal, where, in little, there is Mrs. Stewart's face...and a pretty thing it is, that he should choose her face to represent Britannia by..."

Britannia was now the enduring symbol of British nationhood, outliving kings, lords and the statesmen of Parliament. However, the problem was, she was still aligned with the monarchy rather than the people and thus when the Stuarts brought the monarchy to near disaster, Britannia went with them. For much of the seventeenth century, while she may have been tucked into the nation's purse, she was essentially kept out of the limelight while Britain struggled to find a model of leadership that suited the people, the church and the state. In fact, it took until the start of the Georgian period in 1714 for Britannia to see a revival in her fortunes and public presence as Britain went from strength to strength and regained its national pride. By the time Thomas Arne wrote his epic tune for James Thompson's *Rule Britannia*, Britannia was riding high again: she not only ruled the waves – she reflected her country's newfound confidence. But what would happen next would not only increase her power, it would transform the very nature of her identity by firmly uniting her with her own alter ego: Boudica, the warrior queen.

In many ways it is unsurprising that the mythical warrior queen Britannia and her real classical counterpart, Boudica, made their resurgence in the years where a queen rather than a king sat on the throne. It is also no surprise that under Victoria, her people would look back to other famous queens in history as a metaphor for her own rule – but the mere fact that they did this at all still marked a female monarch out as culturally "different" and challenging in a way that can never be said of a male monarch. What is more surprising is that for the first half of her reign, Boudica and Britannia had a clear connection with the queen in terms of their gender and perceived nationalism but they were still a distinctly *parallel* idea to the idea of Victoria, rather than being merged with her as the personification of her virtue. In other words, for the first part of the new queen's reign, there were three dominant ideas of what a queen should be like – and how she should behave: Boudica's earthy warrior queen, Britannia's elite and nationalistic figurehead and Victoria's "duty to nation and family" figurehead.

"I think the Victorian period is perhaps the key to understanding the reinvention of Boudica," argues Jenny Hall of the Museum of London. "The fact that 'Bouda' meant victory so that both queens shared the same name added an extra fillip, too, but you'll find that an awful lot of the myths surrounding the warrior queen arise from this time. The Victorian period revitalised her image, and it certainly added to her mystique as a legendary hero."

A prime example of Boudica's savage and earthy persona is in the poem, *Boadicea*, written by Alfred, Lord Tennyson in 1859-60. This difficult, challenging and ultimately unpopular work absorbed and almost taunted Tennyson, though it was one of his personal favourites. Wild and naturalistic, it inverts the more traditional Ode of Cowper completely. Not only does it start with a brief introduction to the Druids before giving the main voice to Boadicea herself, the balance of power is also switched: the Druids – and "Druidess" – are portrayed as impotent against the might of the Romans while Boadicea is awesome in her "fierce volubility". But Boadicea's power is not that of a restrained, civilised monarch like Tennyson's own queen: the Icenian queen is terrifying in her storm-force hatred of the foreign invaders – and for her barbarian mob:

Far in the East Boadicea, standing loftily charioted,
Mad and maddening all that heard her in her fierce volubility,
Girt by half the tribes of Britain, near the colony Camulodune,
Yell'd and shriek'd between her daughters o'er a wild confederacy.

"They that scorn the tribes and call us Britain's barbarous populaces,
Did they hear me, would they listen, did they pity me supplicating?
Shall I heed them in their anguish? Shall I brook to be supplicated?
Hear Icenian, Catieuchlanian, hear Coritanian, Trinobant!
Must their ever-ravening eagle's beak and talon annihilate us?
Tear the noble heart of Britain, leave it gorily quivering?
Bark an answer, Britain's Raven! bark and blacken innumerable,
Blacken round the Roman carrion, make the carcase a skeleton,
Kite and kestrel, wolf and wolfkin, from this wilderness, wallow in it,
Til the face of Bel be brighten'd, Taranis be propitiated.

TENNYSON: *BOADICEA*, 1860

Continuing the myth-making that had been going on since Elizabethan times, Tennyson's Boadicea describes herself as the "lover of liberty" – ignoring the fact that she had, in fact, been in the elite of a tribe that had signed over its power to the Romans in order to gain the privileges of "client" status; but the truth did not fit with Boadicea's role as the populist leader of resistance against an empire that would one day be surpassed by the empire of the Britons. To make the story part of "history" work, Boadicea needed to be fighting for freedom and for her people.

But the poet's "lover of liberty" is not yet the heroic figure into which she would be transformed as the Victorian age wore on; here she is savage and barbarian, full of uncontrolled passion and violence. Tennyson's Boadicea is poles apart from the "civilised" Britannia of the glorious elite:

> *"Cut the Roman boy to pieces in his lust and voluptuousness,*
> *Lash the maiden into swooning, me they lash'd and humiliated,*
> *Chop the breasts from off the mother, dash the brains of the little one out.*

In a period of history that worshipped "motherhood" (even though Victoria herself detested the very states of pregnancy and childbirth) and defined women's roles as caring and nurturing the children of the empire, here Tennyson's Boadicea is so distinctly *anti*-maternal that she is stripped of the traditional femininity that would usually clothe her in the romantic poetry of the age. To Tennyson and his audience, Boadicea is no longer behaving like a woman, not even the kind of woman who was emotionally ranting at the start of his poem: here she is portrayed as one of the great child-killers of popular history, like the wicked Medea who killed her own children and anyone else's she could find in revenge for losing her husband to another woman. And just like Medea, this poetic queen is therefore a ruler doomed by her own savagery to failure. In the words of Tennyson, "Out of evil evil flourishes, out of tyranny tyranny buds."

By the time the poem was finished, the Crimean War was over and Victoria-cum-Britannia was riding high on a wave of popularity. Britannia appeared on a new bronze coin in 1860 which portrayed her mastery of the seas; then, in 1861, Victoria's beloved husband died and the queen withdrew from public life in profound grief and distress. For any other monarch, this would have left the nation without an effective emblem of state. But Victoria was different: still wedded in the public's mind to the defender of the nation, the queen could leave Britannia in her place as a visible image of a strong and potent leader. Whereas the queen retreated to her homes at Balmoral in Scotland and Osborne on the Isle of Wight for four months of the year, Britannia flew off the printing press to every corner of the empire.

In the year that Alfred, Lord Tennyson was penning his *Boadicea*, another great work was finishing its production. In 1859, the scientist Charles Darwin published the first edition of his magnum opus, *On The Origin of Species by Means of Natural Selection, or, The Preservation of Favoured Races in the Struggle for Life*. More than any other book of recent time, its ideas would reverberate in almost every domain, from science to religion and politics to culture. Darwin had kept his preparation of the treatise a closely guarded secret realising how incendiary his proposal might be – but even he could not have guessed its global ramifications. His so-called theory of natural selection was picked up, refined, debased and developed by people in all walks of life and then applied to their own situation as a "scientific fact".

Throughout the 1860s, Darwin's ideas were explored by his own cousin, Francis Galton, an independently wealthy young man with an enquiring mind and passion for travel and exploration. By 1869, he had composed his own form of natural selection as a means of "improving" society – a concept that would later be named "eugenics". The basic idea ran as follows: mental as well as physical characteristics are equally inherited from the parents, which meant that by selective breeding programmes, it was possible to "improve" society to a set of desired traits, or equally to debase it by breeding out those traits. This was the classic case of nature overcoming nurture – and a topic of hot concern in the light of the serious social unrest triggered by the Chartist movement for parliamentary reform – a memory that was still painfully fresh for the middle and upper classes.

Slowly but surely, enthusiasm for eugenics gathered pace as a way of "civilising" society, though it proved controversial among many of the social reformers who were battling to improve the appalling living and working conditions which they blamed for "corrupting" the lower classes. However, for many in Britain and her colonies, eugenics offered a fascinating model for the culture and administration of the British empire: it seemed to explain why the white man was superior to the black man ("better" breeding, of course) and offered a way forward to extending Britain's power and influence across the globe. But for any kind of breeding programme to go ahead in the colonies, unless the end result was racial mixing, the first requirement was actually having "suitable" white women living there; females therefore became an essential facet of a growing empire, providing wives for the white settlers and breeding the white children who (naturally) would be superior to their native countrymen.

The trouble was, with the Indian Mutiny in 1857 and the New Zealand uprising in the 1860s, and the Western Canada revolt in 1885, it was growing increasingly hard to attract women to the recesses of the far-flung colonies. The flipside of mass male emigration to the colonies was a Britain with a declining birth rate and paranoid that young women would turn to prostitution because they couldn't find work or a husband to provide them with the stability of a family home. Just like Rome before it, Britain was staring the decline of its empire in the face. The solution, it seemed, was obvious: what the empire needed was a campaign to attract young, moral women to give up the certainty of life in Britain for a new and potentially exciting life overseas: and to achieve that there would have to be a huge recruitment drive which sold the idea as a patriotic duty.

As late as 1922, one colonial commentator wrote:

> "Everyone who knows the tropics is aware that they are full of dark corners where a white man simply cannot live alone ... The average European, exiled without a companion ... soon begins to feel a sense of appalled isolation ... There is one almost unfailing remedy. Give a man a wife ... [she] can evoke the home atmosphere even amongst the uttermost abominations ... They know their business: it is to get a house into order, to domesticate the heart of the wild ... women are directly responsible for the stability of the British administration ..."

ARTHUR GRIMBLE: *WOMEN AS EMPIRE BUILDERS*,

UNITED EMPIRE XIII, 1922

The idea of women's emigration societies to promote and support relocation to the colonies may seem bizarre to a modern audience but at the time, there was genuine fear that both Britain and its females were staring moral and economic degradation in the face. The cause of this potential decline was in white men mixing with indigenous women in the colonies, "diluting" the superiority of the colonial administration and defence. From the 1850s, the *Sidney Herbert's Fund for Promoting Female Emigration*, along with the *Caroline Chisholm's Family Colonisation Loan Society* were both actively supporting the mission, followed by the *Women's Emigration Society* of 1880 and the *British Women's Emigration Association* of 1884 to name just a few of the key players. But while Caroline Chisholm could argue that women were "God's police", a more subtle approach was being deployed to entice women overseas in salvation of the Empire.

Britannia's image was emblazoned over the pamphlets, posters, books and other promotional literature to remind women of their patriotic duty and also to reassure them that they were following in the footsteps of the great classical civilisations, of which Britain was now the moral successor. The fact that Britannia was a warrior queen promised their safety in a strange land; the fact that Britannia was a virgin queen promised them they were heading towards a morally virtuous life; and the fact that here was an elite woman beckoning her sisters across the seas appealed to the Victorian aspiration for self-improvement.

By the time of the Colonial and Indian exhibition of 1886, Britannia's image as the moral and military guardian of the empire was so entrenched that the cover page of the programme showed this symbolic queen raised high on a throne or dais and surrounded by her happy female "courtiers" representing the colonies from around the globe. It was a confident and Arcadian scene from a civilised world; and of all the woman portrayed on the cover, just one of them – located at Britannia's feet – was black.

The image of an omnipotent Britannia was repeated during the Boer War of 1899-1902 by the "Victoria League", which aimed to foster closer relationships between Britain and her colonies: this time, she showed herself in full military armour, leaving little doubt of her intention to fight for their cause and their empire. But Britannia had a problem: while she was a shining example of womankind, everything about her from her classical robes to her symbols of office screamed that she was not just "civilised" but very highly cultured; in other words, she was a member of the topmost stratum of social elite. While aspiration was all well and good, Britannia had little in common with the women who were pondering a future overseas or having to cope with some often profound levels of hardship when they reached their destinations.

As the drive to attract women to fill the empire became ever more pressing, Britannia's more practical, hands-on sister was brought back on to the scene as a female version of the popular hero of the British working man, John Bull: Boudica, dressed in her armour but *also with her children*, was now used in conjunction with Britannia to reassure the children of the empire that they were safe in her hands. As a mother, her subjects could relate to her; as a widow, her symbolism was safe from sexual contamination. Back in Britain, Boudica was being transformed into a national icon once more, featuring in poems, plays and pageants; far from putting writers and artists off, her "realness" as a historical figure now made her hugely attractive as a symbol of Victorian moral virtue. Whereas Britannia represented empire, aspiration and stylised domination, Boudica's power as a public metaphor was rooted firmly in the domestic sphere as a "genuine" British hero, a fighter and a fervent nationalist. Apart from one another, each queenly figure was important; but together they were magnificent. Boudica and Britannia now represented the grit and the culture, the passion and the patriotism: between the two of them, they were all things to all women, and when Victoria recovered from her grief sufficiently to start re-entering public life as a living monarch, the three made a powerful Holy Trinity.

Victoria might not have had the image-management skills of Elizabeth but she had mass production, newspapers and mechanically powered printworks which could churn out the images that would come to define her reign. But perhaps the most enduring symbolism of all is a unique piece of sculpture that stands close to the Houses of Parliament on London's Embankment by Westminster Bridge. This vast work of bronze is the culmination of a seventy-year process to inculcate Victoria into the heart of the British public by means of representation, so it is fitting that it doesn't actually portray the queen at all.

Standing on a large stone plinth in the shadow of Big Ben, Queen Boudica towers in her chariot with her left hand aloft and her right carrying a spear, flanked by her two daughters who crouch like pouncing animals at her feet. Clad in flowing classical robes which billow out behind her, she takes on the mantle of a goddess, summoning up the power to drive her rearing horses without even the use of reins. Below is an inscription drawn from the lines of Cowper and used without any hint of irony:

"Regions Caesar never knew thy posterity shall sway"

The story behind the statue – laid out in a series of letters to *The Times* – is in many ways a fitting epitaph to the queen herself, and certainly gives a fascinating insight to the mood of the times. In 1851, the sculptor Thomas Thorneycroft made a large equestrian statue of Victoria in elegant riding habit for the Great Exhibition that impressed the royal couple so much that he received their full encouragement for what was to become the major work of his career: a heroic and super-scaled bronze group named *Boadicea and her Daughters*.

Thorneycroft began working on the sculpture in the mid-1850s in the Regent's Park studio he shared with his sculptress wife, Mary. The works of the Thorneycrofts were elegantly executed and hugely popular: the Victoria bronze was chosen by the Art Union of London for a series of limited editions, so it's no surprise that Thomas's plans for *Boadicea* found favour with the royals. In fact, the Prince was so enthusiastic that he not only gave his permission to use the royal horses for the modelling, he issued the command that the sculptor "must make … a throne upon wheels". The way Albert saw it, this glorious monument should have pride of place in London and be sited no less than at the entrance to Hyde Park, but with the work progressing slowly over the next few years, Albert died without seeing its completion and his own monument was located in the favoured spot instead.

When Thomas Thorneycroft died in 1885, the sculpture was finished but not yet cast in bronze; in all, it had taken around fifteen years to reach this stage, such was the size and complexity of the work – yet there was no offer of money for the final casting, let alone a suitable home for the group. In the winter

"Boadicea and her Daughters"
Sculpture by Thomas Thorneycroft, erected 1902 at Westminster Bridge, London

of 1894, there was great excitement when it was proclaimed in the press that the burial place of Boudica herself had been found, located under the tumulus on Parliament Hill Fields. Rumours abounded of what lay beneath the soil – was this the lavish grave of the warrior queen? Or was it, as one Professor Hales contended, the battle site between her army and the Romanised Britons of Verulamium who (for some bizarre reason) had chosen to pitch a battle in Hampstead, with the dead conveyed to the site of the tumulus? With debate raging on, the London County Council organised a week-long archaeological excavation of the site which had to contend with weather so appalling that the dig turned into a slurry of mud and clay, with the protective planks too slippery for the workmen even to stand on. No grave was ever found; in fact, nothing was found that even related the site to the early Roman period.

However, with Boudica thrust firmly into the limelight, Thomas Thorneycroft's son John suggested that the infamous site would be the perfect place to locate his father's sculpture – a thoroughly agreeable suggestion until it was realised that not only was the Iceni Queen not buried there, but that even with John Thorneycroft's kind offer to donate the statue, the rumoured cost of the casting was some £6,000. Once again, all plans came to nought and the momentum for casting the group – and then finding a suitable home for it – was lost; John Thorneycroft was left as guardian of the giant model which it seemed was wanted by no one.

Nevertheless, his father's *Boadicea* had won some powerful allies: two years later, an "influential" committee was formed of "well-known members of the legislature, Royal Academicians, London County Councillors, journalists and leading Welshmen" who devised a strategy to raise the necessary funds for completing the work. They started a subscription list – kicked off by a generous donation by John Thorneycroft – with the monies being held by Coutts Bank in the Strand and a public appeal launched in the pages of *The Times* by William Bull, the honourable secretary of the committee. The appeal itself was made in the name of Thomas Thorneycroft who had "specifically stated that [the statue] was intended not only as a memorial to the queen of the Iceni, but as an embodiment of British pluck".

That very same British spirit saw to it that the appeal was an unqualified success. By the start of 1898, the money had been raised and the group cast in bronze by Messrs J W Singer and Sons of Frome for a bargain price of around £2,000. However, the road to *Boadicea's* acceptance continued to prove rocky: the next battle on the hands of the committee was finding a suitable site for the warrior queen and her daughters. A plaster model was placed in a "very conspicuous position" where Westminster Bridge joins the Victoria Embankment. To onlookers, it seemed as though her very horses were on the point of charging the House of Commons – and for many, the placing of the giant bronze in such a prestigious location was a step too far. A flurry of protest letters to *The Times* accused the statue of "awkwardness", of being "extremely conventional" with the modelling leaving "much to be desired"; one particularly snobbish attack sent from the émigré Harry Quilter in Florence decries the entire statuary of London for being devoid of artistic merit – with Thorneycroft's work being "nearly as large, as futile, as irrelevant, and alas! that I must add as inartistic, as all of them put together!" He holds nothing back for his summation, accusing *Boadicea* of being a

> *"noisy, clumsy piece of bravura modelling, which yells at one across the page even in a six-inch black and white reproduction, and which will be as the roar of the tempest if it ever straddles along the old gray stream that I love."*

However, events were to overrun even the forceful erudition of the snooty Mr Quilter. While battles raged about the siting of the statue on the banks of the Thames, on the world stage Britain was descending headlong into a bloody war against the Boers of South Africa – a battle where Boudica once more would be at the forefront of the fighting.

The lands of southern Africa were already the focus for competing imperial ambitions between the Boers and the British but the discovery of huge deposits of gold centred on Johannesburg in 1886 turned up the heat still further. Over the next ten years, the South African gold mines became the richest in the world, with cartels effectively controlling not only the supply of gold but also employing over a hundred thousand migrant workers, including many British. With the massive influx of incomers, yet strict racial voting rights in favour of the Boers, it was almost inevitable that the region would become politically charged. On top of this, conspiracies and covert alliances abounded as imperial and corporate interests vied with each other for power until the region had become so unstable that a full-scale military engagement – engineered by the British – became the only possible result.

On October 11, 1899, Britain went to war against the Boer Transvaal and the Orange Free State in what would prove a desperate, often ill-managed and unbalanced conflict. Back home in Britain, imperial fervour rose to new levels as the motherland expressed its outrage at what it interpreted as an affront to its colonial and economic hegemony. In a mood that would reflect the British war against Argentina almost a century later, a distant war suddenly became deeply personal. The popularity of the queen which had been steadily improving and celebrated in the successive jubilees of 1887 and 1897 and her re-emergence from private grieving now escalated to new heights; in return, Victoria threw herself into public appearances and conspicuous works with visits to military hospitals and army bases, and numerous ceremonies for handing out medals.

Victoria's passion for her empire, displayed in her joy at being made Empress of India by Disraeli in 1876, had proved itself one of her guiding tenets. Now, with her empire under threat, she stopped at nothing to spur her people on to bring an expanded *British* southern Africa back into the fold.

For Britons, the empire wasn't just a passion of their queen, it was part of their national and therefore their own identity; any affront to South Africa was thus a personal slight, and they rose up with unsurpassed levels of patriotism. Now, the whole canon of British imperial symbolism was brought in to support "our boys" – and leading from the front was Victoria herself, the warrior goddess Britannia displaying the Cross of St George or the Union Jack on her shield, and her timeless human incarnation, Queen Boudica.

However, this invincible trinity ended on January 22, 1901 when Victoria died after a short illness in her home at Osborne House on the Isle of Wight. She was just a few months short of her eighty-second birthday and had reigned over Britain for over sixty years – the longest rule of any British monarch. Her death was met by widespread public mourning and an outpouring of grief. As Henry James, always sensitive to nationality and class, commented:

"We all feel a bit motherless today...mysterious little Victoria is dead and fat vulgar Edward is King."

But there was nothing little about her persona or her legacy. Buried next to her beloved Albert in the mausoleum at Frogmore near Windsor, her spirit lived on in her enduring counterparts of Britannia and Boudica, the patron guardian warrior queens of her empire. During her reign, Victoria had presided over the creation of such a strong imperial domain that even with her death, Britain had the confidence and momentum to beat the Boers and win the South African war.

And with Boudica as the uncompromising representation of her earthly dead queen, as well as a symbol of Britain's military success, to denounce her statue as "irrelevant" was tantamount to heresy. The objections of the Mr Quilters of high culture had to bend to the will of the masses: Victoria might now be been dead but from 1902, when the statue was finally set in place, Thorneycroft's *Boadicea and her Daughters* would rise up from the Embankment where they remain to this day as a memento of Victoria, her empire and the evolving symbolism of a two-thousand-year-old rebel leader into an international icon.

CHAPTER 20

THE QUEEN
IS DEAD

Long Live the Queen!

"I'll fight to the end, because I believe I have a role to fulfil, and I've got two children to bring up."

DIANA, PRINCESS OF WALES: BBC *PANORAMA*, NOVEMBER 20, 1995

In 1906, a group of women suffragists marched in London to further their cause for votes for women. Their rallying point was at the statue of Boadicea by Thomas Thorneycroft; in just four years, this had become a powerful landmark in the capital, imbued with symbolism and meaning for the new cause that Boudica would now be championing – not freedom and liberty or the expansion of empire but instead a cause more directly linked to her sex: universal female suffrage. Later, the campaigners and their supporters sat down to an elaborate dinner to welcome their militant comrades back from prison. Boudica came too, carried in on the souvenir artworks that depicted the warrior queen outside the Houses of Parliament, replete with daughters (now dressed), her scythe-wheeled chariot, the scales of justice and a banner above her head which uttered the cry that would help define the age: "Votes for Women".

It is one of the great paradoxes of Victoria's reign that this powerful queen detested the idea of female suffrage and once even declared without any irony that "we women are not made for governing". Yet this female monarch and symbol of empire presided over the largest empire in the history of the world and an era that saw women winning the vote in its colonies as early as 1893 in New Zealand and with Australian women just a year away from winning it by the time of her death in 1901. It would take a further seventeen years for women in the motherland to gain the enfranchisement of their colonial sisters – and then only if they were over thirty; it would take a further decade for the age limit to be reduced to twenty-one, the same as men, in 1928.

The suffragists and their more militant comrades, the suffragettes, carried banners proclaiming their famous ancestor as an early champion of women's heroic potential and achievement. A favourite banner made of velveteen, silk and wool was emblazoned with the name "Boadicea" – but so great was the warrior queen as a meme in public consciousness that the tassled drape didn't have to show her picture at all: by now, her symbol had been reduced a single, scythed chariot wheel and a series of daggers, picked out in orange against the green and purple background that represented the colours of the suffrage movement, the Women's Social and Political Union (WSPU). One of the organisation's leading agitators was Diana Montefiore who ended up in London's Holloway Prison for her actions; she well understood the power and use of imagery. In her 1927 book, "From a Victorian to a Modern", she describes how one of her best suffrage meetings was near to the statue of Boudica in a forbidden part of London – forbidden because no gatherings were allowed to takeplace so close to the Houses of Parliament. However, she recalls how she had always wanted to hold a meeting there as Boudica seemed so threateningly advancing towards the Commons in her chariot – an image which evoked a sense of common cause among the more militant suffragettes.

But why was it that Boudica was selected as the epitome of the warrior queen and not Britannia? Britannia may have ruled the waves but as an icon of authority and elitism, she had little connection with the increasingly rebellious suffragist movement. Boudica, meanwhile, was the very embodiment of the rebel leader, fighting for her people rather than merely an abstract concept of nationhood or empire; in Boudica was a fighting spirit to whom real women could relate – and her many guises as mother, queen, rebel and warrior reflected the complexity of roles that characterised women's lives and would continue to maintain a relevance as the twentieth century progressed.

However, Boudica was not just representative of the national struggle for votes for women; in 1900, the writer Mary Trevelyan published a book that captured the mood of the imperial age. "*Britain's Greatness Foretold: the story of Boadicea, the British Warrior Queen*" hit the shelves at the time when the South Africa war was at its height and was carried along firstly by patriotic fervour and then given added momentum by the wave of nostalgia following the death of Victoria the following year. According to Trevelyan, with her rallying cry, "For Britain, Boadicea and Freedom!", the warrior queen led the brave fight against the Romans in the same way that Victoria inspired her troops in the struggle against the Boers; but much more that that, it was the role of less-heroic women to rise to the challenge to support their warriors and their cause in any way they could.

In the absence of the matriarchal Victoria, Boudica now became a curious amalgam of the "mother" of the nation and the symbol of empire, along with her warrior guise. As ever, the irony that the real historical figure was a *tribal* queen who had fought *against* an empire (and even against some native Britons) was smudged out of her legend: she was a national and now international icon that embodied a uniquely "British" spirit that would only become more acute as its borders and global domination was challenged in the years leading up to the Second World War. In 1937, Lewis Spence wrote one of the first major scholarly studies of the warrior queen; although drawing on the early findings of modern "scientific" archaeology, he cannot escape his own profound slant that in his eyes gives Britain the divine right to rule the world:

"...she was inspired by that spirit of patriotism which is so often the deepest and most vital quality and stimulus of great and powerful natures, making them in all ages the trumpets of the soil, of which indeed they appear to be the familiar mouthpieces. For it is the soil alone that is permanent and man who is its creature – man who, when all is said, is but the soil in action, whose flesh is its clay, whose bones are in its rocks, in whose blood its rivers course, and in whose voice the echoes of its winds are heard. And Boadicea appeals to me peculiarly as a daughter of the soil of Britain, that most noble and indefeasible of all the world's citadels, which I utterly believe, despite the fears and tremors of cravens

and alarmists, to be as impregnable as Eden itself, being guarded, because of its divine mission of liberty, by heavenly might, as well as native and unconquerable fortitude and valour of its folk, though myriads environ it by sea or sky."

LEWIS SPENCE: BOADICEA, WARRIOR QUEEN OF THE BRITONS, 1937

This evocation of the innate superiority of "Britishness" echoes the nationalism that was about to burst out of Germany and Italy and spark the Second World War; just like with Mary Trevelyan in 1900 who was responding to the South African war, any threat to Britain's imperial hegemony over the ages has brought out the much-trumpeted British patriotic spirit. Today it is quite breathtaking to read of the pseudo-science Spence uses to "legitimise" his moral position, but that is the point: his Boadicea was a product of his age and his understanding of the way the world around him functioned – in the same way that Trevelyan's, Tennyson's, Milton's and Tacitus's was of theirs. What we find uncomfortable is that his was an age where theories of race and eugenics were still rampant and "acceptable" in western thinking – and these only became "unacceptable" when the world had to confront their ultimate expression in the extermination camps of the Nazis.

While some used words to make their point, others used imagery and action. In 1909, the Liberal Prime Minister, Herbert Henry Asquith, ordered the force-feeding of suffragette prisoners who had gone on hunger-strike to publicise their cause; two months later, amidst the resultant fury by large tranches of the female population of Britain, *A Pageant of Great Women* opened in London's La Scala Theatre before going on tour nationwide. Written by Cecily Hamilton and directed by Edith Craig, the daughter of Ellen Terry – one of Britain's favourite actresses – the *Pageant* promoted the cause of universal women's suffrage by drawing upon a revival of the popular historical tableaux that were once part of the court of Queen Elizabeth I. And just like Elizabeth's pageantry with its depictions of Amazons and victorious queens, this was designed to show the legacy of "Great Women" such as Elizabeth, Victoria, Joan of Arc and Florence Nightingale for modern civilisation.

Women paraded on stage in groupings by type – and leading the band of

"Warrior Queens" was the perennially popular "Boadicea", dressed in the traditional garb of Dio complete with long, flowing hair, neck torc and menacing spear. However, some of the characters were more controversial than others: many in the audience might have been surprised by the inclusion of the Hindu Queen, the Rhani of Jhansi, who was infamous for the part she played in the Indian Mutiny against the British in 1857-8; meanwhile, there were reportedly problems in one town during the tour finding anyone prepared to play Catherine the Great because while she might have been an esteemed writer and philosopher of her day, she was more infamous for her vast number of lovers. In all, some fifty-two actresses took their audience through the parts played by women in world history – with just man allowed on stage named "Prejudice" and driven off by Boudica and her sisterhood of warriors.

The battle of the sexes continued into the second decade of the twentieth century, with Boudica as the women's iconic champion. Her militancy resonated with that of Emmeline and Christabel Pankhurst – the infamous leaders of the suffragette movement – whose every move to force the Liberal government into accepting women's suffrage was met by obstinate resistance. In 1912, Christabel withdrew to Paris, from where she organised a widespread campaign of arson; in 1913, Asquith presided over the so-called "Cat and Mouse Act" which allowed hunger-striking suffragettes to be freed, only to be re-incarcerated when their health improved so that they would not die in martyrdom in prison. Violence now escalated on both sides. On March 4, 1914, Mary "Slasher" Richardson stole into the National Gallery in London and attacked Diego Velásquez's 1651 portrait of the Rokeby Venus with a meat cleaver.

But Britain's troubles weren't just at home. Across the North Sea, Europe was descending into political and military chaos – and the first of its devastating World Wars. Exactly five months after Richardson's attack on Venus, Germany invaded Belgium and Britain declared itself at war. With the nation in shock, the Pankhursts called an immediate halt to all militant action and urged all supporters of women's suffrage to throw themselves into supporting the British war effort. Patriotically, this was the right thing to do; strategically, it was genius: not only did it win their cause even more popular support, it probably saved Boudica from eternal damnation as the warrior queen who failed to support her

A very maternal depiction of Boudica with her daughters,
unveiled in Cardiff's City Hall, 1916, by James Harvard Thomas

people in a time of national crisis. Instead, like the apparition of the Angel of the Trenches, she now crossed over to the war zone where her courage was invoked by the Royal Navy in the naming of a Destroyer, and by the army for "Boadicea's Redoubt" on the Western Front.

In 1916, her protective maternal image was also celebrated in statue by the sculptor, James Harvard Thomas. Unveiled in Cardiff City Hall, the "Welsh hero" Boudica was shown with her arms draped around the shoulders of her two daughters and not a weapon in sight. This was a far cry from the strident warrior queen of the Victoria Embankment – this time, there were no rearing horses, no scythed chariot wheels; there was no violence at all. Instead, a full-bosomed mother encompassed her family in a reassuring gesture of comfort and reassurance. It couldn't have proved more timely for a nation rent with horror and insecurity; and it would certainly have pleased the "leading Welshmen" who had so staunchly supported Thorneycroft's London statue: at last they had a Boudica of their own.

The warrior queen was poised for her next transformation – and this time it would not merely be in tone or symbolism, but in the very essence of her form. In 1918, Britain emerged shaken but victorious from the Great War in which eight million men died, twice as many were wounded and countless civilians were massacred. Back at home, the war had taken its toll on the balance of the sexes in what became known as "the problem of surplus women"; with a deficit of fit and healthy men in the workforce, the economy relied heavily on female labour to such an extent that the Government could no longer resist the call for female emancipation. That same year, six million women aged thirty and over were finally given the vote, extended to all women over twenty-one a decade later.

The "Roaring Twenties" saw Boudica once again back in the limelight, though this time not for any political reasons but for sheer entertainment. Laurence Binyon's play, *Boadicea*, took to the stage on January 15, 1926, but technology and culture had moved on: later that year, Boudica made her first appearance on the silver screen with the silent black and white movie *Boadicea*. The epic film – unusually long at seventy minutes – was produced by the rather primly named British Instructional Films, with Phyllis Nielson-Terry as the leading lady. Clearly, the daughters' rapes were not considered appropriate for a general audience: expunged from the record, the plot instead focuses on Boadicea's fight to win back her people's freedom and the by-now almost inevitable tryst between her daughter and a Roman soldier so beloved by dramatists throughout the ages. What is interesting is the justification for Boadicea's eventual defeat – she is betrayed by the soldier when loyalty to his country overwhelms his heart: a nationalist message about duty and honour that would not have been lost on British audiences in the year of the General Strike.

Despite Boudica's continued presence and use in the pantheon of British heroes, the question of female equality was yet to be resolved. The Second World War of 1939-45 shook traditional gender roles to the core – and this time women refused to get back into the kitchen. In the period of rebuilding that followed the declaration of peace in Europe on May 8, 1945, the traditional bastions of class and sex and race were steadily broken down to create a new, "modern" society. Britannia, who had clung on to British consciousness during the years of the war and the accession of the popular princess Elizabeth to become the second female monarch of the twentieth century, now quietly began to slip from grace, too heavily tainted with the badge of elitist imperialism to have much relevance to the brave new world of the Commonwealth.

Meanwhile, Boudica was also receiving some post-war flak. In his 1956 *History of the English-Speaking Peoples*, the former Prime Minister and Druid, Sir Winston Churchill, expressed his dislike of the warrior queen by alleging that her revolt against the Romans was possibly the "most horrid episode" in our history. An Establishment figure to the last, he continued,

> *"We see the crude and corrupt beginnings of a higher civilisation blotted out by the ferocious uprising of the native tribes. Still it is the primary right of men to die and kill for the land they live in."*
>
> WINSTON CHURCHILL: *THE HISTORY OF THE ENGLISH-SPEAKING PEOPLES*, 1956

As the British people rejected almost everything to do with war (including Churchill's own government), Boudica lay low, gathering strength for her next calling; but just when she might have expected to rejoin the battle for equal rights with the feminist movement of the 1970s, something bizarre happened. In an atmosphere that combined Roman Saturnalia with the violent fairytale of *Alice in Wonderland*, just as the feminists were taking the country by storm, Britain elected its first female Prime Minister, Margaret Thatcher; however, the trouble for most feminists was, she was not only *a Conservative* but a *right-wing* Conservative at that!

If ever it needed to be proven that the pen of office is mightier than the sword, it was proved by Downing Street and Conservative Central Office between the years of 1979 and 1990 when Margaret Thatcher was in power. Hugely popular after the disastrous Labour governments of 1974–9, her appeal grew further as she started to slash income tax, hobble the militant trade unions, and champion the free market. However, the real turning point in her popularity came in April 1982 with the declaration of war against

Argentina over its invasion of the British Falkland Islands and the Antarctic island of South Georgia.

In the manner of Elizabeth I and by proxy, Queen Victoria, Britain now looked at Margaret Thatcher for what to do next. Ever since the growth of parliamentary power in the seventeenth century, the British crown had been moving towards a constitutional monarchy, governing in association with the Commons and the Lords but fulfilling an increasingly ceremonial role. Queen Victoria had set the trend for successive rulers of being largely symbolic in her power – and Elizabeth II inherited much the same pattern. By the dawn of the twentieth century, it was the role of the Prime Minister to take the nation into war, firstly with Asquith for the Great War, and then Neville Chamberlain and Churchill in the Second World War. All these men had been judged on their performance of leadership at a time of national crisis – but could a woman really lead an army? After all, as the newspapers of the day made much mention of, they were meant to be "the weaker sex". In terms of public perception, the "Iron Lady" now gathered up her spear, emblazoned her shield with the Union Jack, got on to her chariot and went into battle. By June 1982, Margaret Thatcher was re-introduced to the nation as the latest in a long and noble line of British warrior queens.

The cartoonists had a field day: here was plenty of fodder for symbolism. A latter-day Boudica in her scythe-wheeled chariot (a piece of artistic licence by Thorneycroft which had now become an integral but totally fictitious part of the Boudica legend), brandishing her weapon of choice (sometimes a sword, sometimes a spear or trident) and charging proudly into battle. No one seemed to notice that while the iconic figure may have been a victorious heroine, the real Boudica lost the war, her life and her lands; no one seemed to notice that in terms of historical parallels and far-away empires, Britain had more in common with the Romans. Such was the power of the warrior queen *idea*, it could be taken at face value even when the facts didn't actually fit.

Exactly twenty-two years on from Thatcher's reincarnation as Boudica, her former press secretary, Sir Bernard Ingham, kindly reflected on the parallels for this book. It was a sunny June afternoon, redolent of the languid summer when the nation listened to fuzzy reports on transistor radios of a war being played out some seven thousand miles away in the snow and ice of a South Atlantic winter.

Sir Bernard was upbeat, remembering only too well the mood of the day and Prime Minister Thatcher's rebirth in the public imagination as a modern Boadicea. "I didn't cultivate the parallels but I certainly *did* say she was 'a right Boadicea' at times! There's no doubt that she was a warrior Prime Minister in many ways – and not just in terms of the Falklands but with the Cabinet, too. She was a warrior Prime Minister and a patriot – still is, for that matter, so I didn't have any need to cultivate the parallels; it first of all underlined the strength of personality and also the determination to *DO* things. Both women were great British patriots, or at least English ones. And when the cartoons came in we just laughed. The best of all was the one by Jak after her row with Giscard d'Estang which showed him arriving home to his wife with his hair torn, his collar off, sleeve off, totally battered and his wife shouting, 'I told you to stay away from that woman!'"

But did the parallels with an Iron Age queen anger the latter day "Iron Lady" for being too gung-ho and simplistic? Sir Bernard thought not: "She wasn't annoyed by the comparisons with Boadicea; in fact, I think she rather liked being portrayed as someone who bashed men about. I can't recall it ever annoying her, or me for that matter. The parallel wouldn't have occurred to me if it wasn't the truth. I think both were women of strong ideas that were not easily knocked over – successful women, too – and Lady Thatcher certainly had a waspish tongue and was very, very tenacious, which all added up to the perfect cartoonist picture.

"If she'd been in manufacturing, she would have had an iron rolling pin to beat people about the head with but as she was Prime Minister, she had her handbag which she always carried with her and it was always full of documents ready to beat people about the head with. She would say, 'Well, in my handbag I've got a document which says...!' But in terms of her being Boadicea, well, we couldn't object to it because it was the truth – at least in terms of being true to the IMAGE of Boadicea ... and better to be Boadicea than Carti-man-du-a...!"

Clearly, Thatcher's identification with one of the great icons of nationalist pride did no harm at all for her reputation as a leader; by "becoming" Boudica in the public imagination, the prime minister was able to take up the legendary sword of justice as a British warrior queen prepared to risk all to save her people. The fact that Boudica didn't win was irrelevant, as was the fact that while Thatcher was winning hearts for fighting for freedom against tyranny for her people in the Falklands, back home she presided over a fracturing society, the worst unemployment that Britain has seen in modern times, and some of the biggest anti-government riots of the twentieth century. Like heroism and justice, "freedom" and "tyranny" are in the eye of the beholder, and truth is always a good deal more complex than legend.

Margaret Thatcher resigned as leader of the Tories in 1990 after eleven years of continuous rule. It was not a glorious departure: the heroic warrior queen of the Falklands war had come to believe too much in her own individual power and even a warrior queen needs an army; the cabinet revolted, and brought her down with them. Her own deputy, Geoffrey Howe, delivered a resignation speech that has been widely credited with forcing her resignation just three weeks later. Having struggled to negotiate Britain's position in Europe without any real support from Thatcher, he famously declared:

"It is rather like sending your opening batsmen to the crease, only to find ... that their bats have been broken before the game by the team captain."

He went on to urge that his colleagues:

"consider their own response to the tragic conflict of loyalties with which I have myself wrestled for perhaps too long".

The "society" that Thatcher denied even existed throughout her years in government now clearly identified her – not the party – as the source of the problem, re-electing the Conservatives to power in 1992 under its new leader, the young and consensus-building John Major. Major's success in the polls hammered another nail into the coffin of Thatcher's invincibility: she suddenly seemed frail, vulnerable and belonging to a bygone era. Unlike legendary figures

who either adapt to the changing age or simply disappear, humans grow old –
and whereas men might become "*grumpy old* men" the female equivalent of
the stereotype is the more malicious "old hag". Elizabeth I and Victoria had
suffered this fate, now it was the time for Margaret Thatcher. For the former
Prime Minister, there was nowhere else to go: she did some lecturing, continued
her work with companies like British American Tobacco, wrote her memoirs
and started the Thatcher Foundation.

On a freezing cold winter's day, I took the train from Glasgow down through
the ancient landscape of the Brigantes to the University of Durham. I had an
appointment with Dr Richard Hingley – an archaeologist and specialist on
Roman imperialism – whose work raised fascinating questions about Boudica's
links to our sense of national identity. Despite working in an essentially material
discipline, Richard is very much an ideas man and we spent the next few hours
discussing everything from the sexual politics of early Roman Britain to
nationalist pride. By now, I had almost finished my search for Boudica, but
my quest to understand the confused relationship of the British to their Roman
experience of imperialism, and its effect on our relationship with Boudica,
was still unresolved.

Other cultures have their warrior queens – Zenobia, the third-century
queen of the now-Syrian town of Palmyra or the Indian Rani of Jhansi who
led her men against the British in the Indian Mutiny – but few venerate and
update them as a nationalist motif in the way we do with Boudica. My
suspicions were that she was inextricably linked with our bitter-sweet love affair
with imperialism, and Richard was just the man to help me wrestle through the
issues. "Archaeologists can deal pretty well with discovery but they veer away
far too much from the essential 'myths of origin' he began quietly, "yet these are
precisely the things that tell us so much about who we are, or want to be. I came
to my interest in Boudica as a direct result of looking at Britain's imperial
culture in the late nineteenth and early twentieth centuries – the time when
Thorneycroft was producing his giant imperial symbol of Boudica that now
rests by Westminster Bridge. I realised that Boudica enables people to think
about quite complex issues as she engages with all our myths about Roman

Britain. I think we have a culture in Britain where we take the attitude, 'Look what the Romans have done for us,' rather than seeing the huge legacy of what was going on in the native communities of the Iron Age. When it comes down to it, pretty much everything in our modern sense of identity boils down – for better or for worse – to our myths of origin, and we take our point zero as Roman Britain. It's hardly surprising, then, that Boudica is such an imperial figure of inspiration because if you ignore the facts of her being *anti*-Roman then she at least comes from that worshipped period of our history. She's part of our myths of origin, and we need to keep her alive so we don't lose our sense of identity."

But that sense of identity was shifting. With the demise of a powerful political warrior queen in Margaret Thatcher, the representation of the legendary Boudica was once more transformed to suit the mood of the age. On April 27, 1996, a new play premiered at the King's Head Theatre in Islington, North London. Written by Monica Lissak, it was called simply *Boadicea* – a name that reflected the legendary character rather than the historical queen of the Iceni. However, this queen is more like the Jacobean queens of old: distracted and obsessed by passion, she is unwittingly involved in a love triangle and becomes the fool of the Druid Priestess, Morian. Morian manoeuvres the queen into fighting a war she doesn't want or believe in and then ultimately poisons her. Boadicea thus becomes a victim not of war, but of love.

The context of the "softening" of the queen is fascinating. Just five months before the play's debut, another royal had stolen the limelight in a spectacular performance that was the visible culmination of another battle, only this time one of words. On November 20, 1995, Diana, Princess of Wales, gave a frank and emotionally charged interview on BBC television about her turbulent life as the estranged consort to the next in line to the throne. The carefully-staged interview provided some of the best drama – and best-known lines – of the Nineties as the Princess looked up through heavy eyelashes and declared with practised spontaneity:

"There were three of us in the marriage. It was a bit crowded."

Diana's interview came as a retort to one filmed by Prince Charles eighteen months before and was described in the press as an "Exocet missile" in the war of the Windsors. So was Diana taking on the mantle of a new kind of warrior queen – an *anti*-warrior, or at least one who was anti-war, who donned her armoured breastplates and strode across the landmine-strewn battlefields in order to protest against suffering and inhumanity? This was an inversion of the traditional role of being "defender of the nation" that no one else had thought to fill – here was a new emotional landscape filled with victims of war, poverty, abuse and disease, and it suited her perfectly. While she publicly accepted that she would never be the queen of the land of Great Britain, she declared her desire for a more internalised, romanticised monarchy:

"I'd like to be a queen of people's hearts, in people's hearts."

This was the perfect, modern twist to the love that Elizabeth I engendered: Princess Diana had transcended humanity to become a moral idea expressed through love, with a sacred realm that must be defended. And in keeping with this new morality, rather than fighting for her people with a spear or sword, this new kind of warrior queen used words as her weapons, with the media as her battering ram and her press secretaries as her shield. "The enemy" was clearly defined as the "establishment", Charles's staff and "that f***ing family" as she'd allegedly described them in a secretly taped "Squidgy-gate" telephone call – and it was resentment by these factions of her unrivalled popularity that had caused them to apparently declare war on her:

"They see me as a threat of some kind."

This "threat" to the accepted monarchy was much vaunted in the press. Here was a woman who could identify with her people – from an elderly woman dying a hospice, to a young man suffering from AIDS, a child who had been disabled by a landmine; the traditional royals, in stark contrast, were perceived as being out of touch, cold and distant – incapable of the kind of connection that the rebellious Diana could achieve with ease.

Part of Diana's success in becoming "queen of people's hearts" was down to her skill in turning her "victim" status to her advantage. Raising her children in a loveless marriage, living with "the enemy", coping with bulimia and depression – all these were transformed from points of weakness into badges of survival to be worn proudly on her sleeve and to prove that she was a human being just like her subjects (if one could forget about her growing up in a stately home, marrying the future king and becoming arguably the most famous woman in the world). And in her BBC interview, she brilliantly created the aura of having selflessly sacrificed herself for her people; now, as well as proving she, too, could be vulnerable, she was lifted up to heroic levels:

> *"I think every strong woman in history has had to walk down a similar path, and I think it's the strength that causes the confusion and the fear. Why is she strong? Where does she get it from? Where is she taking it? Where is she going to use it? Why do the public still support her?"*

Diana could have been describing Boudica's journey through the ages instead of herself. But not only was the head of this latter-day warrior queen up there in the pantheon of the great women, her feet were still planted firmly on the ground, where she stood in unity with her people:

> *"I want to reassure all those people who have loved me and supported me throughout the last fifteen years that I'd never let them down...I'll fight to the end, because I believe I have a role to fulfil, and I've got two children to bring up."*

DIANA, PRINCESS OF WALES: BBC *PANORAMA* INTERVIEW, NOVEMBER 20, 1995

The television interview was an incredible performance that attracted one in three people in the UK to tune in. Less than two years later, the profound sense of national and international shock at the death of the princess proved her point: on September, 6, 1997, around two and a half billion people around the globe – that's about a third of the world's population – watched the television footage of her funeral. Diana had managed to create her own queenly realm with her loyal subjects pledging their hearts in a modern-day equivalent of courtly love that would never be requited. But, as with Elizabeth I over four hundred years previously, it was enough just to *be* in love with this new-style warrior queen.

CHAPTER 21
FROM BARBARITY TO CELEBRITY
The Cult of the Warrior Queen

"Women grow up and want something more substantial than the role models offered to them in celebrity magazines. Women's lives are multi-faceted and we want deeper, more meaningful role models who reflect this: women with experience, who have really lived – women like Boudica or even Madonna. You look at them and think 'wow - they are just phenomenal'! I've been fascinated by Boudica since childhood: she was so inspirational with such pure, naked energy that her renaissance has to happen; she won't ever fade away – she's too strong a role model, an icon, a metaphor for modern women. I adore the imagery of Boudica in her chariot, defiant having given birth and killed. I love that contradiction: the power to give and take life. Back in her day, women were warriors, they were leaders. I think the greatest conspiracy in the history of mankind has been to deny women their power – but that's exactly what has been happening. For me, she's the last remaining vestige we have of that ancient and primal capacity. She is the ultimate role model."

TOYAH WILLCOX: SINGER, ACTRESS, BUSINESSWOMAN, AUTHOR, PRESENTER AND WIFE. INTERVIEW WITH AUTHOR, APRIL 2005

In the Athens Olympic Games of 2004, three British women sailors stood on the podium after winning gold medals in the *Yngling* class. These were Britain's first gold medals of the games and the media spotlight was shining brightly as Shirley Roberston, Sarah Webb and Sarah Ayton bowed their heads to receive their award. As the last chord of the national anthem was being drowned out by the roars of delight from the packed stadium, the women stripped off their jackets to reveal a bold message painted on their T-shirts: "Britannia rules the waves." Even the commentators had to laugh.

During the late 1990s, attempts were made to launch the image of "Cool Britannia", but of course to define something as "cool" sets the clock running on its longevity as a fashion statement. It was not a great success: the enduring image of Britannia is one that still embodies the spirit of Britain and its maritime heritage – an image so cleverly and cheekily updated on the podium at the 2004 Olympics.

The sea-faring theme has also been drawn upon in a range of gold and silver coins commissioned by the Royal Mint. The basic design is of Britannia, who has resided on coins since the days of Hadrian – but here she has undergone some modernisation to make her relevant to the twenty-first century. The limited-edition coins were designed by the artist and sculptor, Philip Nathan, who has striven over his forty years of working with the Mint to give the classic Britannia a more modern flavour in some designs: her dress is less like that of the Greek Athena and in his own words more "Celtic", her helmet is reduced to a simpler, more north European style and there is a great deal of movement in the

Philip Nathan's beautiful Britannia coin combines classic Britannia imagery with Boudica's trademark chariot

flowing lines of her clothes. However, the most interesting new twist was seating Britannia not on her throne but in a chariot that was being driven through the waves: Britannia and Boudica have become as one.

This is a powerful and graphic expression of a trend that has been occurring for the last two hundred years as the relationship between Boudica and Britannia has drawn ever closer. But Nathan's motivation for conflating the two adds a fascinating slant to the story of the warrior queens: to his mind, there was a natural affinity between Boudica and Britannia which he did not resist as the two converged as a coin design. Boudica made Britannia "more Anglicised" as she was a true *British* heroine, rather than a Greek goddess adopted by the British. The distinction is important for this self-confessed Eurosceptic: his coins represent an identity for a Britain that he calls "proud, independent and democratic" – qualities that many Britons would call the very essence of being British. Symbols used on his other Britannia coins include a lion, Union Jack shield and La Tène style Celtic borders – all powerful motifs in a nationalist consciousness.

The power of the image has never been stronger and it has fed the latest movement that has swept through western culture in the last twenty years: the cult of celebrity. In its own way, the deification of figures like Princess Diana or gold medallists like the sailors or the latest pop or movie star, is little different from the Age of Romance of Cowper or Coleridge, which served to praise both the individual and the heroic – it's just that the mode and speed of delivery of information has changed beyond even these poets' wildest imaginations. Now, apparently, we can't live without knowing every latest, intimate detail of the lives of the latest king or queen of pop/rock/soap (*delete as appropriate) and whenever young children are interviewed about what they want to be when they grow up, they no longer want to be teachers or doctors – in fact, they don't seem to want to *do* anything: now the aspiration is merely to "be famous". However, the images of the rich and famous being broadcast on screen or covering the pages in women's magazines are really nothing more than the twenty-first century version of Henry Peacham's "emblem book" of 1603 – a pattern-book of aspirations and moral examples of how to behave, or in some cases how *not* to behave.

We know that these images are potent: research from studies carried out in the last decade has shown that after looking at pictures of models in women's magazines, readers tend to exaggerate their perceived body size by up to fifteen per cent, regardless of how thin or overweight they really are. One American study of affluent, educated female students concluded that even looking at the images for as little as thirteen minutes made the students feel worse about their body shape. Imagery works, for better or for worse.

So what does this mean in terms of Boudica's image as a warrior queen, mother, hero and historical figure – and what is her relevance today? In the mid-1990s, I ripped a cartoon out of a newspaper article on women bosses. The cartoon depicted a sharp-featured dominatrix dressed in a business suit and brandishing whips; her male colleagues were jumping headlong into a fiery pit to avoid her wrath, while to her left a female colleague quipped, "She's a marvellous boss really, once you get to know her." It struck me at the time that Boudica's imagery is never really far away: the warrior queen stereotype embodies all the frissons of gender, sex and power. Today, more than two centuries after Mary Wollstonecraft's 1792 ground-breaking work, *A Vindication of the Rights of Woman*, we are still unsettled about the prospect of a woman doing a man's job whether on a national, business or even household level. It seems that women's suffrage, feminism, equal opportunities legislation and even the "Girl Power" of the Nineties pop icons, the Spice Girls, haven't been able to resolve this fundamental "problem" in our cultural imagination.

Though we might like to think that "sex was invented in the 1960s", there clearly is nothing new about sex wars: Tacitus and Dio were well aware of Boudica's gender and we have seen how she has been used by both men and women to champion their cause. And how we react to the legend of this woman who took on the Romans depends not only on the mood of the age but often on whether we are male or female. During the pamphlet wars of the puritanical seventeenth century, a man named Joseph Swetnam published the pamphlet, *An Arraignment of Lewde, Idel, Froward (sic), and Unconstant Women* (1615) in which he criticised women as lacking in morality and worth. The attacker did not get away unscathed from his abuse: in response two years later, someone calling themselves "Ester Sowernam" (a pun on "Sweet-nam") published a reply called *Ester hath Hang'd Haman...or the arraignment*

Cartoon by Clare Mackie, "She's a marvellous boss really, once you get to know her..." The Guardian June 10, 1996

of lewd, idel, froward, and unconstant men, and husbands. The title refers to the Jewish heroine, Ester, who helped prevent the genocide of her race and instead had the executioner executed; inside the pamphlet, "Sowernam" delights in her revenge (though "she" could easily have been a "he"):

> *If I should recite and set down all the honorable records and Monuments for and of women, I might write more Books than I have yet written lines...I will only mention some few examples of our own Country and Kingdom, which have been incomparably benefited and honored by women.*
>
> *Among the old Britains, our first Ancestors, the valiant* Boadicea, *that defended the liberty of her Country, against the strength of the* Romans, *when they were at the greatest, and made them feel that a woman could conquer them who had conquered almost all the men of the then known world.*
>
> FROM ESTER SOWERNAM (1617): ESTER HATH HANG'D HAMAN: AN ANSWERE
> TO A LEWD PAMPHLET, ENTITLED *THE ARRAIGNMENT OF WOMEN* WITH THE
> ARRAIGNMENT OF LEWD, IDLE FROWARD, AND UNCONSTANT MEN, AND HUSBANDS.

Almost half a millennium on, the different opinions of male and female commentators towards Boudica are still apparent. In his scholarly account of the two thousand years of Boudican history, Richard Hingley commented on the gender differences even within the study of Boudica herself:

> *"Most of the archaeological and ancient historical work regarding Boudica has been produced by men, while works concerned with her historical representations since the Renaissance are primarily produced by women. Apparently, the gender of writers continues to be a significant factor in how they approach Boudica or Boadicea."*

RICHARD HINGLEY & CHRISTINA UNWIN: *BOUDICA, IRON AGE WARRIOR QUEEN*, 2004

But of course it's not just in the battle of the sexes where Boudica has been a prominent agitator; other cultural forces have kept her legend alive long after her real life had been snuffed out – including patriotism, nationalism and imperialism. In fact, Boudica's appeal has endured through two millennia without any apparent diminution – and at the time of writing there are currently four Hollywood films about the warrior queen rumoured to be in production. Now billed as "Braveheart with a bra", her reincarnation ranges from a peasant girl who rises up to military fame and is posthumously named queen, to glamorous battle goddess fighting against the powers of evil. The films are variously entitled *Warrior*, *Warrior Queen*, *Queen Fury* and *My Country* and the race is on to see which studio can get theirs out first. As ever, the friction that drives the narrative is the modern equivalent of the Romans' festival of Saturnalia or the Celts' Hallowe'en – a time when normal behaviour is suspended and, for a limited period only, there's an inversion of the normal structure of power.

Another plus of having a female Hollywood hero is that she comes ready-packaged with sex appeal. It's a perennial truth of women on screen that you have to be young and attractive to get the leading roles and the multi-million pound deals; once you turn forty, you're no longer considered a draw. In this sense, Boudica fits the bill perfectly as she conveniently died before she could weather into a hag, probably in her mid- to late thirties. But the sex appeal of Boudica has long been an issue to those representing her in literature or the arts. Again, the issue of sex raises uncomfortable questions with a warrior queen who has already given up much of her femininity. In the 1938 painting by C Gill, now hanging in Essex County Council Chambers, Boudica is almost completely defeminised, with mannish hair, stern gaze, high neckline and the classic pose of Britannia, complete with her spear. In contrast, the woman kneeling captive before her is a "true" woman, tender-cheeked, her robe falling off her shoulder seductively and her hair swept up in a knot. In Gill's painting, what is sexually attractive is Boudica's power. Like a dominatrix, she is the one giving the orders – and that can prove highly attractive.

The dichotomies over the sexuality of the warrior queen are played out in the classic 1982 cartoon of Margaret Thatcher by the *Daily Express*'s Griffin. This shows the then Prime Minister riding her chariot, sword held high in a defiant gesture – and with two enormous metal breasts for breastplates. So was Griffin commenting that sex appeal had to be "bolted on" to the female warrior? Or was he merely trying to emphasise that the Iron Lady had impressive Iron Breasts? In this cartoon, they certainly come as an added extra, rather than being an inherent characteristic of a woman. However, the message that there's a frisson of sexual desire for the female in a position of power is absolutely unmissable – and that's something that Hollywood is guaranteed to exploit to the full.

As well as the dramatic and sexual tension of a world turned upside down by a woman fighter, there's another reason why Boudica's transition on to the silver screen might be relatively easy: her "brand recognition" is high (particularly under her Victorian/Edwardian name of Boadicea) so people will see her name and know instantly the headline of the film. This helps with marketing and advertising the finished product as the majority of the target audience will already be receptive to the basic storyline as vaguely familiar. However, here Boudica scores a bonus: while most people in the English-speaking west will know her name, few people actually know much more than that – perhaps one or two sketchy details about her fighting the Romans, that's all.

But this is probably the key to why Boudica has remained such a powerful figure for the last two thousand years: we know enough to be curious but not enough to get bored and feel there is nothing left to discover. What's more, in spite of being on billboards and celluloid across the western world, she is likely to survive her time at the altar of the cult of celebrity. Unlike the Hollywood actor being caught *in flagrante* with her co-star, the chances of Boudica besmirching her legend are practically zero unless a totally new line of evidence appears in some forgotten library or corner of the soil. Meanwhile, there are still enough gaps in her story for her to live in our imaginations and therefore suit our own agendas and purposes. Because we don't actually know the fine detail of her story, our thirst for Boudica will never be sated. It's a truism that Shakespeare knew only too well:

> *If all the year were playing holidays, To sport would be as tedious as to work; But when they seldom come, they wish'd for come, And nothing pleaseth but rare accidents.*
>
> WILLIAM SHAKESPEARE: *HENRY IV: PT 1, ACT 1*

And Boudica *is* a rare accident: had Tacitus not written of her, she would have died forever in AD 60/61 but now, like a horoscope, she has the perfect balance of concrete and general information to be relevant to our modern lives. She also still acts as a cultural reference point: she is a mother, a queen, a warrior, a victim, a hero – but the rest of her life is made from unknowns and extrapolation. The result? That she can be whoever you want her to be. The Texan model Jerry Hall infamously said that to keep her marriage strong she was "a cook in the kitchen, a maid in the living room and a whore in the bedroom" – and in many ways, Boudica-the-legend has provided the same flexible service for us over her long history. The real difference is that Jerry Hall is free to act as she chooses, whereas the image of Boudica-the-legend is completely at our behest: we're not her partner, we're her pimp.

So what are the futures of Boudica the historical woman and Boudica the legend? For the real Boudica, the future looks brighter than it has ever been before. Over the last few decades of the twentieth century, more and more artefacts have been discovered by metal detectorists, ordinary men and women finding the small but telling objects that have been lost or thrown away or simply buried in the sediment of time. Significantly, changes in the law regarding treasure and in the setting up of Finds Liaison Officers at local museums under the Portable Antiquities Scheme have resulted in a coming together of amateurs and professionals to the benefit of both knowledge and understanding. From

Norfolk, Colchester, London and St Albans to the British Museum, the story is the same: they are becoming inundated with new finds, each one of which has the possibility to shed some light into the voids of late Iron Age history. Now, the only trouble is cataloguing the increased number of finds and then finding the funds to purchase the very best of them.

New or unique discoveries are clearly exciting in their own right but in many ways the more humdrum finds are just as important. By simply recording where they were found this geographical data can show the distribution of coins and coin-mints, pottery, brooches – even possible manufacturing sites and trade links. By mapping what might seem inconsequential, patterns start to emerge which can tell us about the ways in which Boudica, her people and her neighbouring tribes lived their lives both before – and after – the Roman invasions. And what we are learning is that life in the Iron Age was a great deal more complex and dynamic than the crude barbarian lifestyles suggested by Roman propaganda.

Ordinary British people digging up extraordinary British history: it's a story that fits perfectly into this era of "people's histories", "people's peers" and even the "people's princess". As the old aristocracies are being broken down, or at least, revised and re-named, the new word for our time is "democratisation" – and Boudica's story can be made to fit perfectly. She may be of royal blood but, as she says via the pen of Tacitus,

"it is not as a woman descended from illustrious ancestry, but as one of the people that I am avenging lost freedom, my lashed body, the outraged honour of my daughters."

And this is the force behind the legendary Boudica – that she can be all things to all mankind because she is a living oxymoron: noble yet one of us, a mother but a warrior, a stateswoman though barbarian, and loyal yet a rebel, dead but very much alive.

However, there is one final and surprising twist to her tale. In the late 1990s, the hugely influential rap/soul group, The Fugees, sampled a track called *Song of Boadicea* by the Irish singer, Enya; the trouble was, they did it without permission and then put their own track, *Ready or Not*, out as a single. In the furore that followed, Enya – who didn't seem to know of The Fugees despite their growing fame – had to be reassured that they weren't a "gangsta" group condoning drugs and violence, and only when happy that they were explicitly against these evils, the two sides came to an agreement. Legalities aside, the issue raises two fascinating insights into Boudica's ability to "fit" with cultures that have been traditionally oppressed by the British, despite the fact her image once promoted British imperialism: the first point is that Enya's *Song of Boadicea* is on an album called *The Celts*, written for the BBC series of the same name – so here is an Irish woman claiming Boudica as an exemplar of a Celt when we know that the ancient Britons never called themselves by that name and regarded themselves as distinct from their Celtic neighbours in mainland Europe; meantime and more ironically, while Boudica was being appropriated to shore up Enya's *Celticness*, The Fugees – some of the most respected artists in urban music – were actively sampling New Age Celtic music to make it their own style of *black*. It seems that Boudica – now portrayed as the underdog – has finally managed what that other great imperialist icon, Britannia, never could: being picked up by a foreign culture that was being oppressed, and then recycled and reclaimed as one of their own.

Today, her many faces reflect the complexity of modern women's lives. It is not in spite of her inherent contradictions but because of them that the symbol of Boudica has the power to survive until our current culture moves on to its next phase, and *her* next reincarnation. Perhaps it is fitting that we've never found the Iceni Queen's grave, for her story isn't yet over: her earthly bones may have turned to dust but Boudica the legend is here to stay. After all, her story is the story of Britain – of its search for a national identity throughout the last two thousand years. The fact that she lost her brave fight against the Romans gave us an enduring role model for the "great British underdog"; her conflation with Britannia gave us a role model for maternalistic imperialism; and now she's held up as a champion in the fight against cultural oppression.

The story of Boudica is thus the perfect metaphor for our struggles to define where we came from and who we really are, and while our culture might alter with each new generation, our history – by its very nature – must stay the same. It's only our *interpretations* of that history that change, just as they did in AD 60 when a client queen of the Romans rebelled against her foreign masters and rose up to become Britain's legendary warrior queen.

ACKNOWLEDGEMENTS

The last eighteen months has been the hardest period in my life, with prolonged ill-health, the early arrival of my son and the premature death of my young sister-in-law, Sheona, whose bravery was an inspiration to everyone around her. The fact that this book was completed at all is therefore down to the support of a wide range of people – and these thank-yous barely plumb the depth of my appreciation.

Firstly, I am profoundly grateful for the encouragement and assistance given to me by both professional and amateur archaeologists and historians who have given so freely of both their time and experience in interviews, conversations, emails and sometimes even some extensive guided tours. Very special thanks must go to Colchester Archaeology Trust's Philip Crummy; John Davies, chief curator at Norfolk Museums who runs the superb Boudica Gallery and who has been a constant source of information, contacts and advice; Jenny Hall from the Museum of London; J D Hill – Iron Age guru at the British Museum (who also generously let me read his work in progress); Bill Hanson at Glasgow University; Richard Hingley at Durham University; Philip de Jersey from Oxford University – Celtic coin supremo and much-valued friend and sounding-board; Verulamium expert Rosalind Niblett; Paul Sealey at Colchester Museum; and finally to Alison Sheridan at the National Museums of Scotland for her boundless enthusiasm and suggestions.

I am also hugely grateful to the amateurs who have contributed so knowledgably not just to my research but the wider field of archaeology, particularly Trevor Austin, John Talbot, John and Pat Wells and Eflyn Owen-Jones, daughter of the late William Roberts of Anglesey. Historical researcher Ruth Boreham kept my papers in logical order and gathered materials from far and wide, while Margaret Sweenie and the team at Lochwinnoch Library also provided unswerving service in tracking down reams of obscure texts through the inter-library loan scheme. Thanks, too, must go to Prof. Barry Cunliffe, Sir Bernard Ingham – former chief press secretary to Margaret Thatcher, the sculptor Philip Nathan, Druid priestess Emma Restall Orr, the novelist Manda Scott and Toyah Willcox for generously giving interviews for this book.

A collective thank-you must go to my friends and family in Scotland and England who have kept me afloat over the last year and a half. Donna and Eric Watt have scooped up their grandson at a moment's notice whenever they were needed, while my own parents Gordon and Irene have not only helped with childcare but also driven round southern England visiting sites I couldn't reach. If only he could talk, Archie would like to say his own thanks to Michelle McNeillie and now the wonderful Charlotte McGuiness for their loving care. And to my "Cally Girls" and amazing female friends, thank you for keeping me included despite being absent in brain and/or body for large periods of time.

Two remaining sets of people have made fundamental contributions to the production of this book: my agents, Vicki McIvor and Sara Cameron at Take 3 Management, have as usual gone beyond the call of duty in their friendship, expertise – and occasional baby-sitting services – while Hannah MacDonald and fantastic publishing team at Ebury Press have been a constant source of ideas, encouragement and passionate commitment since we first began the project. Profound thanks to you all for your professionalism and your humanity.

Finally to my beloved partner, Al, who at times felt like he'd not only lost his sister but his partner, too: Til a' the seas gang dry, my dear, and the rocks melt wi' the sun…

Ness Collingridge
March 2005

SELECT BIBLIOGRAPHY

Abdy, Richard Anthony: *Romano-British Coin Hoards*, Shire Publications, 2002

Alessio, Dominic David: "Domesticating 'The Heart of the Wild': female personifications of the colonies", *Women's History Review*, 6:2, 1997

Allason-Jones, Lindsay: *Women in Roman Britain*, British Museum Press, 1989

Allen, DF: "Coins of the Iceni". *Britannia*, Vol 1, 1970

Bede: *The Ecclesiastical History of the English Nation*, Michael Maclagan transl., Basil Blackwell, 1949

de la Bédoyère, Guy: *Defying Rome – the Rebels of Roman Britain*, Tempus, 2003

Beresford Ellis, Peter: *A Brief History of The Druids*, Constable & Robinson, 1994

Birley, Robin: *Vindolanda Guide Book*, The Vindolanda Trust, 2004

Black, EW: "The first century historians of Roman Britain", *Oxford Journal of Archaeology*, 20:4, 2001

Bradford, E: *Cleopatra*, Penguin Books, 1971

Braund, David: "Observations on Cartimandua", *Britannia*, 15, 1984

Braund, David: *Ruling Roman Britain*, Routledge, 1996

Caesar, Julius: *Seven Commentaries on the Gallic War*, OUP, 1996

Camden, William: *Britannia*, 1586 (various edns)

Carey & Scullard: *A History of Rome*, 3rd ed, Palgrave, 1975

Carroll, KK: "The Date of Boudicca's Revolt", *Britannia*, 10, 1979

Crawford, Julie: "Fletcher's 'Tragedie of Bonduca' and the Anxieties of the Masculine Government of James I", *Studies in English Literature, 1500-1900*, Vol 39, The John Hopkins University Press, Spring 1999

Creighton, John: "The decline and fall of the Icenian monetary system" in Melinda Mays (ed) *Celtic Coinage: Britain and Beyond*, Oxford Tempus Raparatum, 1992

Crummy, Philip: *City of Victory – the story of Colchester –Britain's first Roman Town*, Colchester Archaeological Trust, 1997

Cunliffe, Barry: *Fishbourne: A Guide to the Site*, Sussex Archaeological Society, 2003

Cunliffe, Barry: *Iron Age Communities in Britain*, 3rd edn, Routledge, 1991

Cunliffe, Barry: *Iron Age Britain*, Batsford/English Heritage, 1994

Cunliffe, Barry: *Facing the Ocean – the Atlantic and its Peoples*, OUP, 2001

Davies, John A (ed): *The land of the Iceni: the Iron Age in northern East Anglia*, Studies in East Anglia History, 4, University of East Anglia, 1999

Davies, John: *Venta Icenorum – Caistor St Edmund, Roman Town*, Norfolk Archaeological Trust, 2001

Davies, John A & Gregory, Tony: "Coinage from a civitas: a survey of Roman coins found in Norfolk and their contribution to the archaeology of the Civitas Icenorum", *Britannia*, 22, 1991

Dept for Culture, Media & Sport: *Treasure Annual Report*, DCMS, 2002

Dimon, Nobby: *Cartimandua*, North Country Theatre, 2000

Dio, Cassius: *The Roman History – the Reign of Augustus*, Penguin Classics, 1987

Dio, Cassius: *The Roman History – the Reign of Nero*, Bill Thayer online

Dunnett, Rosalind: *The Trinovantes*, Duckworth, 1975

Elizabeth I: *Speech to her army encamped at Tilbury, 1588* via www.tudorhistory. org

Flamarion, Edith: *Cleopatra: from history to legend*, Thames & Hudson, 1997

Fletcher, John: *Bonduca* (1647), Malone Society Reprints via OUP, 1951

Fraser, Antonia: *The Warrior Queens: Boadicea's Chariot*, Phoenix Press, 1988

Frere, Sheppard & Fulford, Michael: "The Roman invasion of AD 43", *Britannia*, 32, 2001

Gardiner, J: *Women in Roman Law and Society*, Croom Helm, 1991

Geoffrey of Monmouth: *Historia Britonum*, (various edns incl. Rev Peter Roberts (1811) reproduced Llanerch Publ., 2000)

Gildas: *A description of the State of Great Brittain, written eleven hundred years since…*, John Hancock publ, London, 1652

Glover: *A Short History of Boadicea, the British Queen…* W Reeve, Fleet Street, 1754

Green, Miranda: *Celtic Goddesses – Warriors, Virgins, Mothers*, British Museum Press, 1995

Green, Miranda: *Dictionary of Celtic Myth and Legend*, Thames & Hudson, 1992

Green, Miranda: *Celtic Myths*, British Museum Press, 1993

Green, Miranda: *Exploring the World of the Druids*, Thames & Hudson, 1997

Hanson, WS & Campbell DB: "The Brigantes: from clientage to conquest", *Britannia*, 17, 1986

Haywood, John: *The Historical Atlas of the Celtic World*, Thames and Hudson, 2001

Higham, NJ: "Brigantia Revisited", *Northern History*, 23, 1987

Hill, JD: *Re-thinking the Iron Age*, Scottish Archaeological Review, 6, pp16–24

Hill, JD: *The Dynamics of Social Change in Later Iron Age Eastern and South-Eastern England c. 300 BC to AD 43* (paper in progress)

Hingley, R and Unwin, C: *Boudica: Iron Age Warrior Queen*, Hambledon and London Ltd, 2004

Hobbs, Richard: *Treasure: Finding our Past*, British Museum Press, 2003

Hopkins, Charles: *Boadicea: Queen of Britain, A Tragedy*, 1697, reprinted Chadwyck Healey, 1994

Hunt, Richard: *Queen Boudicca's Battle of Britain*, Spellmount, 2003

Jackson, Guida: *Women who Ruled*, ABC-Clio, 1990

Jackson, Kenneth: "Queen Boudicca?", *Britannia*, 10, 1979

James, Simon: *Exploring the World of the Celts*, Thames and Hudson, 1993

James, Simon: *The Atlantic Celts: Ancient People or Modern Invention*, British Museum Press, 1999

Jarman, AOH: *Aneirin: Y Gododdin – Britain's Oldest Poem*, The Welsh Classics, 1988

de Jersey, Philip: *Celtic Coinage in Britain*, Shire Publications, 1996

Jiminez, Ramon L: *Caesar against the Celts*, Spellmount, 1996

Kightly, Charles: *Folk Heroes of Britain*, Thames and Hudson, 1984

Laver, Henry: "The Coinage of Prasutagus, King of the Icenians", *British Numismatic Journal*, 39, 1882

Lefkowitz, MR & Fant, MB: *Women's life in Greece and Rome*, Duckworth, 1992

Lindsay, Sir Coutts: *Boadicea: A tragedy*, London, 1857

Lissak, Monica: *Boadicea*, Onion Shed, London 1997

Manley, John: *AD43 The Roman Invasion of Britain: A reassessment*, Stroud, 2002

McEvedy, Colin: *The New Penguin Atlas of Ancient History*, Penguin, 2nd end, 2002

Mikalachki, Jodi: *The legacy of Boadicea: gender and nation in early modern England*, Routledge, 1998

Millet, Martin: "Boudicca, the first Colchester Potters' Shop and the dating of Neronian Samian", *Britannia*, 18, 1987

Niblett, Rosalind: *Verulamium: The Roman City of St Albans*, Tempus, 2001

Niblett et al: *Roman Verulamium*, St Albans District Council, 2000

SELECT BIBLIOGRAPHY

Piggott, S: *The Druids*, Thames & Hudson, 1985

Portable Antiquities Scheme: *Annual Report 2003/4*, Museums, Libraries & Archives, 2004

Potter, TW: *Roman Britain*, British Museum Press, 1997

Potter, TW & Johns, Catherine: *Roman Britain*, British Museum Press, 1992

Powell, TGE: *The Celts*, Thames and Hudson, new edn, 1980

Pucitta, V: *Boadicea: A New Serious Opera, in two acts*, King's Theatre Haymarket, 1813

Renfrew, Jane: *Food & Cooking in Roman Britain*, English Heritage, 1985

Richmond, IA: "Queen Cartimandua", *Journal of Roman Studies*, 44, 1954

Ritchie, WF & JNG: *Celtic Warriors*, Shire Publications, 1997

Robinson, Tony & Willcock, D: *In Search of British Heroes*, Channel 4 Books, 2003

Scullard, HH: *Roman Britain − Outpost of the Empire*, Thames and Hudson, 1979

Sealey, Paul: *The Boudican Revolt against Rome*, Shire Publications, 1997

Sitwell, Norman: *The World the Romans Knew*, Hamish Hamilton, 1984

Spence, Lewis: *Boadicea, Warrior Queen of the Britons*, Robert Hale, 1937

Stead, IM: *Celtic Art*, British Museum Press, 1997

Suetonius: *The Twelve Caesars*, ed. Michael Grant, Penguin Classics, 2003

Tacitus: *The Agricola and the Germania*, transl. H Mattingly, rev. SA Handford, Penguin Classics, 1970

Tacitus: *The Annals and Histories*, ed. Moses Hadas, Modern Library/Random House, 2003

The Times Digital Archive 1785-1985, Thomson Gayle

Todd, Malcolm: *55 BC-AD 400: The Province beyond Ocean*, Fontana, 2nd edn, 1997

Trow, MJ: *Boudicca the Warrior Queen*, Sutton Publishing, 2003

Warner, Marina: *Monuments and Maidens: The allegory of female form*, Atheneum, 1996

Webster, Graham: *Boudica − The British Revolt against Rome*, Routledge, 1978

Webster, Graham: *Rome against Caratacus*, Taylor and Francis, 1993

Zeigler, Michelle: "Brigantia, Cartimandua and Gwenhwyfar", *The Heroic Age*, 1, Bellville, 1999

Maps

Ancient Britain Historical Map & Guide, Ordnance Survey, 1996

Roman Britain Historical Map & Guide, Ordnance Survey, 2001

Londinium: a descriptive map & guide to Roman London, Ordnance Survey, 1981

Museums & Sites of Interest

The British Museum, Great Russell Street, London WC1B 3DG. Tel: 020 7323 8000

Butser Ancient Farm, Chalton Lane, Chalton, Waterlooville, Hants. Limited public opening. Tel: 023 9259 8838

Colchester Castle Museum, Castle Park, Colchester (incl Temple of Claudius). Tel: 01206 282939

Danebury Iron Age Hill Fort, near Stockbridge, Hampshire. For further infrmation: Tel: 01962 860948

Museum of the Iron Age, Andover Museum, 6 Church Close, Andover, Hamsphire. Tel: 01264 366283

Museum of London, London Wall, London EC2Y 5HN. Tel: 0870 444 3852

Norwich Castle Museum and Art Gallery (incl Boudica Gallery), Castle Meadow, Norwich, NR1 3JU. Tel: 01603 495897 (info desk)

Lunt Roman Fort, Baginton, Coventry, West Midlands CV1 5RN. Tel: 02476 303567

Verulamium Roman Museum, St Michael's Street, St Albans, Hertfordshire, AL3 4SW. Tel: 01727 751810

INDEX

INDEX

BOUDICA

Swanton Morley 259–60
Swetnam, Joseph 372
swords
    bronze 65
    of the Roman army 233
Syracuse, Sicily 32
Syria 364

Tacitus 10–11, 287, 296, 356, 372, 376–7
    on the aftermath of Boudica's uprising 247, 262, 272
    and Boudica's attack on London 215, 216, 219
    on Britons as barbarians 307
    on Calgacus 60
    on Caratacus 123, 131–2
    on Cartimandua 128–9, 136–7, 139–47, 150
    on the casualty figures of Boudica's attacks 227
    on Catus 264–5
    on Classicianus 263
    on the Druids of Anglesey 167
    Elizabeth I's reading of 285–6
    on the Iceni 172–9, 186, 193, 196, 199, 206
    influence on Boece 293
    influence on Vergil 285
    lessening of contemporary dependence on 249
    on Paulinus and Boudica's final battle 228–31, 234–5, 240, 243–4
    Renaissance treatment 290, 291
    on Turpilianus 264
    on women 246, 278, 283
Talbot, John 72–3
Taliesin 327
Tarentum 32
Tasciovanus 22, 101–2, **102**, 103, 221
taxation 100, 122, 141, 220, 268
Teesdale, Henry 335
Temple of Aphrodite, Aphrodisias 337–8
Temple of Claudius, Camulodunum 196–8, 199
Temple of Mithras 101
temples 101, 137, 196–9, 316, 323–4, 337–8
Tennyson, Alfred 303, 341–3, 356
terrets (bronze rings) 202–3, 255
Terry, Ellen 356
Teutoburg Forest 109
Thames 85–6, 119, 120, 210, 211, 270
Thatcher, Margaret 5, 360–4, 365, 375
theatre
    Jacobite 297–8
    under Charles II 301, 302–3
Thenua 253
Thetford 183–4, 258
Thomas, James Harvard 359–60
Thompson, James 328, 340
Thomsen, C J 250
Thorneycroft, John 349
Thorneycroft, Mary 347
Thorneycroft, Thomas 347–50, 352–3, 359, 365
Thracian Cavalry 204
Threxton 259–60
Tiber 20, 21, 22, 28
Tiberius 110–12, 161
Tilbury 278, 285
Times, The (newspaper) 332, 347, 349, 350
Tincomarus 97–8
Togodumnus 104, 118–19, 123
Toland, John 315

torcs 7–8, **7**, 68, **181**, 182, 253
Towcester 231–2
Transalpine Gaul 37
trescle mounts 70, 245–6
Trevelyan, Mary 355, 356
Triads (bardic poems) 123, 129
Trinovantes 94, 100, 103, 109, 189, 222
    attack on Camulodunum 194
    attack on London 210, 213
    and the Catuvellauni 73, 222
    join the Iceni in revolt 184–5, 187
    and Julius Caesar 83, 85, 86, 105
    lands of 72, 83, 85, 124
    post-Boudican revolt 248, 259, 260, 274
triplets 235
Trireme Trust 50
triremes 49–51, **52**, 54
triumvirate
    first 55, 89, 106
    second 106–9
Troy 21, 22
Tulingi 39, 40–1
Tullius, Servius 42
Turpilianus, Petronius 264, 267
Tuscany 29

Umbria 29
underwear, leather 270–1, **271**
United Ancient Order of Druids (UAOD) 317, 321
Universal Druidic Bond (UDB) 315
Unwin, Christina 374

Veii 28–9
Velásquez, Diego 357
Vellocatus 146–7, 148
Veneti 48, 52–4, 60, 63
Venta Icenorum (Caistor St Edmund) 259–60, 274–5
Venus 20, 35
Venutius 139–40, 142, 146
    at war with Cartimandua 143, 145–8
    as new rebel leader of Britain 148–9, 163–4
Veranius 164
Vercingetorix 89–90, 91, 97
Verdi 322
Vergil, Polydore 285, 291, 292
Verica 98–9, 103, 111, 115, 120
Verlamion 221–2
Verulamium (now St Albans) 100–3, 118, 348
    Boudica's attack on 221–6
    as *municipium* 222
    post-Boudican rebuild 269, 272–3
Vespasian (Titus Flavius Vespasianus) 119, 148, 149, 268–70
Vestal Virgins 32
Victoria Cross 336
Victoria League 346
Victoria, Queen 332–7, 340–1, 346–7, 357, 364
    ascension to the throne 325, 332
    and the Boer War 351, 355
    and Britannia 336–7, 340, 341, 352
    burial place 351–2
    death 351
    and the death of Albert 343
    dislike of suffragists 353–4
    initial unpopularity 333–4
    made Empress of India 351
    marriage 332–3
    mother role 334–6
    popularity increases 334

re-enters public life following Albert's death 346
symbolic power 361
villas 128, 180, 260–1
Virgil 293, 312
Voada 293
Voadicia 293
Vocontii 219
Volisios 140
Volusenus, Gaius 57
'Votes for Women' 353–5, 359

Wagner, Richard 322
Walbrook skulls 217–18
Wales 275
    and the Celts 318–19
    and Druidism 318, 320–1
    identity crisis 310
    search for a history/national identity 318–21
Wallace, William 3
Walpole, Horace 327
Walpole, Hugh 323–4
Walter, Archdeacon of Oxford 289
warrior culture 68
Watling Street 222, 227, 229, 231
wattle-and-daub huts 13, 20, 103
Webb, Sarah 369
Webster, Graham 231
Wells, John 70–1, 245–6
Wells, Pat 70
Welsh Cultural Societies 319
Welsh language 309
West, Richard 327
West Stow 183, 258
Western Canada revolt (1885) 344
Western Front 358
Westhall 255
Wetwang Slack 138–9
Wheathampstead 100, 101, 221
Wheeler, Sir John Mortimer 11, 101, 143, 199
"wicker man" 157
Willcox, Toyah 369
William I (the Conqueror) 294
William IV 325, 333
Williams, Edward 319–21
Winchester Torcs 253
Wollstonecraft, Mary 372
women's magazines 371–2
Women's Social and Political Union (WSPU) 354
Woollestone, Derek 255
Wordsworth, William 329, 331–2
world maps, Roman **18**, **33**
Wren, Sir Christopher 304

York 149, 150

Zenobia 364

390